DESMOND MORRIS

MANWATCHING

A Field Guide to Human Behaviour

TRIAD GRANADA

Published by Triad/Granada in 1978

Reprinted 1978, 1979 (four times), 1980 (twice)

ISBN 0 586 04887 1

Triad Paperbacks Ltd is an imprint of Chatto, Bodley Head & Jonathan Cape Ltd and Granada Publishing Ltd.

First published in Great Britain by Jonathan Cape Ltd 1977

PLANNED AND PRODUCED BY

Elsevier International Projects Ltd, Oxford, in co-operation with Jonathan Cape Ltd, London.

Publishing controller
Herman Friedhoff

Designed and edited by
Grendon Desebrock

Advisory editor
Peter Hutchinson PhD

Managing editor
Andrew Ivett

Picture research
Ann Davies

Artwork production
Andrew Lawson
John Brennan

Production
John Sanders

SPECIAL ACKNOWLEDGEMENT

The Publishers would like to acknowledge the assistance of Magnum Photos Inc, Paris, the photographers' co-operative, source of a large proportion of the photographic illustrations.

PRODUCTION

Filmset by:
Keyspools Ltd, Golborne, Lancashire.

Colour origination:
Colour Workshop, Hertford.

Black-and-white origination:
City Engraving Ltd, Hull, and
Jolly & Barber Ltd, Rugby.

Printed and bound by:
Arnoldo Mondadori, Officine Grafiche, Verona, Italy.

CONTENTS

INTRODUCTION 8

ACTIONS 10

INBORN ACTIONS 12
Actions we do not have to learn

DISCOVERED ACTIONS 17
Actions we discover for
ourselves

ABSORBED ACTIONS 18
Actions we acquire
unknowingly from our
companions

TRAINED ACTIONS 21
Actions we have to be taught

MIXED ACTIONS 21
Actions acquired in several
ways

GESTURES 24

INCIDENTAL GESTURES 24
Mechanical actions with
secondary messages

EXPRESSIVE GESTURES 26
Biological gestures of the kind
we share with other animals

MIMIC GESTURES 28
Gestures which transmit signals
by imitation

SCHEMATIC GESTURES 29
Imitations that become
abbreviated or abridged

SYMBOLIC GESTURES 30
Gestures which represent
moods and ideas

TECHNICAL GESTURES 33
Gestures used by specialist
minorities

CODED GESTURES 34
Sign-language based on a
formal system

GESTURE VARIANTS 36
Personal or local variations on
gestural themes

MULTIMESSAGE GESTURES 39
Gestures that have many
meanings

GESTURE ALTERNATIVES 41
Different gestures that transmit
the same signal

HYBRID GESTURES 43
Signals made up of two original
gestures

COMPOUND GESTURES 45
Actions made up of a number of
distinct elements

RELIC GESTURES 47
Gestures that have survived
long after their primary
contexts have vanished

REGIONAL SIGNALS 53
The way signals change from
country to country and district
to district

BATON SIGNALS 56
Actions that emphasize the
rhythm of words

GUIDE SIGNS 64
Pointing and beckoning—how
we show the way

YES/NO SIGNALS 68
Ways in which we signal
agreement and acceptance, or
denial and refusal

GAZE BEHAVIOUR 71
Staring eyes and glancing eyes—
the way we look at one another

SALUTATION DISPLAYS 77
Hello and goodbye—greetings
and farewells

POSTURAL ECHO 83
The way friends unconsciously
act in unison

TIE-SIGNS 86
Signals that display personal
bonds to others

BODY-CONTACT TIE-SIGNS 92
The way companions touch
each other in public

AUTO-CONTACT 102
Self-intimacies—why and how
we touch ourselves

NONVERBAL LEAKAGE 106
Clues that give us away without
our knowing

CONTRADICTORY SIGNALS 112
Giving two conflicting signals
at the same time

SHORTFALL SIGNALS 116

When we under-react despite
ourselves

OVERKILL SIGNALS 118

When we over-react

STATUS DISPLAYS 121

Ways in which we signal our
position in the social peck order

TERRITORIAL BEHAVIOUR 126

The defence of a limited area

BARRIER SIGNALS 133

Body-defence actions in social
situations

PROTECTIVE BEHAVIOUR 136

Reactions to dangers—both
real and imaginary

SUBMISSIVE BEHAVIOUR 142

How we appease our critics or
attackers

RELIGIOUS DISPLAYS 148

Actions performed to placate
imagined deities

ALTRUISTIC BEHAVIOUR 153

How do we help others at our
own expense?

FIGHTING BEHAVIOUR 156

Pulling punches and throwing
punches—the biology of human
combat

TRIUMPH DISPLAYS 161

How winners celebrate and
losers react

CUT-OFF 164

Actions that block in-coming
visual signals when we are
under stress

AUTONOMIC SIGNALS 166

Actions and other changes
resulting from body-stress

PUPIL SIGNALS 169

Pupil dilations and
constrictions indicating
changes of mood

INTENTION MOVEMENTS 173

Get-ready actions that signal
future intentions

DISPLACEMENT ACTIVITIES 179
Agitated fill-in actions
performed during periods of
acute tension

REDIRECTED ACTIVITES 182
Actions diverted on to a
bystander

RE-MOTIVATING ACTIONS 184
Actions which stimulate a new
mood as a way of eliminating
an old one

INSULT SIGNALS 186
Sneers and snubs—the ways we
show disrespect and contempt

THREAT SIGNALS 195
Attempts to intimidate without
coming to blows

OBSCENE SIGNALS 198
The symbolism of sexual insults

TABOO ZONES 204
Regions of the human body
that are out of bounds

OVEREXPOSED SIGNALS 207
Going too far—breaking
through the etiquette barrier

CLOTHING SIGNALS 213
Clothing as display, comfort
and modesty

BODY ADORNMENT 222
Social mutilations and cosmetic
decorations

GENDER SIGNALS 230
Masculine and feminine signals
that help to label or emphasize
the sex of the signaller

BODY SELF-MIMICRY 239
Ways in which we imitate
ourselves anatomically

SEXUAL SIGNALS 245
The courtship and pre-
copulatory sequence of the
human animal

PARENTAL SIGNALS 252
Maternal and paternal
messages of loving care and
safety

INFANTILE SIGNALS 256
The babyface syndrome, and
the signals of crying, smiling
and laughing

ANIMAL CONTACTS 260
From predators to pets—
human involvement with other
species

PLAY PATTERNS 267
Play signals, play rules and
playfulness

METASIGNALS 272
How one signal can tell us
about the nature of other
signals

SUPERNORMAL STIMULI 274
The creation of stimuli stronger
than their natural equivalents

AESTHETIC BEHAVIOUR 278
Our reactions to the beautiful—
in nature and in art

LATERALITY 284
Lefthanded versus righthanded

LOCOMOTION 288
The twenty basic ways of
moving from place to place

AQUATIC BEHAVIOUR 294
Was man more aquatic in his
ancient past?

FEEDING BEHAVIOUR 299
How and where and what we
drink and eat?

SPORTING BEHAVIOUR 305
The biology of sport—a modern
hunting ritual

RESTING BEHAVIOUR 311
The postures of relaxation and
the nature of sleeping and
dreaming

REFERENCE 316

INDEX 318

ACKNOWLEDGEMENTS 320

INTRODUCTION

Just as a bird-watcher watches birds, so a man-watcher watches people. But he is a student of human behaviour, not a voyeur. To him, the way an elderly gentleman waves to a friend is quite as exciting as the way a young girl crosses her legs. He is a field-observer of human actions, and his field is everywhere—at the bus-stop, the supermarket, the airport, the street corner, the dinner party and the football match. Wherever people behave, there the man-watcher has something to learn—something about his fellow-men and, ultimately, about himself.

We are all man-watchers to some extent. We occasionally make a mental note of a particular posture or gesture and wonder how it can have originated, but we seldom do anything about it. We say things like: 'So-and-so makes me uneasy—I don't know why, but he just does', or 'Wasn't she behaving strangely last night?' or 'I always feel completely relaxed with those two—it's something about their manner.' And there we leave the matter. But the serious man-watcher wants to know why these feelings are aroused. He wants to know how we come to act the way we do. This means carrying out long hours of field-work and looking at people in a new way.

There is nothing especially technical about this approach. All that is needed is an understanding of a number of simple concepts, and it is these concepts that this book aims to present. Each one tells us about a special type of behaviour, or a special way in which behaviour develops, originates or changes. To know these concepts makes it possible to recognize certain patterns of behaviour much more clearly the next time they are encountered. And it enables the observer to see beneath the surface of what is taking place whenever people meet and interact.

So this is a book about actions, about how actions become gestures, and about how gestures transmit messages. As a species we may be technologically clever and philosophically brilliant, but we have not lost our animal property of being physically active; and it is this bodily activity that is the primary concern of the man-watcher. Frequently the human animal is unaware of his actions—which makes them all the more revealing. He concentrates so hard on his words that he seems to forget that his movements, postures and expressions are telling their own story.

It should be added, though, that this book is not intended as an aid to dominating one's companions by reading their secret thoughts. A bird-watcher does not study birds in order to shoot them down. In the same way, a man-watcher does not take unfair advantage of his special understanding of human behaviour. True, a proficient, objective observer can utilize his knowledge to transform a boring social occasion into an exciting field-trip, but his primary aim is to come to a deeper understanding of human interactions and of the remarkable predictability of much of human behaviour.

As with all scientific research there is, of course, the danger that new knowledge can lead to new forms of exploitation of the ignorant by the knowledgeable, but in this particular case there is perhaps a greater chance that it can instead be the source of increased tolerance. For to understand the significance of another man's actions is to gain an insight into his problems; to see what lies behind his conduct is perhaps to forgive it, where previously one would have attacked it.

Above all, it must be stressed that there is nothing insulting about looking at people as animals. We *are* animals, after all. *Homo sapiens* is a species of primate, a biological phenomenon dominated by biological rules, like any other species. Human nature is no more than one particular kind of animal nature. Agreed, the human species is an extraordinary animal; but all other species are also extraordinary animals, each in their own way, and the scientific man-watcher can bring many fresh insights to the study of human affairs if he can retain this basic attitude of evolutionary humility.

ACTIONS

All animals perform actions and most do little else. A great many also make artifacts—constructed or manufactured objects—such as nests, webs, beds and burrows. Among the monkeys and apes there is also some evidence of abstract thinking. But it is only with man that artifaction and abstraction have run riot. This is the essence of his success story. With his massive brain, man has increasingly internalized his behaviour through complex processes of abstract thought—through language, philosophy and mathematics. With his weak body, he has dramatically externalized his behaviour, scattering the surface of the globe with his artifacts—his implements, machines, weapons, vehicles, roads, works of art, buildings, villages and cities.

There he sits, this thinking, building animal, his machines humming gently all around him and his thoughts whirring inside his head. Artifaction and abstraction have come to dominate his life. One might almost suppose that action—simple animal action—would be beneath him, surviving only as a remnant from his primeval past. But this is not so. Throughout it all, he has remained a creature of action—a gesticulating, posturing, moving, expressive primate. He is as far today from becoming the disembodied, plasma-fed,

Action, artifaction and abstraction— represented by a leaping ice-skater (below), an array of scientific instruments (right) and a mathematician's symbols (above right). Human behaviour has become increasingly internalized through abstract, or symbolic, thinking and externalized through 'artifaction'—the making and use of tools— but man remains as much as ever a creature of vigorous bodily actions.

giant superbrain of science fiction as he was back in his prehistoric hunting past. Philosophy and engineering have not replaced animal activity, they have added to it. The fact that we have developed a concept of happiness and have words to express it, does not stop us from performing the action-pattern of stretching our lips into a smile. The fact that we have boats does not stop us swimming.

Our hunger for action is as strong as ever it was. The city-dweller, however deeply impressed he may be by the achievements of abstraction and artifaction, still takes his pleasures in age-old fashion. He eats and makes love; he goes to parties where he can laugh, frown, gesture and embrace. When he takes his holidays his machines bear him away to a few snatched weeks in forests, on hills and on seashores, where he can re-live his animal past in the pursuit of simple physical activity, walking, climbing and swimming.

Viewed objectively, there is a curious irony about a human animal flying a thousand miles in a machine costing several millions in order to splash about in a rock-pool looking for sea shells; or another, who has spent all day operating a huge computer, spending the evening playing darts, dancing in a discotheque, or laughing over a drink with a few friends. Yet this is what people do, tacitly accepting the irresistible need to express themselves in simple bodily actions.

What form do these actions take, and how are they acquired by each individual? Human behaviour is not free-flowing; it is divided up into a long series of separate events. Each event, such as eating a meal, visiting a theatre, taking a bath, or making love, has its own special rules and rhythms. Between our birthday and our deathday we can expect to pass through a total of over a million such behaviour events. Each of these events is itself subdivided into numerous distinct acts. Basically these acts follow one another in a sequence of posture-movement-posture-movement. Most of the postures we adopt and the movements we make we have made thousands of times before. Most of them are performed unconsciously, spontaneously and without self-analysis. In many cases they are so familiar, so much taken for granted, that we do not even know how we do them. For example, when people interlock their fingers, one thumb rests on top of the other. For each person there is a dominant thumb in this action and whenever left and right hand interlock, the same thumb rests uppermost. Yet hardly anyone can guess which is their dominant thumb without going through the motions of interlocking their hands and looking to see which thumb comes out on top.

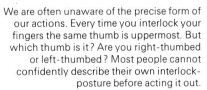

We are often unaware of the precise form of our actions. Every time you interlock your fingers the same thumb is uppermost. But which thumb is it? Are you right-thumbed or left-thumbed? Most people cannot confidently describe their own interlock-posture before acting it out.

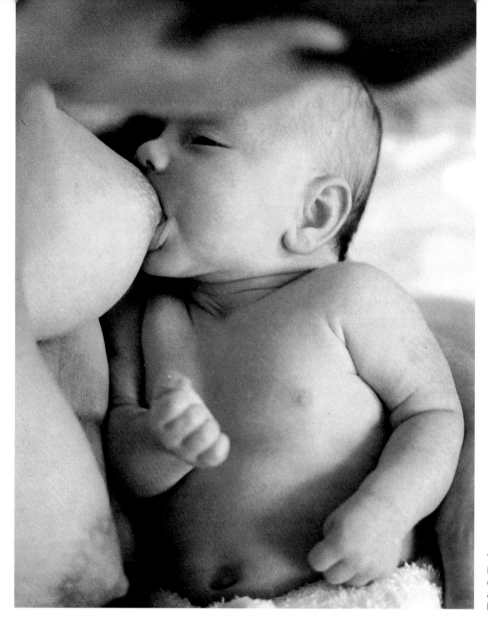

The inborn sucking response of the baby at the mother's breast. As with other young mammals, the human infant responds to the maternal stimulus without the involvement of a learning process.

The changing facial expressions of children born blind and deaf reveal that these actions occur independently of copying or learning and must therefore be inborn. (After Eibl-Eibesfeldt.)

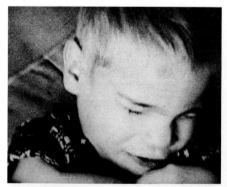

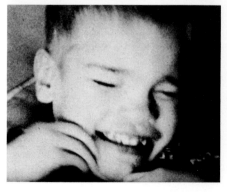

Over the years, each person has developed a fixed pattern of interlocking without realizing it. If they try to reverse the positions, bringing the dominant thumb beneath the other, the hand posture will feel strange and awkward.

This is only a trivial example, but almost every body action performed by adults has a characteristic fixed pattern. These Fixed Action-Patterns are the basic units of behaviour that the human field-observer employs as his points of reference. He watches their form, the context in which they occur, and the messages they transmit. He also asks questions about how they were acquired in the first place. Were they inborn, requiring no prior experience whatever? Were they discovered by personal trial and error as each person grew older? Were they absorbed as people unconsciously emulated their companions? Or were they acquired by conscious training, being learned by deliberate effort based on specific analytical observation, or active teaching?

INBORN ACTIONS
Actions we do not have to learn

Man's greatest genetic gift is his vast capacity for learning from his environment. Some have argued that, as a result of this one inborn ability, he has no need for any others. Rival opinion claims that, on the contrary, man's behaviour is rich in inborn patterns and that his behaviour can only be fully understood if this fact is appreciated.

People all around the world perform a rapid eyebrow-flash action when greeting. The eyebrows are momentarily raised and then lowered. Even though it does not provide conclusive proof, the global distribution of this facial movement strongly suggests that the action is inborn. (After Eibl-Eibesfeldt.)

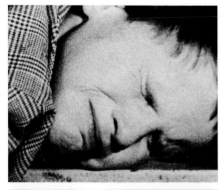

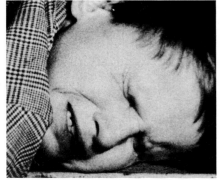

In support of the idea that the human brain learns everything and inherits nothing, is put the observation that different societies all over the world show widely differing behaviour patterns. Since we all belong to the same species, this can only mean that men everwhere are learning to behave rather than following some fixed set of genetic instructions.

Against this and in support of the idea that, as it was recently expressed, 'man is pre-programmed to a decisive extent', is put the observation that cultures are not as different as they seem. If you look for differences you will find them, but if you look for similarities you will find plenty of those, too. Unfortunately the natural inclination has been to notice the differences and overlook the similarities. It is rather like a tourist visiting a foreign country. He is impressed by the few unfamiliar elements he encounters and ignores the many familiar ones. This very understandable bias has also influenced much of the field-work carried out by anthropologists in the past. The often striking, superficial variations in social behaviour have been mistaken for fundamental differences.

These are the two conflicting views. Since no one is arguing about the fact that we do learn a great deal during our lives, the debate must concentrate on those particular actions which are claimed to be inborn.

How does an inborn action work? Essentially the idea is that the brain is programmed, rather like a computer, to link particular reactions with specific stimuli. The stimulus *input* triggers off the reaction *output* without any prior experience—it is pre-planned and operates successfully the very first time you encounter the stimulus.

The classic example is the newborn baby reacting immediately to its mother's nipple by sucking. A number of infantile reactions seem to be of this type and are clearly essential to survival. There is no time to learn. But what about actions that appear later on, when there has already been ample time for learning to have taken place? How about smiling and frowning? Does the young child copy these from its mother, or are they, too, inborn? Only a child that has never seen its mother can provide the answer. If we look at children born blind and deaf we find that they do indeed show smiling and frowning at appropriate moments in their daily lives. They also cry even though they cannot hear themselves doing so.

So these actions are also apparently inborn, but what about adult behaviour patterns? Here, even the blind-deaf cannot help us to solve the problem because, by this stage, they will have learned to communicate by special touch sign language and will be too sophisticated, too knowing. They will have learned to feel expressions on faces with their fingers, so they can no longer provide valid evidence in favour of inborn actions.

The only method left to support the idea that an adult action is inborn is to demonstrate that it occurs in every human society, regardless of varying cultural pressures. Do all people, everywhere, stamp their feet when they are angry, or bare their teeth when enraged, or flick their eyebrows momentarily up and down when they greet a friend? Some intrepid research workers have scoured the globe for remote tribes in an attempt to answer this point and have been able to confirm that even Amazonian Indians who have never met white men before do indeed perform many small actions precisely as we do. But does this really prove that the actions are inborn? If remote tribesmen flash their eyebrows in greeting like we do, and like everyone else does, can we be sure that this means the reaction must be 'built-in' to our brains before birth?

The answer is that we cannot be certain. There is no reason why, with particular actions, we should not *all* learn to behave in the same way. It seems unlikely, but it cannot be ruled out, and so the argument is, for the present, bound to be inconclusive. Until we can read the human behaviour genes like a book—and modern genetics is still many years away from that ideal condition—there is little point in dwelling at length on the problem of whether a particular action is inborn or not. Even if a global tour revealed that an action was *not* world-wide in distribution, this would equally be of little help to the rival philosophy. An action that truly is inborn might be suppressed in whole cultures, giving it the false appearance of having only local significance. So either way the arguments remain suspect.

To put this in perspective, consider nuns and weapons. Nuns live out non-sexual lives, but no one would argue that sexual behaviour is a non-biological, cultural invention on the part of the rest of the world merely because some communities can live without it. Conversely, if it could be shown that every single culture on earth uses weapons of some kind, it would not follow that weapon-use, as such, was an inborn pattern for mankind. Instead we would argue that the nuns are successfully suppressing an inborn sexual urge, while the weapon-users are utilizing a learning pattern so ancient that it has diffused throughout the entire world.

To sum up, until the study of genetics has made massive advances, we can only be *certain* of inborn actions in man in those cases where movements are performed without any prior experience, either by newborn babies or by blind-born children. This restriction limits this category of activity severely, but at the present stage of knowledge it is inevitable.

In saying this it would be wrong to give the impression that zoologists who have studied the human animal have come to the conclusion that there are only a few, infantile ways in which man's behaviour is guided by his genetic make-up. On the contrary, the general impression is that man, like other animals, is well endowed with a rich variety of inborn behaviour patterns. Anyone who has studied a number of primate species, including the human species, is bound to feel this way. But a feeling is not a certainty, and since there is no way of obtaining scientific proof or disproof where adult behaviour patterns are concerned, the matter is hardly worth pursuing in depth at this stage.

This is the considered view of most zoologists today, but sadly the inborn/learned debate has not remained in the scientific arena—it has escaped into the world of political opportunism. The first abuse was to grab hold of the idea that man has powerful inborn tendencies and distort it. It was easily warped by selecting only those tendencies that suited the political needs. One in particular was stressed—aggression. The approach here was to suggest that if mankind has an inborn urge towards unprovoked aggression, then warlike behaviour is natural, acceptable and unavoidable. If man is programmed to fight, then fight he must, and off we go to war with heads held high.

The flaws inherent in this view are obvious enough to anyone who has studied animal aggression and the way it is organized. Animals fight, but they do not go to war. Their fighting is done on a personal basis, either to establish a dominant position in a social hierarchy, or to defend a personal territory. In either case, physical combat is reduced to a minimum and disputes are nearly always settled by display, by threat and counter-threat. There is a good reason for this. In the tooth-and-claw fury of close combat, the ultimate winner is likely to be wounded almost as badly as the loser. This is something a wild animal can ill afford and any alternative method of settling disputes is clearly to be preferred. Only under conditions of extreme overcrowding does this efficient system break down. Then the fighting becomes intense and bloody. In the case of crowded hierarchies, there are just too many members of the 'peck-order' and personal relationships of dominance and subordination cannot be stabilized. Fighting continues unabated. In the case of crowded territories, everyone appears to be invading everyone else's territory, even when they are only sitting on their own. Once again fighting rages, this time in a futile attempt to clear the defended spaces of supposed intruders.

To return to the human situation, it is evident that if mankind does possess inborn aggressive urges, they are hardly going to explain the occurrence of modern wars. They may help us to understand why we go red in the face and

There are striking superficial differences between human cultures, but these sometimes obscure the many basic similarities. Young lovers the world over (top) indulge in intimate body-contact actions. Specific greeting rituals may have to be learned, but the need to perform some kind of salutation display (middle) when meeting or parting is common to all people. Also worldwide is the display of status differences in small groups (right), where the actions of dominant individuals contrast conspicuously with those of their followers.

shout and shake our fists at one another when we are angry, but the cannot possibly be used to explain the bombing of cities or the mass invasion of friendly neighbours by dictatorial warlords. The chances are that men do possess inborn aggressive urges of the special, limited kind we see in other primates. It would be strange if we, unlike all other mammals, were genetically unequipped to defend ourselves or our offspring when under attack, and it would be surprising if we lacked the urge to assert ourselves to some degree in competitive social situations. But self-defence and self-assertion are one thing; mass murder is quite another. The savagery of twentieth-century violence can only properly be compared to the bloodshed witnessed when animal groups become hopelessly overcrowded. In other words, the extremes of human violence, even when they appear to be unprovoked and stemming from some inner, inborn urge to kill, are probably being strongly provoked by the unnatural conditions prevailing at the time.

This effect can be rather indirect. For instance, one of the results of animal overcrowding is that parental care suffers and the young do not receive the usual love and attention that is normal for their species. This happens in human populations, too, with the result that juveniles are ill-treated in a way that leads to later revenge of a violent kind. This revenge is not taken on the parents who caused the damage because they are now old or dead. Instead it is taken on parent-substitutes. Violence against these individuals appears to be senseless, and their innocence leads to comments about the 'animal savagery—unprovoked brutality of a wild beast' perpetrated by the attacker. It is never clear which wild beast is being cast in this role, or why the wild beast should want to make an unprovoked attack, but the implication is obvious enough. The violent man who performs the assault is being pictured as someone who has given in to his primeval, inborn urge to attack his companions and try to kill them. Judges are repeatedly quoted as describing thugs and muggers as 'wild animals' and thereby reviving the fallacy that man is naturally violent, and that only if he suppresses his natural urges can he become a helpful, co-operative member of society.

Ironically, the inborn factor that is most likely to be making the major contribution to the savageries of modern war is the powerful human inclination to co-operate. This is a legacy from our ancient hunting past, when we had to co-operate or starve. It was the only way we could hope to defeat large prey animals. All that a modern dictator has to do is to play on this inherent sense of human group-loyalty and to expand and organize this group into a full-scale army. By converting the naturally helpful into the excessively patriotic, he can easily persuade them to kill strangers, not as acts of inborn brutality, but as laudable acts of companion-protection. If our ancestors had not become so innately co-operative, it might be much more difficult today to raise an army and send it into battle as an organized force.

Rejecting the idea that man is an inborn killer of men and that he goes looking for a fight even when all is well, we must now move over to the other side of the inborn/learned debate. For there is a potential danger in the rival claim that for man all is learned and nothing is genetically inherited. Statements, like a recent one that 'everything a human being does as such he has had to learn from other human beings' are as politically dangerous as the 'innate killer' errors of the opposing extremists. They can easily feed the power-greed of totalitarian dictators by giving them the impression that society can be moulded into any shape they may desire. A young human life is seen merely as a blank canvas on which the state can paint any picture it wishes, the word 'state' being a coy word meaning 'party leaders'. To say that man has no genetic influences whatsoever on his behaviour patterns is so bizarre, zoologically speaking, as to make one wonder at the true motives of the scientists who have ventured such opinions.

If, as seems much more probable, the truth is that man still possesses a wide range of valuable inborn behaviour patterns, then dictators are sooner or later going to find resistance to extreme forms of social organization. For a

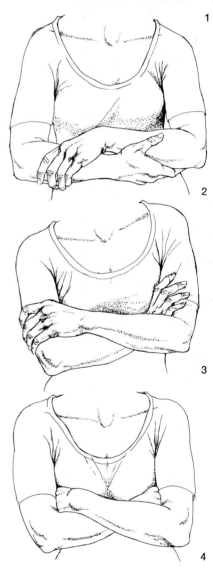

1

2

3

4

Folding the arms is a Discovered Action. It does not show any major changes as one moves from one culture to another, but it does show slight variation from person to person. This is because we do not learn the action from others, but discover it for ourselves without knowing quite how. How do you fold your arms? You may fold left-over-right or right-over-left, and you probably cannot reverse the movement without feeling strangely awkward. There are seven basic kinds of arm-folding, each with a mirror-image counterpart. (1) The Arm-crook/Chest Clasp and its mirror-image. (2) The Forearm/Forearm Clasp. (3) The Upper-arm/Arm-crook Clasp. (4) The Chest/Chest Clasp. (5) The Upper-arm/Elbow Clasp. (6) The Upper-arm/Chest Clasp. (7) The High Upper-arm/High Upper-arm Clasp.

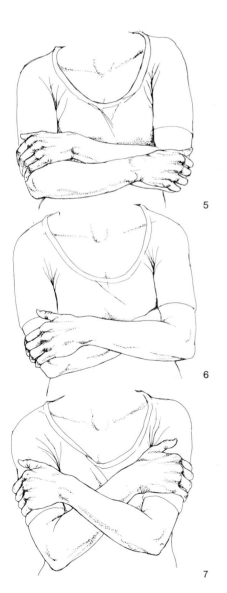

5

6

7

while they may—and have—dominated large populations with extremist doctrines, but not for long. As time passes, people begin to revert, either by sudden upheaval or by slow, creeping changes, to a form of daily life more in tune with their animal inheritance. It is doubtful whether the day-by-day social intercourse of man in the twentieth century is very different from that of prehistoric man. If we could return, by time machine, to an early cave-dwelling, we would no doubt hear the same kind of laughter, see the same kind of facial expressions, and witness the same sorts of quarrels, love affairs, acts of parental devotion and friendly co-operation as we do today. We may have advanced with abstraction and artifaction, but our urges and our actions are probably much the same.

We should examine carefully the myth that our cave-man ancestors were inarticulate, violent, raping, club-swinging louts. The more we learn about ape and human behaviour, the more this story looks like a moralizer's confidence trick. If our friendly, loving actions are inborn, then, of course, the moralizers can take little credit for them, and if there is one thing moralizers seem to love above all else it is taking credit for society's good behaviour.

Artifaction and the advance of technology is another question. It has brought us many admitted advantages. But it is worth remembering that many technological advances are geared to the reduction of the stress, pollution and discomfort caused by . . . technological advances.

When examined closely, technology can usually be found to be serving one or other of our ancient action-patterns. The television set, for example, is a miracle of artifaction, but what do we see on it? Mostly we watch simulations of the quarrels, love affairs, parental devotion, and other age-old action-patterns just mentioned. Even in our TV armchairs we are still men of action, if only at second hand.

DISCOVERED ACTIONS
Actions we discover for ourselves

If there is doubt as to whether an action is inborn or not, there can be little doubt as to whether the features of our anatomy are genetically inherited. We cannot learn an arm or a leg, in the way that we can learn a salute or a high kick. The prize fighter and the chronic invalid have precisely the same set of muscles. In the fighter they are better developed, but they remain the same muscles none the less. The environment cannot alter a man's basic anatomical make-up during his lifetime, except in such extreme cases as mutilation or surgery. It follows that, if we all inherit basically similar hands, arms and legs, we will all be likely to gesticulate, fold our arms, and cross our legs in much the same way in every culture.

In other words, when we observe a New Guinea tribesman folding his arms exactly like a German banker or a Tibetan farmer, we may not be observing a truly inborn action, but rather a Discovered Action. The tribesman, the banker and the farmer each inherit a pair of arms of the same design. At some stage in their lives, by a process of personal trial-and-error, they each discover the possibility of folding their arms across the chest. So it is the arms that are inherited, not the action. Given those particular arms, however, it is almost inevitable that, even without copying from their companions, they will arrive at the arms-fold action. This is halfway to being inborn; it is an action based on a 'genetic suggestion', via the anatomy, rather than on a direct genetic instruction.

Our Discovered Actions are unconsciously acquired as we get to know our bodies during the long process of growing up. We are not even aware of their addition to our childhood repertoire and in most cases we have no idea precisely how we perform them—which arm crosses over which, or which way our hands move as we speak.

Many Discovered Actions are so widespread that they could easily be

Many postures are absorbed from the social environment in which we live. The tough, legs-apart posture of the aggressively masculine screen cowboys (left) contrasts strikingly with the somewhat effeminate standing pose of the two males seen below.

mistaken for inborn patterns and it is this fact that has given rise to many of the needless arguments about inborn-versus-learned behaviour.

ABSORBED ACTIONS

Actions we acquire unknowingly from our companions

Absorbed Actions are those which are unconsciously copied from other people. As with Discovered Actions, we are not aware of how or when we first acquired them. Unlike Discovered Actions, however, they tend to vary from group to group, culture to culture, and nation to nation.

As a species we are strongly imitative and it is impossible for a healthy individual to grow up and live in a community without becoming infected with its typical action-patterns. The way we walk and stand, laugh and grimace, are all subject to this influence.

Many actions are first performed solely because we have observed them in our companions' behaviour. It is difficult to recognize this in your own behaviour, because the process of absorption is so subtle and you are seldom aware that it has happened, but it is easy to detect in minority groups within your own society.

Homosexual males display a number of actions peculiar to their social group, for example. A schoolboy who will eventually join this group shows none of these, and his public behaviour differs little from that of his school friends. But as soon as he has joined an adult homosexual community in a large city he rapidly adopts their characteristic action-patterns. His wrist-actions change and so does his walking and standing posture. His neck movements become more exaggerated, throwing his head out of its neutral position more frequently. He adopts more protrusive lip postures and his tongue movements become more visible and active.

It could be argued that such a male is deliberately behaving in a more feminine manner, but his actions are not precisely female. Nor are they absorbed from females, but from other homosexual males. They are passed on, time and again, from one male to another in his social group. In origin these actions may be pseudo-female, but once they have become established in a homosexual group they grow away from the typically female and, by repeated male-to-male transfer, become more and more modified until they

Among young adults the 'flop-out' posture of recent years (top) contrasts strikingly with the neatly-alert postures of the 1950s. It became such a dominant social feature during the 1960s and early 1970s that it, along with other postures of extreme casualness, even invaded city squares and streets (above).

develop a character of their own. In many cases they are now so distinct that a true female could, by miming them accurately, make it quite clear that she was not acting in a feminine way, but was instead pretending to be a male homosexual.

Of course, not all homosexual males adopt these exaggerated actions. Many do not feel the need to display in this way. Bearing this in mind, it is significant that whenever a comedian wishes to be derisive at the expense of homosexuals, he mimics the limp-wristed, head-tossing, lip-pouting variety, and whenever serious actors portray homosexuals sympathetically, they reduce or omit these elements. It would seem that the heterosexual's intolerance is aroused more by homosexual manners than by homosexual love, which is an intriguing comment on the strength of our reactions to so-called 'trivial' mannerisms.

Human beings are not alone in this tendency to absorb actions from their companions. There are several field studies of monkeys and apes which reveal similar trends, with one colony of animals performing actions that are missing from other colonies of the same species, and which they can be shown to have learned by absorption from inventive individuals in their particular groups.

Both in monkeys and men, it is clear that the status of the individual emulated is important. The higher his or her status in a group, the more readily he or she is copied by the others. In our own society we absorb most from those we admire. This operates most actively among close personal contacts, but with mass media communications we also absorb actions from remote celebrities, public figures, and popular idols.

A recent example of this is the spread of the 'flop-out' resting posture among certain young adults. A sprawling posture when relaxing has become highly infectious in the past decade. Like many postural changes, this owes its origin to a change in clothing. The use of neatly pressed trousers for male casual wear lost ground steadily during the 1960s, with blue jeans taking their place. Jeans, originally modified tent-cloth provided for hard-riding American cowboys, were for many years considered to be suitable only for manual labour. Then high-status, idolized Californian males began to display them as ordinary day-wear. Soon they were adopted by many young adults of both sexes right across America and Europe, and following this trend came the flop-out posture. The young in question began to sit or lie on the floors of their rooms instead of in conventional seating, and also on the steps and pavements of cities, their legs sprawled out on rough or unclean surfaces that only jeans could defy.

Each summer now in Amsterdam, Paris and London, the squatting, reclining figures can be seen in their hundreds, and the postural contrast with previous generations is striking. A manifestation of this change was to be seen in the 1960s at open-air pop-music festivals, where whole days were spent lying on the ground and no attempt was made to provide any form of seating.

Jeans are not the whole story, however. The process has gone beyond clothing. There is a deeper change, a change in philosophy, that influences the postural behaviour of the young. They have developed an open-mindedness and a relaxed style of thinking that is reflected in a reduction of tension and muscular tonus in their actions. To the elderly, the body postures and actions that have accompanied this change appear slovenly, but to the objective observer they constitute a behaviour style, not a lack of style.

There is nothing new about this type of change. For literally thousands of years authors have been recording the dismay of older generations at the 'decaying' manners of the young. Sometimes the complaint has been that they have become too foppish or dandyish; at others that they have become too effeminate or perhaps too boisterous or brusque. On each occasion the postures and gesticulations have changed in various ways, and by a process of rapid absorption the new action-styles have spread like wild-fire, only to

It becomes increasingly difficult to acquire new skills as we approach adulthood, and excellence is normally achieved only by those who begin training while young. The child (left), unconsciously improving his ability to co-ordinate eye and hand, may eventually acquire the skills of an artist. Many deceptively simple actions are impossible to perform without several years of intensive training—as with the acrobatic skills of Olympic gymnasts, demonstrated (above) by Olga Korbut.

Such is the human passion for training that from time to time in the past elaborate attempts were made to teach 'oratorial gesticulation', despite the fact that few people need such instructions.

Many small actions, such as winking, have to be deliberately learned, and some individuals, unlike the three seen here, find the wink difficult to perform, even as adults.

burn out and be replaced by others. Already there are signs that the modern flop-out style is changing yet again, but no one can predict which behaviour styles will be the ones to be eagerly emulated and absorbed by the young adults of the twenty-first century.

TRAINED ACTIONS
Actions we have to be taught

Trained actions are consciously acquired by teaching or self-analytical observation and practice. At one end of the scale there are difficult physical achievements such as turning mid-air somersaults, or walking on your hands. Only expert acrobats can master these activities, after long hours of training.

At the other end of the scale there are simple actions such as winking and shaking hands. In some cases these might almost fall into the category of Absorbed Actions, but if children are watched closely it soon becomes clear that the child must first teach itself, deliberately and consciously, many of the actions we adults take for granted. The hand-shake, so natural to adults, seems unpleasant and awkward to small children and, at the outset, they usually have to be coaxed to offer a hand and then have the appropriate shaking action demonstrated to them. Watching a child first trying to master a knowing wink provides another vivid reminder of how difficult some apparently simple actions can be. Indeed, some people never do master the wink, even as adults, though it is hard for a winker to understand why.

Snapping the fingers, whistling and many other trivial acts fall into this category, in addition to the more obvious, complex skills.

MIXED ACTIONS
Actions acquired in several ways

These, then, are the four ways in which we acquire actions: by genetic inheritance, by personal discovery, by social absorption, and by deliberate training. But in distinguishing between the four corresponding types of actions, I do not wish to give the impression that they are rigidly separated. Many actions owe their adult form to influences from more than one of these categories.

To give some examples: Inborn Actions are often drastically modified by social pressures. Infantile crying, for instance, becomes transformed in adult life into anything from silent weeping or suppressed sobbing to hysterical screeching and piteous wailing, according to local cultural influences.

Discovered Actions are frequently influenced in the same way, being strongly modified by the unconscious emulation of social fashions. Sitting with the legs crossed, for instance, may be privately discovered as a pleasing, convenient posture, but the exact form it takes will soon come under the influence of unwritten social rules. Without realizing it, children, as they grow older, start crossing their legs like other members of their own sex, class, age-group and culture.

This will happen almost unnoticed. Even when it is noticed, it will probably not be analysed or understood. A member of one group, mixing with another, will feel ill at ease without realizing why. The reason will be because the others are moving, posturing and gesticulating in an alien manner. The differences may be subtle, but they will be detectable and will register. A member of one group can be heard referring to another group as lazy or effeminate or rough. When asked why, he will reply: 'You've only got to look at them.' The chances are that he is unconsciously misreading their actions.

To continue with the example of leg-crossing—certain American males have been reported as saying that they find European males slightly effeminate. When this reaction is analysed it turns out to have nothing to do with the sexual behaviour of European males, but rather with the fact that they often sit with one knee crossed over the other knee. To the European this is such a normal posture that he cannot even see it as a posture. It is just a natural way to sit. But to the American male it appears effeminate because, at home, it is more often performed by his female than his male companions. The American male prefers—if he is going to cross his leg—to perform the ankle-knee cross, in which the ankle of one leg rests high up across the knee of the other leg.

A valid objection to this observation could be that many European males often adopt the ankle-knee cross posture and that American males, especially those from major cities, can sometimes be seen sitting with one knee crossed over the other. This is true, but it only underlines the sensitivity of the unconscious reactions people give to the behaviour of their companions. The difference is only a matter of degree. More European males happen to behave in the one way, more Americans in the other. And yet this minor difference is enough to give a visiting American a distinct feeling that European males are in some way effeminate.

In addition to these unconscious modifications there are also many conscious influences. Delightful examples of these can be tracked down in etiquette books from the past, especially in those from the Victorian period, when strict instructions were issued to young adults faced with the behaviour-minefield of correct deportment and good manners at social functions. With regard to an inborn pattern such as crying, there might be ruthless demands for total suppression. No strong emotions may be shown. Hide your feelings. Do not let go.

If a Victorian young lady responded to a tragedy with a few stifled sobs, she might be modifying her inborn urge to weep and scream, either by unconscious emulation of her 'betters', or by conscious adherence to a manual of conduct. Probably in most cases both were involved, making the final action a mixture of Inborn, Absorbed and Trained.

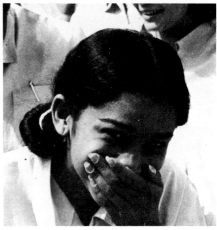

Looking again at leg-crossing, the same situation applies. A Victorian girl was bluntly informed that 'a lady never crosses her legs'. By the earlier part of the present century the rules were relaxed, but only for the most informal of contexts, and girls were still advised to avoid leg-crossing if possible. If they felt compelled to do it, then they were requested to restrict themselves to a modest form of the action, such as the ankle-ankle cross, rather than the knee-knee cross.

In the latter part of the twentieth century this might seem rather irrelevant—almost ancient history—in view of the current revolutions in social behaviour. If, for example, it is possible to see a naked girl having her pubic hair combed by a naked young man on the London stage, then, surely, someone will argue, degrees of leg-crossing are strictly the concern of great-grandmothers? But any serious field observer of human behaviour would instantly deny this. Not only are such prim subtleties still very much with us today, but they are adhered to even by the most liberated individuals. It is all a matter of context. Take the actress who permitted her pubic hair to be groomed on stage, clothe her, and set her down in a TV discussion studio, and you will find her obeying all the polite rules of standard leg-crossing. Present her to the Queen at a Charity Show, and this same girl will fall back immediately upon medieval manners and dip her body in an ancient curtsey.

So one must not be misled by cries of total cultural revolution. Old action patterns rarely die—they merely fade out of certain contexts. They limit

Victorian ladies were advised never to cross their legs; but today leg-crossing has become increasingly acceptable. Even so, royalty still restricts itself in public to the modest ankle-ankle cross.

The globally observed action of laughing may be suppressed or exaggerated. The stifled giggles of inhibited laughter, with hand-to-mouth cover-up (below left), contrast strongly with the unrestrained mirth of a London borough's Pearly Queen at a streetvendors' harvest festival (left). The inborn crying response is also modified by social pressures, in some cases (below) becoming tense, contorted sobbing—in others (right) silent, almost expressionless weeping.

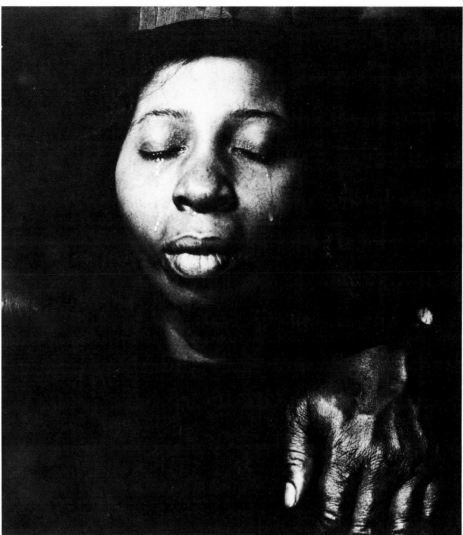

their social range, but somehow, somewhere, they usually manage to survive.

So tenacious are they, that we are still today giving the sign that the imaginary gladiator may not be spared—when we give the thumbs-down—as if we are ancient Romans, or doffing our imaginary hats—when giving a casual salute—as if we are still clad in bygone headgear.

We may no longer be aware of the original meanings of many of the actions we perform today, but we continue to use them because we are taught to do so. Frequently the teacher tells us no more than that it is polite, or the 'done thing', or the correct procedure, to perform a particular action, but he omits to say why. If we ask him, he does not know. We acquire the act, copying it slavishly, and then pass it on to others, who remain equally ignorant of its origins.

In this way, the early history of many actions is rapidly obscured, but this does not hamper their acquisition by new generations. Soon, they are being passed on, not because they are formally taught, but because we see others doing them and unthinkingly do likewise. They are therefore Mixed Actions of a special kind—they are historically mixed. They began as Trained Actions, obeying specific etiquette rules (= the medieval act of doffing the hat as part of the formal bow); then they became modified by abbreviation (=the modern military salute in which the hand is brought smartly up to touch the temple); until eventually they became so casually treated that they slipped into our general repertoire of Absorbed Actions (=hand raised to near the temple as a friendly greeting). They are therefore Mixed Actions when viewed across an historical time span, though not necessarily at any one point.

GESTURES

A gesture is any action that sends a visual signal to an onlooker. To become a gesture, an act has to be seen by someone else and has to communicate some piece of information to them. It can do this either because the gesturer deliberately sets out to send a signal—as when he waves his hand—or it can do it only incidentally—as when he sneezes. The hand-wave is a Primary Gesture, because it has no other existence or function. It is a piece of communication from start to finish. The sneeze, by contrast, is a secondary, or Incidental Gesture. Its primary function is mechanical and is concerned with the sneezer's personal breathing problem. In its secondary role, however, it cannot help but transmit a message to his companions, warning them that he may have caught a cold.

Most people tend to limit their use of the term 'gesture' to the primary form—the hand-wave type—but this misses an important point. What matters with gesturing is not what signals we think we are sending out, but what signals are being received. The observers of our acts will make no distinction between our intentional Primary Gestures and our unintentional, incidental ones. In some ways, our Incidental Gestures are the more illuminating of the two, if only for the very fact that we do not think of them as gestures, and therefore do not censor and manipulate them so strictly. This is why it is preferable to use the term 'gesture' in its wider meaning as an 'observed action'.

A convenient way to distinguish between Incidental and Primary Gestures is to ask the question: Would I do it if I were completely alone? If the answer is No, then it is a Primary Gesture. We do not wave, wink, or point when we are by ourselves; not, that is, unless we have reached the unusual condition of talking animatedly to ourselves.

INCIDENTAL GESTURES
Mechanical actions with secondary messages

Many of our actions are basically non-social, having to do with problems of personal body care, body comfort and body transportation; we clean and groom ourselves with a variety of scratchings, rubbings and wipings; we cough, yawn and stretch our limbs; we eat and drink; we prop ourselves up in restful postures, folding our arms and crossing our legs; we sit, stand, squat and recline, in a whole range of different positions; we crawl, walk and run in varying gaits and styles. But although we do these things for our own benefit, we are not always unaccompanied when we do them. Our companions learn a great deal about us from these 'personal' actions—not merely that we are scratching because we itch or that we are running because we are late, but also, from the way we do them, what kind of personalities we possess and what mood we are in at the time.

Sometimes the mood-signal transmitted unwittingly in this way is one that we would rather conceal, if we stopped to think about it. Occasionally we do become self-consciously aware of the 'mood broadcasts' and 'personality displays' we are making and we may then try to check ourselves. But often we do not, and the message goes out loud and clear.

For instance, if a student props his head on his hands while listening to a boring lecture, his head-on-hands action operates both mechanically and gesturally. As a mechanical act, it is simply a case of supporting a tired head—a physical act that concerns no one but the student himself. At the same time, though, it cannot help operating as a gestural act, beaming out a visual signal to his companions, and perhaps to the lecturer himself, telling them that he is bored.

In such a case his gesture was not deliberate and he may not even have

Since a gesture is an action that sends information to an onlooker, even a sneeze (left) can act as a gesture: it tells us about the condition of the sneezer, although that is not its primary function. It is an Incidental Gesture and contrasts with a Primary Gesture such as a wave or a beckon, where signalling is the only function. Supporting a tired head (above) is a simple, mechanical act, but since an interested audience is usually alert, slumped bodies confronting a speaker cannot help sending signals of boredom. As with sneezing, the head-propped posture therefore acts as an Incidental Gesture.

been aware that he was transmitting it. If challenged, he would claim that he was not bored at all, but merely tired. If he were honest—or impolite—he would have to admit that excited attention easily banishes tiredness, and that a really fascinating speaker need never fear to see a slumped, head-propped figure like his in the audience.

In the schoolroom, the teacher who barks at his pupils to 'sit up straight' is demanding, by right, the attention-posture that he should have gained by generating interest in his lesson. It says a great deal for the power of gesture-signals that he feels more 'attended-to' when he sees his pupils sitting up straight, even though he is consciously well aware of the fact that they have just been forcibly un-slumped, rather than genuinely excited by his teaching.

Many of our Incidental Gestures provide mood information of a kind that neither we *nor our companions* become consciously alerted to. It is as if there is an underground communication system operating just below the surface of our social encounters. We perform an act and it is observed. Its meaning is read, but not out loud. We 'feel' the mood, rather than analyse it. Occasionally an action of this type becomes so characteristic of a particular situation that we do eventually identify it—as when we say of a difficult problem: 'That will make him scratch his head', indicating that we do understand the link that exists between puzzlement and the Incidental Gesture of head-scratching. But frequently this type of link operates below the conscious level, or is missed altogether.

Where the links are clearer, we can, of course, manipulate the situation and use our Incidental Gestures in a contrived way. If a student listening to a lecture is not tired, but wishes to insult the speaker, he can deliberately adopt a bored, slumped posture, knowing that its message will get across. This is a Stylized Incidental Gesture—a mechanical action that is being artificially employed as a pure signal. Many of the common 'courtesies' also fall into this category—as when we greedily eat up a plate of food that we do not want and

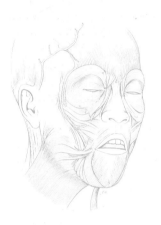

which we do not like, merely to transmit a suitably grateful signal to our hosts. Controlling our Incidental Gestures in this way is one of the processes that every child must learn as it grows up and learns to adapt to the rules of conduct of the society in which it lives.

EXPRESSIVE GESTURES
Biological gestures of the kind we share with other animals

Primary Gestures fall into six main categories. Five of these are unique to man, and depend on his complex, highly evolved brain. The exception is the category I called Expressive Gestures. These are gestures of the type which all men, everywhere, share with one another, and which other animals also perform. They include the important signals of Facial Expression, so crucial to daily human interaction.

All primates are facially expressive and among the higher species the facial muscles become increasingly elaborate, making possible the performance of a whole range of subtly varying facial signals. In man this trend reaches its peak, and it is true to say that the bulk of non-verbal signalling is transmitted by the human face.

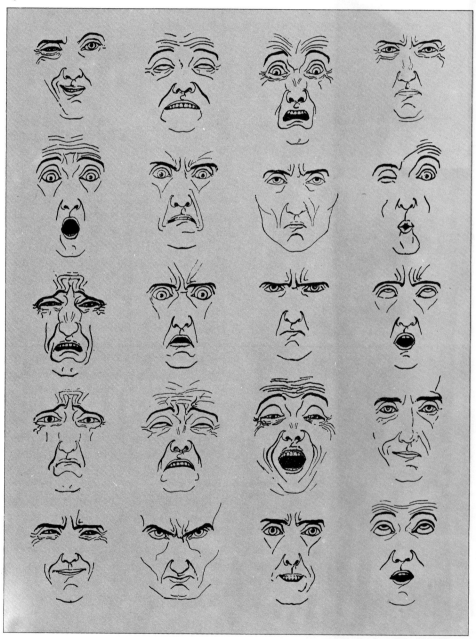

A shouting man, a smiling woman and a grimacing child. The human face has the most complex and highly developed set of facial muscles in the entire animal world. Some of our animal relatives are capable of a fair range of expressions, but none can match the subtlety or variety of human facial expressions and the moods they transmit. The array of Expressive Gestures (left) is from a book on the art of pantomime by Charles Aubert; and the drawing of the muscles of the face (far left) is from a study by Ernst Huber of the evolution of the face.

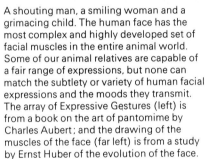

The human hands are also important, having been freed from their ancient locomotion duties, and are capable, with their Manual Gesticulations, of transmitting many small mood changes by shifts in their postures and movements, especially during conversational encounters. I am defining the word 'gesticulation', as distinct from 'gesture', as a manual action performed unconsciously during social interactions, when the gesticulator is emphasizing a verbal point he is making.

These natural gestures are usually spontaneous and very much taken for granted. Yes, we say, he made a funny face. But which way did his eyebrows move? We cannot recall. Yes, we say, he was waving his arms about as he spoke. But what shape did his fingers make? We cannot remember. Yet we were not inattentive. We saw it all and our brains registered what we saw. We simply did not need to analyse the actions, any more than we had to spell out the words we heard, in order to understand them. In this respect they are similar to the Incidental Gestures of the previous category, but they differ, because here there is no mechanical function—only signalling. This is the world of smiles and sneers, shrugs and pouts, laughs and winces, blushes and blanches, waves and beckons, nods and glares, frowns and snarls. These are the gestures that nearly everyone performs nearly everywhere in the world. They may differ in detail and in context from place to place, but basically they are actions we all share. We all have complex facial muscles whose sole job it is to make expressions, and we all stand on two feet rather than four, freeing our hands and letting them dance in the air evocatively as we explain, argue and joke our way through our social encounters. We may have lost our twitching tails and our bristling fur, but we more than make up for it with our marvellously mobile faces and our twisting, spreading, fluttering hands.

In origin, our Expressive Gestures are closely related to our Incidental Gestures, because their roots also lie in primarily non-communicative actions. The clenched fist of the gesticulator owes its origin to an intention movement of hitting an opponent, just as the frown on the face of a worried man can be traced back to an ancient eye-protection movement of an animal anticipating physical attack. But the difference is that in these cases the link between the primary physical action and its ultimate descendant, the Expressive Gesture, has been broken. Smiles, pouts, winces, gapes, smirks, and the rest, are now, for all practical purposes, pure gestures and exclusively communicative in function.

Despite their worldwide distribution, Expressive Gestures are nevertheless subject to considerable cultural influences. Even though we all have an evolved set of smiling muscles, we do not all smile in precisely the same way,

to the same extent, or on the same occasions. For example, all children may start out as easy-smilers and easy-laughers, but a local tradition may insist that, as the youngsters mature, they must hide their feelings, and their adult laughter may become severely muted as a result. These local Display Rules, varying from place to place, often give the false impression that Expressive Gestures are local inventions rather than modified, but universal, behaviour patterns.

MIMIC GESTURES

Gestures which transmit signals by imitation

Mimic Gestures are those in which the performer attempts to imitate, as accurately as possible, a person, an object or an action. Here we leave our animal heritage behind and enter an exclusively human sphere. The essential quality of a Mimic Gesture is that it attempts to copy the thing it is trying to portray. No stylized conventions are applied. A successful Mimic Gesture is therefore understandable to someone who has never seen it performed before. No prior knowledge should be required and there need be no set tradition concerning the way in which a particular item is represented. There are four kinds of Mimic Gesture:

First, there is Social Mimicry, or 'putting on a good face'. We have all done this. We have all smiled at a party when really we feel sad, and perhaps looked sadder at a funeral than we feel, simply because it is expected of us. We lie with simulated gestures to please others. This should not be confused with what psychologists call 'role-playing'. When indulging in Social Mimicry we deceive only others, but when role-playing we deceive ourselves as well.

Second, there is Theatrical Mimicry—the world of actors and actresses, who simulate everything for our amusement. Essentially it embraces two distinct techniques. One is the calculated attempt to imitate specifically observed actions. The actor who is to play a general, say, will spend long hours watching films of military scenes in which he can analyse every tiny movement and then consciously copy them and incorporate them into his

final portrayal. The other technique is to concentrate instead on the imagined mood of the character to be portrayed, to attempt to take on that mood, and to rely upon it to produce, unconsciously, the necessary style of body actions.

In reality, all actors use a combination of both these techniques, although in explaining their craft they may stress one or other of the two methods. In the past, acting performances were usually highly stylized, but today, except in pantomime, opera and farce, extraordinary degrees of realism are reached and the formal, obtrusive audience has become instead a shadowy group of eavesdroppers. Gone are the actor's asides, gone are the audience participations. We must all believe that it is really happening. In other words, Theatrical Mimicry has at last become as realistic as day-to-day Social Mimicry. In this respect, these first two types of mimic activity contrast sharply with the third, which can be called Partial Mimicry.

In Partial Mimicry the performer attempts to imitate something which he is not and never can be, such as a bird, or raindrops. Usually only the hands are involved, but these make the most realistic approach to the subject they can manage. If a bird, they flap their 'wings' as best they can; if raindrops, they describe a sprinkling descent as graphically as possible. Widely used mimic gestures of this kind are those which convert the hand into a 'gun', an animal of some sort, or the foot of an animal; or those which use the movements of the hand to indicate the outline shape of an object of some kind.

The fourth kind of Mimic Gesture can best be called Vacuum Mimicry, because the action takes place in the absence of the object to which it is related. If I am hungry, for example, I can go through the motions of putting imaginary food into my mouth. If I am thirsty, I can raise my hand as if holding an invisible glass, and gulp invisible liquid from it.

The important feature of Partial Mimicry and Vacuum Mimicry is that, like Social and Theatrical Mimicry, they strive for reality. Even though they are doomed to failure, they make an attempt. This means that they can be understood internationally. In this respect they contrast strongly with the next two types of gesture, which show marked cultural restrictions.

SCHEMATIC GESTURES
Imitations that become abbreviated or abridged

Schematic Gestures are abbreviated or abridged versions of Mimic Gestures. They attempt to portray something by taking just one of its prominent features and then performing that alone. There is no longer any attempt at realism.

Schematic Gestures usually arise as a sort of gestural shorthand because of the need to perform an imitation quickly and on many occasions. Just as, in ordinary speech, we reduce the word 'cannot' to 'can't', so an elaborate miming of a charging bull becomes reduced simply to a pair of horns jabbed in the air as a pair of fingers.

When one element of a mime is selected and retained in this way, and the other elements are reduced or omitted, the gesture may still be easy to understand, when seen for the first time, but the stylization may go so far that it becomes meaningless to those not 'in the know'. The Schematic Gesture then becomes a local tradition with a limited geographical range. If the original mime was complex and involved several distinctive features, different localities may select different key features for their abridged versions. Once these different forms of shorthand have become fully established in each region, then the people who use them will become less and less likely to recognize the foreign forms. The local gesture becomes 'the' gesture, and there quickly develops, in gesture communication, a situation similar to that found in linguistics. Just as each region has its own verbal language, so it also has its own set of Schematic Gestures.

To give an example: the American Indian sign for a horse consists of a gesture in which two fingers of one hand 'sit astride' the fingers of the other hand. A Cistercian monk would instead signal 'horse' by lowering his head slightly and pulling at an imaginary tuft of hair on his forehead. An Englishman would probably crouch down like a jockey and pull at imaginary reins. The Englishman's version, being closer to a Vacuum Mimic Gesture, might be understood by the other two, but their gestures, being highly schematic, might well prove incomprehensible to anyone outside their groups.

Some objects, however, have one special feature that is so strongly characteristic of them that, even with Schematic Gestures, there is little doubt about what is being portrayed. The bull, mentioned above, is a good example of this. Cattle are nearly always indicated by their horns alone, and the two horns are always represented by two digits. In fact, if an American Indian, a Hindu dancer, and an Australian Aborigine met, they would all understand one another's cattle signs, and we would understand all three of them. This does not mean that the signs are all identical. The American Indian's cattle sign would represent the bison, and the horns of bison do not curve forward like those of domestic cattle, but inward, towards each other. The American Indian's sign reflects this, his hands being held to his temples and his forefingers being pointed inward. The Australian Aborigine instead points his forefingers forward. The Hindu dancer also points forward, but rather than using two forefingers up at the temples, employs the forefinger and little finger of one hand, held at waist height. So each culture has its own variant, but the fact that horns are such an obvious distinguishing feature of cattle means that, despite local variations, the bovine Schematic Gesture is reasonably understandable in most cultures.

Because Schematic Gestures select one special feature of the thing to be portrayed and present this in a stylized way, they are not always clear to strangers who are ignorant of local gestural conventions. Some objects, however, have one feature so obvious that it is nearly always chosen. Thus cattle are represented schematically as a pair of horns in cultures as widely separated as those of the Australian Aborigine and Hindu dancer (above) and the North American Indian (opposite).

SYMBOLIC GESTURES

Gestures which represent moods and ideas

A Symbolic Gesture indicates an abstract quality that has no simple equivalent in the world of objects and movements. Here we are one stage further away from the obviousness of the enacted Mimic Gesture.

How, for instance, would you make a silent sign for stupidity? You might launch into a full-blooded Theatrical Mime of a drooling village idiot. But total idiocy is not a precise way of indicating the momentary stupidity of a healthy adult. Instead, you might tap your forefinger against your temple, but this also lacks accuracy, since you might do precisely the same thing when indicating that someone is brainy. All the tap does is to point to the brain. To make the meaning more clear, you might instead twist your forefinger against your temple, indicating 'a screw loose'. Alternatively, you might rotate your forefinger close to your temple, signalling that the brain is going round and round and is not stable.

Many people would understand these temple-forefinger actions, but others

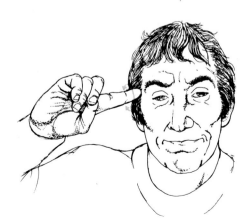

would not. They would have their own local, stupidity gestures, which we in our turn would find confusing, such as tapping the elbow of the raised forearm, flapping the hand up and down in front of half-closed eyes, rotating a raised hand, or laying one forefinger flat across the forehead.

The situation is further complicated by the fact that some stupidity signals mean totally different things in different countries. To take one example, in Saudi Arabia stupidity can be signalled by touching the lower eyelid with the tip of the forefinger. But this same action, in various other countries, can mean disbelief, approval, agreement, mistrust, scepticism, alertness, secrecy, craftiness, danger, or criminality. The reason for this apparent chaos of meanings is simple enough. By pointing to the eye, the gesturer is doing no more than stress the symbolic importance of the eye as a seeing organ. Beyond that, the action says nothing, so that the message can become either: 'Yes, I see', or 'I can't believe my eyes', or 'Keep a sharp look-out', or 'I like what I see', or almost any other seeing signal you care to imagine. In such a case it is essential to know the precise 'seeing' property being represented by the symbolism of the gesture in any particular culture.

So we are faced with two basic problems where Symbolic Gestures are concerned: either one meaning may be signalled by different actions, or several meanings may be signalled by the same action, as we move from culture to culture. The only solution is to approach each culture with an open mind and learn their Symbolic Gestures as one would their vocabulary.

As part of this process, it helps if a link can be found between the action and the meaning, but this is not always possible. In some cases we simply do not know how certain Symbolic Gestures arose. It is clear that they are symbolic because they now represent some abstract quality, but how they first acquired the link between action and meaning has been lost somewhere in their long history. A good instance of this is the 'cuckold' sign from Italy. This consists of making a pair of horns, either with two forefingers held at the temples, or with a forefinger and little finger of one hand held in front of the body. There is little doubt about what the fingers are meant to be: they are the horns of a bull. As such, they would rate as part of a Schematic Gesture. But they do not send out the simple message 'bull'. Instead they now indicate 'sexual betrayal'. The action is therefore a Symbolic gesture and, in order to explain it, it becomes necessary to find the link between bulls and sexual betrayal.

Historically, the link appears to be lost, with the result that some rather wild speculations have been made. A complication arises in the form of the 'horned hand', also common in Italy, which has a totally different significance, even though it employs the same motif of bull's horns. The horned hand is essentially a protective gesture, made to ward off imagined dangers. Here it is clear enough that it is the bull's great power, ferocity and masculinity that is being invoked as a symbolic aid to protect the gesturer. But this only makes it even more difficult to explain the other use of the bull's-horns gesture as a sign of a 'pathetic' cuckold.

Symbolic Gestures are often difficult to interpret because their origins have been obscured. But some can be guessed, as in the case of signs symbolizing 'stupidity'. These vary from place to place, but nearly always indicate 'something wrong with the brain'. Examples (below, left to right) are the Temple Tap, the Temple Rotate, the Temple Screw, the Forehead Tap, the Eyes Flap and the Forehead Scrub. The last is confined to certain North American Indians, but the others are more widespread.

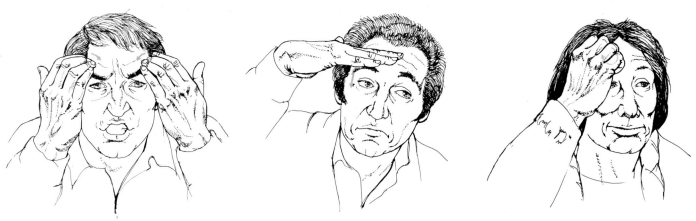

The Cuckold Sign from Italy, seen in an 18th-century drawing (above) and performed by a 19th-century Harlequin (below). The symbolic origins of this ancient action—a gross insult to an Italian—are lost, but several conflicting theories have been proposed. Opposite: symbolic finger-crossing actions. The act of kissing crossed forefingers when swearing an oath is not difficult to trace to its origin, the crossed fingers clearly representing the Christian Cross. Less obviously sharing the same origin is the familiar 'good luck' sign of crossing the first two fingers of one hand.

A suggested explanation of this contradiction is that it is due to one gesture using as its starting point the bull's power, while the other—the cuckold sign—selects the bull's frequent castration. Since the domestication of cattle began, there have always been too many bulls in relation to cows. A good, uncastrated bull can serve between 50 and 100 cows a year, so that it is only necessary to retain a small proportion of intact bulls for breeding purposes. The rest are rendered much more docile and easy to handle for beef production, by castration. In folk-lore, then, these impotent males must stand helplessly by, while the few sexually active bulls 'steal their rightful females'; hence the symbolism of: bull = cuckold.

A completely different explanation once offered was that, when the cuckold discovers that his wife has betrayed him, he becomes so enraged and jealous that he bellows and rushes violently about like a 'mad bull'.

A more classical interpretation involves Diana the Huntress, who made horns into a symbol of male downfall. Actaeon, another hunter, is said to have sneaked a look at her naked body when she was bathing. This so angered her that she turned him into a horned beast and set his own hounds upon him, who promptly killed and ate him.

Alternatively, there is the version dealing with ancient religious prostitutes. These ladies worshipped gods who wore 'horns of honour'—that is, horns in their other role as symbols of power and masculinity—and the gods were so pleased with the wives who became sacred whores that they transferred their godly horns on to the heads of the husbands who had ordered their women to act in this role. In this way, the horns of honour became the horns of ridicule.

As if this were not enough, it is also claimed elsewhere, and with equal conviction, that because stags have horns (antlers were often called horns in earlier periods) and because most stags in the rutting season lose their females to a few dominant males who round up large harems, the majority of 'horned' deer are unhappy 'cuckolds'.

Finally, there is the bizarre interpretation that bulls and deer have nothing to do with it. Instead, it is thought that the ancient practice of grafting the spurs of a castrated cockrel on to the root of its excised comb, where they apparently grew and became 'horns', is the origin of the symbolic link between horns and cuckolds. This claim is backed up by the fact that the German equivalent word for 'cuckold' (*hahnrei*) originally meant 'capon'.

If, after reading these rival claims, you feel that all you have really learned is the meaning of the phrase 'cock-and-bull story', you can be forgiven. Clearly, we are in the realm of fertile imagination rather than historical record. But this example has been dealt with at length to show how, in so many cases, the true story of the origin of a Symbolic Gesture is no longer available to us. Many other similarly conflicting examples are known, but this one will suffice to demonstrate the general principle.

There are exceptions, of course, and certain of the Symbolic Gestures we

make today, and take for granted, can easily be traced to their origins. 'Keeping your fingers crossed' is a good example of this. Although used by many non-Christians, this action of making the cross, using only the first and second fingers, is an ancient protective device of the Christian church. In earlier times it was commonplace to make a more conspicuous sign of the cross (to cross oneself) by moving the whole arm, first downwards and then sideways, in front of the body, tracing the shape of the cross in the air. This can still be seen in some countries today in a non-religious context, acting as a 'good luck' protective device. In more trivial situations it has been widely replaced, however, by the act of holding up one hand to show that the second finger is tightly crossed over the first, with the crossing movement of the arm omitted. Originally this was the secret version of 'crossing oneself' and was done with the hand in question carefully hidden from view. It may still be done in this secret way, as when trying to protect oneself from the consequences of lying, but as a 'good luck' sign it has now come out into the open. This development is easily explained by the fact that crossing the fingers lacks an obvious religious character. Symbolically, the finger-crossing may be calling on the protection of the Christian God, but the small finger action performed is so far removed from the priestly arm crossing action, that it can without difficulty slide into everyday life as a casual wish for good fortune. Proof of this is that many people do not even realize that they are demanding an act of Christian worship—historically speaking—when they shout out: 'Keep your fingers crossed!'

TECHNICAL GESTURES

Gestures used by speciaiist minorities

Technical Gestures are invented by a specialist minority for use strictly within the limits of their particular activity. They are meaningless to anyone outside the specialization and operate in such a narrow field that they cannot be considered as playing a part in the mainstream of visual communication of any culture.

Television-studio signals are a good example of Technical Gestures in use today. The studio commentator we see on our screens at home is face to face with a 'studio manager'. The manager is linked to the programme director in the control room by means of headphones and conveys the director's instructions to the commentator by simple visual gestures. To warn the commentator that he will have to start speaking at any moment, the manager raises a forearm and holds it stiffly erect. To start him speaking, he brings the forearm swiftly down to point at the commentator. To warn him that he must stop speaking in a few seconds, the manager rotates his forearm, as if it were the hand of a clock going very fast—'Time is running out fast.' To ask him to lengthen the speaking time and say more, he holds his hands together in front of his chest and pulls them slowly apart, as if stretching something—'stretch it out.' To tell the speaker to stop dead this instant, the manager makes a slashing action with his hand across his throat—'Cut!' There are no set rules laid down for these signals. They grew up in the early days of television and, although the main ones listed here are fairly

Technical Gestures are used by specialists and do not constitute part of the gestural repertoire of a whole society. Examples include signals given to British crane-drivers (below) or exchanged by firemen (below right).

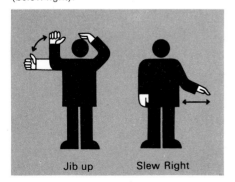

Jib up   Slew Right

Water on

Increase pressure

Reduce pressure

Make up all gear

widespread today, each studio may well have its own special variants, worked out to suit a particular performer.

Other Technical Gestures are found wherever an activity prohibits verbal contact. Skindivers, for instance, cannot speak to one another and need simple signals to deal with potentially dangerous situations. In particular they need gestures for danger, cold, cramp and fatigue. Other messages, such as yes, no, good, bad, up and down, are easily enough understood by the use of everyday actions and require no Technical Gestures to make sense. But how could you signal to a companion that you had cramp? The answer is that you would open and close one hand rhythmically—a simple gesture, but one that might nevertheless save a life.

Disaster can sometimes occur because a Technical Gesture is required from someone who is not a specialist in a technical field. Suppose some holiday-makers take out a boat, and it sinks, and they swim to the safety of a small, rocky island. Wet and frightened, they crouch there wondering what to do next, when to their immense relief a small fishing-boat comes chugging towards them. As it draws level with the island, they wave frantically at it. The people on board wave back, and the boat chugs on and disappears. If the stranded holiday-makers had been marine 'specialists', they would have known that, at sea, waving is only used as a greeting. To signal distress, they should have raised and lowered their arms stiffly from their sides. This is the accepted marine gesture for 'Help!'

Ironically, if the shipwrecked signallers had been marine experts and had given the correct distress signal, the potential rescue boat might well have been manned by holiday-makers, who would have been completely nonplussed by the strange actions and would probably have ignored them. When a technical sphere is invaded by the non-technical, gesture problems always arise.

Firemen, crane-drivers, airport-tarmac signalmen, gambling-casino croupiers, dealers at auctions, and restaurant staff, all have their own special Technical Gestures. Either because they must keep quiet, must be discreet, or cannot be heard, they develop their own sets of signals. The rest of us can ignore them, unless we, too, wish to enter their specialized spheres.

CODED GESTURES

Sign-language based on a formal system

Coded Gestures, unlike all others, are part of a formal system of signals. They interrelate with one another in a complex and systematic way, so that they constitute a true language. The special feature of this category is that the

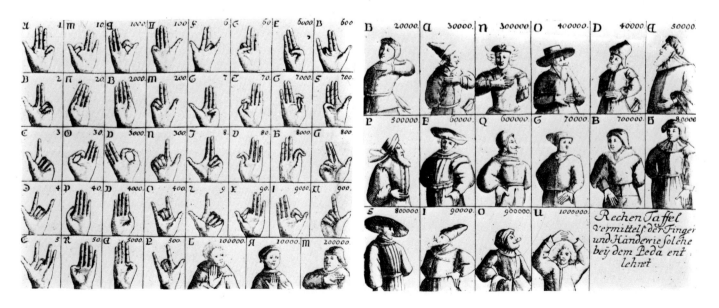

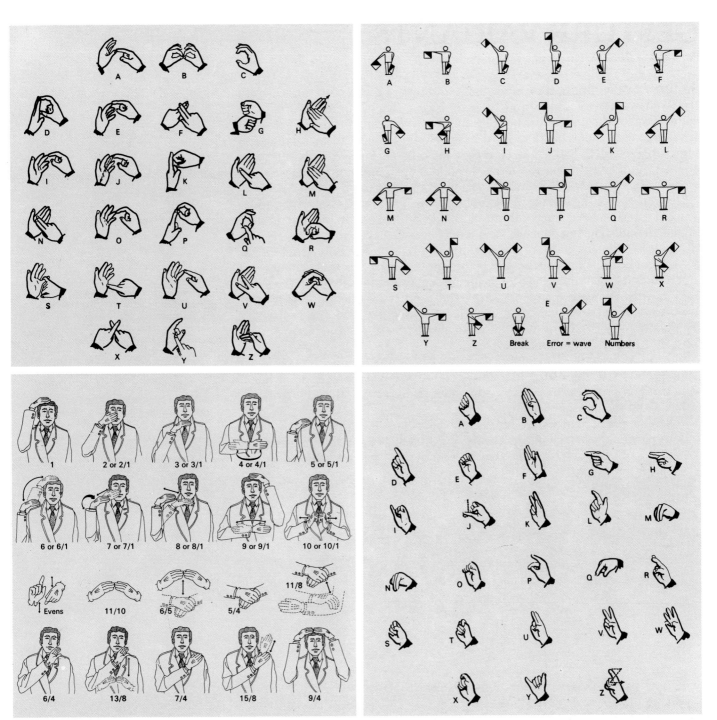

Coded Gestures only have meaning as part of a planned, structured signalling system. Examples include the two-handed and one-handed deaf-and-dumb codes (top left and bottom right), the semaphore code employed for naval communications (top right), and the tic-tac system used on race-courses for describing the betting odds (after Brun). There are also many gestural counting systems, such as this early one at left, dating from 1724.

individual units are valueless without reference to the other units in the code. Technical Gestures may be systematically planned, but, with them, each signal can operate quite independently of the others. With Coded Gestures, by contrast, all the units interlock with one another on rigidly formulated principles, like the letters and words in a verbal language.

The most important example is the Deaf-and-dumb Sign Language of hand signals, of which there is both a one-handed and a two-handed version. Also, there is the Semaphore Language of arm signals, and the Tic-tac Language of the race course. These all require considerable skill and training and belong in a totally different world from the familiar gestures we employ in everyday life. They serve as a valuable reminder, though, of the incredibly sensitive potential we all possess for visual communication. It makes it all the more plausible to argue that we are all of us responding, with greater sensitivity than we may realize, to the ordinary gestures we witness each day of our lives.

GESTURE VARIANTS

Personal or local variations on gestural themes

Gestures, by definition, transmit signals, and these signals must come across clearly if we are to understand their messages. They cannot afford to be vague and woolly; they must be crisp and sharp and difficult to confuse with other signals. To do this they have to develop a 'typical form' that shows comparatively little variation. And they must be performed with a 'typical intensity', showing much the same speed, strength and amplitude on each occasion that they are brought into action.

It is rather like the ringing of a telephone bell. The signal goes on sounding at fixed intervals, at a fixed volume, and with a fixed sound, no matter how urgent the call. The telephone system treats a casual call in just the same way as one that happens to be a matter of life and death. The only difference it permits is the length of the ringing, before the caller gives up. This may seem inefficient, and one sometimes longs for a telephone bell that gets louder and louder, with increasing urgency. But the rigidity of the ringing tone is important in one major respect: it reduces ambiguity. No one confuses a telephone bell with a front-door bell or an alarum clock. Its fixed form and its fixed intensity make it unmistakable.

This process is at work in human gestures. They can never hope to perfect a completely fixed intensity, like the bell, but they can and do achieve something approximating it in many cases. Here again, the ambiguity is reduced and the message is clear.

When an angry man shakes his fist, the chances are that the speed, force and amplitude of each shake, as the fist jerks back and forth in mid-air, are much the same on each occasion that he employs this gesture. And there is a

Fist-shaking is performed in much the same way wherever it occurs, and is easy to understand because its form of expression has developed a 'typical intensity'—it conforms to a general rule. Below: the fist-shaking of political demonstrators.

Gesture Variants are departures from the general rule. Right: three variants of a gestural theme, the Forearm Jerk. This is a phallic insult common to many Western countries, but the precise form it takes varies from place to place and from person to person. For example, it may appear in a flathand version, a palm-down-fist version, or a palm-up-fist version.

Personal Gesture Variants provide each of us with an individual 'body-style'. We all smile, but some of us have supersmiles, exposing gums as well as teeth—like President Carter (above right)—while others show only a narrow-gap grin.

reasonable likelihood that his speed, force and amplitude will be similar to those of any other fist-shaker. If, as an experiment, you were to perform a fist-shaking gesture in which you slowed down the movement, decreased the force, and increased the distance travelled by the clenched fist, it is doubtful if your signal would be understood. An onlooker might imagine you were exercising your arm, but it is doubtful if he would read the message as a threat display.

Most of our gestures have grown into typical presentations of this kind. We all wave in much the same way, clap our hands at roughly the same speed, beckon with much the same amplitude, and shake our heads with the same sort of rhythm. This is not a conscious process. We simply tune in to the cultural norm. Unwittingly, we smooth the path of the hundreds of tiny messages that fly between us whenever we meet and interact. Somehow we manage to match up our gestures with those of our companions, and they do the same with ours. Together we synchronize the intensities of our gesturings until we are all operating in concert, as if under the control of an invisible cultural conductor.

As always with human behaviour, there are exceptions to this general rule. We are not automatons. We show personal idiosyncracies—individual variations on the cultural themes. One man, with a particularly fine set of teeth, shows an exaggeratedly intense, open-lipped smile, and he does this even in mild situations. Another man, with bad teeth, gives a more closed

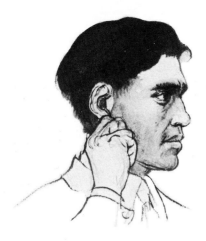

The Italian Ear Touch gesture, meaning that a man is considered to be effeminate, exists in several variant forms. The ear may be held, flicked or (as seen here) pulled. All these actions have the same meaning and in this case, because of the absence of other ear-touching signals, the variations do not create confusion.

The Hand Purse gesture has many variant forms in different countries. Here, performed by a Sardinian, it means 'What's the matter with you?' In this version, the hand is jerked rapidly up and down.

smile, even when strongly stimulated. One man bellows with laughter, while another titters, in reaction to the same joke. These are the Gesture Variants and they provide each of us with a behavioural 'style', or body-personality. They are small differences compared with our general gesture-conformity, but they can become important personal labels none the less.

There is another type of Gesture Variant, and that is the one that exists because a particular gesture is rather rare and is unlikely to be confused with any other gesture. It fails to develop a typical form, through lack of use and lack of ambiguity. A good example is the Italian Ear Touch. This gesture always has the same meaning throughout Italy: it is a sign that someone, a male, is considered to be effeminate or homosexual. It occurs infrequently and there are no other ear-touching gestures with which it can be confused. The result is that it lacks a typical form. The ear can be pulled, tugged, flipped, flicked or merely touched, and yet the message is always the same. The observer is not confused by these variations, as he might be with other gestures that have close similarities with one another. There is no pressure on the gesturer to narrow the action down to a precise movement. The gesture owes its origin, incidentally, to the fact that women wear ear-rings, the gesture representing the touching of an imaginary ear ornament and therefore implying a female trait.

Although the Gesture Variants in this particular case cause no confusion, the situation becomes much more complicated with certain other gestures. The Hand Purse signal is a case in point. In origin this is a hand action which is used to emphasize a statement being made during the course of conversation. The thumb and fingertips are brought together in a cone, pointing upwards. The hand beats time in this posture as the key words are uttered, and in this form the gesture can be observed in almost every country in the world. But in certain regions specific variations of this basic gesture have been developed, each with its own particular, local meaning. In Greece and Turkey the action has come to mean 'good'; in Spain it means 'lots of . . .' something; in Malta it implies heavy sarcasm; in Tunisia it indicates the caution: 'Slowly, slowly'; in France it says: 'I am afraid'; and in Italy, where it is extremely common, it is usually an irritated query, saying: 'What's the matter, what's up?' In each of these cases the action is performed in a special local variant form of the basic action. In Malta, for instance, the hand is pulled heavily down through the air once; in Tunisia, the hand moves down several times very slowly; in France, it is done with the fingers opening and closing very slightly; and in Italy the hand is jerked up and down rapidly.

The truth is that the original Hand Purse gesture has grown into a whole series of quite distinct actions, each of which should be considered as a separate gesture. These are not true Gesture Variants of one gesture, they are now a whole family of gestures. This works well enough within any one culture. But when a man moves from one of these countries to another, he is very likely to become confused. He sees the foreign gesture as merely a Gesture Variant of his own, and therefore cannot understand why it should have a totally different meaning. He reads the variation as a personal or local idiosyncrasy and imagines that the foreigner he is observing simply has a rather odd way of performing his old familiar gesture.

Were there a great deal of contact between two such cultures there is little doubt that over a period of time the gesture differences would start to widen until no confusion was possible, but without this, errors do occur. This underlines the reason why, within one culture, typical action-patterns do develop and how, in so doing, they avoid signalling ambiguity. Except in special cases, Gesture Variants constitute a threat to this system and tend to be eliminated or reduced. In this way, each culture develops its own clear-cut repertoire of discrete visual signals, each unit being clearly differentiated from all the others. Only when our wanderlust and our modern mobility lead us into foreign parts does this efficient communication system start to break down.

MULTIMESSAGE GESTURES

Gestures that have many meanings

A Multimessage Gesture is one that has a number of totally distinct meanings, depending on the time and the place.

When an American wants to signal that something is OK, fine, perfect, great—he raises his hand and makes a circle with his thumb and forefinger. This circle-sign has only one message for him, and he might be surprised to discover that in other countries it can mean something quite different.

In Japan, for instance, it is the gesture for money. In France it means 'zero' or 'worthless'. In Malta it means that someone is a 'pooftah'—a male homosexual. In Sardinia and Greece it is an obscene comment or insult to either a male or female.

Apart from the fact that such differences can obviously lead to all kinds of misunderstandings when foreigners meet, it is puzzling that such contradictory messages should have arisen in the first place. To find the explanation we have to look at the basic symbolism used in each case.

The American sign for something perfect is derived from the hand posture for precision. If we want to say that something is precise or exact, we make the movement of holding something very small between the tips of our thumb and forefinger. People all over the world do this unconsciously when speaking about some fine point. The object they hold is imaginary—they merely go through the motions of holding it, and in this way they automatically form a ring or circle with the thumb and forefinger. In America this unconscious gesticulation became amplified into a deliberate signal, the expression of exactness developing into the message 'exactly right', or 'perfect', and the famous OK sign was born.

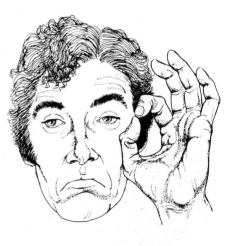

The Japanese sign for money starts from a completely different source. Money means coins and coins are circular. Therefore, making a circular hand-sign comes to symbolize money. It is as simple as that.

The French sign for 'nothing', or 'worthless', also starts from a simple equation, but this time the circle represents not a coin, but a nought. Nought = zero = nothing = worthless.

The sexual examples are related to one another and have the same basic symbolism. Here the ring made by the thumb and forefinger stands for a body orifice. Because it is circular, the hand posture is strongly anal, hence its significance in Malta as a gesture meaning male homosexual. In Sardinia and Greece it is used more as a general obscene comment or insult to either sex, but the meaning is still basically anal. These uses of the gesture have a long and ancient history and have certainly been operating for more than two thousand years. An early vase painting shows four athletes bathing outside a gymnasium, with one of them clearly insulting the others by making the orifice gesture.

The Circle-sign made by forming a ring with the thumb and forefinger of one hand. It carries different messages for different people. An Englishman knows only one meaning for this sign; for him, both drawings (above) carry an 'OK' message. But for many Frenchmen only the smiling picture is signalling 'OK', while the other signals 'zero' or 'worthless'. To a Japanese (below) the same sign may mean 'money'.

So the simple, circular hand-sign can stand for a precision grip, a coin, a nought, or an orifice, according to its country of origin. And these visual comparisons then lead on to the five different symbolisms of perfection, money, worthlessness, homosexuality, or sexual propositioning.

This situation is complicated enough, but it becomes even more complex when one particular message starts spreading into the range of the others. The American OK sign has become so popular that it has invaded Europe. In England there was no local circle-sign in use, so the American OK sign could move in without resistance. No Englishman today would use the gesture for any other purpose. But in France the situation was different. They already had the zero sign, so that the arrival of the OK gesture created a problem. Today, many Frenchmen still use the circle-sign as a 'zero' signal, others as an OK. The 'zero' message predominates in the south of France, while the OK is more common in the far north of the country. Although this can lead to difficulties, confusion is usually avoided by taking into account the context

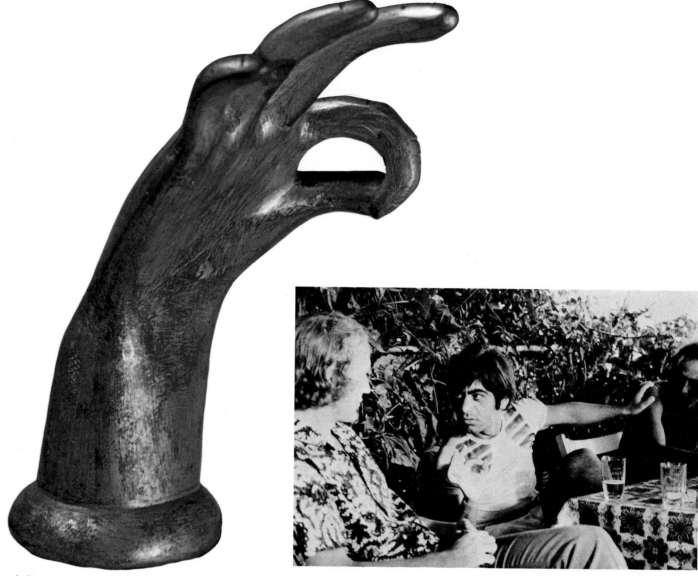

of the gesture. If the gesturer looks happy, it is likely that he means 'OK'; if not, he means 'zero'.

This raises an important point, for in England, or America, where there is only one dominant meaning for the circle-signal, the facial expression would make little difference. The message is so clear that it overrides the context. If an Englishman deliberately makes a grim face while giving the OK sign, the sign is so powerful that the face would be ignored, or interpreted as a joke—a mock-sadness that is not really being felt.

This phenomenon of 'context override' usually comes into operation wherever there is a single, clear, dominant meaning for a particular gesture. But as soon as you move into a region where more than one meaning is possible, the context becomes vitally important.

Multimessage Gestures with as many meanings as the circle-sign are comparatively rare, but there are large numbers of signs that have more than one basic message. Wherever the action involved has a built-in ambiguity, there we are likely to find alternative meanings if we look far enough afield.

For example, actions in which the finger touches the temple or forehead usually symbolize some condition of the brain, but the condition varies from case to case. Sometimes it means 'clever'—'good brain'—and sometimes it means 'stupid'—'bad brain'; actions in which the mouth is touched may mean 'hunger', 'thirst', 'speech' or 'lack of speech'; actions involving pointing at the eye may refer to 'seeing well' or 'seeing badly'. The generality of the basic gesture leads to different paths of symbolism, spreading out in different directions.

As an obscene comment or insult, the circle-sign, demonstrated above by a Sardinian, has been active in the Mediterranean region for over two thousand years, and can be found in ancient paintings, as amulets and as sculptures such as the one shown (above left).

GESTURE ALTERNATIVES

Different gestures that transmit the same signal

Just as one gesture can have many different meanings, so can many different gestures have the same meaning. If a message is basic enough and of sufficient importance to appear in widely varying cultures, the chances are high that it will be transmitted by gestures that are strikingly different both in form and in origin.

If two men are standing on a street corner and they see an attractive girl walking past, one may turn to the other and signal his appreciation by a simple gesture. Even within one particular culture there are usually several ways in which he can do this; but when we cast our net wider and observe this fleeting incident on street corners in many different countries, the list of possible signals becomes even more impressive. The illustrations show twelve ways of saying: 'What a beautiful girl!'—and reveal the many different sources that are drawn upon when performing this brief act of praise.

Gestures 1–4 are ways of commenting on the girl's attributes.

1. The Cheek Stroke. The forefinger and thumb of one hand are placed lightly on the gesturer's cheek-bones and then stroked gently down towards the chin. The gesture symbolizes the smooth roundedness of the face of a beautiful girl, and is said to have originated in ancient Greece, where an egg-shaped face was the ideal of female beauty. Greece remains to this day the area where the gesture most commonly occurs, but it is now also found in Italy and Spain.

2. The Cheek Screw. A straight forefinger is pressed into the middle of the cheek and rotated. There are two possible origins. One idea is that the action symbolizes something delicious to eat, which is extended to mean that the girl is 'delicious'. The other sees the gesture as emphasizing the dimpling of a beautiful girl's cheek. Today, the Cheek Screw is in common use throughout Italy, including Sicily and Sardinia, but is rare elsewhere.

3. The Breast Curve. The hands describe the forward curve of the female breasts. The origin is obvious and the action is common over a wide range.

4. The Waist Curve. The hands sweep down through the air describing an exaggerated female-trunk outline, emphasizing the narrow waist-line and the wide hips. Again, an obvious origin for an action that is widely understood and especially common in English-speaking countries.

Gestures 5–8 are comments by the man on his reactions to the girl.

5. The Eye Touch. The man places a straight forefinger against his lower eyelid and may pull it slightly downwards. This action occurs in many countries and has many meanings, but in certain areas, such as parts of South America and a few districts in Italy, it is a signal that a girl is 'an eyeful'.

6. The Two-handed Telescope. The hands are curled and the man peers

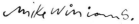

9

10

11

mike williams.

7

8

12

through them as if using a telescope to gaze at the girl. The symbolism is based on the idea that the girl deserves a closer look. This gesture is found in particular in Brazil.

7. The Moustache Twist. The thumb and forefinger are squeezed together in the cheek region and twisted round, as if twiddling the tip of an imaginary moustache. The symbolism derives from the male's need to preen himself in preparation for his advances towards the girl, stimulated by her beauty. This is primarily an old Italian gesture, surviving into modern times despite the absence of long mustachios.

8. The Hand-on-Heart. The man places his right hand flat on to his chest in the heart region. The symbolism indicates that the girl is so beautiful that she makes his heart beat faster with emotion. In English-speaking countries this would be considered too 'formal' a gesture, but in some South American countries it is employed in informal contexts in a more spontaneous way.

Gestures 9–12 are comments by the man on what he would like to do to the girl.

9. The Fingertips Kiss. The man kisses his fingertips and then fans them out, flinging them towards the girl. This action of throwing a kiss could, of course, be done as a salutation or a direct act of praise, but it is also seen as a signal performed for the benefit of his male companion, when the girl is not watching. The gesture is aimed at the girl, but the message is directed at his friend. This is particularly common in France, but is also found today in many other countries.

10. The Air Kiss. The man makes a kissing movement with his lips, in the direction of the girl. Again, this is done for the benefit of his companion, to indicate what he would like to do to the girl, because she is so beautiful; and it is most likely to be performed at a moment when the girl cannot observe him. It is common in English-speaking countries as an alternative to the more 'Continental' Fingertips-Kiss.

11. The Cheek Pinch. The man pinches his own cheek as if he were doing it to the girl. This action is most commonly used in Sicily, but is also seen elsewhere.

12. The Breast Cup. The hands make a cupping movement in the air, as if holding the girl's breasts and squeezing them. This obvious gesture is popular in Europe and elsewhere and is easily understood even by those who do not employ it themselves.

There are many other gestures that signify female beauty, but this selection suffices to make the point that a message as basic as the male's response to feminine appeal will inevitably find a wide variety of forms of expression, both within cultures and between them. As with other basic messages, the inventiveness of human symbolizing gives rise to a bewildering array of Gesture Alternatives. This makes the task of assembling a comprehensive international dictionary of human gestures a daunting prospect, and one that has so far not been seriously attempted.

HYBRID GESTURES

Signals made up of two original gestures

A Hybrid Gesture is one that combines two separate gestures, with distinct origins, in a single action.

A popular threat display is the cutting through the air of a stiffly flattened hand—the Hand Chop gesture, common in Italy and various other countries around the Mediterranean. Its meaning is obvious enough—I will chop off your head. In Tunisia this gesture often becomes grafted on to the French sign meaning 'zero' or 'worthless' which is performed by making a ring from the thumb and forefinger. Tunisians, when threatening, often combine these two gestures into a Hand Ring-Chop gesture. The thumb and forefinger form the circle, while the other three fingers are held stiffly flattened. In this posture the hand is chopped repeatedly through the air. The message is 'I will kill you tomorrow'. It is a combination of the two parent messages 'worthless' and 'kill'. In effect, the signal says: 'You are so worthless that I will kill you tomorrow.'

Hybrid Gestures of this kind are extremely rare in ordinary social gesturing. When giving a visual signal, people tend to do one thing at a time. Gesture communication is unitary rather than a language that combines visual 'words' into visual 'sentences'. Of course, we may perform a whole stream of gestures, one after the other, and we may grimace while gesticulating, but that is not the same as welding together two distinct gestures into a new double-unit. The few examples that do exist nearly all combine two actions that both have the same general meaning, but are brought together in the hybrid form to produce a double-strength signal. The insulting Forearm Jerk gesture, for instance, may be combined with the equally insulting Middle-finger Jerk, or with the obscene Fig Sign. Usually these are given separately, but when done together they intensify the insult that is being hurled at the victim.

Only when we move into the specialized area of North American Indian Sign Language or the Deaf-and-Dumb Sign Language does this type of combination occur with any frequency. The Indian sign for beauty, for example, consists of raising one hand, like a mirror, and looking into it, while bringing the other hand, palm-down, across to touch the chest. This second gesture means 'good', so that the combination reads as: looking good = beautiful.

The North American Indian sign for 'beauty' is a Hybrid Gesture combining the sign for 'looking' (gazing into a mimed mirror) with the sign for 'good' (placing the palm-down hand to the chest). The Hand Chop gesture (below left)—a simple threat—and the Hand Ring gesture—here meaning 'zero' or 'worthless'—may be combined as a Ring-Chop gesture (below). This Hybrid Gesture signals, in Tunisia, the double message: 'You are worthless and I will kill you'.

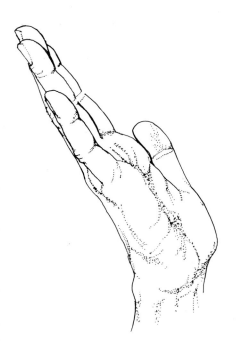
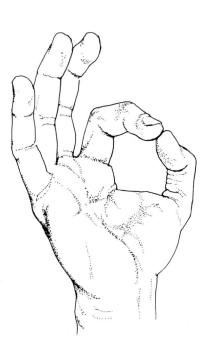
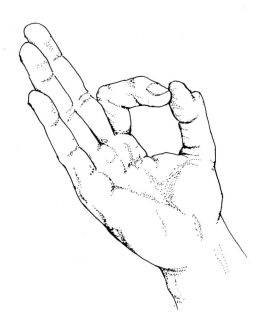

COMPOUND GESTURES
Gestures made up of a number of distinct elements

A Compound Gesture is one that is made up of a number of separate elements, each of which has at least some degree of independence.

Many human gestures have only one element. If a man is busy working at his desk and someone asks him if the work is going well, he may answer by giving a thumb-up sign. He can do this without looking up and without pausing in his work. He merely extends a hand with the thumb raised. The rest of his body contributes nothing, and yet the message is understood.

This is a simple gesture and it contrasts sharply with more complex ones involving related but discrete features. Human laughter, or, rather, what happens when a man laughs, is a good example of a Compound Gesture. When the display occurs at its very highest intensity, the laugher simultaneously: (1) emits a hooting or barking sound; (2) opens his mouth wide; (3) pulls back his mouth-corners; (4) wrinkles up his nose; (5) closes his eyes; (6) shows crinkle lines at the outer corners of his eyes; (7) weeps; (8) throws back his head; (9) raises his shoulders; (10) rolls his trunk about; (11) clasps his body; and (12) stamps his foot.

Whenever you observe someone laughing, it should be possible to score them on this 12-point scale. Extreme scores are rare. It is possible to score only one point—by laughing with the mouth shut and with the body immobile—and it is possible to score a full 12—as with uncontrollable, cheek-streaming belly-laughter. But it is much more common to observe a middle-range laugh of about 6 to 8 points. These will not always be the same elements. Even the laughing sound itself can be omitted—think of silent laughter or a picture of a laughing man—and yet the message of the display still comes across.

A Compound Gesture is made up of three kinds of elements. First, there are the *essential elements*. These are the ones that *must* be present if the display is to be understood. In the case of a simple gesture, such as the thumb-up, the essential element *is* the gesture—there is nothing else. But with Compound Gestures, such as laughing, there need be no essential elements at all. Each element may be expendable provided there are enough of the other elements present. Not one of the 12 laughter signals listed above is absolutely essential to the message. Each can be replaced by other features.

Second, there are the *key elements*. These do not have to be present, but they are the most important features of a display, and their special quality is

Human laughter in its most fully developed form is a Compound Gesture made up of twelve major elements. The New Guinea highlander (opposite) is performing a high-intensity laugh which includes throwing back the head, closing the eyes and hunching the shoulders. Low-intensity laughter (above top) involves fewer elements. There are many different ways of laughing: two common forms (left) are the snigger and the guffaw. The sniggerer shows exaggerated nose-wrinkling and eye-creasing but no head-tilting; the guffaw involves a marked throwing back of the head but less nose-wrinkling. At very high intensity, laughter includes the element of weeping (above), and when examining photographs it is sometimes difficult to distinguish between crying and intense laughing.

that they can, by themselves, in the absence of all the other elements, still transmit the message. Although the sound of laughter is not an essential element in the display, it is a key element, because it can operate on its own in the absence of all the visual elements.

Third, there are the *amplifiers*, or supporting elements. These cannot operate on their own, and only transmit the message if other elements are present. For instance, if a man retracts his neck, or throws his head back, these actions alone do not mean 'laughter' to an onlooker. Most of the visual aspects of laughing are of this type, but with some other Compound Gestures this is not the case.

With the shrug gesture, for example, there are more key signals than amplifiers. The full shrug involves (1) a brief hunching of the shoulders, (2) a twisting of the hands into a palm-up posture, (3) a tilting of the head to one side, (4) a lowering of the mouth-corners, and (5) a raising of the eyebrows. Four of these five are key elements and can work alone. I can perform a perfectly understandable shrug merely by raising and then lowering my shoulders. I can even do it by briefly hunching just one shoulder while keeping the other still. The same applies to my hands. I can shrug expressively with one or both hands, simply by twisting them momentarily into the palm-up posture. Or I can transmit the same message by an exaggerated lowering of my mouth-corners, remaining immobile in every other respect. I can even do it with an upward jerk of my eyebrows. Only the head-tilting element would fail to work in isolation and this is therefore the only amplifier in the case of the Compound Gesture of shrugging.

Inevitably this means that there are many possible styles of shrugging, depending on which key elements are used. These styles vary from person to person and from culture to culture. Travelling around the Mediterranean, an expert shrug-watcher can quickly identify the local 'shrug-dialects', as he moves from country to country.

RELIC GESTURES

Gestures that have survived long after their primary contexts have vanished

This Greek car-sticker, representing a gestural relic from Byzantine times, is intended to offer a *moutza* insult to the driver of the car behind should he approach too closely.

Certain gestures have outlived the situations that created them. This Neapolitan gesture of self-preening consists of the twiddling of the tips of an imaginary moustache. As a grooming action it is a relic from the days when waxed or pointed moustaches were common in Italy.

The shrug is another Compound Gesture involving many independent elements. A shoulder shrug (top left) may occur by itself, without other elements; a mouth shrug (left) is often combined with an eyebrows shrug, but the eyebrows shrug itself (above left) often appears with a hand-shrug element and a side-tilt of the head.

A Relic Gesture is one that has outlived its original situation. It might be an historic relic, surviving long after the period that gave birth to it, or a personal relic, such as an infantile pattern lasting into adulthood.

There is usually a special reason for the survival of a gesture from an earlier historical period—some slight advantage it has over its modern equivalent. Without this, it would die out along with the context that created it. A good example is the telephone gesture. The telephone rings and the caller asks to speak to someone who is on the far side of a noisy, crowded room. The person who has taken the call asks the caller to wait and struggles across the room. Halfway across he catches the eye of the person he wants and gestures to him: 'You are wanted on the telephone.' How does he do it? The modern telephone does not lend itself to miming, but he may try to act out the posture of holding the receiver to his ear. Or he may silently mouth out the word 'telephone', exaggerating his lip movements as much as possible. Long ago, a more primitive kind of telephone was operated by cranking a handle, and this provided the basis for a much more easily identifiable hand gesture. One hand was held near to the ear and then rotated forwards in tight circles. This gestural abbreviation—cranking+ear—supplied the information: 'Someone has *cranked* their telephone to get the exchange to call your number, so please come and put your *ear* to the phone.' This gesture was efficient because it could not be confused with any other action. Because it was more explicit than its modern equivalent, it managed to outlive changes in telephone design. Even today, many years after the demise of the last of the cranked telephones, it still survives in certain parts of southern Europe and South America. Now totally emancipated from its original mechanical source, the mime lives on, handed down from generation to generation. As an historical Relic Gesture, it is used today by people who may never even have heard of a cranked telephone and who do not understand where the action stems from.

A similar Relic Gesture is the rude sign used in Britain to say that something stinks, or is rubbish. This consists of reaching up to pull an imaginary lavatory chain, as if in the act of flushing something down the drain. Old-fashioned lavatories with a high-level water-tank are rapidly disappearing and being replaced by low-level suites, where the bowl is flushed by turning a small handle or pressing a button. As with the modern telephone, the hand actions involved in turning the handle or pressing the button are far less characteristic or specific. To mime them would be ambiguous and, as rude signs, they would be quite meaningless. So, once again, the early technology and its accompanying action live on in the form of a Relic Gesture. In this case, the old-fashioned lavatory chains have not as yet vanished altogether, like the cranked telephones, but there is every likelihood that, even when they have been completely superseded, the gesture will persist.

Some ancient gestures have managed to survive for centuries after the disappearance of the occasions that gave birth to them. In modern Greece, the rudest gesture it is possible to make is the *moutza*, which had its origins in the Byzantine era. It consists of thrusting an open hand towards the insulted person's face. To a non-Greek this seems harmless enough, but to a Greek it is a gross act of ridicule. It produces such an angry response that it is largely confined to traffic disputes, where one driver is telling another to get lost, and where the insulted driver is unable to retaliate physically. To understand the potency of this gesture we have to turn the clock back hundreds of years to the ancient city streets, where captured criminals were paraded in chains through the crowded thoroughfares so that the populace could torment and abuse them. The favourite way of doing this was to scoop up a handful of filth

This Japanese earthquake victim sits hunched beside her ruined home, rocking back and forth and weeping like a lost child. When caught in a disaster, many adults revert to relic behaviour of this kind, stemming from their infancy.

and thrust it into the helpless captive's face. In Britain and other countries, criminals placed in a public pillory or stocks were often abused in a similar way, but only in Greece has the smearing action survived as an historical Relic Gesture. It says something for the persistence of Relic Gestures that the moutza has retained its savage message despite the fact that it is now performed (1) with a clean hand, (2) at a distance from the face, (3) hundreds of years after the last true 'smearing' took place, and (4) by people who, in most instances, have little idea about its original meaning.

A more delicate Relic Gesture is the twiddling of the tips of an imaginary moustache. With the notable exception of the painter Salvador Dali, few men today wear long moustaches with finely pointed, upward-sweeping tips, but in earlier times, when this fashion was popular and widespread, especially among the European military, a man could express his amorous arousal to his companions by a little deft moustache-grooming. These actions can still be observed today in various European countries, performed by clean-shaven men who live in towns that have not seen a fine, pointed moustache for many a year.

A completely different kind of Relic Gesture is the one which survives not from past history, but from the personal past of an individual's lifetime. These personal behaviour relics are nearly always infantile actions that survive, disguised, into adulthood, and occur at moments when the inner mood of the adult suddenly matches one of the special conditions of childhood. The disaster victim, sitting beside the corpses of loved ones or the shell of a destroyed home, rocks back and forth, back and forth, in a desperate attempt at self-comfort. As the body rocks rhythmically to and fro, the hands clasp the knees or the trunk. The eyes weep and the voice sobs. All these actions are rare among adults in ordinary day-to-day life, but they are commonplace in infancy. The desolate adult victim, in an unconscious attempt to console himself, reverts to infantile patterns which once spelled safety and security. The parental arms, so large in relation to the small child's body, so all-enveloping and protective, have long since vanished. Now, the agonized adult must replace the parental hug of reassurance with the self-hug of his own arms; and the gentle rocking of his mother's embrace with the rhythmic tilting of his own, solitary body. The self-hugging and the self-rocking are personal relics from the days of dependency and, inadequate though they may be as substitutes, their latter-day revival in moments of crisis clearly provides some small consolation.

A less dramatic example is the simple Head Cock. An adult who wishes to appear appealing to another adult, from whom it is hoped to wheedle some reward or advantage, often gives a soft smile and tilts the head on to one side, while continuing to gaze hopefully in their direction. This is not an action to be found among liberated feminists: it is the teasing, cajoling action of the woman who is playing the 'little girl' role to break down a man's resistance. Although adult, she is playing the part of his young daughter, and the Head Cock action is a Relic Gesture stemming from the juvenile movement of laying the head against the parent's body, when seeking comfort or rest, or during tender moments of body-contact loving. In the adult, relic version, the head is no longer directed towards the companion's body, but the cocking movement itself is sufficiently evocative to arouse protective feelings. Without knowing why, the companion feels his reluctance draining away.

The Head Cock is not confined entirely to situations of wheedling persuasion. It can also be observed in many 'appealing girl' photographs, where the smiling subject tilts the head provocatively to one side, as if to say: 'I would like to lay my head on your shoulder.' Certain males also employ the device, again unconsciously, when at their most sympathetic and reassuring, as if they are trying to convey the feeling that 'I am not really a hard-bitten, ruthless adult, but merely a helpless little boy'.

Perhaps the most important of all the personal Relic Gestures are those whose source can be traced back to those very early moments when, as

Oral-contact is the most widespread and common form of Relic Gesture. Contact with the mouth during moments of tension makes it possible to re-live momentarily the comforts known at the mother's breast. Among children, oral-contact often takes the form of thumb-sucking (top left). Thumb-sucking vanishes with adulthood, but finger-sucking (left) survives and becomes extended to pen-sucking (middle left), pipe-sucking, cigar-chomping and cigarette-smoking. In the family group (above), the comfort of the mother's nipple has been replaced, for the child, by a plastic 'comforter', and, for the adults, by their own nicotine 'comforters.'

babies, we are nursed at the breast—or at the bottle. We all experience our first great moments of comfort during these early feeding sessions, and they appear to leave a lasting impression on us that leads to the later re-surfacing of a variety of oral-comfort actions. In adult life these actions are usually heavily disguised and it is hard to convince an elderly businessman, sucking on his unlit pipe or squeezing his cigar between his lips, that he is in reality comforting himself with a sophisticated version of a baby's dummy. Thumb-sucking among children—often quite old children—is fairly transparent in its relation to sucking at the breast, and its frequency increases and decreases with the rise and fall of moment-by-moment tensions; but once adulthood has been reached we have to put away childish things—or, at least, those that are detectably childish—and the oral-comfort actions have to undergo a metamorphosis. The nipple-sucking and teat-sucking of babyhood, after being transformed into the comforter-sucking of infancy and then the thumb-sucking of childhood, becomes the nail-biting and pencil-sucking of adolescence, which later becomes the gum-chewing, sunglass-sucking, cigarette and cigar-sucking, and pipe-sucking of adulthood. The nicotine pleasures of the various forms of smoking fall very far short of explaining the full reward which these activities bring, just as sucking sweets is more than a matter of taste-bud reward. The oral contact involved and the sucking movements of the tongue and mouth are also vitally important, as we relive our earliest infantile comforts.

It has been argued that even our Head Shake action for No can be traced back to these early moments. The infant who is not hungry rejects the breast, or food offered on a spoon, by a sharp turning of the head to the side. In other words, the Head Shake begins as an act of rejection, a negative No to food. From these beginnings, it is argued, has come our adult sign for negation, which we accept without questioning its origin and without ever considering that it, too, might be a relic from our personal past.

Apart from rejecting food by turning the head to the side, the baby also pushes it away by using its tongue. Protruding the tongue becomes another very basic rejection movement. Later in life we use it in two distinct ways: when concentrating hard on some difficult task or skill, or when being deliberately rude to someone. Sticking out the tongue as a rudeness is obviously related to the rejection act in infancy, but the showing of the tip of the tongue during moments of intense concentration is not at first sight so easy to explain. However, careful studies of this action, not only in human adults, but also in nursery-school children—and in great apes, such as gorillas—have revealed that here too we are in the realms of Relic Gesturing.

Observers noticed that the nursery-school children protruded their tongues slightly whenever they wanted to avoid a social contact. If they were busy doing something and suddenly it looked as if they were about to be interrupted, out would come the tongue. This is not the full protrusion of the deliberately rude 'sticking-out-the-tongue' gesture, but an unconscious action in which only the tip of the tongue is showing from between closed lips. The gesture gradually revealed itself, not so much as a pure 'concentration' gesture, but as a 'please-leave-me-in-peace' gesture. This explains why children sometimes show the tip of the tongue when doing difficult homework or other complicated manual tasks. Once the action was understood as a social rejection gesture, it began to fit in with the infantile, breast-rejection movement and also the deliberately rude one. Turning their attention to apes, the observers found that the same rules applied here, too, indicating that this particular Relic Gesture has an even wider significance.

Critics were quick to point out that sticking out the tongue can, in certain, more erotic circumstances, function as a 'come-on' signal rather than a rejection device. But a closer examination of these sexual tongue gestures shows them to be of rather a special kind. Here, the tongue is not pushing something away. Instead, it is curling and moving, as if searching for something. These actions, it seems, can be related to what happens when a

The three forms of tongue-protrusion: the Concentration Tongue (above), the Rude Tongue (below) and the Sexy Tongue (opposite). As with oral-contact gestures, each is a Relic Gesture having its origins in infantile moments at the mother's breast.

baby's tongue is searching for the nipple, rather than trying to push it away. They are the tongue actions of pleasure-seeking moments from our infancy and are Relic Gestures of a totally different kind.

Kissing comes into this category. In early human societies, before commercial baby-food was invented, mothers weaned their children by chewing up their food and then passing it into the infantile mouth by lip-to-lip contact—which naturally involved a considerable amount of tonguing and mutual mouth-pressure. This almost bird-like system of parental care seems strange and alien to us today, but our species probably practised it for a million years or more, and adult erotic kissing today is almost certainly a

Relic Gesture stemming from these origins. In this case, however, it is a relic not of our personal past, since we no longer feed infants this way, but of our ancient prehistoric past. Whether it has been handed down from generation to generation, like the Greek insult sign, or whether we have an inborn predisposition towards it, we cannot say. But whichever is the case, it looks rather as though, with the deep kissing and tonguing of modern lovers, we are back again at the infantile mouth-feeding stage of the far-distant past. Many other adult actions could, perhaps, be traced back in a similar way.

Some writers give the impression that the discovery of a relic element in adult actions somehow makes them ridiculous or superfluous. But in fact quite the opposite seems to be true. If we perform Relic Gestures today, as modern adults, it is because they are of value to us *as* modern adults. For some reason they still assist us in our daily lives. To understand their origins is to clarify their value for us, not to condemn them as 'childish' or 'old-fashioned'. If the disaster victim rocking to and fro feels the comfort of being rocked again in his mother's arms, this feeling may help him to cope better with the disaster that has befallen him. If the young lovers exploring each other's mouths with their tongues feel the ancient comfort of parental mouth-feeding, this may help them to increase their mutual trust and thereby their pair-bonding.

These are valuable patterns of behaviour, and although they are, to use a Freudian term, 'regressive', they clearly have a functional role in adult life. If Freudian theory is often critical of them, this is because psychoanalysts encounter them in extreme forms, with patients who have reverted extensively to childhood patterns as a substitute for adult living. But to attack all relic actions, as Freudians tend to do, is rather like saying that no one should take an aspirin to relieve a headache because some people are advanced hypochondriacs. The man-watcher, making his observations in everyday life, rather than the clinic, is perhaps better placed to avoid such errors.

Mothers once weaned their babies by passing chewed-up food mouth-to-mouth (above) (after Eibl-Eibesfeldt) and this appears to be the origin of erotic tongue-kissing between adult lovers.

REGIONAL SIGNALS

The way signals change from country to country and district to district

A Regional Signal is one that has a limited geographical range. If a Norwegian, a Korean and a Masai were marooned together on a desert island, they would easily be able to communicate their basic moods and intentions to one another by their actions. All humanity shares a large repertoire of common movements, expressions and postures. But there would also be misunderstandings. Each man would have acquired from his own culture a special set of Regional Signals that would be meaningless to the others. If the Norwegian were shipwrecked instead with a Swede and a Dane, he would find his task much easier, because their closer origins would mean a greater share of these regional gestures, since localized actions, like many words, do not follow precisely the present-day national boundaries.

This comparison of gestures with words is significant because it reveals immediately our state of ignorance as regards gestural geography. We already know a great deal about linguistic maps, but we know far too little about Gesture Maps. Ask a linguist to describe the distribution of any language you like to name and he will be able to provide accurate, detailed information for you. Take any word, and he will be able to demonstrate its spread from country to country. He can even present you with local dialect maps for some parts of the world and show you, like Professor Higgins in Pygmalion, how slang expressions are limited to certain small areas of big cities. But ask anyone for a world-wide gesture atlas, and you will be disappointed.

A start has already been made, however, and new field work is now beginning. Although this research is only in its infancy, recent studies in Europe and around the Mediterranean are providing some valuable clues about the way gestures change as one travels from locality to locality. For example, there is a simple gesture in which the forefinger taps the side of the nose. In England most people interpret this as meaning secrecy or conspiracy. The message is: 'Keep it dark, don't spread it around.' But as one moves down across Europe to central Italy, the dominant meaning changes to become a helpful warning: 'Take care, there is danger—they are crafty.' The two messages are related, because they are both concerned with cunning. In England it is *we* who are cunning, by not divulging our secret. But in central Italy it is *they* who are cunning, and we must be warned against them. The Nose Tap gesture symbolizes cunning in both cases, but the source of the cunning has shifted.

This is an example of a gesture keeping the same form over a wide range, and also retaining the same basic meaning, but nevertheless carrying a quite distinct message in two regions. The more gestures that are mapped in the field, the more common this type of change is proving to be. Another instance is found in the Eye Touch gesture, where the forefinger touches the face just below the eye and pulls the skin downwards, opening the eye wider. In England and France this has the dominant meaning: 'You can't fool me—I see what you are up to.' But in Italy this shifts to: 'Keep your eyes peeled— pay attention, he's a crook.' In other words the basic meaning remains one of alertness, but it changes from 'I am alert' to 'You be alert'.

In both these cases, there is a small number of people in each region who interpret the gesture in its other meaning. It is not an all-or-none situation, merely a shift in dominance of one message over the other. This gives some idea of the subtlety of regional changes. Occasionally there is a total switch as one moves from one district to the next, but more often than not the change is only a matter of degree.

Sometimes it is possible to relate the geography of modern Regional Signals to past historical events. The Chin Flick gesture, in which the backs of the fingers are swept upwards and forwards against the underside of the

The Nose Tap gesture. In England this is a signal for conspiracy or secrecy, but in Italy the meaning changes and it becomes a friendly warning: 'Take care, there is danger.'

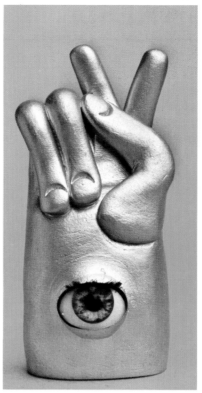

chin, is an insulting action in both France and northern Italy. There it means 'Get lost—you are annoying me.' In southern Italy it also has a negative meaning, but the message it carries is no longer insulting. It now says simply 'There is nothing' or 'No' or 'I cannot' or 'I don't want any'. This switch takes place between Rome and Naples and gives rise to the intriguing possibility that the difference is due to a surviving influence of ancient Greece. The Greeks colonized southern Italy, but stopped their northern movement between Rome and Naples. Greeks today use the Chin Flick in the same way as the southern Italians. In fact, the distribution of this, and certain other gestures, follows remarkably accurately the range of the Greek civilization at its zenith. Our words and our buildings still display the mark of early Greek influence, so it should not be too surprising if ancient Greek gestures are equally tenacious. What is interesting is why they did not spread farther as time passed. Greek architecture and philosophy expanded farther and farther in their influences, but for some reason, gestures like the Chin Flick did not travel so well. Many countries, such as England, lack them altogether, and others, like France, know them only in a different role.

Another historical influence becomes obvious when one moves to North Africa. There, in Tunisia, the Chin Flick gesture once again becomes totally insulting: a Tunisian gives a 'French' Chin Flick, rather than a 'Southern Italian' Chin Flick, despite the fact that France is more remote. The explanation, borne out by other gesture links between France and Tunisia, is that the French colonial influence in Tunisia has left its imperial mark even on informal body-language. The modern Tunisian is gesturally more French than any of his closer neighbours who have not experienced the French presence.

This gives rise to the question as to whether gestures are generally rather conservative, compared with other social patterns. One talks about the latest fashions in clothing, but one never hears of 'this season's crop of new gestures'. There does seem to be a cultural tenacity about them, similar to the persistence found in much folklore and in many children's games and rhymes. Yet new gestures do occasionally manage to creep in and establish themselves. Two thousand years ago it was apparently the Greeks who were the 'gesturally virile' nation. Today it is the British, with their Victory-sign

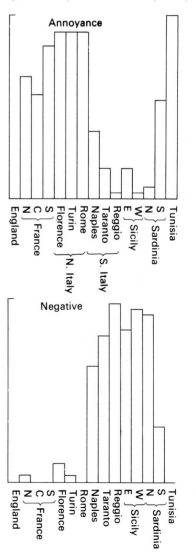

Many gestures have only a limited geographical range, while others are known across wide areas. These ten Neapolitan gestures published by Andrea de Jorio in 1832 have, or had, the following meanings: (1) silence; (2) negative; (3) beauty; (4) hunger; (5) derision; (6) tiredness; (7) stupidity; (8) beware; (9) dishonest; (10) crafty. Some, such as (1) and (5), will be known to at least all Europeans, while others, such as (9) and (10), may not be understood at all outside Italy.

The Eyelid-pull gesture—see drawing (8)—changes its meaning slightly when the traveller crosses the border between France and Italy. In France it means: 'I am alert'; while in Italy it means: 'You be alert.' Both cases have to do with cunning, with having one's eyes open, but in France it is I who am cunning, while in Italy it is they who are cunning. This difference is expressed in the two charts (below). (All charts from Morris et al: *Gesture Maps*.)

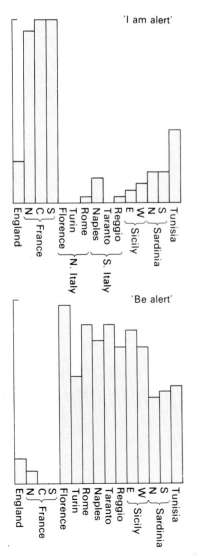

and their Thumbs-up, and the Americans with their OK Circle-sign. These have spread right across Europe and much of the rest of the world as well, making their first great advance during the turmoil of the Second World War, and managing to cling on since then, even in the gesture-rich countries of southern Europe. But these are exceptions. Most of the local signs made today are centuries old and steeped in history.

BATON SIGNALS
Actions that emphasize the rhythm of words

Baton Signals beat time to the rhythm of spoken thoughts. Their essential role is to mark the points of emphasis in our speech, and they are so much an integral part of our verbal delivery that we sometimes gesticulate even when talking on the telephone.

Batons account for the bulk of the gesticulations that accompany conversation or public speaking. An animated speaker's hands are seldom still, but flick, swish and dip as he conducts the 'music' of his words. He is only half-conscious of these movements. He knows his hands are active, but ask him for an exact description of his Baton Signals and he will be unable to give it. He will admit to 'waving his hands about', but there the description will end. Show him a film of himself batoning to his speech and he will be surprised to see that his hands perform a veritable ballet of airborne movements and shifting postures.

It is these posture changes that are of special interest. If Baton Signals did no more than beat time to words there would be little to say about them. But each time-beat is performed with the hand in a particular position and these positions vary from occasion to occasion, from person to person, and from culture to culture. The beating of the hand says: '*This* is the point I am making, and *this*, and *this*'. The posture of the beating hand says: '. . . and this is the mood in which I am making these points'. It is possible to make a detailed classification of these beating postures and then to study their natural history in the field. Here are some of the most important types:

1. The Vacuum Precision-grip. The human hand has two basic holding actions—the precision-grip and the power-grip. In the precision-grip it is the

Some of the more distinctive hand batons used by gesticulating speakers. The Air Grasp baton, emphasizing the need for control, was used so often by President de Gaulle (right) that it became one of his best-known idiosyncrasies.

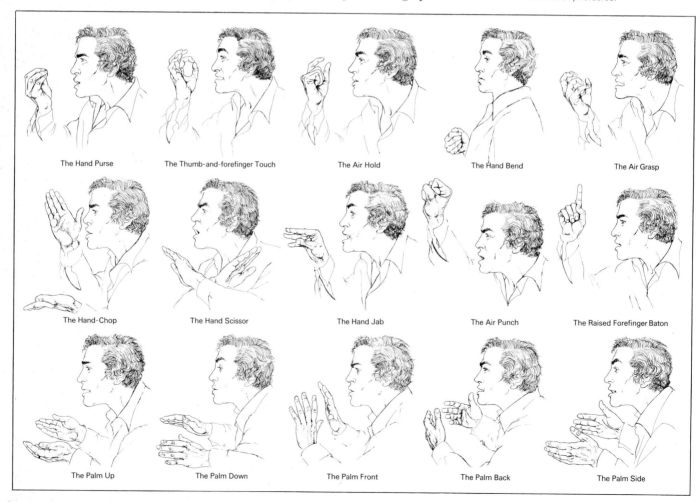

The Hand Purse	The Thumb-and-forefinger Touch	The Air Hold	The Hand Bend	The Air Grasp
The Hand-Chop	The Hand Scissor	The Hand Jab	The Air Punch	The Raised Forefinger Baton
The Palm Up	The Palm Down	The Palm Front	The Palm Back	The Palm Side

The delicate Thumb-and-forefinger Touch underlines the precision of a point made— on this occasion, by a German politician. Superficially it resembles the familiar American OK sign.

During an informal discussion, the Shah of Iran reaches out as if to touch the listener. The resulting Palm Side baton reinforces his desire to project his ideas.

tips of the thumb and fingers that are used; in the power-grip the whole hand is involved. We employ the precision-grip when holding small objects delicately and manipulating them with accuracy, as when writing or threading a needle. When batoning during speech, we often adopt a precision-grip hand posture, even though the hand in question is empty. In other words, we perform the precision-grip in vacuo. This form of baton reflects an urge on the part of the speaker to express himself delicately and with great exactness. His hand emphasizes the fineness of the points he is stressing.

There are two popular versions of the Vacuum Precision-grip: the Hand Purse and the Thumb-and-forefinger Touch. In the Hand Purse the tips of all five digits are brought together until they touch in a tight circle, like the mouth of a string-closed purse.

In the Thumb-and-forefinger Touch, the tips of only these two digits are brought into contact with each other. This appears to be the most popular form of the Vacuum Precision-grip, requiring slightly less muscular effort than the Hand Purse.

2. The Intention Precision-grip. In this baton posture, the hand makes the intention movement of delicately taking hold of an imaginary, small object, but does not follow the action through to the point where the thumb-tip and finger-tips meet. It is an Air Hold posture and the mood it reflects is more one of a quest for precision than precision itself. There is usually an element of questioning or uncertainty on the part of the gesticulator, as if he is searching for something. The hand, beating the air, almost closes on the answer, but not quite.

3. The Vacuum Power-grip. We employ the power-grip for crude, forceful manipulations such as grasping or hammering. The digits are curled tightly around the held object. When this is done in vacuo, the result, in mild cases, is a bent hand and, in strong cases, a tight fist.

In the Hand Bend posture the curled fingers only lightly touch the palm. This is a rather insipid baton posture, reflecting neither precision of thought, nor forcefulness. The Tight Fist, in contrast, although it lacks delicacy, does signal considerable determination and strength of thought.

Of all the baton hand-positions, the Tight Fist carries the most obvious mood-message, so much so that it is the most likely of the different forms to be used as a deliberate, contrived act. A political speaker who is indecisive and confused may purposely and deceitfully adopt a Tight Fist baton-posture in order to convince his audience of his mental vigour and determination. In other words, the action is too well understood to be a reliable indicator of the underlying mood.

4. The Intention Power-grip. The speaker who is seeking control and is striving in his speech to master the situation, but has not yet done so, performs his batons with his hand held in the frozen intention movement of the power-grip. This is the Air Grasp posture, with the digits stiffly spread and slightly bent. The hand grabs at the air but does not follow through.

5. The Vacuum Blow. The hand acts, not as a holding machine, but as a blunt instrument. Instead of gripping, grabbing, or grasping, it chops, jabs or punches. But again it does this in vacuo, chopping, jabbing or punching the air rather than a solid object.

The Hand Chop, with the straight hand rigid and slashed downwards through the air like an axe, is the baton posture of the aggressive speaker who wants his ideas to cut through the confusion of the situation, to an imposed solution. A special variant of the Hand Chop is the Hand Scissor, where the forearms cross over each other horizontally, then both chop outwards. The Hands Scissor baton adds a strong flavour of denial or rejection to the mood of the speech. It is as if, with this variant, the speaker is cutting his way through a hostile barrier, negating the opposition by striking it away from him, both to the left and to the right.

The Hand Jab baton, where the fingertips are prodded sharply towards the

The Hand Chop, in which the flattened hand slices through the air, emphasizing the speaker's need to cut through a problem.

The Palm Up baton of the speaker who implores his audience to agree with him. His hands adopt the posture typical of a begging man.

listener, is also aggressive, but here the aggression is more specific. It has to do with the listener rather than with the general problem.

The Air Punch is the most aggressive of the baton postures, and when the hand is beaten in the air as a clenched fist there is little doubt of the mood of the performer. There is a similarity between this type of batoning and the Tight Fist of the Vacuum Power-grip, but it is usually possible to distinguish between them. The Tight Fist shows the hand gripping the air, while the Air Punch shows it punching into the air. In both cases the hands may beat time aggressively, but only in the Air Punch is there a sense that the fists are delivering blows.

6. The Hand Extend. Instead of imaginary gripping or hitting, the batoning hand may simply be extended in front of the body and held there in a rather neutral posture, fingers together and flat. The important clue in such cases is the direction of the palm. The Palm Up: the imploring hand of the beggar. Hand batons in this posture beg the listener to agree. The Palm Down: the restraining hand of the cool-headed. Hand batons of this type reveal an urge to damp down or lower the prevalent mood—to control it by reduction. The Palm Front: the repelling hand of the protester. The hand faces forwards as if to protect the speaker or push away some imaginary object approaching from the front. The mood reflected is one of rejection. The Palm Back: the embracing hand of the comfort-seeker. This baton is usually performed with both hands at once, palms towards the chest. They are held in front of the body as if embracing an invisible companion. Their posture reflects an attempt to embrace an idea, to encompass the concept under discussion, or to pull the other person metaphorically closer to the speaker. The Palm Side: the reaching hand of the negotiator. The hand is held out in the hand-shake position, where it beats the air in a baton-action that seems to reflect the urge to stretch out and touch the companion. The predominant mood appears to be a strong desire to bridge the gap between speaker and listener—to 'reach' the other person's mind with the idea being expressed in words.

7. The Intention Touch. When the fingers are spread out in a radiating shape—the hand-fan posture—the baton takes on a special flavour. This Air Touch posture is especially popular amongst professional communicators. The speaker widens his hand as if each finger tip is reaching out to touch a

The aggressive Air Punch lends an added vehemence to a speaker's words: an American Civil Rights leader in full cry.

different section of his audience. It is a delicate action related, because of its tip-touching emphasis, to the precision-grip batons mentioned earlier. The difference is that here, instead of the tips touching one another, as in the Hand Purse, they make the intention movement of touching the listeners.

8. The Hands together. If the speaker joins his left and right hand in some sort of hand-to-hand contact, this tends to replace batoning. Instead of beating time to his thoughts, he now enjoys the comforting sensation of 'holding hands with himself' while continuing to talk.

This self-intimacy often clashes with the urge to emphasize a point, however, and speakers can be observed in a state of conflict, with their linked hands rebelling against their conjoined repose. Without pulling apart, they jerk and jump with the shift of spoken thoughts. These muted batons are common among individuals made anxious and insecure by the tension of the social situation in which they find themselves, but who nevertheless have a strong urge to communicate to their companions.

9. The Forefinger Baton. Hand batons usually employ all the digits working together, but there is one common baton posture in which a single digit—the forefinger—plays a dominant role. This is the extended-forefinger posture.

There are two popular versions: the Frontal Forefinger Baton and the Raised Forefinger Baton. In the frontal case the forefinger is jabbed towards the listener or towards some object under discussion. Pointing at an object may be merely a way of emphasizing the importance of that object for the discussion, but pointing directly at a listener is an assertive, authoritarian act and when it becomes extended as a rhythmic baton, the impact on the listener is one of open hostility or domination. The jabbing forefinger may only assault the air, but the listener can almost feel it stabbing into his ribs.

The Forefinger Baton is usually employed assertively by a domineering speaker: boxer Muhammad Ali, weighing in for a world heavyweight title fight, predicts the outcome. This baton is aggressive enough to make even a fragile signaller (below) appear firm and authoritative.

The Raised Forefinger Baton is also seen as threatening or domineering, but for a slightly different reason. Here the forefinger is acting as a symbolic club or stick, raised ready to deliver a symbolic blow. The beating-time action of the speaker who holds his hand aloft in this position is menacing because it relates to the ancient overarm blow of our species.

It is known that both very small children and our closest ape relatives employ the overarm blow as a fundamental attack movement and that when human adults indulge in informal violence, as in a city riot, they too invariably resort to this particular action. It seems probable that it is an example of an inborn action pattern for the human species. The use of the warning finger, raised high and beating the air like a miniature blunt instrument, is therefore likely to trigger off a deep-seated intimidation response in the speaker's audience, even though the forefinger itself is such a puny symbolic substitute for a real weapon.

10. The Head Baton. The hands are undeniably the most important baton organs, but other parts of the body also beat time to the spoken ideas. The head often plays a supporting role, making small dipping movements to add further emphasis. Each Head Dip involves a sharp down-jerk, followed by a softer up-jerk return. There is a small forward movement as the head dips, giving it a slightly attacking quality. In fact, this form of baton is usually reserved for rather forceful, aggressive statements and the Head Dip action appears to have originated from a lunging intention movement.

11. The Body Baton. Similar to the Head Baton, but involving the whole body as well, is the Body Jerk. This is seen in the most dramatic cases of batoning, where the speaker literally throws himself into his role of communicator. The musical baton-waver—the orchestra conductor—shows the most exaggerated form of this type of beating-time action, but it can also

The Tight Fist, a Baton Signal popular among politicians, is used to transmit an impression of unshakable determination. A Head Dip reinforces its effect.

be observed in cases of extravagantly intense public speakers, who are rather aggressively desperate in their attempts to convince their audiences.

Another Body Baton, popular among singers, is the Body Sway, in which the trunk tilts to the side, first one way, then the other, keeping in time with the emphasis of the sung words, which will also, inevitably, be the tempo of the song's music.

12. The Foot Baton. Feet play little part in ordinary speech batoning, but there is one special exception—the Foot Stamp. This Foot Baton is almost exclusively connected with passionate, violent emphasis, when the speaker is almost at temper-tantrum level. The foot is banged down hard with each point of verbal emphasis, with the result that this particular baton, like fist-thumping on a table, is heard as well as seen.

These, then, are the major Baton Signals. In each case the underlying mood has been suggested, but these suggestions must not be interpreted too rigidly. They represent probabilities rather than certainties and there is a good reason for this, namely the 'personal fixation' factor. Each of us is likely to develop personal preferences for certain types of Baton Signal and then, as the years go by, display these more and more to the exclusion of others. Our batoning style will still vary with our mood-changes, but in a less precise way, with our favourite hand postures covering a rather wider range of moods than might be expected from the simplified classification given here.

Other differences in batoning behaviour have been noted as well. It is claimed that some nationalities gesticulate more than others, that lower classes gesticulate more than upper classes, and that the inarticulate gesticulate more than the articulate. National differences certainly do seem to exist, and studies of film sequences confirm that most Mediterranean peoples gesticulate more freely than northern Europeans. The trend is not so much national as geographical, and the obvious implication is that it has something to do with temperature differences but, as yet, no one has been able to explain why this should be.

Class differences may also exist, but these have been exaggerated. It is true that upper-class Victorians frowned on all forms of social disinhibition and the lively use of the arms and hands 'as auxilliaries to the voice' was considered 'vulgar' by the author of The Habits of Good Society, published in London a hundred years ago. However, the Victorian public speaker was noted for his manual gestures and was even able to buy books on how to gesticulate more effectively when addressing an audience. So the precise social context was relevant, and even in Victorian times the matter was not as simple as it might seem at first sight. Today there are still some lingering influences from this earlier era, with certain individuals taught that it is unseemly to gesticulate emotionally, but there is no longer any clear-cut division between one social group and another. In all social strata there are wild gesticulators and non-gesticulators.

As regards the articulation claim, there seems to be little supporting evidence. The idea was that verbal clumsiness was counterbalanced by manual gesturing, that the inarticulate are groping with their hands for words that elude them. Again, the truth is not that simple. Some articulate men are rather body-static, but many more are highly animated. Some of the most brilliant wordsmiths alive are also the most gesticulatory. Conversely, many of the least articulate individuals are such blunted personalities that their hands are as inexpressive as their words.

Apart from group-to-group differences and person-to-person differences, there are also variations in batoning frequency from occasion to occasion for the same individual. Since batons are concerned with both emphasis and mood, it follows that in situations where spoken comments are rather matter-of-fact, such as when ordering groceries, the words will be accompanied by fewer batons than when someone is arguing about some passionately held belief. Also, he is more likely to gesticulate if he is an enthusiast rather than a cynic. The enthusiast wants to share his excitements and feels a powerful

Baton signalling is so compulsive that often we continue to use hand batons to emphasize words, even when the listener is clearly unable to see them.

need to emphasize every point that he considers important. The cynic is so negative in all his attitudes that he feels no such urge.

The enthusiast's behaviour provides another clue. His batons beat out his eagerness to arouse similar enthusiasm in his listeners. The more feedback he gets from them, the more successful he will feel. The more successful he feels, the less he will be driven—unconsciously—to emphasize his verbal statements. So, the reaction of his audience to his speech is a vital factor in influencing the intensity of his baton signals. A demonstrative and totally sympathetic listener will tend to damp down his gesticulations. But give him an attentive yet critical audience and his hands will start to dance. He must win over the listener and to do this he must emphasize his words over and over again. Bearing this in mind, it suddenly becomes clear why public speakers addressing large groups of people gesticulate so much more than private conversationalists. The same man talking to a single friend or addressing a big audience shows many more batons in the public situation than in the private encounter. The reason is that, paradoxically, he gets less feedback from the crowd than he does from the solitary friend. The friend keeps on nodding and smiling and the speaker knows all the time that his words are getting across. No need then to add much manual emphasis. But the members of a large audience do not show their minute-by-minute appreciation with smiles and nods. Being part of a crowd makes their relationship with the speaker impersonal. They stare at him and save their reaction for the end, when they applaud with hand-clapping. For the speaker, the sea of faces is a challenge—they are not nodding as a close friend would do, so what precisely *are* they thinking? Are the ideas getting across or are they failing to make any impact? Unconsciously, the speaker decides that the only safe course of action is to step up the emphasis, just to make sure. And so it is that moderate gesticulators in private become intense gesticulators on the public platform.

Finally, in addition to differences in frequency, there is also much subtle variation in baton style. But little research has been done on this subject so far, and for a detailed report on baton 'dialects', we must await the results of field studies yet to come.

The Palm Back baton is used by gesticulators attempting to 'embrace' a concept. The hands appear to embrace an invisible companion.

GUIDE SIGNS

Pointing and beckoning—how we show the way

Guide Signs are actions which indicate direction. They guide the attention of the onlooker, or his actual movements. In a word, they are pointers. In the scientific literature they have been given the name Deictic Signals, but this seems unnecessarily obscure.

When we point at something it seems such a simple thing to do that we tend to take this type of action for granted. Yet other animals are poor pointers and the extensive use of Guide Signs is uniquely human property. Pointing is, in fact, a speciality of our species and we perform it in many different ways.

The most simple Guide Sign is the Body Point, and this is the only form of pointing which we do share with other species. If some sudden stimulus alerts one animal in a group and it swings its body quickly to face the stimulus, this action may guide the attention of its companions so that they too turn to face in the same direction, even though they themselves may not yet have spotted the source of interest. We have made special use of this animal Body Point in one instance—the gun-dog aptly called the 'Pointer'.

Human body-pointing can be observed at any social gathering where an important personage is present. We can detect his position as we enter the room by the cluster of bodies surrounding him and all facing towards him. Street clusters of this kind also arouse our curiosity, when we see a circle of inward-facing bodies obscuring some focal point of interest. When there has been an accident, people run towards such a cluster, guided by the inward body-pointing, so that the clump of onlookers quickly swells to a dense crowd.

Human body-pointing is only an incidental gesture. We do not do it as an intended signal—it is secondary to what else is going on. The most popular form of deliberate guide-signing in our species is undoubtedly the Forefinger Point. When someone stops us in the street and asks the way, we may give a perfectly adequate verbal answer, but we rarely omit to add a Forefinger Point in support of those words. Even when the pointing is clearly

The Forefinger Point (below far left) is a Guide-sign showing the position of something, while the Hand Point (below left) is used to indicate the course to be taken. The farther away the object, the higher the forefinger points (below), as if it were an arrow about to be fired at a target.

The Forefinger Hop, in which the finger loops forward once for each future day. The sign shown here means 'the day after tomorrow'.

The thumbs-compressed and the thumbs-down signs. The Romans' sign for 'slay him' was the thumbs-down and their signal for 'spare him' was the thumbs-compressed—not, as is usually believed, the thumbs-up.

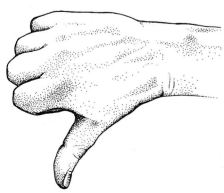

superfluous we still feel compelled to do it, and it is an action that is observable in almost all countries in the world. In certain places, where finger-pointing is taboo, it is replaced by the Head Point, in which the head is jerked in the appropriate direction, combined with an opening and closing, or pouting, of the lips. Head-pointing is most likely to be encountered in Central and South America, in black Africa and among Gurkhas and North American Indians.

A special form of the Head Point is the secretive Eyes Point. If I wish to warn you that someone has just entered the room, out of your line of vision, I may glance quickly in their direction, pause with an intense stare for a fraction of a second, then return my gaze to you again to see if you have understood. The chances are that I will have to repeat this special glance several times before you get the message. This is a deliberate and intensified version of the ordinary Eyes Glance action, but it requires delicate handling. If I perform the action too intensely, it may be observed by the third party, and if I do not intensify it enough you may overlook it.

Returning to the most important human pointer—the hand—there are some variants there, too. In addition to the Forefinger Point, there is also the Hand Point, in which all five digits are aimed, flat-handed and with the fingers together. The difference between the Forefinger Point and the Hand Point is subtle. If I ask someone in the street 'Where is the station?' and he replies 'It is down there', he is likely to point with his forefinger. If I ask 'How do I get to the station?' and he replies 'You walk down there', he is more likely to indicate the direction of my walk by pointing with the whole of his hand, thumb uppermost and all four fingers stretched out.

In other words, the pointing hand is a Guide Sign indicating the course to be taken, while the pointing finger is more concerned with indicating the position of the goal you are seeking. It is as if the forefinger is an arrow about to be fired at your destination. So relevant is this analogy, that in certain tribal societies, the distance of the destination is indicated by the angle of the forefinger. If I ask 'Where is the nearest waterhole?' and it is close by, the forefinger will point almost horizontally; but if it is far away, then the forefinger will be tilted slightly upwards. The farther away it is, the higher the pointing finger is tilted up, just as an arrow would be fired higher to make it go farther.

In Greece and parts of Italy there is a special version of this symbolism—The Forefinger Hop. In this action, the extended forefinger is jumped forward in an arc, each jump representing one day ahead of the present day. This is a Guide Sign indicating a direction in time rather than space and, with its aid, a boy and girl can make a date across a crowded room without exchanging a word. The question and answer goes something like this:

BOY: Unspoken words: Can we meet tomorrow at five? Actions: (1) points at girl, points at himself (=we); (2) hops forefinger once (=tomorrow); (3) holds up five fingers (=5 pm).

GIRL: Unspoken words: No, but I can manage five, the day after. Actions: (1) tosses head back (=no); (2) hops forefinger twice (=day after tomorrow); (3) holds up five fingers (5 pm).

The Two-fingers Point, employing the first and second fingers, is not a common Guide Sign, but is used sometimes as an intermediate between goal-indicating forefinger-pointing and course-indicating hand-pointing.

Finally, there is the Thumb Point, with an ancient and bloody history. In Roman times this was a Guide Sign that could spell death. When a gladiator was defeated in combat in the arena, he might be spared or he might be killed on the spot by his victor. The crowd of spectators could influence the decision by the position of their thumbs. It is popularly believed that the life-or-death thumb gestures were thumbs-up for life and thumbs-down for death, but this appears to be based on a misinterpretation of ancient writings. A re-examination of these writings makes it more likely that the 'thumbs-up' posture was really a 'thumbs-cover-up'—with the thumbs hidden inside the closed hands—while the 'thumbs-down' was really a 'thumbs-point-down'. The crowd was seated above the arena, so if they pointed their thumbs towards the gladiator they would automatically be pointed downwards. So the life-or-death gesturing was either thumbs-hide for life, or thumbs-point for death.

We are so used to the modern version of thumbs-up and thumbs-down that this explanation of the ancient signs seems highly improbable, but the fact remains that the original phrase for thumbs-up—*pollice compresso*—means literally 'thumbs compressed', which is hardly the way we would describe the modern thumb sign indicating approval. The origin of the ancient actions appears to be based in simple mimicry. The thrusting downwards of the thumb, with the fingers closed, is an imitation of the killing action of thrusting the sword down into the victim. It is a swordless sword-thrust performed by the onlookers to encourage the winner to do likewise to the loser. To give the opposite signal—spare him, do *not* make the sword-thrust—they hold out their hands with the thumbs clearly hidden inside their closed fingers.

The sarcastic Forefinger Beckon, a favourite gesture of Oliver Hardy's.

Perhaps because of their ancient heritage, Italians today are far less likely to use the thumbs-up gesture meaning 'OK', 'fine', 'good', when compared with, say, Englishmen or Frenchmen. When quizzed on this point, 95 per cent of Englishmen and Frenchmen agreed that they used the sign in this way, but the figure for Italians was as low as 23 per cent. What is more, many of the Italians referred to the sign as the 'English OK' signal, and mentioned that they had seen it in films or on television. So it looks as if the popular thumbs-up, which started out as a mistranslation from the literature of ancient Rome, is now 'returning' to the city from which it never really came in the first place.

Apart from this special use of the thumb, there is also a more general, directional thumb-point. It has the flavour of a rather surly action—a grumpy or irritated gesture. If I am busy and someone interrupts me to ask where an object is, I may respond by jerking my thumb in the appropriate direction. Such an action is considered rather impolite, and it is worth asking why. I am, after all, providing the required information. I am not ignoring the questioner, so why should he feel that my jabbing thumb is slightly insulting? The answer seems to be connected with the role of the thumb as the 'brutal digit', or 'power digit'. If we want to press down on something as hard as we can, we use the thumb rather than any of the fingers. When we grip an object firmly, the thumb's strength has to balance the strength of all four fingers put together. We talk of having a person 'under our thumb' when we mean they are under our control, in our power. So the directional thumb-jab is a statement unconsciously associated with physical strength. As a gesture that hints at hidden power it is definitely not for use by subordinates towards their superiors. No one in a junior role would indicate direction to a senior colleague by means of a thumb-jerk, unless he were being deliberately rude.

The only exception to this rule is when the direction being indicated is over the shoulder of the pointer. If he were being polite, he would turn right round and point with his forefinger, but if it is difficult for him to turn, then a thumb-point over his shoulder is acceptable. A special case of this is the hitch-hiker, who thumb-points down the road behind him as he faces the on-coming traffic.

In addition to the gestures we call 'pointing', there is another special category of Guide Signs that we refer to as 'beckoning'. Here there is only one direction involved—towards oneself. These are the 'come here' or 'come hither' signals and there are several variants.

The most common form of beckoning is the Hand Beckon in which all four fingers open and close together. Some people do this with the palm facing upwards, and others do it in the opposite way, with the palm facing downwards. Which of these positions you use depends on where you live. If

Beckoning is done with the palm up in some countries and the palm down in others. The charts show how the preference changes as you travel from England across Europe to North Africa (Charts after Morris et al: *Gesture Maps*).

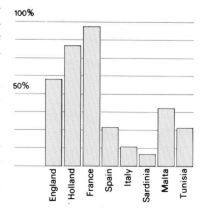

you are an Englishman or a Frenchman you always use the palm-up posture for beckoning, but if you are an Italian you nearly always use the palm-down posture. This is because Italians employ a good-bye wave that looks almost exactly like the Anglo–French beckon. If they beckoned in the Anglo–French style it could lead to confusion.

In the rest of the world, the palm-up Hand Beckon is seen in most areas, but the palm-down variant is found in certain parts of Asia and Africa, and in Spain and the South American Countries.

The Forefinger Beckon is much less common than the Hand Beckon, and in England it has a slightly teasing or sarcastic flavour. This is not so marked in France and it is twice as common there as in England. In Italy it is rare, but even less common is the palm-down Forefinger Beckon which was used by only 5 out of 300 Italians questioned on the subject (1.7 per cent).

Another rare variant is the Two-finger Beckon, which was found in only 8 per cent of Englishmen and Frenchmen and not at all in Italy. Its lack of popularity may well be due to its resemblance to the Two-finger Jerk, which is a widespread obscenity.

If a beckoner wishes to be more insistent—a parent signalling to a child in the distance, for example—he often employs a full arm movement which makes the message more conspicuous. The Sideways Arm-sweep is the most popular version of this gesture, which says, not so much 'Come here', as 'Come on!'. Another long-distance beckon signal is the Raised-forefinger Rotation gesture. In this, the arm is raised above the head, the straightened forefinger stretched up to the sky. The finger is then rotated vigorously. This is observable in many military contexts, but is also reported to be used by certain Bedouins in North Africa—who may prove to be the original source from which the military borrowed the action.

Another North African speciality that has been observed is numbered beckoning. If you see a group of people and you wish to beckon only one of them to come over to you, you use a forefinger only. If you want two of them to come to you, you employ the second finger as well as the forefinger. If you want three of them, you use the first, second and third fingers. This beckoning 'oddity' was discovered in Tunisia, but whether it was a local peculiarity, or whether it has a wider importance is not yet clear.

A theatrical and rather sarcastic, 'school-masterish' beckon is the Finger-by-finger Beckon. In this the fingers do not close together, but one after the other in a wave motion, starting with the little finger and ending with the forefinger. Some comedians use this as a mocking sign of 'patient exasperation'. In origin it appears to be a hybrid between an ordinary Hand Beckon and a grasping action.

Finally, there is the Head Beckon, which is normally used only when the hands are full and unable to perform the more usual beckoning movements. A special exception is the collusive Head Beckon which gives a sexual 'Come Hither' signal. This involves no more than a very slight head jerk and implies a sexual invitation, although it is now used more in a joking context of pretended sexuality, rather than in a truly erotic situation.

Apart from pointing and beckoning there are various hand and arm movements that act as general Guide Signs. The Hand-repel gesture, with the hand held up, palm-front, and pushing away from the signaller, guides the companion to go back. The directional Hand Flap ushers the companion in the direction of the moved hand. The Hand Lift directs upwards, and the Hand Downbeat directs downwards.

Put together, all these Guide Signs confirm the claim that man is the best and most elaborate pointer in the animal kingdom. We take it all for granted, and yet when one considers all the subtle distinctions between the different types of directional signalling, it is clear that even here there is a whole complex world of gesture communication, enabling man to express with just the right degree of precision the 'whereness' of the objects, places and people around him.

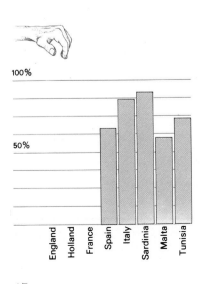

100%

50%

England Holland France Spain Italy Sardinia Malta Tunisia

YES/NO SIGNALS

Ways in which we signal agreement and acceptance, or denial and refusal

Many people believe that there is only one way to signal YES and one way to signal NO—the Head Nod and the Head Shake—and that these actions are global in their distribution. This is close to the truth, but it is not the whole truth. In certain regions there are other, less well-known head movements that are used locally to signify affirmatives and negatives, and unless these are understood, travellers may find themselves in difficulties. There are five main head actions.

1. The Head Nod. The head moves vertically up and down one or more times, with the down elements stronger than the up elements. Essentially this is an incipient bowing action, with the head starting to make a bow and then stopping short. Since bowing is part of a worldwide system of submissive body-lowering, it is not surprising to find that the Head Nod occurs almost everywhere and that whenever it does occur, it is always a YES sign, never a NO. Even remote tribes, such as the Australian Aborigines, were found to be using the Head Nod for YES, when first encountered by white men, so that it must either be thousands of years old or have developed independently in different places at various times. Its wide range certainly cannot be explained as a recent colonial or tourist import.

In addition to the Aborigines, the Head Nod has also been recorded in the Amazonian Indians, Eskimos, Fuegians, Papuans, Samoans, Balinese, Malays, Japanese, Chinese, and a number of African Tribes. It is also used by nearly all whites in Europe, North and South America, Australia and New Zealand, and it has even been recorded in people born deaf and blind, and in microcephalic individuals incapable of speech. This impressive list, which could doubtless be greatly extended, strongly suggests that affirmative Head Nodding may well be an inborn action for our species. If this is so, then the exceptions to the rule—those people who employ some other head movement for YES—require a special explanation. The chances are that they are adding to rather than replacing the nodding gesture. In Ceylon, for instance, the Head Nod was said by some travellers to be replaced by a Head Sway. When agreeing to some proposal, the local inhabitants were seen to sway the head from side to side instead of nodding it up and down. Closer study revealed that this was only the case where agreement was concerned and that if a factual question was put, it was answered with the familiar Head Nod. So it depended on the type of YES involved. For most people there is simply a 'blanket response' to all questions requiring an affirmative signal, but for others, the precise kind of YES is relevant. There are several basic varieties of YES:

The Acknowledgement Nod: 'Yes, I am still listening.'
The Encouraging Nod: 'Yes, how fascinating.'
The Understanding Nod: 'Yes, I see what you mean.'
The Agreement Nod: 'Yes, I will.'
The Factual Nod: 'Yes, that is correct.'

If, in any particular locality, one of these types of Nod is replaced by some other head action, then this is likely to be the one that catches the eye of the casual traveller, simply because it is different; and he will return with inaccurate stories of a totally different signalling system for affirmations.

2. The Head Shake. The head turns horizontally from side to side, with equal emphasis left and right. This is the most common form of negative response, covering a wide range of NOs, from 'I cannot' and 'I will not' to 'I disagree' and 'I do not know'. It can also signify disapproval or bewilderment.

Like the Head Nod, the Head Shake is virtually global in range and, again like the Head Nod, it usually manages to survive in those areas where some other negative action is operating. In origin, as mentioned earlier, it is

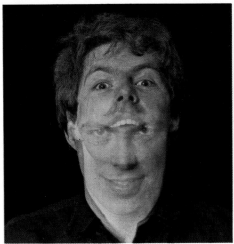 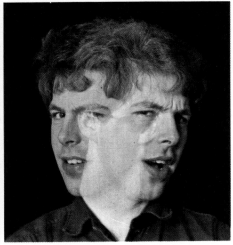

The Head Nod and the Head Shake, the two most widespread signs for 'yes' and 'no'. Many people mistakenly believe that these are the only two gestures employed for affirmations and negations.

thought to stem from the infantile action of rejecting the breast, the bottle, or a spoonful of food. When the parent tries to persuade the baby to feed, the negative response to the offering is to twist the head first to one side and then to the other, turning the head away from the unwanted object. This alternate turning is seen as the starting point for the adult Head Shake, and explains why, wherever it occurs, it is always a negative signal.

3. The Head Twist. The head turns sharply to one side and back again to the neutral position. This is half a Head Shake and means much the same. It is employed as a NO sign in parts of Ethiopia and elsewhere, and is even more clearly related to the child's action of refusing food which is being pressed to the mouth.

4. The Head Sway. The head tilts rhythmically from side to side, describing an arc as if it were an inverted pendulum. To most Europeans, this action would mean 'Maybe yes, maybe no', with the head mimicking the alternating actions of going 'this way or that way'. But in Bulgaria and parts of Greece, Yugoslavia, Turkey, Iran and Bengal, this rocking movement of the head is reputed to be a replacement for the more familiar Head Nod. In these areas it is said to mean YES, rather than maybe, and the movement is sufficiently similar to the more common Head Shake to cause some confusion.

When Head-shaking Russian soldiers were occupying Bulgaria in the last century, they had trouble understanding the local inhabitants. The Bulgarian YES looked so much like a Russian NO that complications arose. To solve the problem the Russians trained themselves to sway their heads when they meant YES and to suppress their own negative Head Shakes. This should have worked well, but even greater misunderstandings arose because the Bulgarians were never sure whether the Russians had remembered to switch to their system, or whether they had reverted momentarily to their own. At this point, all head signalling broke down.

The Bulgarian language contains several phrases which give the clue to the origin of the Head Sway movement as an affirmative. There are sayings such as 'I give you my ear' and 'I am all ears', and the suggestion is that the swaying movement is a stylized form of tilting the ear to the companion to offer him your attention. Affirming your interest then becomes a generalized affirmation.

5. The Head Toss. The head is tilted sharply back and returns less sharply to the neutral posture. This is like an inverted Head Nod, and is a special way of saying NO for many regions. Many signals work on the *antithesis principle*, and this is one of them. The principle states, quite simply, that if two signals mean the opposite of each other, then the actions on which they are based will also be opposite in form or direction. For example, in a dominant posture, the body is held high, while in a submissive posture it crouches low. Similarly, if the Head Nod means YES, then one might expect the sign for NO to be the

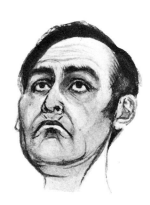

By flicking the backs of the fingers of one hand forward against the underside of the chin, a southern Italian (left) indicates a negative answer. This gesture—the Chin Flick—is an amplification of the upward Head Toss (above).

The wagged forefinger (top) or the laterally shaken hand (middle) often act in place of the simple Head Shake. These are examples of Substitute Signals, where one part of the body (the forefinger or the hand) replaces the usual organ (the head) involved in sending the signal. In a similar way, the North American Indian sign for 'yes' is a dip of the forefinger (above), with this movement substituting for a nod of the head.

opposite of it. There are two ways of opposing the downward nodding movement—one is the sideways shaking action, the Head Shake, and the other is upward Head Toss.

Perhaps because it is less distinctive than the Head Shake, the Head Toss has a much more limited range. Its main centre is in Greece, and it is sometimes referred to as the 'Greek NO', but it also spreads out around many parts of the Mediterranean and can be seen today not only in Greece, but also in Cyprus, Turkey, Yugoslavia, some Arab countries, Malta, Sicily and southern Italy. As with the Chin Flick (one of the Regional Signals discussed earlier), its present-day range is remarkably similar to the territorial spread of ancient Greece in its heyday, and it looks very much as though this is an ancient Grecian gesture that has survived in those places that were once Greek colonies, despite the passage of over two thousand years. To test this, a special study was made in central Italy. It was found that, despite the mobility of modern populations in Italy and the existence of a national television network covering the whole country, modern Romans still say NO with a Head Shake, and Neapolitans still say NO with a Head Toss. Travelling through the villages between the two cities, it became clear that there was a fairly sharp dividing-line coinciding with the first mountain range north of Naples. South of this, nearly everyone used the Head Toss; north of it they used the Head Shake. As far as the Head Toss is concerned, it is almost as if the Greeks never left the south of Italy.

For most people in the south, however, the Head Toss is not used for every kind of negative statement. A little Head Shaking still goes on, especially for factual NOs. The Head Toss has the flavour of an emotional NO—'No, you may not', 'It's no good', 'No!!!'. It is sometimes emphasized by the addition of lip-pursing, eye-raising and eyebrow-raising, and a clicking sound. At a distance, it is also augmented by a flicking movement in which the backs of the fingers scrape forward under the chin—the Chin Flick.

To confuse matters further, there is a totally different meaning for the Head Toss in certain other parts of the world. Among the Maoris of New Zealand, the Tagals of the Philippines, the Dyaks of Borneo, and certain Ethiopians, the Head Toss means, not NO, but YES. This remarkably scattered distribution is hard to understand, but the way in which the tossing back of the head can come to mean YES is not impossible to guess. There is an 'Aha!' response, involving an up-and-back tilt of the head, which we all give when we have just solved a problem with a flash of insight. It is a movement of pleased surprise: 'Ah, yes, of course!', and the 'Ah, yes' can presumably develop into a simple YES signal. This is what seems to have happened in several isolated cases, and it provides another reason why the Head Toss is not a more popular, world-wide sign, like the Head Nod and the Head Shake. It lacks their specificity.

The five main YES/NO signals are all movements of the head—but there are other ways of saying YES or NO, involving the hands. A parental warning to a child not to do something is often performed, not with a shaking head, but instead with a wagging forefinger. This is an example of a Substitute Signal, with one part of the body 'standing in' for another. Here, the forefinger is being shaken in imitation of the shaken head. The hand, so to speak, borrows the action from the head and, in so doing, is able to speed it up and add more vigour to it. If the parent is anxious or angry, the child can be given a more forceful, agitated and rapid shaking signal with the finger than would be possible with the head. Another version is the shaking hand. The same action is performed, but with the flat palm of the hand facing the companion.

According to students of North American Indian sign language, the Indian hand signal for YES is a downward dip of the forefinger—another Substitute Signal, this time a 'Hand Bow' or 'Hand Nod', with the dipping down of the hand standing in for the dipping of the affirmative head. The Indian NO is a flicking *up* of the hand, again a copy of a typical head movement, in this case, the upward Head Toss.

GAZE BEHAVIOUR

Staring eyes and glancing eyes—the way we look at one another

When two people meet and make eye contact, they find themselves in an immediate state of conflict. They want to look at each other and at the same time they want to look away. The result is a complicated series of eye movements, back and forth, and a careful study of this Gaze Behaviour can reveal a great deal about their relationship.

To understand why the rules of human 'glancing' are so complex, it is necessary to appreciate that there is not one, but several reasons why we may want to look at someone, and several other reasons why we may want to look away. In the case of young lovers experiencing the first intense emotions of mutual attraction, there are some very noticeable patterns of gazing. If both boy and girl are acutely shy, they may spend a lot of time looking far away from each other. As they talk, they exchange only the briefest of glances. For most of the time they will stare down at the ground or gaze in opposite directions. Sometimes their deflected gaze is so intent that it seems there must be something fascinating lying on the ground near their feet. Their eyes are rivetted there, as if concentrating hard on some tiny speck of dust. Internally, it is the conflict between fear and sexual attraction that is

During friendly social encounters, eye contact is held fractionally longer than usual by individuals who find their companions appealing. This extended gaze is usually performed unconsciously and its message is received in the same way. The companions are aware of the unusual warmth of the encounter but they do not analyse the signals involved.

The Gaze Behaviour of young lovers passes through several distinct phases. Initially, shyness involves much looking away and a reluctance to meet the companion's eyes. Then there are the sidelong glances in which the eyes gaze at the partner, but the head is still turned away. Sometimes this posture is deliberately adopted as a joking display of flirtation, as can be seen here.

creating the problem of where to direct their eyes. As the courtship progresses, there is less fear and the lovers meet each other's eyes more often. Even so, there is still some shyness and instead of turning full-face to look at each other, they continue to show typical, side-long glances (sometimes called making 'sheep's eyes'). But these nervous glances are now more frequent and last a little longer. If one of the lovers becomes bolder than the other, there is a period of rapt attention, with one staring long and longingly at the other, who may still be concentrating on that important speck of dust on the ground. 'He could not take his eyes off her', and 'He kept on staring at me', are the phrases used to describe this phase of a relationship.

Eventually, when the lovers have grown truly intimate and all fear is gone, they may sit close together, gazing deeply into each other's eyes for long periods of time, with only occasional glances away, talking softly and making gentle physical contacts. This progression, from the shy beginnings, to the one-sided longing, to the powerful, mutual attachment, involves a massive increase in the amount of time spent looking at each other, and inevitably labels 'long-looking' as a sign of loving.

Switching to an entirely different kind of emotional encounter: what

The agonized staring of the adoring fans of a pop star idol (above) contrasts with the softer mutual gaze of young lovers (below): but both cases illustrate the way in which loving attachment is linked with a dramatic increase in the amount of direct gazing.

Intense staring at close quarters occurs in threatening as well as in loving situations. The actively hostile dominant male (right) thrusts his face close to that of the intimidated subordinate, who dare not meet his gaze. Where two opponents are both actively threatening, the close staring becomes mutual and the arguing pair face each other eye to eye (above).

happens to the eyes when status rather than love is the dominant element? Suppose a subordinate has done something stupid, and he is called to the office of a superior to be reprimanded. As he enters, he is watching the dominant one's face closely for signs of his mood, but the superior sits quietly behind his desk, staring out of the window. With hardly a glance at the subordinate he tells him to sit and then begins to attack him verbally, still looking out of the window. Suddenly the subordinate's replies annoy him and he swivels round to glare intently at the unfortunate man, fixating him with a threatening expression. He holds this prolonged stare and now the subordinate cannot meet his eyes. In his nervousness, the weaker man looks away, glancing back only occasionally to check any change in mood. As he looks away more and more, his face is lost to view—he is literally 'losing face'. The dominant is threatening with phrases such as 'I am keeping my eye on you', while he does precisely that, his eyes boring into the head of the now submissive employee. But he goes too far and the subordinate loses his temper. Leaping up, he starts shouting at the dominant figure. With his sudden change of mood, to open hostility, his Gaze Behaviour is transformed. Now he too is staring hard at his opponent, and they fixate each other. Out of control, the subordinate leaps round the desk and begins hitting the older man, who falls to the floor. With the dominant man's rapid change to panic and fear for his physical safety, there is a major change in facial expression, but he keeps his eyes fixed on his angry opponent. In this situation, however, his stare is one of fearfulness, not aggression. He dare not take his eyes off his assailant for a second if he is to protect himself.

This escalating scene involves several distinct changes in Gaze Behaviour. It shows that *passive* dominance and *passive* submission both involve exaggerated looking away. Before the superior was roused to action, he haughtily ignored the subordinate and stared out of the window as if the employee were hardly worth a glance. The subordinate, for his part, looked away dejectedly when being glared at, and submissively lowered his eyes. It also shows that *active* aggression and *active* fear both involve intense looking towards the opponent. The angered superior, the outraged subordinate and, finally, the panic-stricken superior, in each case, fixated their opponent, either as a direct threat, or as a means of keeping alert for signs of attack.

Summing up these highly-charged scenes of love and hate, it can be said that a direct stare indicates intensely active feelings of an amorous, hostile, or fearful kind, while a deflected gaze is linked with shyness, casual superiority, or downcast submissiveness. Since there are basically only two kinds of gazing—away and towards—it is left up to the accompanying facial expressions to signal which of the three major moods is involved—love, anger, or fear. In the strongly emotional situations described, these facial expressions will be undiluted and unmistakable, but these are comparatively rare occasions. The vast majority of social encounters are, by comparison, mild and muted affairs. Even if slight feelings of sexual arousal, hostility, or anxiety are present, they tend to remain submerged beneath a mask of social politeness. At a party, a meeting, a dinner, or some other gathering, the man who finds the woman to whom he is talking exceptionally appealing will probably not reveal the fact by adopting an obviously lecherous facial expression. Instead, he will carry on his conversation at what he hopes will look like a merely friendly level. Another man, who finds his host especially irritating, will likewise suppress his hostile facial expressions, and a third, who feels unduly intimidated by his impressive companion, will not permit his face to break out into an expression of naked anxiety.

Under these more moderate conditions, the less intense emotions can be controlled and the outward display is flattened out to one of almost uniform 'nodding-and-smiling'. But smiles are more easy to discipline than glances. We are hardly aware of changes in our pattern of eye movements as we chat and sip our drinks. What is happening is that slightly, very slightly, we increase the amount of time we spend looking away from, or towards, our companions as we engage them in conversation. The man who finds a beautiful colleague unusually arousing may not show his feelings in other ways, but his gaze, when their eyes meet, holds hers fractionally longer than usual. Another man, forced to talk to his singularly unappealing hostess, will reveal his inner reactions to her not by his beaming smile, but by the brevity of his glances in her direction. In the same way, the smiling but rather hostile, domineering guest, tends to fixate his companions with over-long glances, with the result that his smiling but secretly rather nervous victims will divert their eyes much more than in the average encounter.

The obvious problem with these situations is trying to tell whether the guest who 'super-gazes' you fancies you or actively dislikes you. This is too much to ask of Gaze Behaviour. All the eye directions can tell you is whether you are getting slightly more or slightly less attention than usual. The precise

Because humans engage in prolonged verbal encounters face-to-face the signals of gaze direction have become especially important for our species. In connection with this, we have developed distinctive 'whites' to our eyes, making the direction of our glance more conspicuous. These 'whites' are lacking in our nonverbal relatives, such as the chimpanzee.

Such is the impact of the close-quarters gaze that the schoolboy game of stare-you-out is extremely difficult to maintain over a long period of time.

nature of that attention must be sought in other nonverbal clues—those that may remain unmasked by the polite smile. But even though the small increases and decreases of direct gazing are only general indicators, carrying little mood-specificity, they are nevertheless vitally important social clues to which we all respond unconsciously every time we meet and talk with a companion.

So important are they, that we have evolved a special facial element—the white of the eye—that serves to make our glancings more conspicuous. Other primates lack this and their shifts of eye-direction are much less obvious. But they, of course, do not stand hour after hour in a face-to-face relationship, talking to one another. It is, in fact, the evolution of speech that has made eye contact such a significant and useful human signalling device.

Watch the eyes of any two people engrossed in conversation, and you will observe a highly characteristic 'dance' of gaze shifts. The speaker starts his statement with a glance at his companion. Then, as he gains momentum of thought and word, he looks away. As he is coming to the end of his comment, he glances back again to check the impact of what he has said. While he has been doing this, his companion has been watching him, but now, as the listener takes over the talk and becomes the speaker, he, in turn, looks away, glancing back only to check the effect of his words. In this way, the talk and the eyes go back and forth, in a remarkably predictable pattern.

In ordinary conversation, it is the moments where the eyes make brief contact, at the point of handing over the speaking role, that the variations in attention start to make themselves felt. It is there that the amorous male

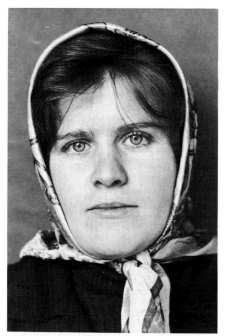

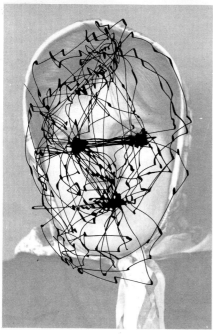

When we stare closely at a human face, we do not remain fixated on exactly the same spot for any length of time. Our eyes scan the features of the face, but concentrate most on the eyes and mouth, as revealed by this experimental record of eye-movements made by a subject staring for three minutes at a photograph of a young girl's face. (After Yarbus.)

holds on a little too long. As he answers the beautiful girl's last statement he begins talking and reaches the point where normally he would look away, but instead he is still staring at her. This makes her uncomfortable, because she is forced either to lock eyes with him, or to look away from him while *he* is talking. If he continues to talk and stare while she deflects her eyes, it puts her into the 'shy' category, which she resents. If she boldly locks eyes with him, then he has forced her into a 'lover's gaze', which she also resents. But the chances are that he will not go this far. He will only increase his gaze-time by a tiny amount, just long enough for the message to get across without creating any embarrassment.

There are several other variants that can be seen in almost any social gathering. For instance, there is the verbose companion who talks so much and for so long that he cannot wait for the end of his statement to check reactions to what he is saying, and has to keep glancing back during the course of his speech. Then there is the shifty-eyed man, whose nervousness fluctuates rapidly between nervous attention (glance towards) and nervous submission (glance away). His eyes dart back and forth wildly, creating acute discomfort in his companion. Or there is the gushing 'fan', whose rapt interest in an admired companion means that he cannot take his eyes off him for a second, whether talking or listening. This forces the admired one either to lock eyes, or to gaze, like a passive dominant, into the distance.

These special cases disrupt the typical back and forth balance of the Gaze Behaviour of the ordinary social encounter, a balance which expresses interest without the implication of intense emotional involvement, and does it with great delicacy and finesse without our ever being consciously aware of it. Only when we encounter an unusually distorted pattern of gazing do we notice what is happening. One situation in which this always occurs is the giving of a lecture or talk to a large audience. The speaker mounts the platform and immediately sees before him a sea of eyes, all staring at him. As he starts to speak, he inevitably feels threatened by their massed stare and he gazes away, up into the air, or down at his notes. An experienced lecturer knows that this is bad technique, and learns to correct it by forcing himself to look directly at the audience from time to time, as he would do if conversing with a single companion. This is important because to each of the listeners he is, in effect, a one-to-one companion. If he does not look in their direction occasionally, they feel ignored. The expert lecturer's solution is to sweep the audience slowly with his eyes at frequent intervals.

The exact opposite problem faces the television newscaster. For him, there are no staring eyes, only a camera lens. Over the lens is an automatic device called an auto-cue, on which the words he must speak roll slowly past. To read these words he need never look away from the lens — indeed it is difficult to do so without him losing his place in the text. But for the viewer at home he appears to be performing a prolonged, unrelenting stare, which gives an unnatural feel to his delivery. His problem is solved by having a sheaf of notes on his newsdesk, to which he can glance occasionally and thereby relieve the tension of his super-stare. Other expert auto-cue users, standing in a studio and pretending to speak off the cuff, develop the technique of deliberately glancing away from the camera from time to time for a similar reason. They have no notes to look at, but they can gaze upwards or to one side of the camera, treating it as if it were a human companion, and thereby create a much more natural relationship with the viewers in their homes.

Our sensitivity to prolonged staring is such that the child's game of stare-you-out is extremely difficult to keep going for any length of time. Direct, eyeball-to-eyeball staring seems to have a deeply threatening effect, even when we consciously tell ourselves that it is only a game. Before long, something in us snaps and we have to look away. It is almost as if we feel that we will somehow be damaged by the staring eye, and this feeling has given rise to many superstitious practices — the most famous being the powerful and widespread belief in the Evil Eye.

SALUTATION DISPLAYS

Hello and goodbye—greetings and farewells

A Salutation Display demonstrates that we wish someone well, or, at the very least, that we wish them no harm. It transmits signals of friendliness or the absence of hostility. It does this at peak moments—when someone is arriving on the scene, departing from it, or dramatically changing their social role. We salute their comings, their goings and their transformations, and we do it with rituals of greeting, farewell and celebration.

Whenever two friends meet after a long separation, they go through a special Greeting Ritual. During the first moments of the reunion they amplify their friendly signals to super-friendly signals. They smile and touch, often embrace and kiss, and generally behave more intimately and expansively than usual. They do this because they have to make up for lost time—lost friendship time. While they have been apart it has been impossible for them to send the hundreds of small, minute-by-minute friendly signals to each other that their relationship requires, and they have, so to speak, built up a backlog of these signals.

This backlog amounts to a gestural debt that must be repaid without delay, as an assurance that the bond of friendship has not waned but has survived the passage of time spent apart—hence the gushing ceremonies of the reunion scene, which must try to pay off this debt in a single outburst of activity.

Once the Greeting Ritual is over, the old relationship between the friends is now re-established and they can continue with their amicable interactions as before. Eventually, if they have to part for another long spell, there will be a Separation Ritual in which the super-friendly signals will once again be displayed. This time they have the function of leaving both partners with a powerful dose of befriendedness, to last them through the isolated times to come.

In a similar way, if someone undergoes a major change in social role, we again offer them a massive outpouring of friendliness, because we are simultaneously saying farewell to their old self and greeting their new self. We do this when boy and girl become man and wife, when man and wife become father and mother, when prince becomes king, when candidate becomes president, and when competitor becomes champion.

We have many formal procedures for celebrating these occasions, both the

Salutation Displays occur when friends meet after a period of separation (above) or when companions are undergoing a transformation ceremony, such as marriage (below).

The salutation at a wedding has a double function: it says farewell to the old role and welcome to the new role. There is little difference between the human displays of greeting, congratulation and departure. In all three cases there are the same contact elements of hand-shaking, patting, embracing or kissing.

The Inconvenience Display. The first element of a planned greeting is a show of inconvenience in which the greeter moves off his home territory. He may travel to the airport or may go no farther than his front doorstep (right). Or he may remain doggedly in the centre of his territory and have his visitor brought to him.

The Distant Display. When human greeters first establish eye contact with one another they perform some kind of recognition display. This may be a Palm-hidden Wave, typical of Italians (far left top), which to other eyes may resemble an act of beckoning; or a simple hail, with a raised hand, as in the old man from Hong Kong (far left middle); or it may be a Vertical Wave, as shown by the young Russian boy (above left), or a Lateral Wave, performed here by Egyptians greeting President Nixon (left).

physical arrivals and departures and the symbolic comings and goings of the social transformations. We celebrate birthdays, christenings, comings-of-age, weddings, coronations, anniversaries, inaugurations, presentations and retirements. We give house-warmings, welcoming parties, farewell dinners, and funerals. In all these cases we are, in essence, performing Salutation Displays.

The grander the occasion, the more rigid and institutionalized are the procedures. But even our more modest, private, two-person rituals follow distinct sets of rules. We seem to be almost incapable of beginning or ending any kind of encounter without performing some type of salutation. This is even true when we write a letter to someone. We begin with 'Dear Mr Smith' and end 'Yours faithfully', and the rules of salutation are so compelling that we do this even when Mr Smith is far from dear to us and we have little faith in him.

Similarly we shake hands with unwelcome guests and express regret at their departure, although we are glad to see the back of them. All the more reason, then, that our genuine greetings and farewells should be excessively demonstrative.

Social greetings that are planned and anticipated have a distinctive structure and fall into four separate phases:

1. The Inconvenience Display. To show the strength of our friendliness, we 'put ourselves out' to varying degrees. We demonstrate that we are taking trouble. For both host and guest, this may mean 'dressing up'. For the guest it may mean a long journey. For the host it also entails a bodily shift from the centre of his home territory. The stronger the greeting, the greater the inconvenience. The Head of State drives to the airport to meet the important arrival. The brother drives to the airport to greet his sister returning from abroad. This is the maximum form of bodily displacement that a host can offer. From this extreme there is a declining scale of inconvenience, as the distance travelled by the host decreases. He may only go as far as the local station or bus depot. Or he may move no farther than his front drive, emerging from his front door after watching through the window for the moment of arrival. Or he may wait for the bell to ring and then only displace himself as far as his doorway or front hall. Or he may allow a child or servant to answer the door and remain in his room, the very centre of his territory, awaiting the guest who is then ushered into his presence. The minimal Inconvenience Display he can offer is to stand up when the guest enters the room, displacing himself vertically but not horizontally. Only if he remains seated as the guest enters and approaches him, can he be said to be totally omitting Phase One of a planned social greeting. Such omissions are extremely rare today and some degree of voluntary inconvenience is nearly always demonstrated. If, because of some accident or delay, it is unavoidably omitted, there are profuse apologies for its absence when the meeting finally takes place.

At the time of farewell, the Inconvenience Display is repeated in much the same form. 'You know your own way out' is the lowest level of expression here. Beyond that, there is an increasing displacement from territorial base, with the usual social level being 'I will see you to the door'. A slightly more intense form involves going outside the house and waiting there until the departing figures have vanished from sight. And so on, with the full expression being an accompaniment to the station or airport.

2. The Distant Display. The main moment of greeting is when body contact is made, but before this comes the moment of first sighting. As soon as host and guest have identified each other, they signify this fact with a recognition response. Doorstep meetings tend to curtail this phase, because contact can be made almost immediately the door is opened, but in most other greeting situations the Distance Display is prominently demonstrated. It consists of six visual elements: (1) the Smile; (2) the Eyebrow Flash; (3) the Head Tilt; (4) the Hail; (5) the Wave; and (6) the Intention Embrace.

The first three of these almost always occur, and they are performed simultaneously. At the moment of recognition, the head tilts back, the eyebrows arch up, and the face breaks into a large smile. The Head Tilt and the Eyebrow Flash may be very brief. They are elements of surprise. Combined with the smile, they signal a 'pleasant surprise' at seeing the friend. This basic pattern may or may not be augmented by an arm movement. The simplest such action is the Hail—the raising of one hand. A more intense version, typical of long-distance greetings, is the Wave, and a still more intense expression is the Intention Embrace, in which the arms are stretched out towards the friend, as if the greeter cannot wait to perform the contact-embrace that is about to take place. A flamboyant speciality

The Close Display. Following the recognition display there is an approach phase leading to the body-contact actions of a Close Display. This may vary from a simple handshake to a full embrace (far left). In some cultures, elements of cheek-pressing and nose-rubbing (above) (from Eibl-Eibesfeldt) are common, while in others they are suppressed. Again, in some areas such as France and Russia male-to-male greeting kisses (left) are common, while in other regions such contacts are avoided.

sometimes added is the Thrown or Blown Kiss, again anticipating the contact to come.

As before, the same actions are repeated during the farewell Separation Ritual, but with Intention Embraces less likely and Thrown or Blown Kisses more likely.

Of these Distant Displays, the Smile, Head Tilt and Eyebrow Flash appear to be worldwide. They have been observed in remote native tribes that had never previously encountered white men. The raising of an arm in some form of Hail or Wave salute is also extremely widespread. The exact form of the arm movement may vary from culture to culture, but the existence of *some* kind of arm action appears to be global for mankind. The actions seems to stem, like the Intention Embrace, from an urge to reach out and touch the other person. In the Hail, the arm is raised up rather than reached out, because this makes it more conspicuous from a distance, but the movement is essentially a stylized version of touching the distant friend. More 'historical' explanations, such as that the hand is raised to show it is empty of weapons or that it is thrust up to mime the action of offering the owner's sword, and therefore his allegiance, may be true in certain specific contexts, but the action is too widespread and too general for this interpretation to stand for all cases of Hailing.

The Wave takes three main forms: the Vertical Wave, the Hidden-palm Wave, and the Lateral Wave. In the Vertical Wave, the palm faces the friend and the hand moves repeatedly up and down. This appears to be the 'primitive' form of waving. In origin, it seems to be a vacuum patting action, the hand patting the friend's body at a distance, again in anticipation of the friendly embrace to come. The Hidden-palm Wave, seen mainly in Italy, is also a patting action, but with the hand moving repeatedly towards the waver himself. To non-Italians, this looks rather like beckoning, but it is basically another form of vacuum embracing. The Lateral Wave, common all over the world, consists of showing the palm to the friend and then moving it rhythmically from side to side. This appears to be an improved form of the other waves. The modification is essentially one of increasing the visibility and conspicuousness of the patting action. In turning it into a lateral movement, it loses its embracing quality, but gains dramatically in visual impact from a distance. It can be further exaggerated by extending it to full arm-waving, or even double-arm-waving.

3. The Close Display. As soon as the Distant Display has been performed, there is an approach interval and then the key moment of actual body contact. At full intensity this consists of a total embrace, bringing both arms around the friend's body, with frontal trunk contact and head contact. There is much hugging, squeezing, patting, cheek-pressing and kissing. This may be followed by intense eye contact at close range, cheek-clasping, mouth-kissing, hair-stroking, laughing, even weeping, and, of course, continued smiling.

From this uninhibited display, there is a whole range of body-contacts of decreasing strength, right down to the formal handshake. The precise intensity will depend on: (1) the depth of the prior relationship; (2) the length of the separation; (3) the privacy of the greeting context; (4) the local, cultural display-rules and traditions; and (5) the changes that have taken place during the separation.

Most of these conditions are obvious enough, but the last deserves comment. If the friend is known to have been through some major emotional experience—an ordeal such as imprisonment, illness, or disaster, or a great success such as an award, a victory or an honour—there will be a much more intense greeting and stronger embracing. This is because the Salutation Display is simultaneously a greeting and a celebration and is, in effect, double-strength.

Different cultures have formalized the close greeting performance in different ways. In all cases, the basis of the display is the full embrace, but

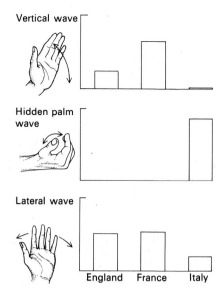

Vertical wave

Hidden palm wave

Lateral wave

England   France   Italy

The three basic forms of hand waving. As you travel from England through France to Italy the favoured wave changes. In England the Lateral Wave dominates the scene, while in France it is overtaken in popularity by the Vertical Wave. In Italy the local Hidden-palm Wave largely replaces them. The columns show the percentage of people using each wave, from samples taken in each country. (From Morris et al: *Gesture Maps*)

when this is simplified, different parts of it are retained in different places. In some cultures, the head-to-head element becomes nose-rubbing, cheek-mouthing, or face-pressing. In others, there is a stylized mutual cheek-kiss, with the lips stopping short of contact. In others again, there is kissing between men—in France and Russia, for example—while in many cultures, male-to-male kissing is omitted as supposedly effeminate.

While these cultural variations are, of course, of interest, they should not be allowed to obscure the fact that they are all variations on a basic theme—the body embrace. This is the fundamental, global, human contact action, the one we all know as babies, infants and growing children, and to which we return whenever the rules permit and we wish to demonstrate feelings of attachment for another individual.

4. The 'Grooming' Display. Following the initial body contacts, we move into the final stage of the greeting ceremony, which is similar to the social grooming performances of monkeys and apes. We do not pick at one another's fur, but instead we display 'Grooming Talk'—inane comments that mean very little in themselves, but which demonstrate vocally our pleasure at the meeting. 'How are you?', 'How nice of you to come', 'Did you have a good journey?', 'You are looking so well', 'Let me take your coat', and so on. The answers are barely heard. All that is important is to pay compliments and to receive them. To show concern and to show pleasure. The precise verbal content and the intelligence of the questions is almost irrelevant. This Grooming Display is sometimes augmented by helping with clothing, taking off coats, and generally fussing with creature comforts. On occasion there is an additional Gift Display on the part of the guest, who brings some small offering as a further, material form of salutation.

After the Grooming Display is over, the friends leave the special site of the greeting and move on to resume their old, familiar, social interactions. The Salutation Display is complete and has performed its important task.

By contrast, unplanned greetings are far less elaborate. When we see a friend in the street, or somewhere away from home, we give the typical Distant Display—a smile and a wave—and perhaps no more. Or we approach and add a Close Display, usually a rather abbreviated embrace, but more usually a mere handshake. As we part, we again display, often turning for a final Distant Signal, as we move off.

Introductory Greetings take yet another form. If we are meeting someone for the first time, we omit the Distant Display, simply because we are not recognizing an old friend. We do, however, offer a minor form of Close Display, nearly always a handshake, and we smile at the new acquaintance and offer him a Grooming Display of friendly chatter and concern. We treat him, in fact, as though he were a friend already, not a close one but a friend none the less, and in so doing we bring him into our orbit and initiate a social relationship with him.

As a species of primate, we are remarkably rich in greetings and farewells. Other primates do show some simple greeting rituals, but we exceed them all, and we also show farewell displays which they seem to lack entirely. Looking back into our ancestry, there seems to have been a good reason for this development. Most primates move around in a fairly close-knit group. Occasionally, they may drift apart and then, on reuniting, will give small gestures of greeting. But they rarely part deliberately, in a purposeful way, so they have no use for Separation Displays. Early man established himself as a hunting species, with the male hunting group leaving for a specific purpose at a specific time, and then returning to the home base with the kill. For millions of years, therefore, we have needed Salutation Displays, both in the form of farewells, as the group split up in its major division-of-labour, and in the form of greetings, when they came together again. And the importance of success or failure on the hunt meant that these were not trivial, but vital moments in the communal life of the primeval tribe. Little wonder that today we are such a salutatory species.

POSTURAL ECHO
The way friends unconsciously act in unison

When friends of equal status and similar opinions meet face-to-face, they often adopt almost identical postures. This Postural Echo is illustrated here by examples showing echo-head-propping (top) and echo-leaning.

When two friends meet and talk informally they usually adopt similar body postures. If they are particularly friendly and share identical attitudes to the subjects being discussed, then the positions in which they hold their bodies are liable to become even more alike, to the point where they virtually become carbon copies of each other. This is not a deliberate imitative process. The friends in question are automatically indulging in what has been called Postural Echo, and they do this unconsciously as part of a natural body display of companionship.

There is a good reason for this. A true bond of friendship is usually only possible between people of roughly equal status. This equality is demonstrated in many indirect ways, but it is reinforced in face-to-face encounters by a matching of the postures of relaxation or alertness. In this way the body transmits a silent message, saying: 'See, I am just like you'; and this message is not only sent unconsciously but also understood in the same manner. The friends simply 'feel right' when they are together.

The precision of the Postural Echo can be quite remarkable. Two friends talking in a restaurant both lean on the table with the same elbow, tilt their bodies forward to the same angle and nod in agreement with the same rhythm. Two other friends reclining in armchairs both have their legs crossed in exactly the same way and both have one arm across their lap. The two friends chatting while standing by a wall both lean against it with the same body slope and both have one hand thrust deep into a pocket and the other hand resting on the hip.

More surprising is the fact that they frequently synchronize their movements as they talk. When one uncrosses his legs, the other soon follows suit, and when one leans back a little, so does his companion. When one lights a cigarette or gets a drink, he tries to persuade the other to join him. If he fails he is disappointed, not because he really cares if his friend smokes a cigarette or takes a drink, but because if they do not both smoke or drink at the same time, there will be a slight loss of synchrony in their actions. In such situations we frequently see one friend insisting that the other join him, even when it is obvious that he is not interested. 'I don't want to drink alone' and 'Am I the only one smoking?' are phrases often heard in this context; and, quite often, the reluctant companion gives in, despite his wishes, in order to keep up the synchrony.

'Do come and sit down, you look so uncomfortable standing there' is another common invitation that helps to increase the chances for Postural Echo, and groups of friends usually try to arrange themselves in such a way that they can lock in to one another's body postures and movement rhythms. The subjective sensation gained in such cases is one of being 'at ease'. It is simple enough for one person to destroy such ease, merely by adopting an alien posture—stiff and formal, or jerky and anxious.

Similarly, an intensely active, excited gathering of friends soon becomes critical if one of their number is slumped lethargically in an unmatching posture. They will plead with him to join in the fun and if, for some private reason, he cannot do so, they will refer to him as having been a 'wet blanket' and spoiling the evening. Again, the person in question has *said* nothing hostile and has done nothing that directly interfered with the actions of the others. He has merely destroyed the group's Postural Echo.

Because acting in unison spells equal-status friendship, it can be used by dominant individuals to put subordinates at their ease. A therapist treating a patient can help him to relax by deliberately copying the sick person's body displays. If the patient sits quietly, leaning forward in his chair, with his arms folded across his chest and staring at the floor, the doctor who sits near him in a similar, quiet pose is more likely to be able to communicate successfully

Three further examples of Postural Echo: echo-leg-hugging (left); echo-elbows-resting on a table (far left); and echo-hand-clasping on walking sticks (below left).

with him. If instead he adopts a more typical dominant posture behind his desk, he will find it harder to make contact.

Whenever a dominant and a subordinate meet, they signal their relationship by their body postures and it is a simple matter for a subordinate to manipulate such a situation. Just as the dominant doctor deliberately climbed down from his high status role by echoing the patient's body posture, so a subordinate can, if he wishes, unnerve a dominant individual by copying his body actions. Instead of sitting on the edge of his chair or leaning eagerly forwards, he can sprawl out his legs and recline his body in imitation of the high status posture he sees before him. Even if verbally he is politeness itself, such a course of action will have a powerful impact, and the experiment is best reserved for moments immediately prior to tendering one's resignation.

Sometimes it is possible to observe two distinct sets of Postural Echoes in the same group. Usually this is related to 'taking sides' in a group argument. If three of the group are disputing with the other four, the members of each sub-group will tend to match up their body postures and movements but keep distinct from the other sub-group. On occasion, it is even possible to predict that one of them is changing sides before he has declared his change of heart verbally, because his body will start to blend with the postures of the opposing 'team'. A mediator, trying to control such a group, may take up an intermediate body posture as if to say 'I am neutral', folding his arms like one side and crossing his legs like the other.

Recent studies of such situations, employing slow-motion film to record the subtle changes in posture, have revealed that there is even a 'microsynchrony' of small movements, so sensitive that it is hard to see with the naked eye. Tiny, momentary dips and nods of the head, tensing of the fingers, stretching of the lips, and jerks of the body, are all beautifully matched when a pair of friends are in a condition of strong rapport. The rhythm of this matching is so extraordinary that only detailed film analysis reveals it clearly. Yet, despite this, it seems that the human brain can absorb the general message of the synchrony and respond appropriately with feelings of warmth towards those who echo our postures and our body movements.

One eight-year study of slow-motion films of people talking informally together has shown us that the precision of the matching of the rhythmic movements they make as they speak and listen is often perfected to within a 48th of a second. When film shot at 48 frames per second is analysed frame by frame, it is possible to see the way in which sudden, small movements start simultaneously, on exactly the same frame of film, with both the speaker and the listener. As the speaker jerks his body with the emphasis he makes on different words, so the listener makes tiny, matching movements of some part of the body. The more friendly the two people are, the more their rhythm locks together. In such cases, however, the echo is in the rhythm, rather than the exact posture. The two are not necessarily copying each other's precise actions, but rather their rate of delivery. The speaker may, for instance, be 'beating time' to his words with small head-jerks or hand movements, while the listener is echoing the rhythm with minute tilts of the body. An important discovery was made when similar films were taken of conversations with mentally disturbed patients. Here there was little or no body synchrony—the echo had vanished and with it the rapport. And it was this particular quality that contributed so strongly to the feeling of 'strangeness' when encountering and attempting social contact with these patients.

Recent American slang includes the two terms 'good vibes' and 'bad vibes'—'vibes' meaning vibrations—and it looks as if these expressions, referring to feeling at ease, or not at ease, with someone, may reflect an intuitive recognition of the fundamental importance of Postural Echo and the unconscious synchrony of small body movements in everyday social life.

TIE-SIGNS

Signals that display personal bonds to others

A Tie-sign is any action which indicates the existence of a personal relationship. If two people walk arm-in-arm down the street, their linked-arm action is a sign to onlookers that they are personally 'tied' to each other in some way. There are many different Tie-signs of this kind and, as social mammals, we are acutely responsive to every subtle variation, judging not only that a personal link exists, but also the nature of that link.

The most obvious form of Tie-sign is simple body proximity in which, although they do not touch each other, two people move, stand, sit, or lie close together. But in our crowded modern world this can be misleading. In any densely populated situation, close proximity can become meaningless. Even in less cramped conditions, there are so many strangers about that a close body-encounter may reflect no more than a fleeting, impersonal communication. Two men observed talking to each other in the street and walking together to the corner may be old friends, or they may be perfect strangers, with one merely asking the other the time or the way to the nearest post-office. To be certain, we need to study more than simple proximity.

The clues we use are subtle and complex. Take, for instance, the case of the fragile old lady being helped across the road by a young man, or the drunk being helped out of a bar. How do we read the signs in such cases? How can we tell whether the old lady is a complete stranger who has solicited the young man's aid, or whether she is his favourite aunt? How can we tell whether the drunk is unknown to his helpers, or their life-long drinking companion?

The fact is that we *can* usually tell in such cases, but if asked how we do it, we would be at a loss to explain. We are all expert Tie-sign readers, even though we may never give the matter a moment's thought. To see how it is done, it is best to start with the initial formation of a 'tie'. Since the definition of the term requires that each side should know the other personally, the most obvious beginning for any social tie is an exchange of names. As an accompaniment there is often a hand-shake and, in the early stages of the relationship, a great deal of smiling and nodding of please and thank-you, and considerable mutual attentiveness. As the tie strengthens, usually over several meetings, there is a progressive exchange of biographical information. This exchange strengthens the bond because it acts as a verbal substitute for shared activities. By telling each other of past experiences, the new twosome can artificially extend their relationship backwards in time.

The initial stage of a tie—whether it is between friends, colleagues or lovers—therefore has a number of special features. When we observe these, we can be fairly certain that we are witnessing a young or half-formed tie.

With the fully formed tie there are obvious differences. Old friends and long-term lovers or spouses reduce the pleasantries of the tie-formation stage. To take the features one by one: (1) The use of personal names declines. After progressing from 'Who is he?' to 'Mr Smith', to 'John', and perhaps to 'Johnny', the stage arrives where the man becomes referred to as an unidentified category, such as: darling, dear, chum, buddy, mate, or simply as 'you', according to the nature of the relationship. The use of first names does not disappear completely, of course, but is now reserved largely for third-party use—'Have you seen John?'—and for hailing from a distance—'John, are you there?' (2) Hand-shaking also declines. Between lovers and spouses it disappears completely as a greeting or farewell and surfaces only occasionally, when making joke-pacts or wagers. Between old friends it is used less and less, except when meeting after a long separation. Curiously, there are national differences on this point, the French in particular resisting this decline in hand-shaking frequency. (3) Sustained good humour, with

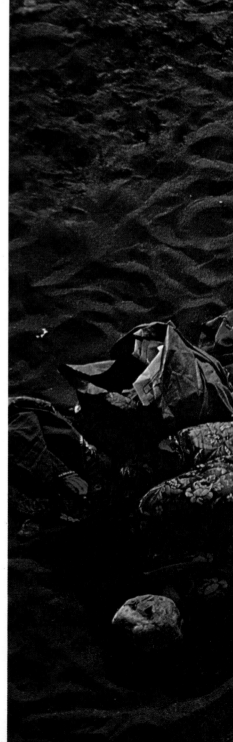

Tie-signs indicate personal relationships. The simplest form of Tie-sign is body proximity. This need not involve body contact but merely the act of standing (right) or lying closer to a companion than to other individuals nearby.

endless conversational smiling and nodding, becomes restricted to limited periods in social encounters. A sign of old friendships or pair-bonds is that two people can sit together in a peaceful silence without feeling the need to keep up a stream of cheerful chatter. (4) Attentiveness wanes. Long-established ties do not exhibit postures of prolonged, rapt attention. The engrossed exchanges of the initial stages give way to a more relaxed, off-hand manner. (5) The exchange of personal histories becomes exhausted—the partners have heard it all before.

The striking overall feature of the change from initial ties to long-term ties is that the members of well-established pair-bonds often express themselves more like strangers to one another. If we look at three couples sitting in the park, the pair who are strangers and the pair who are an old married couple outwardly have much in common. They sit silently ignoring each other for much of the time. The third couple are obviously young lovers or new friends, because they never pause in their mutual attentiveness. If they are potential lovers who have not yet made love together, they will not only be attentive to each other, but will probably also keep up a more or less non-stop conversation. If they have actually made love, then the tie will already be tighter and they will now be likely to enjoy periods of silence. But if they do, their mutual attentiveness will not wane with their words, as it does with the old married couple. They will show it by means of a variety of body actions, especially intimate body contact.

If so many Tie-signs are reduced with long-term bonding, how are long-established relationships to be detected? The answer is that although the fully 'tied' couple are less demonstrative, they nevertheless transmit many small, restrained clues that reveal the depth of their bond. Knowing each other as well as they do, they can sense each other's intentions with great subtlety. They do not sign-post their forthcoming actions—there is no need. The married couple who are about to leave a social gathering can synchronize their leave-taking by an almost imperceptible exchange of glances. Or, a flicker of a smile lasting a fraction of a second, on the faces of a pair of old friends as they look across a room at each other, is sufficient to communicate a shared reaction. The way in which one partner of a pair, when changing direction in the street, is copied by the other partner without an exchanged

Long-established bonds show less intense Tie-signs than newly forming ones. Older married couples sit quietly together with little demonstration of the mutual attentiveness so common between young lovers (right).

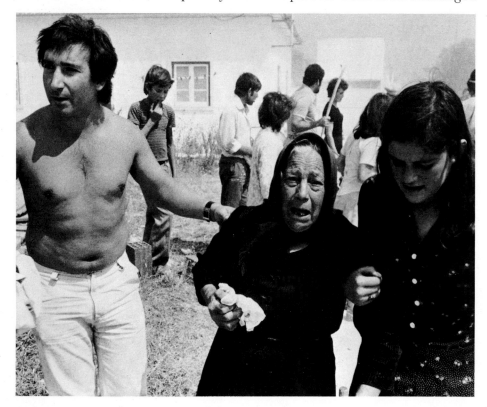

An old lady being helped across a road after a fire in north Portugal. When we look at this scene a Tie-sign tells us about the nature of the relationship between the woman and the young man. The way he reaches out to support her suggests that she is a stranger rather than a close relative.

Indirect Tie-signs. Objects shared by two people, such as a glass when drinking, act as Tie-sign indicators. Even in the absence of the couple, such signs can continue to signal the existence of a past bond—as with the pierced hearts drawn on walls or carved on trees.

comment—almost as if they were members of a shoal of fish—immediately reveals the unspoken, mutual understanding.

Returning now to answer the questions asked at the outset: how can we tell if the young man helping the elderly lady across the road is her nephew or a complete stranger? And how can we tell if a drunk is being supported by old friends or by strangers? These are difficult examples because people in trouble provoke unusually intimate responses, even from individuals they do not know. A helpless adult transmits pseudo-infantile signals that produce pseudo-parental responses. So the old lady and the drunk will be supported with helper-actions that look like Tie-signs, whether personal ties exist or not. To tell the difference it is necessary to look for special, inconspicuous clues.

Taking the case of the old lady first, if the young man is a stranger he will probably take *her* arm, supporting it by grasping it under the elbow, and he will walk her across the street with a slight separation between his trunk and hers. If she is his aged aunt, she will probably take *his* arm, linking her hand through the crook of his elbow, and they will cross the road with close side-to-side contact.

The reason for this difference is to be found in the initiation of the incident. If the two are strangers, there will be a special politeness at the start of the encounter, with the old lady asking for the young man's help and with him responding by taking her arm. If the two have an old bond between them, the road-crossing will be initiated without ceremony. The old lady will automatically take the young man's arm, and their behaviour will synchronize smoothly, without the need for a verbal exchange.

In the case of the drunk being helped out of a bar, the same rule may apply, but here there is the added problem that the drunk may be too uncoordinated to be able to cling on to his friends and therefore to initiate the supporting actions. If he is in this advanced state of oblivion, other clues must be sought, and they can be found not in the support itself, but in the faces of the supporters. If he is an old drinking companion, they will be smiling and joking and attempting to reduce the gap between their controlled behaviour and their friend's loss of control by converting the episode from a serious into a playful one. If the drunk is a stranger, the faces will display far less humour, more concern, and possibly even unconcealed distaste. This difference is sometimes exploited by thriller writers in search of a plausible method of removing a corpse from a building under the eyes of witnesses. By laughing and joking about the dead man supported between them, the counterfeit 'helpers' can convincingly give the impression that he is a drunken friend with whom they have a close personal tie, and that they are helping him home to 'sleep it off'. The impression of a personal tie is important in such a case in order to reduce the chances of offers of help. If a close bond is simulated, outsiders will feel less inclined to interfere, because they will feel less social responsibility for the helpless man.

In these and a hundred other ways, we read the Tie-signs of the people we see around us. Here it has been possible to select and discuss only a few of the many features we notice in forming tie-judgements. In practice, at any one moment we may be responsive to a dozen or more separate clues, balancing them unconsciously in our minds and coming out with the right answer. This is especially true of people whose occupations tend to make them acutely sensitive to Tie-sign subtleties. Perhaps the greatest masters of relationship-detection are the hotel receptionists, who see couples come and go daily and who can tell almost at a glance whether they are married to each other, both married but not to each other, one married and one single, both single but pretending to be married, or both just-married and on honeymoon. In all these cases the man and woman will probably try to behave like the ordinary married couple, but to an expert eye their Tie-signs will let them down. The biggest mistake of an illicit couple is to be too demonstrative towards each other. The second biggest is to over-compensate by being too casual. They

may know enough to fake a matter-of-fact, off-hand attitude, but in doing so they may overlook the need for the almost terse synchrony of the truly established pair.

There are many other instances of attempted Tie-sign deception and some of these subterfuges require special training or expertise. The shadowy world of espionage is full of such concealments, where agents must meet and exchange information without appearing to do so and must conceal true bonds and pretend others. Police on undercover duty have to be equally expert at hiding their connexions. A single gesture-error here could cost a life.

Occasionally this danger can be reversed and put to work. A criminal's reputation can be deliberately tarnished by a contrived Tie-sign trick. All that is necessary is for him to be seen by an associate in a 'friendly' interaction with a member of the police. The true, private encounter between the criminal and the policeman may have been genuinely hostile but if, as the criminal is leaving, a policeman deliberately smiles and winks at him, or pretends to whisper something in his ear, and this is observed by one of his criminal contacts, he may have a hard time convincing his underworld friends that there is no secret link between him and the law. One brief Tie-sign, in such a case, can speak louder than a thousand words.

False Tie-signs are also the stock-in-trade of the smuggling fraternity. A single man being naturally suspect, the professional smuggler adorns himself with a set of family Tie-signs, passing through customs with a 'wife', a squabbling brood of children, a babe in arms, and heroin in the talcum powder.

Extreme Tie-signs of this kind may be more common in fiction than in real life, but less dramatic subterfuges are used every day by law-abiding citizens who wish to enhance their social status. We have all encountered the man who, within minutes of meeting, is reeling off the names of his important friends, exaggerating, by implication, the intimacy of the ties he has established with them. Being seen with the 'right' people is another widespread device for the socially ambitious, as is not being seen with the 'wrong' people. Exclusive clubs and societies rely on this for their very existence.

In a more domestic atmosphere, the Tie-signs of ordinary titles operate everywhere. When a Miss becomes a Mrs, she carries with her a permanent Tie-sign, even in the absence of her mate. In addition to her new title, displayed whenever she is introduced and faced with the possibility of a new Tie-sign development, she also wears a wedding-ring, a symbolic Tie-sign which stands for the bodily Tie-signs she would be performing if her husband were present. Symbols of this kind are to be found in every society. In some, the unmarried women wear a different kind of hat, or some other adornment, to distinguish them from the married ones. In others, a widow will always display the tie with her dead husband by wearing black for the rest of her life.

Recently, in America especially, certain women have rebelled against these symbolic Tie-signs and have insisted on the apellation Ms, to replace both Miss and Mrs; but the device has not succeeded because nearly every Ms is either a Miss or an ex-Mrs, so that Ms remains in general a 'non-Mrs' title and has therefore failed to achieve the desired lumping of mated and unmated females under one heading. The Tie-sign remains.

In complete opposition to the Ms trend is the device, more common in provincial areas, of displaying a Tie-sign where no true bond exists. For an adult female to be left 'on the shelf' can be such a social slur that even a tie-less Tie-sign is preferable to no Tie-sign. A young girl without a boy-friend may even be driven to using her brother as a fake boy-friend in order to appear coupled. Alternatively, she may permit a boy public intimacies, despite the fact that she does not like him, simply in order to display overt Tie-signs to match those of her more fortunate friends. She may even go to the length of marrying him—not for money, not for security, and not for love, but merely to display publically the Tie-signs that are expected of a successful female in her society.

In special cases, the outwardly normal Tie-signs of a marriage may be used as a cover for private homosexuality. A homosexual of either sex will, in certain social contexts, find it easier to indulge in his or her private ties if he or she presents a public set of heterosexual Tie-signs. A marriage of convenience is an obvious solution.

Up to this point Tie-signs have been presented in general terms, without attempting a classification of the different types of sign. The problem is that almost any action can operate as a Tie-sign under certain conditions. Everything that a couple does or does not do together can provide clues about the nature of their personal relationship. Nevertheless, a useful, if somewhat simplified classification can be drawn up as follows:

First, there are the Indirect Tie-signs: objects revealing a bond between two people—(a) when the couple is present. These are objects shared by two people, such as a glass when drinking, a bed when sleeping, a table when dining out, or a towel when bathing. They reflect a bond between the sharers even if action Tie-signs are not observed. (b) When the couple is absent. If one or both members of a tied pair are missing from the scene, certain objects can still signal that a bond exists—the engagement ring, the wedding photo, the entry in the telephone book, the picture of children on an office desk, the 'John-loves-Mary' carved on a tree, the dedication in a book, or the tattoo on the arm of a sailor.

Second, there are the Direct Tie-signs: actions revealing a bond between two people—(a) body-proximity and orientation; (b) shared expressions and gesticulations; (c) verbal exchanges; and (d) body-contact.

This last category—body-contact—is perhaps the most interesting. Here it is possible to observe a wide variety of clear-cut actions, each of which provides information about the nature of a particular relationship. They are examined in detail on the pages that follow.

Tie-signs indicating the bond between a woman and her absent husband. In many countries, the widow wears black from the time of her husband's death and continues to do so for the rest of her life, displaying a permanent bond with her departed mate. In the Canary Islands (below), an unmarried girl wears a white linen hat, while a married woman displays a yellow straw hat. It is possible to distinguish at a glance between the bonded and unbonded females in this group.

BODY-CONTACT TIE-SIGNS

The way companions touch each other in public

A Body-contact Tie-sign is displayed whenever the bond between two people expresses itself in the form of a physical touching of one by the other. When this happens, what we see is the attraction process of the bonding overcoming the natural inclination of each individual to defend his personal space. Because there is a basic conflict between 'keeping your distance' and 'making contact', the result is that there are many varieties and degrees of friendly touching.

Field observations have so far led to the naming of 457 types of body contact, but many of these are rarities and of restricted importance. Others

The Body Guide. This is a contact version of pointing. The hand presses gently on the companion's back, guiding him in the desired direction, while at the same time suggesting a mild form of embrace.

The amplified hand-shake. Because the simple hand-shake is an expected formality, warmth of greeting is expressed by exaggerating the action in various ways. It is progressively amplified (from bottom) by hand-clasping, by arm-clasping, by shoulder-clasping, and by shoulder embracing.

involve specialized touching by such people as doctors, priests, dentists and hairdressers. Still others are private contacts usually confined to the bedroom and not therefore available as public indications of personal bonds. From the remainder—the common, social intimacies—it is convenient to isolate 14 major types. With these we do most of our tie-signing when we make body-contact. They are:

1. The Hand-shake. This appears where a personal bond is absent, weak, or there has been a long separation. Because it is an expected formality when greeting, its interest as a Tie-sign lies not in its basic form, but in the way it is amplified. The strength of the tie-to-be or the tie-that-was is expressed in how far beyond the ordinary hand-shake the action goes. To express strong feeling, the shakers must exceed the formally expected.

The most common hand-shake amplifier is the left-hand-squeeze. As the formal right hands meet, the left hand comes forward, either to clasp the already clasped right hands, or the right arm, or the shoulder. If the action becomes even more intense, the shaking right hands can get sandwiched between converging chests, as left hands circle the shoulders in a one-armed embrace, perhaps with an added cheek-to-cheek pressure or cheek kiss.

This full pattern is the cautious greeter's embrace. He or she expresses, as it were, a rapidly growing warmth towards the other person, the shake swelling into an embrace. By contrast, an instant, intimate warmth upon meeting would have resulted in the unguarded flinging out of both arms as an immediate invitation to a full embrace, both arms ending up encircling the other body, and with the complete omission of the formal hand-shake element.

Slow-motion analysis of more inhibited hand-shakings reveal that, even where the shakers are by personal style non-embracers, there is nevertheless a perceptible body-leaning towards each other—tell-tale, small intention movements of embracing that can go no further.

2. The Body-guide. This is an intimate, contact version of pointing. The companion's direction of movement is guided by a light pressure on their body. The most popular version is a mild pressing of the hand on the back. Also common is the light clasp on the arm, with forward pressure, or the more uninhibited tug of the hand. The guider propels the companion forward, not by force, but by gentle contact-suggestion. Essentially this is a muted adult version of the more active parent-to-child guidance system. Parents often have to lead or nudge their children in one direction or another, and the action has an essential 'I-am-in-control' flavour. It is rarely used by subordinates towards dominant individuals, or by guests towards their hosts. It is, in fact, one of the mild ways in which a host expresses his or her dominance over the guests who are momentarily in a weakened position, being on someone else's territory. Even between spouses it is an expression of momentary dominance, an act of taking charge of a situation. Used by a wife towards a husband, it presents a pseudo-motherly Tie-sign to onlookers. Used deftly by a male, it imparts a 'masterly' air to his actions. Used unwisely, it can quickly become pompous and patronizing.

3. The Pat. Another primarily parental action, the Pat is a kind of miniature embrace performed by the hand alone, without the involvement of the rest of the body. There are greeting pats, congratulatory pats, comforting pats, loving pats and plain friendly pats. Between adults, the action is often pseudo-parental in flavour, like the Body-guide. Children can be patted on almost any part of the body, but with adults the pat must be confined to the hand, arm, shoulder or back, if it is to be 'neutral' in character. Pats on the adult head, buttocks, thighs, or knees are either condescending or sexual. An interesting exception to this is the footballer's head-pat, after a goal has been scored. Other adult head-pats are usually rather mocking—'what a clever boy'—but the footballer's action really is congratulatory. The explanation seems to be that it is a schoolboy hang-over. Boys can be seen to pat one another on the head in imitation of what their fathers do to them and,

in the special context of the football field, this tradition apparently manages to linger on.

4. The Arm-link. Perhaps the most obvious and publically displayed of all Tie-signs, the Arm-link is basically a signal of co-ordinated walking, with one partner expressing mild control over the other. In the majority of cases it is the female who hooks her hand through the bent arm of the male, as if for support and protection. The support and protection are largely symbolic, however, and the act is much less one of physical aid by a strong male to a weak female than a visual display of emotional linkage. In other words, it is done for others to see, rather than for the pair themselves. Only among the elderly and the frail is the physical aspect uppermost. Healthy, younger couples seldom perform the Arm-link when walking by themselves—they reserve it instead for social occasions, some formal, like walking down the aisle of a church, some informal, like strolling down a shopping arcade. As a Tie-sign it could almost be described as a signal of mutual ownership.

5. The Shoulder Embrace. Because men are generally taller than women, this Tie-sign is usually performed by males towards females. Being masculine in flavour, it is also used freely between males expressing a 'buddy'

The Hand-on-shoulder. The need to limit a companion's movement during conversation is often expressed by placing a restraining hand on his shoulder while the toucher continues to engage him in discussion.

The Arm-link. A rather formal Tie-sign when displayed by male and female (far left), or female and female (left), this action develops a special flavour when performed by two males (right).

relationship. It is a half-embrace and, unlike the full-frontal embrace, it can be used as a mobile Tie-sign as well as a static one. If men are to walk together in side-by-side contact, this is the way they are most likely to do it. For many men it will be the only way. Despite this it is not used a great deal, because it hampers even moderately fast progression. A minor version of it—the hand-on-shoulder—is sometimes preferred and is typical of situations where one male is busily explaining or persuading. It enables him to limit the movements of his companion and keep him within close proximity, to receive the full impact of the verbal delivery.

6. The Full Embrace. Being hugged is a powerful childhood experience, and between adults it is reserved for intense emotional moments. Only young lovers perform this dramatic Tie-sign with any great frequency and they are in a more or less permanent condition of intense emotion when they are together. For other adults, it is usually either a private sexual posture, or a 'break-and-remake' Tie-sign. 'Break-and-remake' refers to farewells and reunions, these being the moments when the tie is being severed by physical separation or is re-forming after it. A couple who are parting, especially if it is for a long period, feel a massive urge to give the highest intensity of expression to their bond, a strong enough expression to last, as it were, right through the phase of isolation. It is as if they are trying to make the passionate hug equal to the sum total of all the smaller day-to-day contacts they would have exchanged had they not been parted from each other. And when eventually the same couple are reunited, they go through what amounts to a miniature pair-formation repeat-ceremony, with another massive hug.

Exceptions to this rule include contact-dancing, which is an arena display incorporating a stylized version of the full-frontal body-contact in which the arms-enfolding element is curtailed. Watching a couple revolving on a dance floor is rather like seeing a couple grappling towards a Full Embrace, but failing through hand collision. The frozen half-embrace that results is sufficiently distinct from the true embrace to be considered 'safe' even for comparative strangers. The dancers can enjoy the suggestion of the real thing without its full Tie-sign implications.

A second exception is the triumph ceremony of modern footballers. This may not be a break-and-remake situation, but it is certainly one where intense emotions are on display. Display is the operative word, for the hugging and embracing following a successful goal is aimed primarily at the club supporters. Like the arm-link, this is an action that relies heavily on an audience.

The Shoulder Embrace. Because men are generally taller than women, the shoulder embrace is essentially masculine. Although this makes it available for male-to-male use, it is most commonly seen in male-to-female situations.

The Hand-in-hand (above) is popular among young lovers because they share the action in equal proportions. With older couples it becomes increasingly replaced by the Arm-link, except in cases where the couple wish to express their special attachment to each other.

The Neck Embrace (left) is so similar to a throttling action that it is rarely used and can only be employed where there is total trust and, as in this case, both partners are completely relaxed.

The Full Embrace. The complex embrace of young lovers (right) leaves no doubt about their bonded condition. It is one of the most powerful of all Tie-signs. In certain countries male-to-male embraces also survive with some frequency, as the scene from Russia (far left) reveals. Male embracing can also be observed in the West during moments of elation on the football field (left), where the strongly masculine atmosphere makes such emotioned gestures permissible without danger of misinterpretation.

A final exception is the embracing that can be seen in ordinary party greetings and farewells. Here the situation is the reverse of the football case: there are no very intense emotions, but there is a break-and-remake element. Guests arriving and departing may not arouse powerful passions in one another or in their hosts, but a great deal of embracing occurs none the less. Close examination of the detailed actions involved, however, reveals that the embraces are not all they may seem. Usually, in fact, they are not much better than the dancefloor contacts. Arms half-enfold rather than hug, cheeks are brushed or pecked rather than kissed, the body-fronts hardly even make contact, and the duration of the embrace is severely curtailed. In other words, the party-farewell contact has become almost as formalized as the Hand-shake, expressing neatly a tie-moment which demands more than mere hand-to-hand touching, but less than a passionate hug.

7. The Hand-in-hand. We first experience the act of walking hand-in-hand when we are infants exploring the exciting new world of vertical locomotion. In the very beginning its function is to prevent us falling down. Later, with older children, it is to keep them close when moving through a crowded area, or to stop them running into the street when there is traffic. Even when they are more independent it still survives as a special protection when crossing a busy street. Then, during adolescence, it vanishes as a parent-offspring act and re-surfaces as a 'young lovers' Tie-sign. Its special quality for the lovers is that it is a mutual act. Each member of the adult hand-holding pair is performing the same action and in this way it comes to reflect an equality of involvement. This makes it essentially different, as a Tie-sign, from the Arm-link, where one partner takes the role of the 'dominant supporter' and the other the role of the 'supported'. Hand-holders are not concerned with such matters of status. They are at the delightful stage of offering themselves to each other. Neither is concerned with 'gaining the upper hand' and there is no upper hand in hand-holding.

8. The Waist Embrace. When holding hands the young couple do not make trunk contact. Their bodies walk side-by-side with an intervening space. With the Waist Embrace this space disappears and the couple are now pressing their sides against each other. This gives a much more intimate Tie-sign and the arm-around-waist action is a clear indicator that the bond between the lovers is stronger and deeper. It makes walking more difficult and is limited almost exclusively to sexual strolling by a courting pair. It is as if they want to walk and perform a Full Embrace at one and the same time,

More intimate than the Hand-in-hand is the Waist Embrace (top right). Because it involves close trunk contact and impedes locomotion it is usually confined to strolling couples with time to spare. Above: the Stylized Embrace. In countries where embracing has become an expected formality during family gatherings the action often becomes formalized and abbreviated, as in this French greeting, where the arms fail to enfold the companion and the trunks remain separated. The Kiss as a public Tie-sign (above right) shows variations from country to country. In many, cheek-kissing is more frequent in public than mouth-kissing, which has a greater potential for sexual arousal.

and employ the waist-embraced stroll as a compromise between the two conflicting desires.

Like the Hand-in-hand, the Waist Embrace is nearly always a heterosexual Tie-sign and therefore contrasts strongly with the Shoulder Embrace. The shift from the 'friendly shoulder' to the 'amorous waist' of a simple arm contact marks a huge change in Tie-sign significance. The reason for this appears to be that the waist is so much nearer to the primary genital zone, so that, like the buttocks and the thighs, it inevitably becomes a sexual-contact zone.

9. The Kiss. Touching a companion with the lips is not a simple Tie-sign, but a whole set of signs, according to the area of the body kissed. The most intimate form of kissing to be seen in public, and therefore available as a Tie-sign, is the mouth-to-mouth kiss. As we saw when considering the Kiss as a Relic Gesture, it was once common practice for a mother to premasticate food for her infant before transferring it direct, mouth-to-mouth. This is still done in a wide variety of tribal societies and has been observed in peasant communities in Europe even today. The child reacts to the mouth-offering with special searching movements of its tongue inside the mother's mouth. It would appear that this is an ancient, inborn pattern of our species, and even

In some countries, such as the Yemen, male to male kissing is commonplace (above), while in others it is largely confined to joke contexts, as with these British footballers (below).

though it no longer occurs in civilized cultures as a regular element of recommended child-care, we still have the adult version of it in the form of the deep tongue-kissing of young lovers—a striking example of parent-offspring interaction re-surfacing as an adult intimacy. Partly because of the sexually arousing potential of mouth-to-mouth kissing and partly because of our culture's hygiene-conditioning, this type of kiss is generally limited to strongly bonded pairs. The sexual element means that these pairs are typically heterosexual, but in some countries it is possible to observe adult males kissing passionately on the mouth, with no sexual element whatever being present.

Young lovers who are just beginning to form a bond may also employ mouth-kissing, borrowing it, so to speak, from the later stages of courtship. In this early form it is frequently an abbreviated contact, lacking the tongue element. Older couples who have been bonded on a long-term basis tend to reduce the intensity of the public kiss again, using a brief lip-to-lip touch and confining the act largely to greetings and farewells, except when they are alone together. A couple who are indulging in prolonged, intense mouth-kissing in a public place can safely be said to be at a point in the bonding process where pair-formation is still in progress, though no doubt well

The Hand-to-head. Since the head is one of the most sensitive and protected areas of the human body, being touched in that region indicates a degree of trust that reflects a close bond of attachment, as with these young lovers in Russia.

advanced. The only occasions when an older couple will behave like this in public are when they are parting for a long separation or meeting after one, or have just come through some powerful emotional experience together—a triumph, a disaster, or an escape from danger. These are re-bonding moments, when the mouth-to-mouth Tie-sign reappears unashamedly in full public view.

A deflected version of the mouth-to-mouth kiss is the mutual cheek kiss, which occurs as a low intensity form of it. Married couples employ it as a mild contact occasionally, but it is most typical of greetings and farewells between relatives and friends. The mildness of its signal is the result of the fact that it is not so much a cheek kiss as a failed mouth kiss. Its timidity makes it available for non-sexual contacts, hence its widespread use on social occasions.

Other kisses can be scaled according to how high or low they are on the body. These are the status kisses, starting at the top of the head with the parental kiss down on to the child's crown region. This is a dominant kiss and when it is performed by one adult to another it usually carries a mock-parental message. The same is true of other top-of-the-body kisses, such as the forehead kiss and the nose-tip kiss. Both are typically parental, or mock-parental. Lower down the body, the hand kiss reflects an appropriately lower status. It is the kiss of reverence or formal deference and its subordinate message is boosted by the bow needed to carry it out. In earlier days, where a female had to hand-kissed even by dominant males as part of a rigid social formula, the top males solved the problem by raising the female's hand up to their mouths, thus avoiding the demeaning bow.

10. The Hand-to-head. Touching the partner's head with the hand is a more intimate action than it may at first seem. The intimacy of this Tie-sign is based on the trust it implies, for the head is the most sensitive and damageable part of the body where all the important sense organs are clustered, and the hand is the part of the body that is potentially the most damaging weapon. To allow one to come close to and touch the other therefore requires a strong bond of trust between the toucher and the touched. Go to touch a comparative stranger's arm and he will feel little alarm. Go to touch his head and he becomes immediately defensive. This is obvious enough, and yet behind this obvious statement lies a non-stop, unconscious sensitivity to any physical threat to our head region, no matter how remote or unlikely the threat may be. Only between the closest and oldest of friends, or between lovers, spouses or loving parents, do we permit invasion of this region by hands that are not our own. Even the most fleeting and gentle of hand-to-head touches is therefore a Tie-sign of a much greater and deeper bond than might be imagined from the superficial triviality of the action.

11. The Head-to-head. When one head makes contact with another it is like a 'chronic' version of the 'acute' kiss. Like the hand-to-head, this is seen more with young lovers than with older couples. The special flavour of this

Right: the Head-to-head, another intimate Tie-sign more common among young lovers than older couples. The head contact tends to exclude other companions from the bonded pair.

Far right: the Caress. Body-stroking and caressing is sufficiently arousing to be strictly limited as a public display but sometimes occurs in informal settings between less inhibited partners, where it reflects a high degree of sexual intimacy.

The Body Support. We are supported as infants on our parents' laps, and any similar body action given to an adult immediately recreates a protective atmosphere, with the supported individual automatically transmitting childlike signals, regardless of whether a young female (top) or an older male (above).

Tie-sign is the way it incapacitates the head-to-head couple with regard to other activities. By putting their heads together, or sitting cheek-to-cheek, they are effectively saying: 'It is more important for us to touch each other than to be alert to outside events'. It is a signal that says they are shutting out the rest of the world, a fact that is underlined by the frequent addition of closed eyes. More than any of the other loving Tie-signs, this is an excluding action, cutting the rest of us off from the pair.

12. The Caress. Gentle stroking, rubbing, squeezing and exploring of the partner's body with the hand, or occasionally with some other organ such as the nose, tongue or foot, is nearly always sexual and can easily lead to physiological arousal. In public it is almost always a Tie-sign of young lovers who have reached a point of intensity in their relationship where they are virtually prepared to ignore the rest of the world and concentrate exclusively on the discovery of each other's bodies and responses. Sometimes an exception can be observed at a social gathering where an older, mated pair will indulge momentarily in a mild form of this action. This usually takes the form of an almost absent-minded caressing of some part of the spouse's body, and it then acts as an unconscious signal to the others present of the depth of the bond that exists between the two. It is the tip of the iceberg which they are allowed to see. Just occasionally it is used as a deliberate, contrived signal to show off a bond that the others must be made to appreciate.

13. The Body Support. Children sit on their parents' laps and are carried by them when they are tiny or tired. The pattern is often repeated during playful adolescent interludes, when girl sits on boy, or is carried by him. It is repeated again in a ritual fashion when the bride is carried over the threshold. At other times in the adult world it is confined to situations of helplessness caused by fainting, illness or drunkenness and then, since it has the character of an emergency action, it signifies little or no bond, and can be performed by total strangers. This, then, is an infantile pattern of intimacy which does not, like certain others, survive into adulthood as an important Tie-sign. The reason for this difference is obvious enough, namely the great increase in body weight of the object which sits in your lap or has to be carried.

14. The Mock-attack. Between adults there are many arm-punches, hair-rufflings, ear-nibblings, body-pushes, grabs, squeezes and nudges which are fundamentally aggressive, but which are performed in such a mild and inhibited way that they do not hurt. Instead of being read as hostile contacts, they are interpreted as friendly liberties. As Tie-signs they signify that the mock-attacker is so bonded to the 'victim' that he or she can indulge in these pseudo-hostile actions without the slightest fear that they will be misinterpreted. They are demonstrations of great familiarity, of knowledge that the ruffled or nudged companion 'won't mind'. Sometimes they represent the only way one person can make intimate contact with another — say, a father with an adolescent son — because he knows that a more overtly loving touch would be embarrassing.

This brief survey of a few of the more common social Tie-signs is, of necessity, oversimplified. The great subtlety and variety of such actions is astonishing when analysed objectively. This is because we are such loving, bonding animals and because we have such a complex social life. For each of us there are dozens of different relationships — with mates, children, parents, relatives, friends, neighbours, colleagues, clients, teachers, students, employers, subordinates and so on. We are aware not only of our own relationships with each of the people we know personally, but also of their relationships with one another, and wherever we meet or gather socially our sense organs are constantly feeding into our brains information about these ever-changing bonds. Every day we read off a thousand different Tie-signs and transmit thousands more ourselves to those around us. They are more than just a way of telling us who loves whom and how much — they are also a way of fitting ourselves into the web of social life and of demonstrating that fit to others.

AUTO-CONTACT BEHAVIOUR

Self-intimacies—why and how we touch ourselves

Auto-contact Behaviour occurs whenever we touch our own bodies. It contrasts with Allo-contact, which occurs when we touch someone else's body. Making physical contact with another person is not something we treat lightly and we are usually quite conscious of what we are doing—whether it be a friendly pat, a loving caress, or a hostile blow. But when we indulge in Auto-contact, we are much more likely to take it for granted. If we stroke, clasp, or hug ourselves, we are not invading someone else's body-privacy, and we think little of it. But the unconscious way we employ self-touchings does not mean that they are unimportant or meaningless. On the contrary, it means that they can provide genuine, uncontrived clues concerning our inner moods.

The most common form of Auto-contact can best be called a Self-intimacy, and apart from cleaning and shielding actions, which respectively groom and protect the body, this category accounts for the majority of all touching actions that we direct towards ourselves. Self-intimacies can be defined as movements that provide comfort because they are *unconsciously mimed acts of being touched by someone else*.

When we perform a Self-intimacy we use part of our body as if it belonged to a comforting companion. During our infancy, our parents cuddle and hug us, and rock us gently back and forth if we are frightened or hurt. They pat us, stroke us, and caress us, and make us feel safe and secure, loved and wanted. When we are adults we often feel insecure and in need of gentle loving, but the parental arms are no longer there to protect us. Our own arms are there, however, and so we use them as substitutes. We hug our own bodies and rock ourselves back and forth, or we hold hands with ourselves, clasping one hand tightly in the other.

There are many such ways in which we behave as if we were two people. The majority are only minor Self-intimacies—little more than a fleeting touch—but the clue is there just the same: a little comfort is needed. The most common actions are those in which the hand comes up to touch the head. The city-dweller, in particular, is prone to head-touchings. He has to sit in rooms for so much of his day—at a desk, a table, or with a group of colleagues. Frequently he is stressed, in a state of conflict, indecision, or boredom, and it is then that his hand strays headwards. He may use it to support his head, as if his neck were suddenly too weak to do the job, or he may stroke his face thoughtfully or gently press his knuckles against his lips. The supporting hand recreates the feeling of being able to lay the infantile head against the huge parental body. The stroking hand rekindles the sensation of a parental caress. And the pressed lips, like many other forms of mouth contact, hark back to moments at the maternal breast (or, for that matter, the adult lover's mouth).

By studying hundreds of such hand-to-head actions it is possible to record which are the most favoured solutions to the adult problem of finding minor comforts in a stressed social world. The most common, in order of frequency are: (1) the Jaw Support; (2) the Chin Support; (3) the Hair Clasp; (4) the Cheek Support; (5) the Mouth Touch; and (6) the Temple Support. All these actions are performed by both adult males and adult females, but in the case of hair-touching there is a three-to-one bias in favour of women, and with temple-supporting there is a two-to-one bias in favour of men.

The action of arm-folding, which creates a protective barrier across the chest, also has a comforting element of self-contact about it, as if halfway to being a self-hug. Any action that brings one part of the body into close contact with another can create this effect and give a minor sensation of security. In tense moments, for example, people are much more likely to 'hold hands with themselves', either interlocking the fingers or clasping one

Three forms of Auto-contact Behaviour that provide comfort during moments of tension. The hand pressed to the mouth recalls moments of security as an infant at the mother's breast, while the hand straying to the chin simulates a caress. The self-hug (right) is an extreme form of Auto-contact in which the body enfolds itself, almost as if it were two people locked in an embrace.

Auto-contact Behaviour during moments of social interaction. In this informal group the touching finger tips, the clasped leg and the folded arms pressed against the body are all important aids to individual relaxation.

palm with another. Also, all forms of leg-crossing provide a leg-to-leg Self-intimacy in which one limb-surface feels the comforting pressure of the other. Clamping one leg firmly around the other can increase this sensation and is a sure sign of someone needing comfort.

There are certain leg actions that appear, for some reason, to be almost wholly feminine. These include leg-hugging and thigh-clasping. In leg-hugging, both legs are bent up until the knees touch the chest, and then the arms are wrapped around the legs, and the head is lowered on to the knees. This is perhaps the most impressive way of creating a second person out of one's own body. The doubled-up legs provide a shape that can be embraced, leant against, and rested on. The arms, trunk and head all feel the comfort of body-contact. Despite this, the posture is not popular among men: a random sample revealed that the relevant female/male ratio was 19 to 1. Perhaps the

Models required to adopt sexually inviting poses often exploit the suggestive power of Auto-contact. Here, the hands pressing the thighs and the chin lowered on to the raised shoulder signal the message: 'I want to be touched.'

On more formal occasions head-support and hand-to-mouth contacts tend to occur during moments of concentration or boredom.

reason is that the posture is so extensively self-comforting that it begins to reveal its infantile connections too clearly, and males shy away from it. Another Self-intimacy that is strongly feminine is the head-lowered-on-to-shoulder posture, where the woman's own shoulder is used as if it belonged to her parent or lover. This, too, is rather transparent, and males again avoid it. A third feminine action is hard to explain in this way, however. This is the hand-clasping-thigh posture, which, in a random sample, was found to occur ten times as often among women as among men. Sitting with the hands clamped to the thighs is far less obvious as an 'infantile comforter', and yet, for some reason, males also keep away from this form of self-contact. There may be an erotic element here that can explain the difference. During fondling, in courtship sequences, it is the male who is more likely to move his hand to the female's thighs, and so, during moments of Self-intimacy, it is the female who is more likely to re-create this form of body contact.

Finally, there is the specialized form of sexual self-contact: masturbation. Here the use of the hand as a substitute for a partner is obvious enough. This fact makes masturbation into a transparently makeshift alternative to sexual Allo-contact. Because it therefore reflects the unavailability of a mate and implies the inability to obtain one, it has become associated with shame and unjustly condemned. For those without mates, it provides a perfectly harmless method of relieving sexual tensions and, despite thousands of published statements to the contrary, has no damaging effects whatsoever. Officially, of course, it has not always been condemned because it is a poor substitute for copulation. Many other wildly invented reasons have been given at various times, and everything from blindness to insanity has been claimed as the price that must be paid for repeated 'self-abuse'. Although we can laugh at these crackpot warnings today, they were taken very seriously in their time, and reflect a more general hostility to the whole business of bodily self-comforting. The need for an adult to obtain a pacifying and reassuring sensation by caressing his or her own body has been frowned upon as regressive and immature. This has not stopped adults feeling stressed and anxious, nor has it stopped the more 'masked' forms of Auto-contact. If a Self-intimacy, such as a cheek clasp, is sufficiently obscure in its relation to bodily comfort, then no one frowns upon it or suggests that it will lead to some gross disability. So the minor forms of Auto-contact Behaviour continue unabated, heavily indulged in by both adult females and adult males. Only if their origins or their function become too obvious will they come under attack and be socially condemned. In this way adults the world over, wherever there is a need for a little gentle aid in the form of body-loving, continue to clasp, support, stroke and hug themselves, and benefit richly, if briefly, from the results.

NONVERBAL LEAKAGE

Clues that give us away without our knowing

There are many occasions in our social lives when we wish to hide our true feelings but somehow fail to do so. The bereaved mother who is trying to conceal her sadness from her children is said to be 'putting on a brave face', as if she were wearing a mask of false expressions over a face of true ones. When we fail to deceive in this way, how does the information about our true feelings leak out? What is the source of Nonverbal Leakage and how can we tell if someone is lying?

The case of the bereaved mother is one where the deception fails because there is no great pressure for it to succeed. In fact, there is a positive advantage for it failing to deceive. If the bereaved mother were too successful in concealing her grief, she would be criticized for a lack of feeling. Equally, if she failed to display some visible inhibition of her grief she would be said to lack courage and self-control. Her 'brave face' is therefore an example of pseudo-deception, where the deceiver is happy to be found out. Either consciously or unconsciously, she wants her forced smile to be read as forced.

But what happens if the pressure to deceive is greater? The defendant in a murder trial who knows he is guilty but desperately protests his innocence is under enormous pressure to succeed with his deception. He lies with his verbal statements and must match his words with equally convincing body actions. How does he do it? He can control his words, but can he control his body?

The answer is that he can control some parts of his body better than others. The easy parts to discipline are those whose actions he is most aware of in ordinary day-to-day signalling. He knows most about his smiles and frowns—he sees them occasionally in a mirror—and his facial expressions will come out at the top of his self-awareness list. So he can lie best with his face.

His general body postures can give some valuable clues because he is not always fully conscious of the degree of stiffness of his stance or the degree of slump or alertness. But the value of these body postures is greatly reduced by social rules that require certain rather stereotyped poses in specific contexts. A murder trial defendant, for instance, is traditionally expected to sit or stand rather stiffly, whether guilty or innocent, and this can easily act as a postural 'signal-blunter'.

Hand movements and postures are more useful clues to deception because our murderer will be less aware of them, and there are usually no set rules to blunt his manual expressiveness. Of course, if he were undergoing military interrogation, his hands would be signal-blunted by the strict code of military etiquette: standing at attention makes lying easier for a soldier than for a civilian. But normally there will be gesticulations, and these should be carefully studied for deception clues.

Finally, his legs and feet are of particular interest because this is the part of the body where he is least aware of what he is doing. Frequently, however, the actions of this lower region of the body are obscured from view, so that, in practice, their usefulness is severely limited. Furniture permitting, though, they are a vital give-away area, which is one of the reasons why people feel more comfortable during interviews and business negotiations when sitting behind the lower-body screen of a desk or table. This fact is sometimes exploited in competitive interviews by placing the candidates' chair alone in the centre of the room so that the body of each 'victim' is fully exposed to view.

To sum up, then, the best way to deceive is to restrict your signals to words and facial expressions. The most efficient means of doing this is either to conceal the rest of your body or keep it so busy with a complicated

Nonverbal Leakage is the failure of the social mask. In public we so often 'put on a happy face' when in reality we feel nervous, tense, or frightened. But small actions may accidentally leak the truth to our companions.

The Nonverbal Leakage of the social scene. We all do our best to be polite, but our smiles sometimes let us down. Often our leaked clues will be detected, but allowed to go unchallenged as part of a 'co-operative lie.

mechanical procedure that all its visual deception clues are stifled by the demand for physical dexterity. In other words, if you have to lie, do it over the telephone or when peering over a wall; alternatively, when threading a needle or manoeuvring a car into a parking space. If much of you is visible and you have no mechanical task to perform, then to succeed with your lie you must try to involve the whole of your body in the act of deception, not just your voice and face.

Whole-body lying is difficult for most of us because we lack practice. In our day-to-day living we are only rarely called upon to indulge in bouts of sustained, deliberate deceit. We may deceive ourselves, but that is another matter. And we all indulge in unconscious role-playing, but again that is quite different from knowingly setting out to deceive others. When we do undertake a deliberate lie, we are often clumsy in executing it and only the observational ineptitude of our companions can save us from discovery. Often they are less inept than we imagine, and can detect our deception, but fail to reveal the fact. Our lies are found out, but remain unchallenged. Two possible reasons for this are that either our companions are too embarrassed to expose the falsehood or they are too confused by our actions to be able to identify the exact nature of the lie. In the embarrassment situation, they know perfectly well what is going on, but find it more socially comfortable to go along with the deception than shatter the facade we have erected. This applies especially in the case of trivial deceits practised on friendly social occasions. If, at a dinner party, our hostess offers us a second helping of a horribly unpalatable dish, we refuse with a polite lie. Instead of telling her the truth, we may say that we are full up, or on a diet. If she detects the lie and appreciates the reason for it, she is likely to let us get away with it, rather than risk introducing a note of discord into the evening. Instead of challenging the lie she falls in with it and switches her conversation to the subject of dieting, trying to match her expressed views to those of the polite guest. Now both sides are lying and both sides know it, but the charade is allowed to run its course because each side wants to keep the other happy. This is the Co-operative Lie and it plays a major role in many social engagements.

The second reason for a lie remaining unchallenged is that it cannot be correctly identified. The liar's actions are too confusing for his companions to know how to deal with them. They know he is not telling the truth, because his body actions do not agree with one another, or with his verbal signals, but although they notice the incongruity they cannot detect the truth he is attempting to conceal. When such a man enters a room, his behaviour makes others present feel more and more uncomfortable. If they could only detect the truth behind the unsuccessful lie, they could deal with it—either challenge it or co-operate with it—but they cannot pin it down and so are trapped by it. A good example of this confusion situation is a social gathering at which one guest, having just experienced a private disaster, attempts to behave as if he is perfectly happy and thoroughly enjoying himself. As his true feelings keep surging up inside him, his deceit performance wavers and fluctuates, often swinging from one extreme to another. If throughout the evening his companions avoid challenging him and precipitating a social crisis, they all heave a sigh of relief when he finally departs and they can relax and speculate on his problem.

The fact that we are so reluctant to challenge openly the lies of others means that the quality of ordinary social lying is not what it might be. Not only do we not get enough practice, but when we do we are not tested severely enough. The result is that most of us can be classified as Leakers, and we have a lot to learn from that devious minority group, the Professional Non-leakers.

Non-leakers are those whose working lives involve repeated and prolonged deceptions and, what is more, deceptions that are open to challenge. Unless they are capable of lying successfully and of sustaining their lies, they are doomed to failure in their chosen professions. As a result they have to become adept at contextual manipulation (choosing the right moment to lie) and at whole-body lying. This may require years of training, but eventually, among the very best practitioners, one can observe deceit raised to the level of an art. I am not thinking here merely of the obvious examples—great actors and actresses—but also of those other super-liars, the professional diplomats and the politicians, the barristers and the lawyers, the conjurers and the magicians, the confidence tricksters and the used-car salesmen. For all of these, lying is a way of life, a superb skill that is polished and polished until it sparkles so brightly that the rest of us most of the time actually enjoy being taken in by it.

The gulf between ordinary Leakers and Professional Non-leakers is enormous—much greater than the average Leaker imagines. He can often be heard claiming that 'anyone could act in the movies' or that 'diplomats have a soft life, nothing but champagne and receptions'. But put this average Leaker to the test and he is quickly found wanting. Ask him to walk—what could be easier than walking?—slowly and in a relaxed, natural manner from one side of a stage to the other, while watched by a large audience, and see what happens. Compare his stilted, awkward performance with the way he strolls down the street with a friend, and immediately the professional actor's skill becomes obvious. Watched by a large audience, the Leaker feels anything but relaxed and cannot make his body transmit relaxed signals, no matter how hard he tries. In fact, the harder he tries the worse it gets.

Turning from the would-be deceiver to the would-be detector, what are the specific clues that give the game away? A series of experiments by American research workers have provided some of the answers. They asked trainee nurses both to lie and to tell the truth about certain films they were shown. The young nurses were confronted with filmed scenes of gory operations such as limb amputation, and also with contrasting scenes of a harmless and pleasant nature. At a number of sessions, they were asked to describe what they saw, sometimes truthfully and at other times untruthfully. While they were doing this their every action and expression was recorded by concealed cameras. It was then possible to analyse in detail all the actions that

The Mouth Cover is employed in two distinct contexts. We may use it as an unconscious concealment gesture when lying or when attempting to hide a genuine facial expression. Employed by a liar, the Mouth Cover provides a source of Nonverbal Leakage. Employed by a laugher, as in this picture, it acts as a device to stop leakage.

accompanied truthful statements and all those accompanying deliberate lies, and to study the differences between them.

The nurses tried hard to conceal their lies because they were told that skill at deception was an important attribute for their future careers. This it is, for anxious patients require repeated reassurance that they are on the mend, or that risky operations are really quite safe, or that baffled doctors know exactly what their complaint is. What is more, they ask for this reassurance while at the same time being acutely tuned in for the slightest sign of any half-hidden pessimisms. To be a successful nurse one must learn to be a convincing liar. The experiment was therefore more than an academic exercise—and in fact it turned out that in later training the nurses who came top of their classes were also the ones who were the best body-liars in the film-report tests.

Even the best body-liars were not perfect, however, and the experimenters were able to assemble a set of key-differences in body actions between moments of truth-telling and moments of deception. They are as follows:

1. When lying, the nurses decreased the frequency of simple gesticulations they made with their hands. The hand actions they would normally use to emphasize verbal statements—to drive home a point, or to underline an important moment—were significantly reduced. The reason for this is that the hand actions, which act as 'illustrators' of spoken words, are not identified gestures. We know we 'wave our hands about' when we engage in excited conversation, but we have no idea exactly what our hands are doing. Our awareness that our hands do *something*, but our unawareness of precisely what it is, makes us suspicious of the possible transparency of these actions. Unconsciously we sense that perhaps they will give us away and we will fail to notice, so we suppress them. This is not easy to do. We can hide them, sit on them, stuff them deep into our pockets (where they may still let us down by finding some coins and jingling them), or, less drastically, we can clasp one firmly with the other and let them hold each other down. The experienced observer is not fooled by this—he knows that if those tiny hands are metaphorically frozen, there is something amiss.

2. When lying, the nurses increased the frequency of hand-to-face auto-contacts. We all touch our faces from time to time during conversations, but the number of times these simple actions are performed rises dramatically during moments of deception. Some hand-to-head actions are more popular than others, in this context, and the nature of the hand movement varies according to the part of the head involved. Deception favourites include: the Chin Stroke, the Lips Press, the Mouth Cover, the Nose Touch, the Cheek Rub, the Eyebrow Scratch, the Earlobe Pull and the Hair Groom. During deception attempts any of these may show a marked increase, but two in particular receive a special boost. These are the Nose Touch and the Mouth Cover.

The Mouth Cover is the easier to understand. False words are emerging from the mouth of the speaker, and the part of his brain that is uncomfortable about this sends a message to his hand to 'cover up' what he is doing. Unconsciously, the lying speaker raises his hand as if to gag himself, but somehow he has to let the words continue to emerge from his mouth. The other part of his brain cannot permit the cover-up to work. The verbal lie must continue to flow. The result is an abortive cover-up, with the hand-to-mouth action ending up as no more than a partial contact. There are several typical forms of this; for example, the fingers fanned over the lips, the forefinger resting on the upper lip, or the hand at the side of the mouth.

It is important to add that if you observe someone performing this partial mouth-cover it does not mean that they *must* be lying. It only means that they are more likely to be lying than at times when the hand has not strayed mouthwards.

The Mouth Cover has an obvious weakness—its message is too transparent. Sometimes, when clumsily performed by a child, it may even be directly challenged with phrases such as: 'Stop mumbling behind your hand—what are you trying to hide?' The more sophisticatedly deflected hand-to-mouth actions of adults may avoid this open challenge, but they remain a little too revealing for comfort. This is overcome by an increase in the deflection element, which brings us to the other important action-clue—the Nose Touch.

Several observers have noticed that nose-touching and deceit go together in a remarkable way, but no-one has ventured to suggest why this should be. There appears to be a double answer. First, the hand, coming up to block the mouth-lie, has to be deflected, and the nose is conveniently near by. The hand could go to the chin, but this would fall short of the mouth; or to the cheek, but this would take it away to the side. The nose, however, being protrusive and right above the mouth, is in the ideal position, for the hand has only to travel a few inches up beyond the lips and it can continue to partially cover the mouth region, while ostensibly attending to the nose.

As a disguised mouth-cover, the Nose Touch has become the most overworked of all deceit actions, but there is a second reason for its popularity. When the moment of the deliberate lie occurs, there is, even in the most experienced of liars, a slight increase in tension. This increase leads to minor physiological changes, some of which may affect the sensitivity of the lining of the nasal cavity, making the nose itch. This can be an almost imperceptible sensation—so slight that we are hardly aware of it—but it may help to make the nose more attractive as the site for a hand-touch. It does not necessarily initiate the hand action, but merely helps to direct it to the nose once the mouth cover-up has started and requires deflection.

3. When lying, the nurses showed an increase in the number of body-shifts they made as they spoke. A child who squirms in his chair is obviously dying to escape and any parent recognizes these symptoms of restlessness immediately. In adults they are reduced and suppressed—again because they are so obviously signs of unease—but they do not vanish. Watched closely, the adult liar can be seen to make tiny, vestigial body-shifts and to make them much more frequently than when telling the truth. They are no longer squirmings; instead they are only slight changes in the resting posture of the trunk as the speaker moves from one sitting posture to another.

The Nose Touch, an action associated with momentary stress. At times when a man's inner thoughts do not reflect his outward calm, he may leak the fact by touching (top), rubbing (above) or squeezing (below) his nose. The reason for this is still not clear.

These unobtrusive body-shifts are saying: 'I wish I were somewhere else', the posture-changes being intensely inhibited intention movements of escape.

4. When lying, the nurses made greater use of one particular hand action, namely the Hand Shrug. While other gesticulations decreased in frequency, this became more common. It is almost as if the hands were disclaiming any responsibility for the verbal statements being made.

5. When lying, the nurses displayed facial expressions that were almost indistinguishable from those given during truthful statements. Almost, but not quite, for there were, even in the most self-aware faces, tiny micro-expressions that leaked the truth. These micro-expressions are so small and so quick—a mere fraction of a second—that untrained observers were unable to detect them. However, after special training, using slow-motion films, they were able to spot them in normal-speed films of interviews. So, to a trained expert, even the face cannot lie.

These micro-expressions are caused by the face's all-too-rapid efficiency in registering inner feelings. When a mood-change seeks expression, it can expect to be registered by the alteration in the set of facial muscles in much less than a second. The counter-message from the brain, telling the face to 'shut up', often fails to catch up with the primary mood-change message. The result is that a facial expression begins and then, a split second later, is cancelled by the counter-message. What happens on the face during the split second delay is a tiny, fleeting hint of an expression. It is suppressed so quickly that most people never see it, but if watched for carefully during lying sessions, it *can* be detected and is then one of the best of deception clues.

There is one serious criticism of these experiments. The American research workers set up a laboratory test which, within its own limitations, worked well. It tells us clearly what happens when people try to lie, and it shows us how the body actions fail in their attempt at total deceit. It allows us to pinpoint the small actions that give the game away. But because this is all it does test, it fails to tell us whether this is the only circumstance in which such behaviour-changes occur. It proves that there is an increase in hand-to-face actions and a decrease in gesticulations when people start to lie, but it fails to rule out the possibility that lying is only one of the conditions that produce this effect. In other words, is lying the key, or only part of the key?

Field studies seem to indicate that it is only part of the key. To give an example: two people are talking, when suddenly one of them explodes with a sharp insult. The insult is unexpected and the insulted person fails to reply. He sits dumb for several minutes while the stream of insults continues. Eventually he answers and does so coolly and collectedly. During this verbal exchange, there is a moment of high tension—the moment of the initial insult—and it is precisely then that the insulted person moves his hand up to his face and touches the side of his nose. It is the Nose Touch that we already know occurs at moments of lying. But this nose toucher cannot be lying, because he is silent. Long before he replies, the hand has left the nose, so that when his answer does come, he is once again composed and cool-headed.

A second example: one man is interviewing another. The interviewer asks easy questions and gets straightforward answers. Then he asks a difficult, complex question. As the interviewee starts his answer, rather hesitantly, his finger flicks up to touch his nose. But he is not about to lie. The question is not one which requires a false answer, merely a complicated one which he has to think out carefully.

In these two examples there is no deceit and yet the nose touching seems remarkably reminiscent of the action that occurs during moments of lying. What do the three situations have in common? All involve an initial moment of tension. The insulted nose-toucher remains silent, but inwardly his mind is reeling under the impact of the unanticipated attack. His brain is seething, but outwardly he remains composed. His inner behaviour (his thinking) and his outer behaviour (his inactivity) do not match with each other. Similarly, the person asked a sudden, difficult question experiences a split between his thoughts and his actions. He tries to answer smoothly and easily, but his brain is working furiously to cope with the complexity of the question. Again, his inner thoughts and his outer actions do not match.

Comparing these two situations with a moment of lying, it is now clear that they have a great deal in common. The essence of deliberate deceit is that what is going on in the brain is not reflected in the outward verbal behaviour. We say one thing while thinking another. So perhaps to say that the Nose Touch is a sign of lying is to oversimplify the case. What we should say instead is that the Nose Touch, and other similar actions, are a reflection of the fact that a split is being forced between inner thoughts and outward actions. This can only be described as deceit in a very general way, and active lying is no more than a special case of this general condition. When we struggle to appear calm while grappling mentally with an insult or with a difficult question, we are, in a sense, being deceitful, but we cannot be said to be lying. In other words, there is more to dishonesty than uttering falsehoods. So, if we set up an experiment to test lying, we are in danger of missing the more general significance of the behaviour we find.

What Nonverbal Leakage really shows, therefore, is not merely lying, but a basic inner-outer conflict of an acute kind, with thoughts and actions mis-matching at a moment of tension. But if this means that we cannot be certain that a nose-toucher is lying, we can still be sure that something is going on in his brain which he is failing to externalize and communicate to us verbally. He may not be lying in the strict sense of the word, but he is certainly hiding something from us, and his nose-touching is leaking that fact to us.

CONTRADICTORY SIGNALS

Giving two conflicting signals at the same time

When we are being dishonest our behaviour often fragments. It comes to pieces like a dismantled jigsaw-puzzle. Instead of all our actions fitting together in a harmonious way, they combine in contradictory assemblages that jar on the observer and tell him something is amiss. To give an over-simplified example: a man gives a friendly smile, but at the same time his fists are tightly clenched. His face says 'I am happy', but his hands say 'I am angry'. How are we to react to such conflicting messages? Do we trust one, both or neither of his actions?

To answer this question it is necessary to make a clear distinction between Ambivalent Signals and Contradictory Signals. In both there is a display of conflicting elements, but in the case of Ambivalent Signals the conflict is the result of a mixed mood. Take the situation in which a thug insults a man's wife. The man is genuinely frightened of the thug and equally genuinely angry with him. His fear makes him pull back defensively, but his aggression makes him want to attack. His body obeys both impulses simultaneously, with the result that he adopts an ambivalent threat posture. This Ambivalent Signal is made up of a mixture of intention movements of attacking and intention movements of retreating. He edges away from the thug, but at the same time displays an angry facial expression and a ready-to-strike arm posture. At that moment, the thug, reading both sets of signals, has to balance them against each other. He accepts both as genuine, but has to decide which reflects the stronger impulse. Can he risk a further insult to the man, or will this push him too far and lead to a frenzied attack?

In a situation like that, the two conflicting parts of the Ambivalent Signal are both read as genuine and acted upon accordingly. But what about the other example, where a man was smiling and clenching his fists simultaneously? Can he really be happy and angry at one and the same time, or is one signal genuine and the other false? The chances are that here the man is really very angry but is trying to conceal the fact with a body-lie in the form of a false smile. This, then, is an example, not of an Ambivalent Signal based on a genuinely mixed mood, but a Contradictory Signal based on a single genuine mood that is over-laid with a deliberate outward lie.

It is possible, of course, to reverse the argument and say that the smiling man who clenches his fists is really genuinely friendly, but is pretending, for some reason, to be hostile; that his smile is mood-induced and his clenched fists are deliberately faked. To decide between the two, we have to return to the lessons learned from the studies of Nonverbal Leakage. The rival elements in a Contradictory Signal have to be assessed as belonging to either the easy-lying type or the difficult-lying type. The more aware a performer is of a particular action he is making, the more likely it is to be a body-lie. Actions performed unconsciously are going to escape faking and reflect the true inner mood of the signaller.

Bearing this in mind it is possible to construct a *Believability Scale* for different types of action. Starting with the most believable and ending with the least, it looks something like this: (1) Autonomic Signals; (2) Leg and Foot Signals; (3) Trunk Signals; (4) Unidentified Gesticulations; (5) Identified Hand Gestures; (6) Facial Expressions; (7) Verbalizations.

This is a crude oversimplification, but until we know a great deal more about the subject, it will do as a rough guide. If you observe a Contradictory Signal made up of, say, elements 1, 3, 6, and 7, then it will be reasonably safe to trust the messages being transmitted by 1 and 3 and ignore the messages from 6 and 7. The seven categories can be briefly summarized as follows:

1. Autonomic Signals. These are the safest of all because, even when we are aware of them we can rarely control them. It is almost impossible to sweat at will, or to make your cheeks go pale. Only a great actress can usually weep to

The girl at the centre of this picture is performing two conflicting sets of gestures at the same time: her facial expression suggests that she is not displeased, but her hands and averted head suggest otherwise. Because these gestures are the result of genuinely mixed feelings towards the young man, she is transmitting an Ambivalent Signal; but if one of them was feigned, it would then become a Contradictory Signal.

order and then she does it by forcing herself into a genuinely sad mood. Even with this safest category, however, there are opportunities for faking in one or two instances. For example, the respiratory upsets that occur with autonomic disturbances can be faked. We can all pant and heave and gasp to order. But despite this, we are most unlikely to do so as part of an ordinary deception device. It requires considerable concentration to maintain a false breathing rate while at the same time handling the other elements of a deception. So even breathing patterns are reasonably safe as genuine mood-clues.

These Autonomic Signals resulting from physiological changes that are beyond our deliberate, conscious control are obviously particularly valuable when trying to sort out the true and false elements in a Contradictory Signal, but they are unfortunately limited to the more powerfully emotional situations. For less dramatic moments we have to turn to other body actions.

2. Leg and Foot Signals. During ordinary social intercourse, when sitting talking to one another, it is the lower parts of our body that seem to escape the net of deliberate control most easily. The main reason for this appears to be that our attentions are face-focused. Even when we can see the whole body of a companion, we still focus our concentration on to his head region. The further away some other part of the body is from his face, the less importance we give it. The feet are as far away as you can get, and so there is little pressure on him to exert deliberate control on his foot actions. They therefore provide valuable clues as to his true mood.

The obvious example of a useful foot clue is the case of the man who listens patiently and apparently enthralled to what we are saying, smiling and nodding at us at appropriate intervals, but whose foot is flapping rhythmically up and down as he does so. One famous American television host is so prone to this particular give-away foot action that it was suggested he should have the word HELP printed on the sole of his shoe. Were this in fact done, the magnificently cool composure of his upper-body would be completely shattered by the HELP signal repeatedly flashing out its sign to the audience each time his foot flap brought his sole up into view. Without this verbal aid, however, most people remain blissfully unaware of which interviews he is finding an ordeal and wishes to escape from, because they are completely focused on the upper-body activities.

Other foot actions which give the game away include small, aggressive foot kicks of an abbreviated kind—little toe-jabs into the air—which may accompany friendly upper-body actions. Here the foot hostilities are the more trustworthy elements, and the companion's friendliness can be viewed as suspect. Then there are tense, leg-squeezing postures, which contradict relaxed facial signals. Or restless leg-shifts and repetitive foot-jigglings that indicate a blocked urge to flee in someone who seems otherwise to be happy to stay where he is. Or, finally, sexual leg actions which conflict with upper-body primness. These erotic leg signals include revealing leg postures and auto-contact rubbing and stroking either of one leg by the other, or of a leg by a hand. If these are performed by a girl whose upper-body activities are either totally non-erotic or even anti-erotic, then she is probably feeling more sexually responsive than she cares to admit.

3. Trunk Signals. The general body posture in an informal situation is a useful true-mood guide because it reflects the general muscular tonus of the whole body system. It is difficult for an excited man to sag or slump artificially, no matter how hard he tries. Similarly, someone who is bored finds it hard to keep his body alert. On this last point, it is particularly instructive to watch a bored junior colleague listening attentively to a boring senior colleague. The junior may nod, frown, smile, murmur accord and even lean forwards eagerly with the correct amount of attentiveness, but his trunk signals can still let him down. He cannot afford a full body-sag or body slump, which would be too revealing, and he is capable of extending his awareness-control to his body posture sufficiently to keep up an alert pose. But every so often his trunk-control starts to slip and his body begins, almost imperceptibly, to sink into the bored-slump posture. Before it goes very far, he senses what is happening and pulls himself up with a jerk. If he handles this well, he manages to disguise the pulling-himself-up action as part of a staccato agreement action, nodding his head vigorously as he does it, so that it seems to be part of the affirmation signal. If the senior colleague is engrossed in his boring statements, the junior colleague will probably get away with it. If the tensing-up actions lack finesse, however, the senior colleague will suddenly feel uneasy, without knowing quite why, and will mutter: '. . . but I have been talking far too much . . .', whereupon there will be an immediate verbal denial from the junior, who will muster all his self-control to re-alert his body to the appropriately attentive posture.

4. Unidentified Gesticulations. The hands come under slightly more control than the feet, legs and trunk, if only because they are more often in view. If we wave our hands about while speaking, we can see the movements in front of us. We do not focus on them, but we 'half-see' them, and we are therefore half-aware of them. Many hand actions are indefinite, vague wavings and dippings to which no names have become attached, and these are the least controlled manual elements. The politician who jabs savagely at the air while he talks about the need for peaceful coexistence is giving a Contradictory Signal in which the hands are the elements to be trusted, rather than the voice.

5. Identified Hand Gestures. Many hand actions are precise units that act like small emblems. They are contrived gestures, deliberately performed. The victory V-sign is a good example. We may not plan such gestures, but when we do them we are fully aware of the fact. They differ markedly, then, from the ordinary gesticulations which we are only vaguely aware of as we perform them. Because of this, they cannot be trusted if they appear as part of a Contradictory Signal. There is no guarantee that they are telling the truth. In fact, they are about as suspect as facial expressions and should generally be ignored in favour of the other signals already listed. If a defeated politician performs the victory V-sign it may reflect his indomitable fighting spirit, but it certainly does not reflect his inner emotional condition at the moment of making the sign. Other defeat-signals accompanying the V-sign will tell the true story, body-sag being one of the best clues in such a case.

Opposite top: the one-sided contradictory smile. Cover one side of this face with a sheet of paper and the man smiles; cover the other side and he scowls. His mouth is capable of sending two conflicting messages at one and the same time. This can also be demonstrated by combining each half of the face with its mirror-image, as is done here.

6. Facial Expressions. We are so aware of what our faces are doing that it is easy to lie with facial expressions. When a Contradictory Signal occurs, the face is of little help. But even here there are some clues. Facial expressions fall into two major categories. As with hand actions, there are identified expressions and unidentified ones. The identified ones are, so to speak, 'set pieces' and we can fake them with ease. They include such items as the smile, the laugh, the frown and the pout. Because they have a name we seem to be able to manipulate them with greater facility. We say: 'give him a smile', or 'I am afraid I will laugh', indicating that we carry a ready-made, fixed image of these expressions in our minds, ready to be switched on at a moment's notice, not by our underlying mood but by deliberate calculation. Other facial expressions that we have never identified are much more difficult to fake. Into this category come such facial changes as a slight narrowing of the eyes, an added tension of the forehead skin, a small in-turning of the lips, or a minute tightening of the jaw muscles. The face is so complex, with the capability of hundreds of minor tensions and relaxations, tuggings and pullings, that it can express a change in underlying mood while hardly altering at all in the sense of there being any gross action changes. Putting on a big smile, or a deep frown, will to a large extent overlay these minute muscle changes, but will not exclude them altogether from view.

If, for instance, a fake smile is adopted, and the underlying, genuine mood is one of sadness or depression, the smile will probably be slightly distorted by the small, unidentified tensions in the face. There are two common forms of this distortion. The most widespread is the Mouth-corners-down Smile. For some reason it is much more difficult to fake the raising of the mouth-corners if one is feeling sad or depressed than it is to fake the rest of the smile. The whole face can appear happy, with the eye region cheerfully crinkled, and yet the mouth-corners simply refuse to pull themselves up to the appropriate raised position in relation to the rest of the face. An otherwise radiant face can still give the game away with this one contradictory clue. Less frequent is the case where one side of the mouth obeys the order 'Fake a smile', while the other side of the mouth refuses to do so, producing the well-known one-sided Crooked Smile.

Summing up, it can be said that whenever a Contradictory Signal is transmitted, in which the two conflicting messages cannot possibly both be true, the false one can be identified by referring them to this Believability Scale. Three general principles have emerged. An action is more likely to be reflecting a true mood: (1) the farther away from the face it is; (2) the less aware the performer is of it; and (3) if it is an unidentified, unnamed action that has not become a recognized unit of behaviour among the general population.

Bearing this in mind, it is comparatively easy to detect the real significance of most Contradictory Signals when we encounter them. If we observe a laughing face, but the body is stiff and rigid, we will trust the body, not the face. If we observe an angry face, but the hands are held in the imploring posture of a beggar, we will trust the hands. Even when both conflicting signals come from the head region, we may be able to decide between them. If, for example, we observe a shyly lowered head which nevertheless has the eyes looking boldly up at us from its lowered position, then we can trust the eyes. We can do this because we know that 'hanging the head' shyly down is a set-piece and can therefore be more calculatingly employed. This last case is a perfect example of how Contradictory Signals can jar on the observer. Lowering both the head *and* the eyes is a genuinely shy reaction and is not unappealing. Looking boldly, head-on at someone also has the ring of truth about it. But doing both at once—head-shy and eyes-bold—sets up a jarring contradiction in the observer. When we see this, it makes us feel uneasy and we have invented an insulting name for such behaviour—we call it 'coy' and we say: 'Stop being coy', making a subtle distinction in our language between attractive shyness and unattractive coyness.

A coy expression (above) consists of two conflicting signals: a 'shyly' lowered head and a bold stare. And it is this which distinguishes it from a truly shy expression, in which both head and eyes are lowered.

SHORTFALL SIGNALS

When we under-react despite ourselves

A Shortfall Signal is one that fails to reach its usual level of intensity. In some way, it falls short of the expected.

The On-off Smile is an obvious example. This is the smile that flashes quickly on to an otherwise immobile face and then, just as quickly, vanishes again. The typical smile, in contrast, takes fractionally longer to grow to full strength and to fade away again. Sometimes, when friends meet in the street, they can both be seen still smiling, some time after they have actually passed each other. But the On-off Smile decays with lightning speed the moment the smiler's face is no longer a focus of attention. Such smiles often last for less than a second and can easily be converted into deliberate insults by switching-off rapidly while still in the other person's line of vision.

The glance that is held for a fraction of a second less than it should be is another example of a Shortfall Signal. Reduced eye contact soon makes us feel uncomfortable, and if our companion persists in it we start reacting, often unconsciously, with feelings that we are being deceived.

The reason why Shortfall Signals occur is that the performer's true mood is interfering with his social 'display'. He attempts to simulate the outward signs of inner feelings he is not experiencing, and he fails to perfect his 'act'. He fails because—to return to the case of the On-off Smile—when he is in the real mood to smile, he never has to calculate or become aware of the exact relationship between the strength of his smile and the strength of his inner mood. He knows there is a crude relationship—that when he is mildly pleased he gives a slight smile and that when he is very pleased he gives a big grin—but he never needs to work out the subtle gradations of this relationship.

When he fakes a smile he is therefore liable to produce a signal that is in some small detail a poor copy of the real thing. This shortcoming may vary from case to case. The On-off Smile is only one of the forms of flawed smiling. There is also the Frozen Smile, which falls short in an entirely different way. In the on-off version the strength of the smile is correct, but its duration is wrong; in the frozen version, the duration is right, but the strength falls short. In other words, when producing a forced, or false smile, the performer fails to treat the action as a complex signal. To get it right, he must copy all the elements of the smile to the appropriate degree. This means that he must stretch his lips, raise his mouth-corners, and adjust the rest of his face, all to the correct strength in relation to one another, and for the correct length of time in relation to their intensity. Also, the smile must grow on his face and fade from it at the correct rate for its particular strength of expression. If this sounds complicated, the answer is that it *is* complicated. The wonder is not that we occasionally see a Shortfall Signal which reveals inadequate faking, but that people are so often able to fake a smile to perfection.

Actors and actresses are well aware of this problem, more so than ever before now that the close-up lens has changed the face of their profession. The live-theatre actor has always been forced to over-exaggerate his actions and expressions. If the hero must smile at the heroine or frown at the villain, he must be seen to do so by a customer sitting at the back of the stalls, even though the face he is smiling at is only a few inches away from his own. Given the unnatural task of having to transmit a 12-inch signal a hundred feet or more, he could do nothing but wildly overemphasize it. The same was true of early films, but with the advent of close-up lenses the film or television actor had to forget the Grand Manner and concentrate on the perfect copying of gestures and expressions. This required a special skill and a whole new breed of actors, for in avoiding deliberate over-acting there was the danger that performances would become wooden and under-expressive. Today, in bad film-acting one can see both errors. The performers either over-stress their movements or display repeated Shortfall Signals. In the latter case they

The Frozen Smile that falls short of the expected response. If the human face forces a smile to please a photographer, the false smile soon begins to decay (above). This applies not only to inexperienced subjects but also to professional models and (opposite) famous public figures.

usually get the main signals right, but underplay subsidiary ones. They make their faces work correctly, but fall short with their casual hand actions, for instance. More successful actors seem to have an ability to fake a mood by 'working' themselves into the required frame of mind and then letting their faces—and hands—do the rest naturally.

For those of us who never have to face the problem of film acting these special difficulties do not arise, although we do have to deal with the general problem in ordinary social intercourse when we are called upon to be polite and suppress our true feelings. But there is one classic situation in which we can all appreciate, for a few moments, the enormous challenge faced by the modern actor in front of a camera. That is when we have our photograph taken for a family snapshot. The photographer asks us to smile for our picture and then starts fiddling with his focusing device. We put on a false smile and hold it as best we can but, as any family album will testify, this is not an easy task. The good photographer will amuse you the moment before he presses the button, and there will be a striking difference between the smile in his portrait and the one in the usual family snapshot.

The main reason, then, for the existence of Shortfall Signals is that, being unaware of the subtle complexities of many of our gestures and expressions, we fail to copy them perfectly in all respects when our mood is inappropriate. Another factor is the inner counter-pressure exerted by our true mood. If, as often happens, it is an opposing mood—sad while pretending to be happy, for instance—then the chances are that every 'happy trend' in the body's actions will be suffering a pull in the opposite direction, from the inner mood, and the simulated actions will tend to fall short of the level expected of them.

In referring to 'expected' levels, there is the implication of a generally accepted form for particular actions. In other words, there is a (correct) supposition that we all know a good smile when we see one. This knowledge is derived from our exposure all our lives to other members of our society. To continue with the example of the smile, it is clear from studies of blind-born individuals that this is an inborn response, but anyone who has talked to a blind person will know that the blind smile is a strange smile. It lacks the subtle nuances of an ordinary smile. It would seem that we inherit the crude act and then proceed to polish it with social experience. We do this unconsciously—hence the shortfall problems when we try to fake it. But this polishing process may vary from culture to culture, according to the different Display Rules operating locally. This introduces a new complication into the business of identifying Shortfall Signals when we travel or mix with members of other cultures. One of the major differences imposed by Display Rules is the degree of 'damping' of particular actions that occurs from region to region. In some cultures it may be usual to underplay the smile, even when genuinely happy. If we meet a person from such an 'inscrutable' culture, we may imagine that we are observing a Shortfall Signal indicating deceit, when in reality we are witnessing a genuine but 'damped' display. This kind of problem can set up unconscious confusions in our dealings with foreigners, over and above verbal language difficulties. This is particularly true of tourists who for most of their lives have stayed strictly within their own social group and who then go abroad for a short holiday. If you watch the faces of such people when engaged in conversation with their foreign hosts, you will detect a curious phenomenon. Realizing that they have lost the subtle nuances of their home-town interactions, they avoid the danger of accidental and unintended Shortfall Signalling by employing a device that is both crude and effective: they over-exaggerate everything. They not only talk more loudly and laugh more noisily, but they also smile more intensely, nod more vigorously and generally overplay their friendly gestures. Since they do not have time to learn the local nonverbal 'dialect', they intuitively feel that this is the safest way to behave. But to over-exaggerate a visual signal can be as transparently artificial as to underplay it. With this thought, we move from Shortfall Signals to the opposite side of the coin—to Overkill Signals.

OVERKILL SIGNALS

When we over-react

An Overkill Signal can be seen whenever an action is performed too strongly for its particular context.

The man who laughs too loud and too long at a mildly amusing joke is immediately suspect. We feel intuitively that he is really unamused but wishes to hide the fact, and does so by over-doing his response. Or we sense, perhaps, that his mind was elsewhere and, not having listened properly to our joke, he is over-laughing as a safety precaution. Or perhaps he failed to understand the joke and is trying to conceal this. We cannot be sure of the exact truth, but we are certain, because of his disproportionate response, that he is faking his reaction.

Like Shortfall Signals, Overkill Signals reflect a failure on the part of the performer to judge the right strength of his counterfeit reaction. There were two reasons for Shortfall Signals—the unawareness of the true subtlety of a genuine reaction, and the suppressing force of the hidden inner mood. Overkill Signals share the first reason, but not the second. When 'overdoing' a reaction, we may be revealing our inability to make a perfect copy of the true reaction, but we are certainly not being subdued by our inner mood. On the contrary, we are fighting it too well. It is as if I were saying to myself: 'I am going to pretend that I am not sad by laughing and, since I know that my sadness may show through and weaken my laugh, I will make such a loud, long laugh that even my deep, inner distress will not be able to defeat it.'

Unfortunately this process of compensation all too easily becomes one of

Overkill signals can be seen wherever individuals over-react to a situation—by grimacing (above), posturing (right) or laughing (below right) in an extreme or exaggerated way. What these actions tell us is that the feelings expressed are insufficiently felt: they have set in motion a compensatory mechanism that has gone too far.

A man in an unfamiliar social situation may find it difficult to strike the 'happy medium' expected of him. His behaviour either falls short or overkills—as depicted in this Bateman cartoon of 1920.

overcompensation, and the deception clue is there for all to see. The reason for this failure is the inability of the false-laugher to balance his books. He says to himself (unconsciously, of course): this joke is worth a Strength Four Laugh, but I am suffering from a Strength Three Sadness. To balance this I must give a Strength Seven Laugh, and that will make the equation come right. In theory it should work, but in practice it is extremely difficult to balance different moods and actions in this way, and the faker often goes too far. He is pushed this way because of a feeling that he must erect a really powerful barrier against the collapse of his inhibitions—the inhibitions which are helping him to conceal his true mood.

Shakespeare was aware of this phenomenon when he wrote 'The lady doth protest too much', and there are some clear examples of Overkill Signals in the behaviour of women who protest too much with their sexual, or, rather, anti-sexual signals. The most obvious example is the girl who repeatedly tugs at her skirt, pulling it down again and again, even though it has not ridden up in a revealing way as she sits in her chair. Another example is the girl who crosses her legs too tightly, twining them like tensed rope, or clamping them together as if she were trying to crack walnuts with her thighs. In such cases, the vigour of the girl's actions, in the presence of a male who is neither on his knees peering up her skirts nor trying to force her legs apart with his arms, is clearly over-exaggerated. As a sexual display, such actions are second only in intensity to opening her legs wide and exposing her crotch. They draw attention to her preoccupation with her sexuality just as surely. As non-sexual signals they are, like most anti-sexual signals, a total failure. (This, incidentally, is why the behaviour of over-zealous anti-pornographers is so suspect and disturbing, even to those who, in a moderate way, agree with their views.)

As with Shortfall Signals, so with Overkill Signals there is a danger of misunderstanding when individuals from different cultures meet. If we encounter an individual who laughs too loudly, back-slaps too hard and hand-shakes too long, it may simply be that we are witnessing the norm for his particular cultural background, where Display Rules have not damped these particular actions as much as in our own culture. But although misunderstandings may arise in such instances, they are not as common as might be expected. This is because, in some subtle way, we can soon sense the authenticity of the complete pattern of the man's behaviour. We use such clues as the absence of Contradictory Signals, and assess his actions correctly as lacking deceit. Even so, we may still not feel entirely at ease with him. We will trust him, but find it hard to adjust rapidly enough to his strong signals in a calm social context. We will find him boisterous while he will no doubt tell his friends that he found us stiff, cold and subdued.

In inter-culture debates, defences have been put forward for both the demonstrative type and the reserved type. Demonstrative cultures accuse the visually quiet cultures of being so unresponsive, so display-damped, that deceit is easy for them. If they show so little emotion, they can easily conceal whether it is there or not. The reserved culture counterattacks by saying that the more flamboyant gestures of the others means that they show so much emotion over trivia that it is impossible to tell when they are seriously intense and when they are not. Anyone who has lived in both types of culture for any length of time will know that both these views are mistaken. Within each culture there is a perfectly clear range of visual expression, from mild to intense, and it is merely a case of learning to tune in to the particular wavelength of the culture in which you find yourself. Once this has been done—and it is no easier than learning a foreign language—it is perfectly possible to detect the moments of deceit and to identify examples of Non-verbal Leakage, Contradictory Signals, Shortfall Signals and Overkill Signals. These basic principles, by which 'the game is given away', are fundamentally the same across all cultures, no matter how supposedly inscrutable or razzle-dazzle their different gesture-patterns may be.

STATUS DISPLAYS

Ways in which we signal our position in the social peck order

A Status Display is a demonstration of a level of dominance. In primitive conditions dominance is achieved by a show of brute force. The strongest member of a group goes to the top of the 'peck order' and the weakest goes to the bottom. In modern human societies physical strength has been replaced by other forms of dominance. Muscle power has given way to inherited power, manipulative power and creative power. The top muscle-men have been superseded by top Inheritors, top Fixers and top Talents. These are the three high-status types we encounter today, and each has his own special way of displaying his dominance. Instead of showing off his bulging muscles, the inheritor shows off his ancestry, the fixer his influence, and the talent his works.

It has sometimes been said that money has replaced muscle as the greatest Status Display of all, but this is not strictly true. It is possible to be a penniless aristocrat, a poorly paid politician, or an impoverished genius, and still command considerable respect because of your background, power, or creative skill. But it has to be admitted that to be rich and titled, rich and powerful, or rich and brilliant, makes you doubly blessed in the 'rat race' for high status. It also makes you the subject of great envy, with a halo that has only a short distance to fall to become a noose. The result of this is that Status Displays have become increasingly subtle. In earlier days, the overlords were able to display their dominance as brashly as they liked. Their clothes, their jewels, their palaces and their entertainments were ostentatiously exposed to view. This was made possible by their guards, their torturers and their dungeons—which dealt effectively with any objectors. In a sense, they were only one step away from bulging their muscles. But then, a few hundred years ago, subordinates began to discover the trick of ganging up on their masters. Strength in numbers was the solution, and the old-style tyrants were knocked from their pedestals. Ever since, the new-style dominants have been forced to play the game of high-status living with cunning and finesse. It is this that makes the study of modern Status Displays such a fascinating pursuit.

For the inheritors, the new situation has meant pomp without power, and for the fixers, power without pomp. Surviving royal families still display the trappings and rituals of the old days, providing a splash of colour and pageantry in a grey world, but without wielding any real governing power; and while political leaders still exercise great power, they are careful to be

Opposite: pomp without power. Modern royalty and nobility in full costume display, but lacking in real political power: Queen Elizabeth II opening a British parliamentary session. Below: power without pomp. Modern presidents possess great power, but dress in dull, simple costumes. The costume display may however, be transferred to the attendant guards. Above: an intermediate stage. An enthroned African chieftain wears a Western lounge suit under his traditional robe.

It is unnecessary for some individuals to express their status in flamboyant displays. The power to call a press conference that attracts the reporters of the world is evidence enough.

Opposite top: for a male to be closely attended by subordinate females — especially in a harem-like setting to which he controls access — has always operated as compelling Status Display. In this case, the high-status male is a successful American businessman.

Opposite bottom: for many high-status individuals, the motor car has replaced the opulent costumes of earlier times.

High status is often displayed in the form of extravagantly unnecessary gadgets, such as this silver drink dispenser on a millionaire's dining table.

seen doing so in grey flannel suits. In other words, a high-status display can still be blatant, provided it is little more than a theatrical performance; but if it is backed by real power, it must be suitably muted.

This muting of Status Displays takes several forms. One is to transfer the display away from the person. A president or head of state dreses quietly and travels in a black vehicle. Gone are the golden crowns and golden coaches. He smiles and shakes hands. Gone are the lordly manners and the demand for bowing and scraping. But he does all this surrounded by an impressive entourage of advisers and bodyguards. Police smooth his passage and personal staff isolate him from interference.

If we move slightly down the peck order, away from kings and presidents, we find another form of muting. This involves the development of the 'in-thing'. This is an action or object which displays high status merely because it is done or owned exclusively by high-status individuals. It may or may not be expensive, but it is always modish. It may be an in-drink, an in-restaurant, an in-vehicle, an in-holiday-resort, or an in-costume. 'In' is short for 'in-the-know' and only the elite band of high-status individuals are 'in-the-know'. This display device is especially favoured by non-regal inheritors—the heirs and heiresses to family fortunes, the young-of-the-rich, and the socialites. This is the jet-set world, where, as with the royals, there is no real power; there are only social graces. But, unlike modern royalty, the playboys and playgirls avoid formal ritual and public ceremonies. The essence of their world is that it is exclusive—it excludes the outside world and confines its Status Displays within its own sphere of action. Its excesses are muted because they are private. They still work, because within their limited social range they continue to impress near rivals, and this is enough. Naturally, it would be pleasant if the displays could reach a wider audience, but that might be dangerous. Mounting envy might trundle out the guillotine once again, in some new form.

However, since envy's gentler face is imitation, there are problems. The out-people try to copy the in-people. Sitting in a dimly-lit, converted slaughter-house (the latest in-restaurant) are two high-status displayers. They are drinking antler-fizz (the latest in-drink) and wearing Sudanese native beads (the latest in-jewellery) dressed in black boiler-suits (the latest in-costume). Only the very in-people know of these new fashions, but nearby is a gossip columnist, scribbling down the details. In no time at all the word is out and the place is packed with imitators. The in-people must move on, and the cycle begins again.

It would, of course, be naive to imagine that these in-people shun publicity. That is not the point. What they do is to make a *show* of shunning publicity, but ensure that they do it inefficiently. They are then in a position to complain that their favourite haunts have been ruined by becoming too popular, and that their fashions have been destroyed by cheap copying. This gives them the chance of being leaders of social fads and fashions without appearing to *want* to be so. They cannot therefore be accused of brazenly flaunting their Status Displays under the noses of those lower in the social peck order.

Switching from the inheritors to the fixers, we can see a similar device in operation. Here there is the same emphasis on 'restricted display'. Below the level of presidents and prime ministers, the top fixers are the tycoons and impresarios, the administrators and high-powered executives, the union bosses and the financiers. This is the real power-without-pomp brigade — grey, private men with immense influence, who reserve their Status Displays for their immediate inferiors. In the privacy of their offices their power is carefully and subtly demonstrated in a hundred different ways. To the outside world many of these displays would be meaningless, but those close to the seat of commercial power know the signs, and are duly impressed.

To give a few examples: there is the shoe display. Shoes of high-status fixers are immaculately polished and identifiable by expert eyes as coming

from only the top shoemakers. Like all truly dominant primates, the top fixers tend to be beautifully groomed, and pay attention to details that the lower ranks miss out. Then there is the telephone display. This involves having more telephones on the desk than is strictly necessary, including a specially coloured one that does not go through the company switchboard — the high-status direct line with a private number. Telephones are never dialled by high-status fixers — someone else has to do that for them, even if it takes longer to issue instructions than to do the actual dialling. Operating any mechanical device, even a telephone, has a tinge of 'manual labour' about it, and therefore has a low-status flavour. Once the two secretaries have made contact, there is the battle of who-speaks-first. High status demands that the other man come on the line first, so that he has to speak to your secretary, but you do not have to speak to his.

The telephone display has recently been extended to car-phones, so that the top fixer can display how busy he is by making calls in transit. For those in the know, these car-phones require a special aerial which, protruding from the top man's vehicle, acts as a further display of power — so much so, that in the United States one firm has successfully marketed dummy aerials for phoneless vehicles. And no doubt Dominance Mimicry of this kind will again force the top man to move on to a new form of Status Display. Similar moves occur with the choice of vehicle itself, and there is a slow, but constant shift from model to model, as imitators gradually catch up.

There is also the briefcase display. Lower-status executives have to deal with details (inattention to details is an extremely high-status display) and must carry bulky briefcases stuffed with papers. Higher up the peck order, the cases become slimmer in order to display that only vital papers are being carried. But at the very top, nothing is carried at all. In the dominance world of fixers, for high-status individuals to carry business materials of any kind is completely taboo. As someone remarked recently, the briefcase men of the business world are the spear-carriers. Generals they protect; generals they are not.

Office seating is another rich area for status battles. Under the guise of providing expensive, unusually comfortable seating for visitors, top men offer visitors very low, soft chairs into which they sink to near floor level. This means that when both host and guest are sitting, the top man is literally on top, high above his visitor, gazing down at him. It is the modern fixer's equivalent of the ancient ruler's demand for prostration — body-lowering disguised as comfort-giving.

In these and many other ways the top fixers of today display their status. To those right outside the field of battle the subtleties would be lost, and even within the business world there are many differences, both between countries and between companies. Status Displays, having withdrawn from public blatancy under the pressure of modern cultural attitudes, have become increasingly localized and specialized. Many high-status features are completely arbitrary, based entirely on what the highest-status individuals choose as top-level elements. But there are, nevertheless, certain general principles that run all through this labyrinth of dominance-signalling. One is time and the other is service. There should always be less time than is needed and more service than is needed. The top man must always appear to be unbelievably busy. Subordinates must be kept waiting on principle, diaries must be full, interviews strictly curtailed. Once away from the seat of power, the top man can dawdle and linger, but once there, the clock must rule the day. To fail in this is to imply that his personal qualities are in less than enormous demand. The same applies to many inheritors — to socialites who stir up a breathless 'social whirl', and whose scintillating personalities must also be seen to be much sought after.

As regards service, this is even more vital for the truly dominant. Servants have always been important, but in the past they were displayed by the middle as well as the top levels in the human peck order. Now they are

High-status male on low-status vehicle. Though shortly to become Lord Chancellor of England, Quintin Hogg, a former hereditary peer and cabinet minister, rides his bicycle through the streets of London.

thinner on the ground and have, as a result, acquired an even more valuable high-status flavour, the chauffeur-driven car being almost obligatory as a demonstration of real power and authority. There was a flutter of unease among the higher strata of London, recently, when a particularly high-status male bravely took to cycling around the city as an anti-pollution demonstration. Laudable as this was, the thought of cycling becoming a new Status Display was too much for other top males, and they reacted with ridicule. Another top male, an explorer reluctantly promoted to the administration, sometimes insisted on walking to and from appointments, an action that occasionally aroused incredulity and hostility in other high-status colleagues, despite the fact that walking can often prove faster in city centres than crawling through traffic jams. What they objected to, in status terms, was that one walker looks like another, and the service-display of sitting behind a chauffeur and having car doors opened and closed for you is lost.

At the outset, three high-status categories were mentioned: the inheritors, the fixers and the talents. The talents have been left until now because they are a special case. Their Status Displays are their works: the composer displays with his music, the scientist with his discoveries, the sculptor with his statues, the architect with his buildings, and so on. They are ranked according to the quality of the things they make, rather than the way they behave. Typically, inheritors and fixers make nothing. When they die their social events and their business deals die with them, but creative talents live on, remembered by their great works. This gives them such an enormous advantage in status terms that they seldom take much trouble with the other aspects of dominance display. In fact, their lack of regard for the usual Status Displays almost *becomes* a Status Display in itself. Eccentricity of dress and behaviour is commonplace for them and they enjoy social freedoms unknown to other rat-racing citizens. Their works speak for them.

Finally, what of the lower-status members of the social hierarchy? They are not all at the very bottom of the peck order, and there are status differences among them that are expressed in a number of characteristic ways. There is the Imitator. We have already met him—he is the one who indulges in Dominance Mimicry. He copies, in an inferior way, the activities of the high-status individual. To give an example: if he cannot afford a valuable painting, he buys a reproduction of a valuable painting to hang on his walls. If he cannot afford real pearls, he buys his wife imitation pearls. His house is full of fake antiques, imitation leather and plastic pretending to be wood. Instead of honest, simple crafts, he prefers mock-expensive products. Then there is the Boaster. Blatant boasting is the typical Status Display of the small boy—'I did it better than you'; 'No you did not, I did'—but this soon fades with adulthood. Where it persists, it becomes more subtle. It is converted into name-dropping and casually steering conversations boast-wards. High-status individuals are not, of course, immune to this, but they usually contrive to have someone else do the boasting for them, thus providing a social niche for another category: the Flatterer. Dominants like to have a few attendant flatterers to sing their praises, and sycophants can successfully raise their status from low to moderate by judiciously employing this device.

There is also the Joker: another low-status type who manages to increase his dominance slightly by entertaining his companions. By amusing them he puts himself in demand. Unable to gain their serious respect, he gains it by humouring them, in both senses of the word.

There is the Talker: the man who never stops talking and thereby manages to hold the centre of attention for much more than his share of any social encounter. And finally there is the Arguer, who prowls the social scene, waiting to pick a verbal fight. By disrupting the smooth flow of social intercourse he too draws attention to himself and slightly increases his standing in the process.

'Top talents' can act in extravagant ways that it would be unwise for 'top fixers' to emulate. Conventions are broken by Picasso in his excessively informal dress (below) and by Dali (above) not only in his eccentric dress and behaviour but also in the decoration of his Catalan home.

We all know and recognize these types and meet them every day, but we are fortunate if we never meet another form of Status Display that occurs right outside the ambit of ordinary social events: this is the neo-primitive, the man who, driven to desperate measures, reverts to primeval muscle-power to display his personal dominance. This is the mugger/rapist/thug category: not the mugger who is desperate for money, nor the rapist who is desperate for sex, but the man who is desperate, if only for a few brief moments, to feel the thrill of violent domination over another human being. The fact that it is domination achieved by the crudest possible means does not deter him. Usually it is all he is capable of achieving.

In the case of rape, this frustrated need to display dominance is the most common cause. A man who is sex-starved can, after all, find a prostitute to satisfy his need without too much trouble. What the rapist wants is not so much sexual relief as the total, abject subjection of his victim, her humiliation and her degradation. Only if this is extreme can he experience a temporary status-boost. This is Status Sex, and it is not by any means an exclusively human pattern of activity. Sex is used in this way by many other species of primate—as a method of displaying dominance. For other species, it has become a highly stylized procedure, with a few token pelvic thrusts from the mounting animal, who does not even bother with intromission. In fact, the 'rapist' monkey or ape can be either male or female, and the 'raped' animal may also be of either sex. All that is important is that the one on top is dominant and the one beneath is subjected to domination. Tragically, in our species, this stylization is missing, and the rather matter-of-fact monkey or ape gesture becomes a traumatic and brutally damaging assault. Fortunately for most of us, the Status Displays of ordinary social life have left muscle-power behind and have entered the restrained and fascinatingly complex world of verbal exchange and visual ritual.

TERRITORIAL BEHAVIOUR
The defence of a limited area

A territory is a defended space. In the broadest sense, there are three kinds of human territory: tribal, family and personal.

It is rare for people to be driven to physical fighting in defence of these 'owned' spaces, but fight they will, if pushed to the limit. The invading army encroaching on national territory, the gang moving into a rival district, the trespasser climbing into an orchard, the burglar breaking into a house, the bully pushing to the front of a queue, the driver trying to steal a parking space, all of these intruders are liable to be met with resistance varying from the vigorous to the savagely violent. Even if the law is on the side of the intruder, the urge to protect a territory may be so strong that otherwise peaceful citizens abandon all their usual controls and inhibitions. Attempts to evict families from their homes, no matter how socially valid the reasons, can lead to siege conditions reminiscent of the defence of a medieval fortress.

The fact that these upheavals are so rare is a measure of the success of Territorial Signals as a system of dispute prevention. It is sometimes cynically stated that 'all property is theft', but in reality it is the opposite. Property, as owned space which is *displayed* as owned space, is a special kind of sharing system which reduces fighting much more than it causes it. Man is a co-operative species, but he is also competitive, and his struggle for dominance has to be structured in some way if chaos is to be avoided. The establishment of territorial rights is one such structure. It limits dominance geographically. I am dominant in my territory and you are dominant in yours. In other words, dominance is shared out spatially, and we all have some. Even if I am weak and unintelligent and you can dominate me when we meet on neutral ground, I can still enjoy a throughly dominant role as soon as I retreat to my private base. Be it ever so humble, there is no place like a home territory.

Of course, I can still be intimidated by a particularly dominant individual

Where building economy has created impersonal uniformity, the individual strikes back with personal colour-schemes in a brave attempt to re-create a distinctive territorial identity.

The tribal territory of modern times. Liverpool football supporters in full display advertising their ownership of a large section of the grandstand and presenting a scene as vivid and spectacular as any native war-dance or magic ceremonial. Each football display of this kind serves to strengthen group identity, heighten group loyalty and transmit the group image to rival supporters.

who enters my home base, but his encroachment will be dangerous for him and he will think twice about it, because he will know that here my urge to resist will be dramatically magnified and my usual subservience banished. Insulted at the heart of my own territory, I may easily explode into battle — either symbolic or real — with a result that may be damaging to both of us.

In order for this to work, each territory has to be plainly advertised as such. Just as a dog cocks its leg to deposit its personal scent on the trees in its locality, so the human animal cocks its leg symbolically all over his home base. But because we are predominantly visual animals we employ mostly visual signals, and it is worth asking how we do this at the three levels: tribal, family and personal.

First: the Tribal Territory. We evolved as tribal animals, living in comparatively small groups, probably of less than a hundred, and we existed like that for millions of years. It is our basic social unit, a group in which everyone knows everyone else. Essentially, the tribal territory consisted of a home base surrounded by extended hunting grounds. Any neighbouring tribe intruding on our social space would be repelled and driven away. As these early tribes swelled into agricultural super-tribes, and eventually into industrial nations, their territorial defence systems became increasingly elaborate. The tiny, ancient home base of the hunting tribe became the great capital city, the primitive war-paint became the flags, emblems, uniforms and regalia of the specialized military, and the war-chants became national anthems, marching songs and bugle calls. Territorial boundary-lines hardened into fixed borders, often conspicuously patrolled and punctuated with defensive structures — forts and lookout posts, checkpoints and great walls, and, today, customs barriers.

Today each nation flies its own flag, a symbolic embodiment of its territorial status. But patriotism is not enough. The ancient tribal hunter lurking inside each citizen finds himself unsatisfied by membership of such a vast conglomeration of individuals, most of whom are totally unknown to him personally. He does his best to feel that he shares a common territorial defence with them all, but the scale of the operation has become inhuman. It

When the human family ventures from its nest it frequently re-establishes a temporary territory, as in this beach scene. Each base is marked out with personal belongings that protect the 'owned space', even in the absence of its owners.

Personal space—the invisible territorial 'bubble' that surrounds each human body—demonstrated here by the spacing between individuals in a queue. To invade this mobile personal territory is to threaten its occupier and create immediate tension.

is hard to feel a sense of belonging with a tribe of fifty million or more. His answer is to form sub-groups, nearer to his ancient pattern, smaller and more personally known to him—the local club, the teenage gang, the union, the specialist society, the sports association, the political party, the college fraternity, the social clique, the protest group, and the rest. Rare indeed is the individual who does not belong to at least one of these splinter groups, and take from it a sense of tribal allegiance and brotherhood. Typical of all these groups is the development of Territorial Signals—badges, costumes, headquarters, banners, slogans, and all the other displays of group identity. This is where the action is, in terms of tribal territorialism, and only when a major war breaks out does the emphasis shift upwards to the higher group level of the nation.

Each of these modern pseudo-tribes sets up its own special kind of home base. In extreme cases non-members are totally excluded, in others they are allowed in as visitors with limited rights and under a control system of special rules. In many ways they are like miniature nations, with their own flags and emblems and their own border guards. The exclusive club has its own 'customs barrier': the doorman who checks your 'passport' (your membership card) and prevents strangers from passing in unchallenged. There is a government: the club committee; and often special displays of the

tribal elders: the photographs or portraits of previous officials on the walls. At the heart of the specialized territories there is a powerful feeling of security and importance, a sense of shared defence against the outside world. Much of the club chatter, both serious and joking, directs itself against the rottenness of everything outside the club boundaries—in that 'other world' beyond the protected portals.

In social organizations which embody a strong class system, such as military units and large business concerns, there are many territorial rules, often unspoken, which interfere with the official hierarchy. High-status individuals, such as officers or managers, could in theory enter any of the regions occupied by the lower levels in the peck order, but they limit this power in a striking way. An officer seldom enters a sergeant's mess or a barrack room unless it is for a formal inspection. He respects those regions as alien territories even though he has the power to go there by virtue of his dominant role. And in businesses, part of the appeal of unions, over and above their obvious functions, is that with their officials, headquarters and meetings they add a sense of territorial power for the staff workers. It is almost as if each military organization and business concern consists of two warring tribes: the officers versus the other ranks, and the management versus the workers. Each has its special home base within the system, and the territorial defence pattern thrusts itself into what, on the surface, is a pure social hierarchy. Negotiations between managements and unions are tribal battles fought out over the neutral ground of a boardroom table, and are as much concerned with territorial display as they are with resolving problems of wages and conditions. Indeed, if one side gives in too quickly and accepts the other's demands, the victors feel strangely cheated and deeply suspicious that it may be a trick. What they are missing is the protracted sequence of ritual and counter-ritual that keeps alive their group territorial identity.

Likewise, many of the hostile displays of sports fans and teenage gangs are primarily concerned with displaying their group image to rival fan-clubs and gangs. Except in rare cases, they do not attack one another's headquarters, drive out the occupants, and reduce them to a submissive, subordinate condition. It is enough to have scuffles on the borderlands between the two rival territories. This is particularly clear at football matches, where the fan-club headquarters becomes temporarily shifted from the club-house to a section of the stands, and where minor fighting breaks out at the unofficial boundary line between the massed groups of rival supporters. Newspaper reports play up the few accidents and injuries which do occur on such occasions, but when these are studied in relation to the total numbers of displaying fans involved it is clear that the serious incidents represent only a tiny fraction of the overall group behaviour. For every actual punch or kick there are a thousand war-cries, war-dances, chants and gestures.

Second: the Family Territory. Essentially, the family is a breeding unit and the family territory is a breeding ground. At the centre of this space, there is the nest—the bedroom—where, tucked up in bed, we feel at our most territorially secure. In a typical house the bedroom is upstairs, where a safe nest should be. This puts it farther away from the entrance hall, the area where contact is made, intermittently, with the outside world. The less private reception rooms, where intruders are allowed access, are the next line of defence. Beyond them, outside the walls of the building, there is often a symbolic remnant of the ancient feeding grounds—a garden. Its symbolism often extends to the plants and animals it contains, which cease to be nutritional and become merely decorative—flowers and pets. But like a true territorial space it has a conspicuously displayed boundary-line, the garden fence, wall, or railings. Often no more than a token barrier, this is the outer territorial demarcation, separating the private world of the family from the public world beyond. To cross it puts any visitor or intruder at an immediate disadvantage. As he crosses the threshold, his dominance wanes, slightly but unmistakably. He is entering an area where he senses that he must ask permission to do simple things that he would consider a right elsewhere. Without lifting a finger, the territorial owners exert their dominance. This is done by all the hundreds of small ownership 'markers' they have deposited on their family territory: the ornaments, the 'possessed' objects positioned in the rooms and on the walls; the furnishings, the furniture, the colours, the patterns, all owner-chosen and all making this particular home base unique to them.

It is one of the tragedies of modern architecture that there has been a standardization of these vital territorial living-units. One of the most important aspects of a home is that it should be similar to other homes only in a general way, and that in detail it should have many differences, making it a *particular* home. Unfortunately, it is cheaper to build a row of houses, or a block of flats, so that all the family living-units are identical, but the territorial urge rebels against this trend and house-owners struggle as best they can to make their mark on their mass-produced properties. They do this with garden-design, with front-door colours, with curtain patterns, with wallpaper and all the other decorative elements that together create a unique and different family environment. Only when they have completed this nest-building do they feel truly 'at home' and secure.

When they venture forth as a family unit they repeat the process in a minor way. On a day-trip to the seaside, they load the car with personal belongings and it becomes their temporary, portable territory. Arriving at the beach they stake out a small territorial claim, marking it with rugs, towels, baskets and other belongings to which they can return from their seaboard wanderings. Even if they all leave it at once to bathe, it retains a characteristic territorial quality and other family groups arriving will recognize this by setting up their own 'home' bases at a respectful distance. Only when the whole beach has filled up with these marked spaces will newcomers start to position themselves in such a way that the inter-base distance becomes reduced. Forced to pitch between several existing beach territories they will feel a momentary sensation of intrusion, and the established 'owners' will feel a similar sensation of invasion, even though they are not being directly inconvenienced.

The same territorial scene is being played out in parks and fields and on riverbanks, wherever family groups gather in their clustered units. But if rivalry for spaces creates mild feelings of hostility, it is true to say that, without the territorial system of sharing and space-limited dominance, there would be chaotic disorder.

Third: the Personal Space. If a man enters a waiting-room and sits at one end of a long row of empty chairs, it is possible to predict where the next man to enter will seat himself. He will not sit next to the first man, nor will he sit at the far end, right away from him. He will choose a position about halfway between these two points. The next man to enter will take the largest gap left, and sit roughly in the middle of that, and so on, until eventually the latest newcomer will be forced to select a seat that places him right next to one of the already seated men. Similar patterns can be observed in cinemas, public urinals, aeroplanes, trains and buses. This is a reflection of the fact that we all carry with us, everywhere we go, a portable territory called a Personal Space. If people move inside this space, we feel threatened. If they keep too far outside it, we feel rejected. The result is a subtle series of spatial adjustments, usually operating quite unconsciously and producing ideal compromises as far as this is possible. If a situation becomes too crowded, then we adjust our reactions accordingly and allow our personal space to shrink. Jammed into an elevator, a rush-hour compartment, or a packed room, we give up altogether and allow body-to-body contact, but when we relinquish our Personal Space in this way, we adopt certain special techniques. In essence, what we do is to convert these other bodies into 'nonpersons'. We studiously ignore them, and they us. We try not to face them if we can possibly avoid it. We wipe all expressiveness from our faces, letting them go blank. We may

The blinkers posture of the individual who displays his need for a private territory in a public place. His arms form a territorial barrier—a clear warning to others against social trespass.

Thrown together in a confined space, humans defend their territorial identity by studiously ignoring their companions and converting them into non-persons. Eye contact is avoided and faces become devoid of all expression.

look up at the ceiling or down at the floor, and we reduce body movements to a minimum. Packed together like sardines in a tin, we stand dumbly still, sending out as few social signals as possible.

Even if the crowding is less severe, we still tend to cut down our social interactions in the presence of large numbers. Careful observations of children in play groups revealed that if they are high density groupings there is less social interaction between the individual children, even though there is theoretically more opportunity for such contacts. At the same time, the high-density groups show a higher frequency of aggressive and destructive behaviour patterns in their play. Personal Space—'elbow room'—is a vital commodity for the human animal, and one that cannot be ignored without risking serious trouble.

Of course, we all enjoy the excitement of being in a crowd, and this reaction cannot be ignored. But there are crowds and crowds. It is pleasant enough to be in a 'spectator crowd', but not so appealing to find yourself in the middle of a rush-hour crush. The difference between the two is that the spectator crowd is all facing in the same direction and concentrating on a distant point of interest. Attending a theatre, there are twinges of rising hostility towards the stranger who sits down immediately in front of you or the one who squeezes into the seat next to you. The shared armrest can become a polite, but distinct, territorial boundary-dispute region. However, as soon as the show begins, these invasions of Personal Space are forgotten and the attention is focused beyond the small space where the crowding is taking place. Now, each member of the audience feels himself spatially related, not to his cramped neighbours, but to the actor on the stage, and this distance is, if anything, too great. In the rush-hour crowd, by contrast, each member of the pushing throng is competing with his neighbours all the time. There is no escape to a spatial relation with a distant actor, only the pushing, shoving bodies all around.

Those of us who have to spend a great deal of time in crowded conditions become gradually better able to adjust, but no one can ever become completely immune to invasions of Personal Space. This is because they remain forever associated with either powerful hostile or equally powerful loving feelings. All through our childhood we will have been held to be loved and held to be hurt, and anyone who invades our Personal Space when we are adults is, in effect, threatening to extend his behaviour into one of these two highly charged areas of human interaction. Even if his motives are clearly neither hostile nor sexual, we still find it hard to suppress our reactions to his close approach. Unfortunately, different countries have different ideas about exactly how close is close. It is easy enough to test your own 'space reaction': when you are talking to someone in the street or in any open space, reach out with your arm and see where the nearest point on his body comes. If you hail from western Europe, you will find that he is at roughly fingertip distance from you. In other words, as you reach out, your fingertips will just about make contact with his shoulder. If you come from eastern Europe you will find you are standing at 'wrist distance'. If you come from the Mediterranean region you will find that you are much closer to your companion, at little more than 'elbow distance'.

Trouble begins when a member of one of these cultures meets and talks to one from another. Say a British diplomat meets an Italian or an Arab diplomat at an embassy function. They start talking in a friendly way, but soon the fingertips man begins to feel uneasy. Without knowing quite why, he starts to back away gently from his companion. The companion edges forward again. Each tries in this way to set up a Personal Space relationship that suits his own background. But it is impossible to do. Every time the Mediterranean diplomat advances to a distance that feels comfortable for him, the British diplomat feels threatened. Every time the Briton moves back, the other feels rejected. Attempts to adjust this situation often lead to a talking pair shifting slowly across a room, and many an embassy reception

Experiments with library territories revealed that reading material left in a particular place successfully reserved that space for an average of 77 minutes. A jacket on the back of an empty chair extended the period of territorial defence to over two hours.

is dotted with western-European fingertip-distance men pinned against the walls by eager elbow-distance men. Until such differences are fully understood, and allowances made, these minor differences in 'body territories' will continue to act as an alienation factor which may interfere in a subtle way with diplomatic harmony and other forms of international transaction.

If there are distance problems when engaged in conversation, then there are clearly going to be even bigger difficulties where people must work privately in a shared space. Close proximity of others, pressing against the invisible boundaries of our personal body-territory, makes it difficult to concentrate on non-social matters. Flatmates, students sharing a study, sailors in the cramped quarters of a ship, and office staff in crowded work-places, all have to face this problem. They solve it by 'cocooning'. They use a variety of devices to shut themselves off from the others present. The best possible cocoon, of course, is a small private room—a den, a private office, a study or a studio—which physically obscures the presence of other nearby territory-owners. This is the ideal situation for non-social work, but the space-sharers cannot enjoy this luxury. Their cocooning must be symbolic. They may, in certain cases, be able to erect small physical barriers, such as screens and partitions, which give substance to their invisible Personal Space boundaries, but when this cannot be done, other means must be sought. One of these is the 'favoured object'. Each space-sharer develops a preference, repeatedly expressed until it becomes a fixed pattern, for a particular chair, or table, or alcove. Others come to respect this, and friction is reduced. This system is often formally arranged (this is my desk, that is yours), but even where it is not, favoured places soon develop. Professor Smith has a favourite chair in the library. It is not formally his, but he always uses it and others avoid it. Seats around a mess-room table, or a boardroom table, become almost personal property for specific individuals. Even in the home, father has his favourite chair for reading the newspaper or watching television. Another device is the blinkers-posture. Just as a horse that over-reacts to other horses and the distractions of the noisy race-course is given a pair of blinkers to shield its eyes, so people studying privately in a public place put on pseudo-blinkers in the form of shielding hands. Resting their elbows on the table, they sit with their hands screening their eyes from the scene on either side.

A third method of reinforcing the body-territory is to use personal markers. Books, papers and other personal belongings are scattered around the favoured site to render it more privately owned in the eyes of companions. Spreading out one's belongings is a well-known trick in public-transport situations, where a traveller tries to give the impression that seats next to him are taken. In many contexts carefully arranged personal markers can act as an effective territorial display, even in the absence of the territory owner. Experiments in a library revealed that placing a pile of magazines on the table in one seating position successfully reserved that place for an average of 77 minutes. If a sports-jacket was added, draped over the chair, then the 'reservation effect' lasted for over two hours.

In these ways, we strengthen the defences of our Personal Spaces, keeping out intruders with the minimum of open hostility. As with all territorial behaviour, the object is to defend space with signals rather than with fists and at all three levels—the tribal, the family and the personal—it is a remarkably efficient system of space-sharing. It does not always seem so, because newspapers and newscasts inevitably magnify the exceptions and dwell on those cases where the signals have failed and wars have broken out, gangs have fought, neighbouring families have feuded, or colleagues have clashed, but for every territorial signal that has failed, there are millions of others that have not. They do not rate a mention in the news, but they nevertheless constitute a dominant feature of human society—the society of a remarkably territorial animal.

BARRIER SIGNALS

Body-defence actions in social situations

People feel safer behind some kind of physical barrier. If a social situation is in any way threatening, then there is an immediate urge to set up such a barricade. For a tiny child faced with a stranger, the problem is usually solved by hiding behind its mother's body and peeping out at the intruder to see what he or she will do next. If the mother's body is not available, then a chair or some other piece of solid furniture will do. If the stranger insists on coming closer, then the peeping face must be hidden too. If the insensitive intruder continues to approach despite these obvious signals of fear, then there is nothing for it but to scream or flee.

This pattern is gradually reduced as the child matures. In teenage girls it may still be detected in the giggling cover-up of the face, with hands or papers, when acutely or jokingly embarrassed. But by the time we are adult, the childhood hiding, which dwindled to adolescent shyness, is expected to disappear altogether, as we bravely stride out to meet our guests, hosts, companions, relatives, colleagues, customers, clients, or friends. Each social occasion involves us, once again, in encounters similar to the ones which made us hide as scared infants and, as then, each encounter is slightly threatening. In other words, the fears are still there, but their expression is blocked. Our adult roles demand control and suppression of any primitive urge to withdraw and hide ourselves away. The more formal the occasion and the more dominant or unfamiliar our social companions, the more worrying the moment of encounter becomes. Watching people under these conditions, it is possible to observe the many small ways in which they continue to 'hide behind their mother's skirts'. The actions are still there, but they are transformed into less obvious movements and postures. It is these that are the Barrier Signals of adult life.

The most popular form of Barrier Signal is the Body-cross. In this, the

The Body-cross—a temporary barrier formed at moments of tension. When individuals feel exposed or threatened they often form a barrier across the front of the body by making contact with themselves, arm-to-arm. This may be done with a simple armfold (above) or may be disguised as a small grooming action, such as (below) a cufflink adjustment, handbag attention or bracelet checking. This need is felt even by experienced public figures, especially as they cross a threshold on a formal occasion.

hands or arms are brought into contact with one another in front of the body, forming a temporary 'bar' across the trunk, rather like a bumper or fender on the front of a motor-car. This is not done as a physical act of fending off the other person, as when raising a forearm horizontally across the front of the body to push through a struggling crowd. It is done, usually at quite a distance, as a nervous guest approaches a dominant host. The action is performed unconsciously and, if tackled on the subject immediately afterwards, the guest will not be able to remember having made the gesture. It is always camouflaged in some way, because if it were performed as a primitive fending-off or covering-up action, it would obviously be too transparent. The disguise it wears varies from person to person. Here are some examples:

The special guest on a gala occasion is alighting from his official limousine. Before he can meet and shake hands with the reception committee, he has to walk alone across the open space in front of the main entrance to the building where the function is being held. A large crowd has come to watch his arrival and the press cameras are flashing. Even for the most experienced of celebrities this is a slightly nervous moment, and the mild fear that is felt expresses itself just as he is halfway across the 'greeting-space'. As he walks forward, his right hand reaches across his body and makes a last-minute adjustment to his left cuff-link. It pauses there momentarily as he takes a few more steps, and then, at last, he is close enough to reach out his hand for the first of the many hand-shakes.

On a similar occasion, the special guest is a female. At just the point where her male counterpart would have fiddled with his cuff, she reaches across her body with her right hand and slightly shifts the position of her handbag, which is hanging from her left forearm.

There are other variations on this theme. A male may finger a button or the strap of a wristwatch instead of his cuff. A female may smooth out an imaginary crease in a sleeve, or re-position a scarf or coat held over her left arm. But in all cases there is one essential feature: at the peak moment of

Girls wearing skimpy costumes that expose their thighs frequently perform a special Barrier Signal that protects their genital region. This takes the form of clamped arms thrust down between their thighs or knees.

nervousness there is a Body-cross, in which one arm makes contact with the other across the front of the body, constructing a fleeting barrier between the guest and the reception committee.

Sometimes the barrier is incomplete. One arm swings across but does not actually make contact with the other. Instead it deals with some trivial clothing-adjustment task on the opposite side of the body. With even heavier camouflage, the hand comes up and across, but goes no further than the far side of the head or face, with a mild stroking or touching action.

Less disguised forms of the Body-cross are seen with less experienced individuals. The man entering the restaurant, as he walks across an open space, rubs his hands together, as if washing them. Or he advances with them clasped firmly in front of him.

Such are the Barrier Signals of the greeting situation, where one person is advancing on another. Interestingly, field observations reveal that it is most unlikely that both the greeter *and* the greeted will perform such actions. Regardless of status, it is nearly always the new arrival who makes the body-cross movement, because it is he who is invading the home territory of the greeters. They are on their own ground or, even if they are not, they were there first and have at least temporary territorial 'rights' over the place. This gives them an indisputable dominance at the moment of the greeting. Only if they are extremely subordinate to the new arrival, and perhaps in serious trouble with him, will there be a likelihood of them taking the 'body-cross role'. And if they do, this will mean that the new arrival on the scene will omit it as he enters.

These observations tell us something about the secret language of Barrier Signals, and indicate that, although the sending and receiving of the signals are both unconsciously done, the message gets across, none the less. The message says: 'I am nervous but I will not retreat'; and this makes it into an act of subordination which automatically makes the other person feel slightly more dominant and more comfortable.

The situation is different after greetings are over and people are standing about talking to one another. Now, if one man edges too close to another, perhaps to hear better in all the noise of chattering voices, the boxed-in companion may feel the same sort of threatening sensation that the arriving celebrity felt as he walked towards the reception committee. What is needed now, however, is something more long-lasting than a mere cuff-fumble. It is simply not possible to go on fiddling with a button for as long as this companion is going to thrust himself forward. So a more composed posture is needed. The favourite Body-cross employed in this situation is the arm-fold, in which the left and right arms intertwine themselves across the front of the chest. This posture, a perfect, frontal Barrier Signal, can be held for a very long time without appearing strange. Unconsciously it transmits a 'come-no-farther' message and is used a great deal at crowded gatherings. It has also been used by poster artists as a deliberate 'They-shall-not-pass!' gesture, and is rather formally employed by bodyguards when standing outside a protected doorway.

The same device of arm-folding can be used in a sitting relationship where the companion is approaching too close, and it can be amplified by a crossing of the legs *away* from the companion. Another variant is to press the tightly clasped hands down on to the crotch and squeeze them there between the legs, as if protecting the genitals. The message of this particular form of barrier is clear enough, even though neither side becomes consciously aware of it. But perhaps the major Barrier Signal for the seated person is that ubiquitous device, the desk. Many a businessman would feel naked without one and hides behind it gratefully every day, wearing it like a vast, wooden chastity-belt. Sitting beyond it he feels fully protected from the visitor exposed on the far side. It is the supreme barrier, both physical and psychological, giving him an immediate and lasting comfort while he remains in its solid embrace.

The Barrier Signal of the seated man is the crossing of the legs *away* from the companion (below left). If a desk or table is available this is unnecessary — the huge wooden barrier exceeds anything the body itself can provide. Many a businessman would feel naked without his desk barrier to defend him against the world beyond it.

PROTECTIVE BEHAVIOUR

Reactions to danger—both real and imaginary

Like any other species, the human animal tries to protect itself when danger threatens. The human body is extremely vulnerable to damage and lacks almost any kind of natural 'armour'. The nearest approach we have to this is the hard, bony casing around the brain, and the five bony projections—the eyebrow ridges, the cheek bones and the bridge of the nose—which surround the eyes. These help to lessen the damage done by blows to the head and increase the chances that we will be able to think and see clearly following a physical attack.

Supporting this bony defence system are a number of protective actions which appear to be common to all human beings. From the age of four months onwards, every healthy human being displays a characteristic 'startle pattern' when sudden danger appears to be imminent. This is a split-second response and the usual way of demonstrating it is to fire off a gun unexpectedly immediately behind someone who is having his photograph taken. By clicking the camera at the same moment, it is possible to record on film the startle posture of our species. It is always the same: there is a closing of the eyes, a widening of the mouth, a thrusting forward of the head and neck, a raising and bringing forward of the shoulders, a bending of the arms, a clenching of the fists, a forward movement of the trunk, a contraction of the abdomen, and a slight bending at the knees.

This protective pattern is clearly the first stage of a defensive crouching action, with the body starting to make itself smaller and more compact, tensing against an expected blow, and with the eyes given instantaneous protection and the shoulders and arms preparing to protect the head.

An extension of the startle pattern can be seen in any riot situation, or where hard objects are flying through the air. The head is further lowered and the arms are brought up swiftly to protect the face. Even in the formalized situation of the boxing ring, a similar posture is adopted by a defensive fighter, who also gives his head priority when protecting himself against heavy blows.

In another specialized context, the priorities change. Association footballers, forming a wall to block their goal-mouth against a free kick, line

The basic protective response, when time permits, is to hide the body from attack. In this classic war-time photograph (below left) English children, crouching in a trench, take shelter from an air-raid.

When it is impossible to hide from a physical attack, the typical response is to shield the face and head and curl up the body, as demonstrated here by a protestor in Amsterdam (below), and by a fallen jockey on the race-track (below right).

up facing the kicker and are liable to be struck by a ball moving at very high speed. Instead of covering their faces, they now clamp their hands together in front of their genitals. Since, in this case, they can watch the direction the missile takes, and can quickly lower their faces to head the ball away if it flies high, they switch their defensive hand position to an area that is less easy to protect by a sudden body movement. It would take fractionally longer to twist the trunk to one side than it would to lower the head, so that the crotch region, in this particular case, becomes the most vulnerable area. Nevertheless, photographs taken at the moment of the kick reveal that, apart from the changed hand position, the typical startle pattern appears as before, with the shoulders hunching slightly and the tense facial expression. Despite their expert heading abilities the footballers still revert, for a split second, to the classic protective response.

At moments of savage physical attack the victim usually remains silent, but in associated moments of fleeing, panic or temporary respite, another protective response often occurs — the scream. This is an alarm cry which we share not only with apes and monkeys but also with many other species of mammals. As a signal alerting others either to come to the rescue or to protect themselves, it is perhaps the most non-specific in the animal world. It is so uncharacteristic of any one species that we ourselves can recognize its meaning, regardless of the animal that is producing it. It varies from case to case, of course, sometimes sounding more like a squeal and sometimes more like a shriek, but there is no confusing its message of pain and fear. In the human species there appears to be a sex difference not only in the pitch of the screaming, but also in the frequency of its use. Adult males employ the scream when in great pain, but they are less likely to use it in moments of panic and fear. Children and adult females use it in both situations. This difference is underlined by a visit to a large fairground where there are Big Dippers, Giant Wheels and Ghost Trains. Here, the high-pitched screams of females enjoying the 'safe' panic of these rides rends the air repeatedly, but the slightly deeper male screams are absent.

If people are asked to express their most intense fears, and to name those things that cause them most dread and horror, their answers are curiously unrealistic in relation to the modern world in which they live. Instead of listing the true killers of today — the fast car, the explosive weapon, the bullet and the knife, the poisons of pollution and the stresses of urban crowding —

Below right: British footballers lining up to face a free kick protect their genitals rather than their faces. Female footballers in the same context protect their breast region.

Screaming girls on a fairground ride. The female scream is more common in this context than the male scream, which seems to be more confined to moments of great pain, rather than panic.

they tend to dwell on ancient terrors such as slithering, creeping, crawling animals, pests and insects, thunder and lightning, enclosed spaces and great heights. This does not mean that they are unafraid of the modern dangers of civilization, but rather that when asked about their fears, they ignore the obvious and search into the backs of their minds for lurking remnants of inexplicable panic, unease or disgust. What they find is the stuff that horror films are made of—images that, despite their rarity as serious threats in a modern community, persist in haunting the human brain.

The greatest fear by far is that of snakes. This applies not only in countries where there really are dangerous reptiles, but also in places like Britain where, if you spent a year travelling around the countryside, your chances of being killed by a snake would be roughly 500 million to one. In the United States, with its deadly rattlers, your chances would still be about six million to one. Yet even in these countries it is always the snake that comes out on top of the list of private fears. And it does not win the hate race by a short head, but by a long, long neck. Nothing can touch it when it comes to giving people the horrors. Indeed the reaction is so strong that, in Britain, no fewer than 19 per cent of television viewers admitted that they had either to turn off their sets or look away from the screen whenever a snake appeared in a programme.

As a protective response, this avoidance of snakes obviously had a great advantage for our early ancestors, when they came down out of the trees and on to the plains. The advantage would have remained during the several million years while modern man was evolving, and snake hatred would, indeed, be a vital element in the early human success story. But its survival in such an intense form in modern communities seems to indicate that it was not only vital, but went so far as to become an inborn property of the human species. There is no proof of this, but the evidence is strongly suggestive.

The human infant shows no fear of snakes at the age of two, but by three there is some caution and by four a strong fear is already present. This reaches a peak at the age of six and then starts to decline gradually as the child grows from four to fourteen. There is little difference between the sexes, although girls do have a slightly stronger reaction than boys at all ages. And

The strongest animal fear of the human species is of snakes. This applies even in countries where there is more chance of being killed by lightning than by a venomous reptile. Below: a chart showing that snake hatred among British children reaches a peak at the age of six and then begins to decline in both sexes. Puberty seems to have no influence on this response, despite Freudian theories of phallic symbolism. Figures based on information from 11,960 children. (After Morris and Morris).

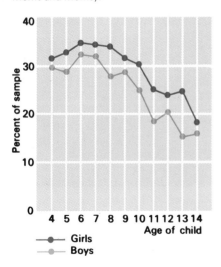

there is no marked change in reaction at puberty. The Freudian explanation of the snake as a phallic symbol does not fit this picture, but something else does. The curve of snake-fear matches very well the child-at-risk situation in a primitive community. The very young child will be more carefully guarded by its mother. The older child will be more able to look after itself. But the intermediate child, the one who even today still shows the strongest fear of snakes, will be the one most likely to wander off and find himself at the greatest risk.

Other strong animal hatreds include spiders and rats, and any small, crawling pests that invade the home. Small creatures actually making contact with the skin provoke an immediate and characteristic protective response in the form of a rapid flicking action of the hand, almost as automatic as the swishing of an ungulate's tail when ridding itself of flies. The reaction is so strong, and in some people so uncontrollable, that it constitutes a serious hazard for drivers, when a wasp or a bee invades a moving vehicle. Even when they have been taught that such insects will not sting unless angered by attacks, they often still find it impossible to restrain their responses, and with their wild swipings to avoid a small sting endanger their very lives in a possible collision or crash. Again, this appears to be a reaction we have inherited from our early ancestors and which we find hard to shed, despite our more sophisticated knowledge of insect life.

It is difficult to be certain which of our present-day reactions can be traced back to our primeval fear of our ancient predators—the large animals that must have once stalked our tribal ancestors. Lions, tigers and crocodiles rate moderately high in the lists of most hated animals by children, but they never approach the intense feelings aroused by snakes and spiders. Perhaps this is because they were more obvious enemies and could be dealt with in a different way. The poisonous snakes and poisonous spiders, creeping into the tribal settlements or appearing suddenly in the grass, were the ones most likely to produce the sudden shudder and the panic, protective reaction, which still lurks today in the mind of modern man.

A form of protective response unique to man is superstition. While he was busy improving the technology of realistic, down-to-earth body-protection, from shields to bullet-proof vests and from suits of armour to fall-out shelters, he was also perpetually occupied with the business of inventing curious, magical acts of self-defence. These superstitious practices appear in every epoch and in every culture. They are so numerous and so varied that whole encyclopedias have been compiled to list them. They are almost all totally meaningless and futile, except in one basic respect; namely, that they make the performers of the actions feel a little less insecure in a hostile and mysterious world. It is unnecessary to catalogue them here. They all consist of some activity which, if performed, is supposed to prevent bad luck in the future. The fact that there is never any logical connection between the act and the outcome does nothing to deter the superstitious. They continue to protect themselves by cautiously performing the acts, 'just in case'. It is easy to start them off. If you tell people that by throwing a coin into a fountain they will have good luck, or that by blowing out all the candles on a birthday cake they will make a silent wish come true, they will be happy to do this. Even if it does not work, it provides an attractive shared procedure which enhances the structure of a social occasion.

The surprising feature of superstitious practices is that they show a remarkably good survival rate, even among the most logical, hard-headed, practical and unromantic of modern urbanites. Almost everywhere there is some small protective pattern surviving today: it may be 'keeping-your-fingers-crossed' for someone (an early Christian act of making the Holy Cross), or 'touching wood' following a boast (touching the sacred oak to placate the god Thor) or saying 'bless you' when someone sneezes (because part of their spirit might be lost in the sudden exhalation), or touching iron for good luck (because iron was once thought to be a magical metal with supernatural powers). There are many such practices to be found as one moves about the modern world of sophisticated civilizations. Each region has one or two favourites and, nearly always, the people using the actions are unaware of their original meanings. They do them with a laugh, saying how stupid it is, but they still do them.

One special category of Protective Behaviour is the wearing of an amulet, talisman, charm or mascot. There are literally hundreds of different 'lucky symbols' that have been carried or worn by people in different countries over the centuries—and, again, the practice is still alive almost everywhere, despite the scientific age in which we live. As before, people smile and admit that it is all 'a lot of nonsense', but they still do it.

One particular type of amulet that is of interest to the man-watcher is the 'frozen gesture'. This is a good luck charm in the shape of a hand which is making a particular sign. By wearing this, the owner of the amulet is, so to speak, making the protective gesture *all the time*. Instead of performing the hand action at the moment when good luck is needed to ward off some ill, the carved hand amulet goes on making it forever and therefore supposedly provides permanent protection. There are at least ten different examples of these frozen gestures on sale in Europe today, if one travels far enough across the continent. They provide their protection in several different ways. Some are simply cheerful, optimistic gestures, such as the V-for-victory sign, the thumbs-up sign, or the circular OK sign. Others, such as the horned hand, or the Greek *moutza* gesture, are directly threatening towards an imagined 'evil'. Then there is a special category that attempts to deflect the 'evil eye'. The basis of the belief in the evil eye is that certain people have a glance that can bring bad luck. As a protection against this, one must either avoid their stare or, alternatively, make their stare avoid you. If you can stop them looking into your eyes you are safe, and so gestures are worn as amulets which are so audacious that they will catch the eye of the 'evil one'. By wearing an obscene gesture such as the fig sign, it is possible to divert the attention of the evil eye, which will be inescapably drawn to the obscenity and will not therefore look straight in to your own eyes. Alternatively, you can wear an amulet of an eye itself, and this will out-stare the evil eye.

Superstitions survive as protective devices, even among the most level-headed and logical of individuals. The thumbs-up sign for good luck is still employed with high frequency in modern times.

The protective 'horned hand' or 'cornuta' gesture is found today over a wide region. In Italy (above) it may be hung in a shop window as a stuffed glove, to ward off evil, or, in Malta (right), be painted on the stempost of a water-taxi.

Far right: a Maltese fishing boat carrying protective eyes to out-stare the 'evil eye' a tradition stretching back to the days of ancient Egypt and still treated seriously in many areas of the Mediterranean.

Belief in the evil eye is still strong in countries around the Mediterranean, where even sophisticated people may take it quite seriously. It usually begins with a simple coincidence. A man visits a house and shortly after he leaves there is a death in the family, or among the animals owned by them, or some other disaster befalls them. They begin to think that perhaps he has the evil eye. If he calls again at a later date and once more there is a tragedy or a disaster, then the thought becomes a certainty, and the family will go to great lengths to avoid the person should he return a third time. If they do have to face him they will take special precautions with amulets and other good-luck charms. Fishermen in certain countries protect their boats against any possible damage from an evil eye by fixing a pair of artificial eyes to the prows of their vessels, so that they will always be ready to out-stare the enemy. This practice, which began in the days of ancient Egypt, is still active in many areas. In other regions, houses are protected from evil by placing a pair of horns on the roof—the horned gesture raised in permanent defiance against unknown enemies.

These protective activities reflect man's obsession with potential dangers and with the anticipation of some kind of unspecified attack. Despite the fact that modern society has instituted specialized protectors in the form of police forces, law courts, insurance companies, commercial safety regulations and the like, which should make us rest easier in our beds, and despite the fact that scientific advances have given us much greater understanding of the world about us and swept away many of the frightening old-wives' tales, we nevertheless retain an animal wariness of the possibility of sudden, inexplicable dangers. And with that wariness we retain a wide variety of Protective Behaviour Patterns.

SUBMISSIVE BEHAVIOUR

How we appease our critics or attackers

The crouched, submissive postures of defeated males taken prisoner during the Six Day War between Israel and Egypt. All human submissive displays involve actions which lower the body and make it appear smaller.

When a man is threatened with attack, he has five alternatives: he can fight, flee, hide, summon aid, or try to appease his assailant. If his attacker is too strong to be challenged, there is nowhere to flee or hide, and no one to come to his aid, then appeasement is the only solution. It is at such moments that Submissive Behaviour occurs.

Passive submission in the human animal is much the same as in other mammals. In extreme cases it takes the form of cringing, crouching, grovelling, whimpering, and attempts to protect the most vulnerable parts of the body. The only uniquely human element added to this display is verbal pleading and begging for mercy.

A cornered human victim driven to these extremes is a pathetic sight, and this is precisely the function of the submissive display, in terms of animal survival. In order for it to succeed, it must present the individual as so incapacitated as to be hardly worth attacking. The display says, as it were: 'This is the condition you would reduce me to if you attacked me, so why go to the trouble—I am there already.' It presents a picture of 'instant defeat' and thereby avoids the damaging physical process of actually being defeated.

Its success depends on the presentation of signals which are the exact opposite of the threat signals of our species. A threatening man will square up to an opponent, his body tense, his chest expanded, his face glaring, his fists clenched, his voice deep and snarling. By contrast, the submissive individual tries to make his body seem as small and limp as possible, with his shoulders hunched, his face wincing, his hands spread, and his voice high and whining. In this way he can switch off all his attack signals and get the message across, many times over, that he is not to be treated as an opponent.

The most important aspect of submission is making oneself appear small. This is achieved in two ways: by curling up the body and by lowering it in relation to the attacker. Both elements are seen in an extreme form in the groveller who is down on the ground whimpering, with his body in a tight ball, but less dramatic versions can be seen in many a walking figure in the street. The long-term loser, the social failure, and the depressed subordinate walk with a permanent stoop, shoulders rounded and neck hunched forward, their posture a non-stop slump. The body-lowering and curling-up is not acute, it is chronic, just as the conditions of submission are chronic. The slumpers' bosses, their superiors, the restrained tyrants who suppress them, never threaten to attack them physically. There is no sudden, savage show-down with fists flying. The domination is a milder, more prolonged affair and the effect it has is reflected in the milder, more prolonged submissive postures.

The language itself is full of references to symbolic bigness and smallness. We say: 'He is a big man in the business'; 'He makes me feel ten feet tall'; 'He has a big name in his field'; or, 'He is a silly little man'; 'He is small fry'; 'He made me feel so small'. In none of these cases are we referring to actual physical height. In each instance the size is a symbol of dominant or subordinate status.

So ingrained is this idea relating smallness to the underdog that it actually affects chances of success. Recent surveys reveal, for example, that bishops are taller, on average, than clergymen; university presidents are taller than college presidents; and sales managers are taller than salesmen. Furthermore, short men who are intensely ambitious, are notorious for the savagery of their assertiveness when they have struggled to the top, indicating the need to compensate for their small stature. Where a tall man at the top can afford to relax, the short tyrant must remain tense, forever re-establishing his position. Napoleon, at 5 foot 4 inches, is the classic example of this; but such men are exceptions to the rule, and are too rare to influence the overall,

average figures which show that if you wish to get ahead it is best to have a tall head.

If being small, even when erect, creates an inevitable impression of submissiveness, then clearly it is possible to signal a temporary mood of submission by a deliberate act of lowering the body. If a beaten man cowers passively on the floor when he has no other choice, then a dominant man who wishes momentarily to relinquish his dominance can do so by performing a brief, stylized gesture of body-lowering. This is voluntary, or active, Submissive Behaviour—the world of bowing and scraping—and it plays an important role in many social contexts, even today. In earlier times it was much more widespread, but despite the increasingly egalitarian social climate of modern times, it still manages to survive in many corners.

Its mildest form is seen when an eager-to-please subordinate leans his body slightly forward as he talks to a high-status companion. Advertisements of the we-aim-to-please variety often show a salesman with a smiling face and his body tilted towards the reader. He is not performing an action as definite as a bow, but his tilt promises that he might. Salesmen in stores and shops are now often surly and upright, but not so many years ago they were repeatedly beaming and bowing to their valued customers, as they greeted them, ushered them through doorways, and bade them farewell. In some old-fashioned stores, even today, the more elderly staff can still be found carrying on this long-standing tradition.

The full bow today is usually reserved for more formal occasions. The bower's body bends from the waist and the head bends to a slightly lower

The bow—an ancient and widespread form of submissive body-lowering in which the eyes are also lowered and the face hidden from view. The example below comes from Iran. Above: 'Two men meet, each believing the other to be of a higher rank'—an early (1903) etching by the Swiss artist Paul Klee, showing exaggerated bowing in which each man tries to make himself smaller than the other.

The modern curtsey, usually reserved for royalty (top), but sometimes offered to other dominant figures (above), was once performed by both males and females, until males replaced it with the bow. In origin the curtsey is an intention movement of kneeling.

angle than the trunk. The bower aims his display straight at the dominant figure, who may reciprocate with a milder version of the same action. The decay of the bowing ceremony has proceeded at different rates in different cultures. It has survived best in Japan and Germany and worst in the United States. Many Japanese and Germans still bow as part of ordinary social introductions, whereas Americans hardly ever bow, except as an act of mockery. In other cultures, very slight head-bowing occurs in social greetings, but the full bow is retained only for special moments, such as greeting important figures at ceremonial occasions. Only in the theatre and the concert hall has bowing survived at full intensity in virtually all cultures, when the performers traditionally lower their bodies in response to the audience's applause.

In areas where men still wear hats, the removal of the hat, with or without a bow, is another method of reducing the body-height and therefore acts as an additional method of token submission. In earlier centuries the bow was so deep that the doffed hat almost touched the floor. Today the gesture, where it survives, is often no more than a touching of the brim of the hat with the fingers—a token token.

In countries where a royal family still presides, there are opportunities for observations on the different forms that bowing takes in its modern, relic-like condition. Local dignitaries tend to greet royal personages with impressively deep bows from the waist, but those closer to the court behave differently. Presumably because they use the bow much more frequently, they abbreviate it to a head bow only, but in order to demonstrate their obedience to the crown they snap the head down and back with rapid, vigorous movements. It is a bow that at once displays their closeness to the crown and yet their subordination to it.

Females presented to royalty still curtsey as a general rule, but this form of body-lowering has not fared as well as the bow and is extremely rare in other, less formal contexts. The modern curtsey, in which the trunk remains upright but the body is bobbed downwards, has a long and interesting history. The body is lowered by stepping back slightly with one foot and then bending both knees. It is an intention movement of kneeling. The full kneel was common in ancient times, when confronting an overlord, and the kneeler then sank to the ground on both knees before the dominant individual. This changed in medieval days, when it was replaced by the less extreme half-kneel, with only one knee sinking to the ground. Men were then specifically instructed that it was proper only to give the full kneel to God and that rulers, having at last become less than God-like, should not be given such an extreme form of lowering.

By Shakespeare's day the trend had gone further, the half-kneel having already been replaced in most situations by the curtsey. Both women *and* men used the curtsey as a token half-kneel, and at this stage there were only minor differences between the sexes. Both sexes bent the knees and at the same time bowed forward. By the seventeenth century this sexual equality was lost, the men concentrating on the bowing element of the display and omitting the knee-bending, while the women retained the knee-bending and omitted or reduced the bowing element. All that usually survived of the bow in the female display was a slight inclination of the body and a lowering of the eyes. This split between the sexes was to survive permanently, except in the theatre, where actresses now often perform a masculine bow alongside their male colleagues.

The general story of submissive gestures, from ancient to modern times, is therefore one of steadily decreasing servility, with the act of body-lowering becoming less and less extreme. Only God seems to have maintained his ancient status and defied this trend. Worshippers in church still accord him the full-kneel, while rulers, who have fared less well, must make do with minor courtesies. One of the few exceptions to this is the ceremony of dispensing knighthoods, where the monarch is still offered a half-kneel and a

The full kneel (above), reserved today for God, was once also offered to kings. Now royalty must be content with a half-kneel (top), as demonstrated here during a knighthood ceremony (at which a Governor-General represents the Monarch).

lowered head. But even here the kneeling action is abbreviated by the provision of a padded stool for the right knee, which does not therefore have to descend fully to ground-level.

In order to find truly grovelling submissive gestures in formal situations, one has to turn back to very early days. If one goes sufficiently far back, even the full kneel begins to look rather churlish. All-powerful emperors and princes frequently demanded and received full prostration from those who wished to approach them. In ancient kingdoms these humbling acts were performed by slaves to their masters, prisoners to their captors, and servants to their overlords. The body was stretched out, face down, flat on the ground—the most extreme form of lowering, and one that can be exceeded only by an act of burial. Prostration became less frequent with the decline of despotic power but, like the full kneel and the half-kneel, it has managed to survive in a few isolated instances, as in the rite of ordination for Catholic priests.

In the Orient, a semi-prostration was the kowtow, in which the body does not lie down flat on the ground but first gives a full kneel and then bends forward until the forehead touches the ground. This, too, has survived as an attitude of prayer but, like the full kneel, is not seen elsewhere today. The salaam appears to be an abbreviated form of the kowtow, just as a dip of the head is a modern token gesture for the full kneel. In the salaam the hand is pressed first to the chest, then the mouth, then the forehead; and this triple touching is followed by a slight bow of the head. The touches symbolize the pressing of the body on to the ground, and the salaam says, in effect: 'I would touch these parts of my body to the ground for you', with the slight bow indicating the intention of doing so. Today, modern Arabs are just as likely to shake hands, but the salaam has not vanished totally. It has, however, become even further abbreviated, with sometimes no more than a quick touch of the hand to the chest. At other times it becomes no more than a rapid touching of the lips. Like all submissive gestures it is slowly being eroded by modern attitudes and relationships.

A similar fate has befallen that specialized form of contact, the kiss. In ancient times, equals kissed equally—that is, head to head, either on the lips or the cheeks—but inferiors were never allowed such liberties with superiors. The lower the rank of the kisser, the lower his kiss had to be. The lowest rank of all was required to 'kiss the dirt'. In other words, he had to kiss the earth near the feet of the lordly one, not being fit even to kiss his feet. As the status of the kisser rose, so did the target of his kissing. From the feet it progressed upwards to the hem of a garment, to the knee, and finally to the hand. In earlier days bishops, for example, were permitted to kiss the Pope's knee, but lesser mortals had to make do with kissing the cross embroidered on his right shoe.

Kissing the hand, being the least extreme of the submissive kisses, has survived best into the present day. In certain countries it is still commonplace for a man to kiss a lady's hand as a greeting ritual, though even this is vanishing among the younger males as the younger females slowly lose their social superiority in their struggle for commercial equality. The Pope has also lost a point or two on the grovel-scale, and those obtaining a private audience are now permitted to kiss the ring on his hand. When doing this, however, they must descend to the full, two-kneed kneel, a formal courtesy which today the Pope shares only with God.

There is one contradiction in this whole matter of submissive body-lowering that cannot be overlooked. Traditionally, when low-rank meets high-rank, he must lower his body in some way; but if high-rank enters a room where low-rank is sitting, low-rank must *rise*. Rising to greet a visitor is still a widespread courtesy in countries where body-lowering in any situation is rare. The more subordinate a person is, the more unlikely he is to remain seated in the presence of a standing companion. Since the act of rising increases rather than reduces the body height, it seems to go against the general trend of: submissiveness = smallness. The explanation is that there are two different systems operating. The first system says that if two people meet, the subordinate must lower himself, and the second system says that if anyone in a group is going to relax, it must be the dominant. Subordinates are not allowed to relax unless the dominant is already relaxing and invites them to do likewise. Since it is more relaxing to sit than to stand, sitting is a more dominant act than standing. Masters sit and servants stand, attending to their master's needs. But clearly these two systems clash, since to sit is to be lower down, in terms of body posture. This is why, when lowering the body in a servile, submissive way, the appeaser has to adopt quite specific postures—the kneel, the bow, the kowtow, the curtsey—which are unmistakably unrelaxed and non-sitting.

The essential nature of a submissive lowering of the body, therefore, is that it should be uncomfortable or incapacitating. By making himself comfortable, a dominant individual can lower himself on to a cushion without lowering his status. And there is one ancient invention that allows him to have it both ways: the throne. By sitting on a special seat, on a raised platform, he can be dominantly seated while at the same time being dominantly higher than his subordinates. Needless to day, this soon became the favourite posture of monarchs, rulers and despots the world over. So basic is its appeal in terms of status signalling that it has been re-invented in countless cultures, wherever high-rank displays have been called for.

Bearing in mind these general principles of Submissive Behaviour, it should be possible to manipulate a situation deliberately to create a successful appeasement. If, for instance, the driver of a car has been flagged down by a policeman for exceeding the speed limit, he is all too likely to react by sitting in his driving seat, arguing with the policeman, making excuses, and refusing to admit his error. This is what usually happens, but the response is essentially that of an unbeaten rival, and the policeman is forced to retaliate. If the speed limit has definitely been broken, then the policeman is in an indisputably dominant position, and the only hope of appeasing him and avoiding a fine is to adopt a totally submissive role. This requires that the driver should: (1) get out of the car—which is his own personal territory and therefore gives him too much status; (2) approach the policeman before he can approach the car—because the more he is made to go out of his way, the more he is being inconvenienced and therefore made hostile; (3) adopt a limp, slumped posture, leaning forward, with an anxious facial expression—because this will transmit inferiority signals; (4) employ verbal submissive devices, such as total admission of error, based on gross personal stupidity, combined with self-attacking jokes and direct flattery of the policeman—because this will lower the driver's mental status and raise the policeman's mental status.

By adopting all these techniques simultaneously, the driver will make it extremely difficult for the policeman to remain hostile and insist on a fine. He will, despite himself, begin to feel appeased. By abandoning the dominant seated posture in the car, retreating from his territorial stronghold, lowering his body once it is standing, and adding the verbal submissiveness of flattery, jokery and self-criticism, the driver will have stripped himself of all the qualities of an 'opponent' and will find himself almost un-attackable.

The deliberate employment of submissive displays of this kind can work wonders in disputes, not only between drivers and police but also between parents and children, neighbours, friends, lovers and relatives. It is astonishing the way in which hostility evaporates when faced with total submission. There is only one catch: for many people even a contrived display of inferiority, consciously assumed to solve a social problem, can be too unpleasant an experience. For it is difficult to act in a servile way without beginning to feel the inner sensation of servility. It is easy enough to recover quickly from this, but momentarily the process can be a painful one, and many a driver would prefer to snarl and pay the fine.

For many religious groups, the kneel is insufficient. Instead, they resort to an even more extreme form of body-lowering—the kowtow—in which the forehead is brought down to touch the ground. This example comes from Malaysia.

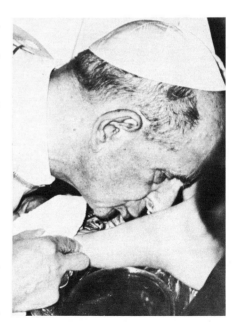

The lower the kiss, the greater the act of submission. The hand-kiss (right) takes the kisser half-way to the ground, but is greatly exceeded in force by the foot-kiss (above), performed here by Pope Paul VI in a symbolic act during Holy Week.

Perhaps the strangest form of submissive behaviour in the entire field of human behaviour is the response of subjects under hypnosis. The hypnotist is said to put someone 'to sleep', but in reality what he does is to trigger off some kind of deep-seated self-subordination mechanism. He achieves this by employing a set of domineering devices, both verbal and visual. There is no such thing as a shy, modest, or hesitant hypnotist. From the very outset he has to be sharp, commanding, forceful and totally in control of the situation. He demands complete obedience: 'Listen to my voice'; 'You will feel . . .'. There is never any 'Please listen . . .' or 'You might feel . . .'; never any doubt or debate, only strict instructions. In some way, these devices bring forth a totally submissive condition and subjects can then be ordered to behave in ways not seen since the days of ancient slavery.

In a much milder form, this is the secret of the success of many of the high-ranking members of modern society. The tycoon, the Mafia godfather, the great actor, the military commander and the political tyrant all emanate a sense of threat of a special kind that somehow locks into our basic submission mechanism and turns on something akin to a slight hypnotic condition. The greatest weapon we have against this is irreverence and disrespect. Any culture which loses these qualities will soon be dangerously awash with Submissive Behaviour.

RELIGIOUS DISPLAYS

Actions performed to placate imagined deities

Religious Displays, as distinct from religious beliefs, are submissive acts performed towards dominant individuals called gods. The acts themselves include various forms of body-lowering, such as kneeling, bowing, kow-towing, salaaming and prostrating; also chanting and rituals of debasement and sacrifice; the offering of gifts to the gods and the making of symbolic gestures of allegiance.

The function of these actions is to appease the super-dominant beings and thereby obtain favours or avoid punishments. There is nothing unusual about this behaviour in itself. Subordinates throughout the animal world subject themselves to their most powerful companions in a similar way. But the strange feature of these human submissive actions, as we encounter them

Religious displays are essentially submissive gestures performed towards a super-dominant figure—the deity. In this Brazilian act of supplication, the worshippers, as in so many religious ceremonies, adopt a subordinate, imploring attitude.

o appease the gods, food offerings, like
these Bornean gifts to the Sea Spirits, and
other forms of sacrifice are made. Attempts
to placate the deity are commonplace
elements in many religions, as if the god-
figure were a powerful member of the tribe
or society.

Religion breeds sects and sectarian
violence, like this confrontation in Northern
Ireland. In this role, religious displays are
operating as isolating mechanisms,
separating one community from another.
Despite preaching love and kindness, many
religious organizations have a long history
of holy wars, repression and intolerance.

today, is that they are performed towards a dominant figure, or figures, who
are never present in person. Instead they are represented by images and
artifacts and operate entirely through agents called holy-men or priests.
These middle-men enjoy a position of social influence and respect because
some of the power of the gods rubs off on them. It is therefore extremely
important to the holy-men to keep the worshippers permanently obedient to
the super-dominant figures, and this is done in several ways:

1. They encourage the social rejection of worshippers of rival deities. This
pressure ranges from mild disapproval to scorn and anger, and often to severe
persecution. Whether or not they preach social tolerance, many religions have
practised intolerance. This is part of the role they play as cultural isolating
mechanisms. The loyalty to the locally shared god-figure demands social
separation from those who worship in a different way. It creates sects and
breeds sectarian violence.

2. They frequently construct convincing evidence that the deities can
hurt the non-submissive. In the past, any natural disaster—flood, disease,
famine or fire—is explained as a token of the deity's anger, sent to punish
insubordinate behaviour. They exploit coincidences which have given rise to
superstitions, and they play on the suggestibility of the worshippers.

3. They invent an afterworld where the subordinates who obey them will
be rewarded and those who do not will suffer torment. There is evidence that
belief in an afterlife existed many thousands of years ago. Ancient burials
occurred with 'grave-goods' supplied for the corpse's journey to the other
world. This practice dates back to the Stone Age and has continued with little
change over the millennia.

It is surprising that otherwise intelligent men have succumbed to these
pressures and fears in so many different cultures and in so many epochs.
There appear to be several factors aiding the agents of the gods:

First, and perhaps most important, is the acquisition by our early
ancestors of a sense of time. Other species can communicate with information
about the present—about the moods they are in at the moment of
communicating—but they cannot consider the future. Man can contemplate

The invention of an afterworld where sinners will be horribly punished is a common threat-device employed by holymen to maintain the required level of submissiveness among worshippers. The scroll painting from Japan (right) shows the fate awaiting Buddhist sinners, while the early Christian mural from Cyprus (below) depicts the tortures of the damned.

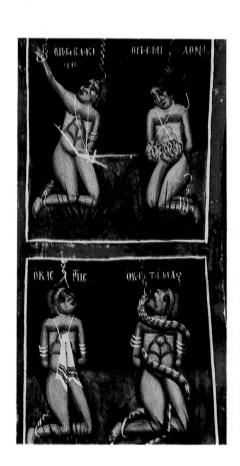

his own mortality and finds the thought intolerable. Any animal will struggle to protect itself from a threat of death. Faced with a predator, it flees, hides, fights or employs some other defensive mechanism, such as death-feigning or the emission of stinking fluids. There are many self-protection mechanisms, but they all occur as a response to an immediate danger. When man contemplates his future death, it is as if, by thinking of it, he renders it immediate. His defence is to deny it. He cannot deny that his body will die and rot—the evidence is too strong for that; so he solves the problem by the invention of an immortal soul—a soul which is more 'him' than even his physical body is 'him'. If this soul can survive in an afterlife, then he has successfully defended himself against the threatened attack on his life.

This gives the agents of the gods a powerful area of support. All they need to do is to remind their followers constantly of their mortality and to convince them that the afterlife itself is under the personal management of the particular gods they are promoting. The self-protective urges of their worshippers will do the rest.

Second, the holy-men are aided by man's neoteny. Neoteny is a biological condition found in certain species in which the juvenile form of the animal becomes increasingly adult. Or, to put it another way, the adults become increasingly juvenile. It is the 'Peter Pan' syndrome—the case of a species that never grows up, but starts to reproduce while still in the juvenile condition. In many ways, man is a neotenous ape. An adult man is more like a young ape than like an adult ape. He has the curiosity and playfulness of a young ape. When the ape becomes mature, he loses his infantile playfulness; but man never loses it.

In the same way, dogs are really neotenous wolves. Man likes his 'best friend' to be playful and so he breeds more and more juvenile dogs. A fully grown domestic dog still leaps and bounds and plays with his master like a young wolf cub. But wolf cubs grow up and stop playing. Young dogs grow up too, but like man they remain infantile in their behaviour—they never stop playing. This means that they will respond to man as if he is a parent. The dog's owner becomes the dog's dominant father-figure, or mother-figure. Being neotenous, the dog can mate and breed, but it still responds to parental

A visitor from outer space flying over earthly towns and villages would come to the conclusion that churches must have very large occupants, since they always tower over the other dwellings. The giants are never at home, apparently, but they are by implication sufficiently impressive to keep their tiny companions in a state of humble subordination.

The power of the gods is reflected in their ability to obtain submissive responses from large numbers of people at one and the same time. This is demonstrated by organizing vast gatherings to witness religious ceremonials (far left), or to participate in shared events (left).

151 RELIGIOUS DISPLAYS

The new gods are also giants, looming over their followers in the form of huge effigies, or lying embalmed like ancient Pharaohs. The titles and phrases change, but the basic features of religious displays remain the same as ever.

domination and obeys its master. This makes it the perfect pet. To the dog, in other words, man is a god.

Man's evolution as a neotenous ape has put him in a similar position to the dog's. He becomes sexually mature and yet he still needs a parent—a super-parent, one as impressive to him as a man must be to a dog. The answer was to invent a god—either a female super-parent in the shape of a Mother Goddess, or a male god in the shape of God the Father, or perhaps even a whole family of gods. Like real parents they would both protect, punish and be obeyed.

It is a fair question to ask why a man's real parents could not play this role themselves. The answer is that, biologically speaking, parents must be bigger than their offspring if they are to remain truly parental. A child must physically look up to its parents. They must have superior strength to be biologically protective. Once the children have grown up and become the same size as their parents, and started to breed like their parents, the true parent-image has gone.

But the gods and goddesses are immense. Like parents, they are 'up there'—we must look up to them in the heavens. And they are all-powerful, like good parents should be. No matter how old we become, we can still call them 'Holy Mother' or 'Father' and put a child-like trust in them (or their agents, who often adopt similar titles for themselves).

Third, the holy-men are aided by man's highly evolved co-operativeness. When our ancient ancestors became hunters, they were forced to co-operate with one another to a much greater degree than ever before. A leader had to rely on his companions for active co-operation, not merely passive submission. If they were to show initiative there was a danger that they would lack the blind, unquestioning allegiance to their leader or to their tribe. The intelligent co-operation that was desperately needed by the hunting group could easily work against the equally necessary group cohesion. How could a leader command both blind faith *and* questioning intelligence? The answer was to enlist the aid of a super-leader—a god-figure—to take care of the blind faith and to bind the group together in a common purpose, while leaving the members of the group free to exercise intelligent co-operation among themselves.

These, then, are the three main factors helping the holy-men in their successful promotion of god-figures and religious behaviour: man's need to protect himself from the threat of death; man's need for a super-parent; and man's need for a super-leader. A god that offers an afterlife in another world, that protects his 'children' regardless of their age, and that offers them devotion to a grand cause and a socially unifying purpose, triggers off a powerful reaction in the human animal.

One of the demands put upon the priests and holy-men is that they should provide impressive rituals. Nearly all religions include ceremonial procedures during which the followers of a particular deity can indulge in complex group activities. This is essential as a demonstration of the power of the gods—that they can dominate and command submissive behaviour from large numbers of people at one and the same time—and it is also a method of strengthening the social bonding in relation to the common belief. Since the gods are super-parents and super-leaders, they must necessarily have large houses in which to 'meet' with their followers. Anyone flying low over human settlements in a spacecraft and ignorant of our ways would notice immediately that in many of the villages and towns and cities there were one or two homes much bigger than the rest. Towering over the other houses, these large buildings must surely be the abodes of some enormous individuals, many times the size of the rest of the population. These—the houses of the gods—the temples, the churches and the cathedrals—are buildings apparently made for giants, and a space visitor would be surprised to find on closer examination that these giants are never at home. Their followers repeatedly visit them and bow down before them, but they themselves are invisible. Only their bell-like cries can be heard across the land. Man is indeed an imaginative species.

A mother, in need herself, clasps her child protectively. Devoted parental care is, in a sense, genetic self-care, since our children carry our genes a step farther down the tunnel of time. Each of us is a temporary, disposable container for this genetic material.

ALTRUISTIC BEHAVIOUR

How do we help others at our own expense?

Altruism is the performance of an unselfish act. As a pattern of behaviour this act must have two properties: it must benefit someone else, and it must do so to the disadvantage of the benefactor. It is not merely a matter of being helpful, it is helpfulness at a cost to yourself.

This simple definition conceals a difficult biological problem. If I harm myself to help you, then I am increasing your chances of success relative to mine. In broad evolutionary terms, if I do this, your offspring (or potential offspring) will have better prospects than mine. Because I have been altruistic, your genetic line will stand a better chance of survival than mine. Over a period of time, my unselfish line will die out and your selfish line will survive. So altruism will not be a viable proposition in evolutionary terms.

Since human beings are animals whose ancestors have won the long struggle for survival during their evolutionary history, they cannot be genetically programmed to display true altruism. Evolution theory suggests that they must, like all other animals, be entirely selfish in their actions, even when they appear to be at their most self-sacrificing and philanthropic.

This is the biological, evolutionary argument and it is completely convincing as far as it goes, but it does not seem to explain many of mankind's 'finer moments'. If a man sees a burning house and inside it his small daughter, an old friend, a complete stranger, or even a screaming kitten, he may, without pausing to think, rush headlong into the building and be badly burned in a desperate attempt to save a life. How can actions of this sort be described as selfish? The fact is that they can, but it requires a special definition of the term 'self'.

When you think of your 'self', you probably think of your living body, complete, as it is at this moment. But biologically it is more correct to think of yourself as merely a temporary housing, a disposable container, for your genes. Your genes—the genetic material that you inherited from your parents and which you will pass on to your children—are in a sense immortal. Our bodies are merely the carriers which they use to transport themselves from one generation to the next. It is they, not we, who are the basic units of evolution. We are only their guardians, protecting them from destruction as best we can, for the brief span of our lives.

Religion pictures man as having an immortal soul which leaves his body at death and floats off to heaven (or hell, as the case may be), but the more useful image is to visualize a man's immortal soul as sperm-shaped and a woman's as egg-shaped, and to think of them as leaving the body during the breeding process rather than at death. Following this line of thought through, there is, of course, an afterlife, but it is not in some mysterious 'other world', it is right here in the heaven (or hell) of the nursery and the playground, where our genes continue their immortal journey down the tunnel of time, re-housed now in the brand-new flesh-containers we call children.

So, genetically speaking, our children are us—or, rather, half of us, since our mate has a half share of the genes of each child. This makes our devoted and apparently selfless parental care nothing more than *genetic self-care*. The man who risks death to save his small daughter from a fire is in reality saving his own genes in their new body-package. And in saving his genes, his act becomes biologically selfish, rather than altruistic.

But supposing the man leaping into the fire is trying to save, not his daughter, but an old friend? How can this be selfish? The answer here lies in the ancient history of mankind. For more than a million years, man was a simple tribal being, living in small groups where everyone knew everyone else and everyone was closely genetically related to everyone else. Despite a certain amount of out-breeding, the chances were that every member of your own tribe was a relative of some kind, even if a rather remote one. A certain degree of altruism was therefore appropriate where all the other members of your tribe were concerned. You would be helping copies of your own genes, and although you might not respond so intensely to their calls for help as you would do with your own children, you would nevertheless give them a degree of help, again on a basis of genetic selfishness.

This is not, of course, a calculated process. It operates unconsciously and is based on an emotion we call 'love'. Our love for our children is what we say we are obeying when we act 'selflessly' for them, and our love of our fellow-men is what we feel when we come to the aid of our friends. These are inborn tendencies and when we are faced with calls for help we feel ourselves obeying these deep-seated urges unquestioningly and unanalytically. It is only because we see ourselves as 'persons' rather than as 'gene machines' that we think of these acts of love as unselfish rather than selfish.

So far, so good, but what about the man who rushes headlong into the fire to save a complete stranger? The stranger is probably *not* genetically related to the man who helps him, so this act must surely be truly unselfish and altruistic? The answer is Yes, but only by accident. The accident is caused by the rapid growth of human populations in the last few thousand years. Previously, for millions of years, man was tribal and any inborn urge to help his fellow-men would have meant automatically that he was helping gene-sharing relatives, even if only remote ones. There was no need for this urge to be selective, because there were no strangers around to create problems. But with the urban explosion, man rapidly found himself in huge communities, surrounded by strangers, and with no time for his genetic constitution to alter to fit the startlingly new circumstances. So his altruism inevitably spread to include all his new fellow-citizens, even though many of them may have been genetically quite unrelated to him.

Politicians, exploiting this ancient urge, were easily able to spread the aid-system even further, to a national level called patriotism, so that men would go and die for their country as if it were their ancient tribe or their family.

The man who leaps into the fire to save a small kitten is a special case. To many people, animals are child-substitutes and receive the same care and love as real children. The kitten-saver is explicable as a man who is going to the aid of his symbolic child. This process of symbolizing, of seeing one thing as a metaphorical equivalent of another, is a powerful tendency of the human animal and it accounts for a great deal of the spread of helpfulness across the human environment.

In particular it explains the phenomenon of dying for a cause. This always gives the appearance of the ultimate in altruistic behaviour, but a careful examination of the nature of each cause reveals that there is some basic symbolism at work. A nun who gives her life for Christ is already technically a 'bride' of Christ and looks upon all people as the 'children' of God. Her symbolism has brought the whole of humanity into her 'family circle' and her altruism is for her symbolic family, which to her can become as real as other people's natural families.

In this manner it is possible to explain the biological bases for man's seemingly altruistic behaviour. This is in no way intended to belittle such activities, but merely to point out that the more usual, alternative explanations are not necessary. For example, it is often stated that man is fundamentally wicked and that his kind acts are largely the result of the teachings of moralists, philosophers and priests; that if he is left to his own devices he will become increasingly savage, violent and cruel. The confidence trick involved here is that if we accept this viewpoint we will attribute all society's good qualities to the brilliant work of these great teachers. The biological truth appears to be rather different. Since selfishness is genetic rather than personal, we will have a natural tendency to help our blood-relatives and hence our whole tribe. Since our tribes have swollen into nations, our helpfulness becomes stretched further and further, aided and

This nun, working in an African leper clinic, is devoting her life to others, but she sees them as her symbolic children, or rather as God's children like herself, and in this way makes them members of her 'family'.

Transactional behaviour. Much of human social life is based on the market-place principle of exchange. But this mutual-aid system is not truly altruistic because it benefits all parties concerned. This is sometimes obscured by the fact that a good turn today is not rewarded until some later date, and the reward process is often indirect.

abetted by our tendency towards accepting symbolic substitutes for the real thing. Altogether this means that we are now, by nature, a remarkably helpful species. If there are break-downs in this helpfulness, they are probably due, not to our 'savage nature' reasserting itself, but to the unbearable tensions under which people so often find themselves in the strained and over-crowded world of today.

It would be a mistake, nevertheless, to overstate man's angelic helpfulness. He is also intensely competitive. But under normal circumstances these rival tendencies balance each other out, and this balance accounts for a great deal of human intercourse, in the form of *transactional behaviour*. This is behaviour of the 'I'll-scratch-your-back-if-you'll-scratch-mine' type. We do deals with one another. My actions help you, but they are not altruistic because they also help me at the same time. This co-operative behaviour is perhaps the dominant feature of day-to-day social interaction. It is the basis of trade and commerce and it explains why such activities do not become more ruthless. If the competitive element were not tempered by the basic urge to help one another, business practices would rapidly become much more savage and brutal than they are, even today.

An important extension of this two-way co-operative behaviour is embodied in the phrase: 'one good turn now deserves another later.' This is delayed, or non-specific co-operation. I give help to you now, even though you cannot help me in return. I do this daily to many people I meet. One day I will need help and then, as part of a 'long-term deal', they will return my help. I do not keep a check on what I am owed or by whom. Indeed, the person who finally helps me may not be one of the ones I have helped. But a whole network of social debts will have built up in a community and, as there is a great division of labour and skills in our species today, such a system will be beneficial to all the members of the society. This has been called 'reciprocal altruism'. But once again it is not true altruism because sooner or later, one way or another, I will be rewarded for my acts of helpfulness.

Anticipation of a delayed reward of this kind is often the hidden motive for a great deal of what is claimed to be purely altruistic behaviour. Many countries hand out official awards to their citizens for 'services to the community', but frequently these services have been deliberately undertaken in the anticipation that they are award-worthy. Comparatively few public honours ever come as a surprise. And many other 'good works' are undertaken with later social (or heavenly) rewards in mind. This does not necessarily make the 'works' any less good, of course, it merely explains the motives involved.

The following table sums up the relationship between competitiveness and helpfulness, and their intermediates:

1 Self-assertive behaviour	Helps me	Harms you	Mild competitiveness to full criminality
2 Self-indulgent behaviour	Helps me	No effect on you	The private, non-social pleasures
3 Co-operative behaviour	Helps me	Helps you	Transaction, trade, barter and negotiation
4 Courteous behaviour	No effect on me	Helps you	Kindness and generosity
5 'Altruistic' behaviour	Harms me	Helps you	Loving devotion, philanthropy self-sacrifice and patriotism

FIGHTING BEHAVIOUR

Pulling punches and throwing punches—the biology of human combat

Fighting represents the failure of threat displays. If intimidation signals cannot settle a dispute, then extreme measures may be called for, and the conflict may develop into full-scale bodily assault. This is extremely rare in human societies, which are remarkably non-violent, despite popular statements to the contrary, and there is a sound biological reason for this. Every time one individual launches a physical attack on the body of another, there is a risk that both may suffer injury. No matter how dominant the attacker may be, he has no guarantee of escaping unscathed. His opponent, even if weaker, may be driven into a desperate frenzy of wild defensive actions, any one of which could inflict lasting damage.

For this reason, threats are far more common than fights in ordinary social life. In fact, unarmed body-struggles are so rare that it is difficult to make accurate observations of them. Most people rely for their information on the stylized brawls depicted in violent cinema or television films. When compared with the real thing, these manly encounters, with hero and villain taking turns to knock each other down, are little more than a ballet performance. The real movements have been slowed down and exaggerated in special ways to make the battle more visually impressive, just as ballet exaggerates ordinary body movements. In a true bar-brawl, once fighting has broken out, everything happens much more quickly. The attacker suddenly explodes with a rapid series of blows and kicks. Each action is quickly followed by another, to block any retaliation. The victim responds in one of three ways. Either he backs away, trying to get out of range, or he protects his body as best he can, or he grabs at the attacker and attempts to convert the assault into a close-hold wrestling situation. If he backs away, flees, or defensively protects himself, the attack may quickly grind to a halt, its goal fully achieved in a few seconds. If he retaliates, then the ungainly grappling sequence may continue for some time, often on the ground, with tearing of hair, scratching and kicking, and even biting, being added to the initial arm-blows and wrestling holds.

In the stylized film-brawl, the film hero frequently begins his assault with a single, massive punch to the jaw of his opponent. This is performed with a wide-amplitude swing of the arm and is not immediately followed up with a second blow. In almost every respect it is nonsensical as a piece of human attack behaviour. The wide swing of the arm would provide far too much warning to the opponent and the approaching fist would never make contact before evasive action was taken. The reach and power of the blow would also leave the puncher unbalanced and vulnerable. The pause following the blow

Real street fighting contrasts strongly with the highly stylized brawls of Hollywood films. Instead of manly punches to the jaw, one is more likely to see ungainly grappling on the ground.

In real fights bystanders stare intently at the action. They surge backwards and forwards as points of violence shift, caught between the conflicting moods of participation and observation, on the one hand, and self-protective retreat, on the other.

would also be fatal and the slowness of the attack disastrous. The film fight then continues with more or less alternating blows from the two combatants, the whole process being performed in what amounts to slow-motion, compared with a real encounter.

When street-fighting or bar-fighting occurs in real life, the combatants are often surrounded by bystanders who experience an intense conflict between watching the action and retreating from its vicinity. The result is a rhythmic surging of the crowd, this way and that, as the fighting pair cut a swathe through the group. As one section of the onlookers bulge forward, another drags back, rather like a disturbed shoal of fish. As the fighting subsides, the crowd now plays a new role, providing a screen from the confrontation for the momentarily separated combatants. This may quickly be used by one or the other to break off the engagement. Again, it is the remarkable speed and brevity of unarmed brawls that accounts for the comparative lack of intervention by bystanders, and accusations that witnesses should have prevented such assaults are usually unjustified.

The fighting behaviour of very young children shows a similar pattern. Disputes among nursery children are nearly always over property. One child tries to take away something belonging to another. There is a rapid assault and then it is all over, with one in possession of the object and the other howling and red-faced. The attack may involve pushing, kicking, biting, or hair-pulling, but the most common action is the overarm blow. In this, the palm-side of the clenched fist beats down on to the opponent's body, the action starting with the arm sharply bent at the elbow and raised vertically above the head. From this position it is brought down hard, with maximum force, on to any part of the other child's body that is near. This beating action seems to be typical of children everywhere and may well be an inborn assault pattern for our species. Interestingly, in later life, after other, more specialized forms of attack have been learned, the overarm blow still re-asserts itself in 'informal' fighting situations. Photographs of street riots, for instance, nearly always show this kind of blow as the predominant mode of assault. In the adult, of course, its damaging effect is much enhanced by grasping a club or stick. Rioters hit police and police hit rioters in the same way, their weapons raining blows on one another's skulls. This looks very much like a case of 'reverting to the primitive' in terms of attack movements, for there are many other, more wounding blows that could be struck, by delivering the hits frontally instead of down from above. A sharp weapon thrust straight into the face, trunk, or genitals of an opponent would undoubtedly do more damage than a blunt one directed down on to the bony skull, and yet these more 'advanced', culturally learned modes of attack are singularly absent from these informal riot occasions.

With the mention of weapons we move into an area of Fighting Behaviour

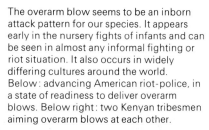

The overarm blow seems to be an inborn attack pattern for our species. It appears early in the nursery fights of infants and can be seen in almost any informal fighting or riot situation. It also occurs in widely differing cultures around the world. Below: advancing American riot-police, in a state of readiness to deliver overarm blows. Below right: two Kenyan tribesmen aiming overarm blows at each other.

that is uniquely human, and which creates special problems for our species. The human body lacks any particularly savage biological weapons, such as sharp claws or fangs, horns or spikes, poison glands or heavy jaws. Many other animals are well equipped, but the human species is a puny object by comparison, unable, in naked body-to-body combat, to inflict lethal injury without a great deal of effort. But when we compare the primeval, unarmed combat of the human animal with its modern, weapon-laden equivalent it is clear that we have long ago outstripped all other species in our killing potential. By inventing fabricated weapons we have brought about several crucial and catastrophic changes in our fighting activities:

1. We have steadily increased the injury-capacity of our attacking actions. By adding blunt instruments, then sharp instruments, then explosive devices, to our body-assaults, we have, over the centuries, made each attack potentially more lethal. Instead of subduing opponents, like other animals, we destroy them.

2. Because of the artificiality of these new weapons we have introduced a possible one-sidedness to hostile encounters. There is no longer any guarantee that both opponents will be equally well equipped. If two tigers fight, they may have sharp, dagger-like claws which naked humans lack in unarmed combat, but *all* tigers possess these weapons and there is therefore an inhibitory balance between fighting opponents. With weapon-carrying humans there can easily arise a grossly unequal situation when any two meet in combat, the superior weapons of one removing his fears of retaliation and thereby unleashing an uninhibited savagery in his assault.

3. The ever-increasing efficiency of artificial weapons means that less and less effort is required to carry out a damaging attack. Instead of being involved in the muscle-straining violence of unarmed combat, the modern weapon-carrier need only perform the tiny, delicate operation of crooking a forefinger, to send a bullet flying into an opponent's body. There is no exhaustion in such an act, no intimate, to-and-fro involvement with the body of the rival. Strictly speaking, to kill a man with a gun is not even a violent act. The effect is violent, of course, but the action is as dainty as picking up a cup of coffee. This lack of exertion makes it a much easier act to perform and again this increases the chances of an attack taking place.

4. We have steadily improved the range at which our weapons can operate successfully. This progression began with throwing an object instead of hitting with it. Then, with the invention of arrows, the sharp points could be fired at the enemy over even greater distances. With the coming of gunpowder the situation took another leap forward. Bullets could be sent to kill at distances at which it was impossible to make out the details of the

Fighting evolved as means of settling personal disputes when all else has failed. Unarmed personal combat is rare in ordinary day-to-day life, and when it does occur it is usually no more than a brief, bloodless scuffle, as in this street-market encounter. Only with artificial weapons and group loyalties can it escalate to tragic proportions for our species.

The development of weapons is a story of gradually increasing distance between the attacker and the attacked. From the close-quarters sword to the thrown spear and the fired arrow we have progressed, if that is the word, via the bullet and the shell to the bomb and the guided missile. The result is the total loss of the personal element in the confrontation—a disastrous situation for a fighting animal.

victim. This added an impersonal element to fighting, eliminating any possibility of appeasement signalling between the combatants. Again, the ordinary animal inhibitions of the hand-to-hand situation were dramatically reduced.

5. We have increased the power of distance weapons to the point where we can destroy not one, but large numbers of victims in a split second. The use of bombs, dropped from the air or deposited with a time-fuse, and the introduction of chemical warfare, has created the ultimate condition of de-personalized and disinhibited fighting. The actions of the attackers are now totally non-violent, usually little more than pressing a button—an even daintier action than squeezing a trigger—and, again, performed at a distance and with a speed that completely rules out any of the usual animal restraints or controls.

Together, these five factors have transformed human Fighting Behaviour from a pattern of violent defeat into one of delicately executed destruction, from beating and dominating a rival to casually disintegrating a horde of unseen strangers. Luckily, however, the latest phase of this chapter of human progress has at last produced a new inhibition of its own. With nuclear devices we are back again at the stage where the attacker may have reason to fear for his own safety, for such is the power of these devices that the dainty button-pusher may well go up in smoke with the rest of us in a globally spreading holocaust. In other words, the destructive potential of these bombs is so great that it has effectively shrunk the world and reduced international disputes to the level of close-quarter brawls. Once again, the impulse to attack involves the immediate arousal of acute fear in the attacker, as it did in the case of unarmed combat. Sadly, however, this new twist in the story of human fighting does not completely eliminate the possibility of a nuclear brawl, it merely reduces the likelihood of it.

One special feature of human conduct which has always been a complicating factor in inter-group mayhem is not the anger of the species but, paradoxically, man's great friendliness. This sense of loyalty to the group has repeatedly led to attacks, not against an enemy, but in support of a companion. It is this co-operative spirit that has made it possible to convert limited personal combat into gang warfare, and gang warfare into military chauvinism. Organized assault forces cannot operate on a personal basis. They require response to discipline and fidelity to the cause, and these are features that have nothing inherently to do with human fighting. They grew originally out of the co-operative male hunting group, where survival depended on allegiance to the 'club', and then, as civilizations grew and flourished and technology advanced, they were increasingly exploited in the new military context.

The combination of attack-remoteness and group co-operativeness, typical of the modern human condition, means that we will always be susceptible to pressures from ruthless leaders urging us to fight for their causes. They will not be asking us to kill with our bare hands, or to exert any great effort to do so, or to do so at close proximity where we can see the expressions of our victims as we attack them. But they *will* be asking us to kill to support our comrades, who will suffer terribly if we do not come to their aid. The argument has worked so well and so often, and tragically it will no doubt do so again. The only defence we have against it is to ask ourselves whether we have any personal argument with the particular individuals we are being asked to kill and whether the 'group' we are being asked to support is really our tribal group, or whether it is not, after all, a quite artificial 'national' group, made up of a mixture of many interwoven 'tribes', some of which hail from our new, so-called enemy. Only if we return to treating the subject of fighting as an extreme form of *personal-dispute* device, which is what it originally was, will we have any hope of escaping from the uncontrolled savagery of our human battlefields to the moderation of animal combat.

TRIUMPH DISPLAYS

How winners celebrate and losers react

Immediately following a moment of victory, there is a surge of feeling that often leads to a Triumph Display. This can vary in its expression from a private, joyous leap in the air, to a full-scale public ceremony. The basis for all these displays is the sudden increase in dominance of the triumphant individual. Before the victory he was still struggling to win; after it, he is the conqueror and his status is instantly raised.

Since high-status postures are taller and higher and larger than low-status postures, it is not surprising to find that in nearly all triumphant moments, the victor expresses his mood by raising his height in some way. This can be done by a wild 'jumping for joy', an excited dancing up and down, or the less dramatic holding high of the head. In many cases there is also a raising of the arms above the head, stretching them up as far as they will go.

The exact nature of the Triumph Display varies with the conquest involved. A team of young children who have won a competition are likely to jump up and down in a rather erratic fashion, shouting and calling. As they grow older this uninhibited display often becomes muted and triumphs are celebrated with a controlled pattern of mock-modesty. Among adults the intensity of the outward display differs strikingly from context to context. For the boxer and wrestler there is the classic 'clasped hands raised above head' posture, traditionally adopted after the winning of a fight. Sometimes this becomes abbreviated to the raising of a single gloved hand and, in certain types of contest, the referee signifies the identity of the winner by taking the victor's hand and raising it up for him.

Politicians, perhaps hoping to acquire by association some of the virility of prize-fighters, have also adopted the pugilistic style of hands-above-head clasping at moments of victory on election nights. They also use the more generalized two-arms spread-and-raise, in which both arms reach for the sky but are slightly angled away from each other, with the hands flat and the fingers stretched stiffly upwards. A variant of this is performed with the fingers held in a victory-V posture.

Footballers are perhaps the most visually rewarding of all conquerors today when it comes to performing Triumph Displays. This was not always the case. Some years ago, in British football, for instance, the scorer of a badly needed goal was met with no more than a pat on the back and a brief word of congratulation. But then, following the development of international football contests and the visits to northern Europe of the more demonstrative Mediterranean clubs, there was a rapid spread of a much more explosive response to the moment of goal-scoring. The scorer himself, as soon as the ball hit the net, was turning and running back towards his companions, with his arms at full stretch. The angle of the arms varied slightly from case to case, because of a conflict between wanting to offer his team-mates an embrace and wanting to reach upwards to the sky in a body-heightening action. Sometimes, as a result of this mixed mood, the scorer's arms would stretch straight in front of him, aimed at his friends, sometimes they were raised vertically, and sometimes they compromised with an intermediate stretching, half reaching and half raised. As he ran, often with his face contorted and his mouth wide open, or at least with a wide smile, the scorer could sometimes be seen to leap in the air and make a downward beat with his raised right fist. This action is similar to the hostile, overarm downbeat seen in riots and brawls, when one man is wildly attacking another with his fist. Here it was being performed in vacuo, a symbolic blow delivered on to the symbolic heads of the opposing team.

As he ran in full display, the footballer was rapidly approached by the other members of his team, who then proceeded to leap at him, hugging him, kissing him, embracing him, ruffling his hair, patting his head and his

Moments of triumph are often marked by body-raising displays. Opposite top: an Olympic athlete celebrates his moment of glory by raising his arms—an action which is also seen in jubilant spectators of sporting events (bottom left). The arms-raised posture of a victorious politician (bottom right) is amplified by his being raised on the shoulders of his equally triumphant supporters. After scoring a decisive goal, a footballer (above) also raises his hands in a Triumph Display, while a team-mate acknowledges his success by embracing him.

shoulders, and generally crowding around him in a dense contact-clump. Occasionally one would leap at him so intensely that he ended up embraced not only by the leaper's arms, but also by his legs, which would be clamped around his body, so that he was effectively carrying his congratulator.

At one time, a few years ago, these congratulatory displays became so intensive that there was almost more danger of being injured after the goal had been scored than before it. Gradually the intensity has subsided, but modified forms can still be observed at almost any professional European match. The whole pattern includes several distinct elements: the increase in height of the victor's body, by leaping and arm-raising; the upsurge of gross body movement, by running rapidly back from the goal-mouth; the symbolic, conquering blow of the overarm downbeat; and the 'loving' contact-actions of the team-mates. This last element is particularly interesting, because the embracing and the touching of the head show a remarkable degree of body-intimacy for northern European males. Under more ordinary, relaxed social conditions, such contacts would be considered positively effeminate if performed between two adult males. This is because of the inevitable association of the full embrace with the actions of amorous lovers. But, here, at the moment of intense emotion following the scoring of a goal, and because of the tough, undeniably virile and masculine nature of the context, the footballers are released from the usual social inhibitions and can give full expression to their feelings of affection towards their triumphant companion. Even if, as sometimes happens, they go to the extreme lengths of actually kissing the scorer, the actions are still 'safely masculine' and in no way misconstrued.

In many sports, it is the practice to carry a victorious individual shoulder-high, or to parade him on top of some kind of vehicle. In some forms of motor-racing the victor sits on top of his car for a special lap of honour, sometimes holding aloft the chequered flag that recorded his moment of conquest as he passed the winning post. Cup winners may also carry out a lap of honour at special events, carrying the cup high around the arena to the applause of their fans. Without realizing it, these modern sportsmen are recreating a simplified version of the ancient Roman Triumph, in which a conquering general and his army entered Rome through a Triumphal Arch and paraded through the city streets, with the victorious general riding on a four-horse chariot decorated with laurel and with a golden crown held above his head by a slave. Dressed in the attire of a god, and with his face reddened with vermillion to simulate the blood of sacrificial victims, the general was given

Arm-raising associated with triumph is sometimes amplified by holding aloft emblems such as flags and banners. These enable supporters to identify more closely with the achievements of their idols, whether they have been successful in a political campaign (above) or in an Olympic event (above right). Appropriately enough, the celebrations of political success are taking place in front of a permanent Triumph display—the Arc de Triomphe.

the highest possible Status Display that Rome could offer. Such triumphs were rare and required success in the field involving the death of at least 5000 of the enemy, the winning of a war and the enlargement of Roman territories by the addition of the vanquished foreign country. Such was the formality of these Roman Triumph Displays that they lost all immediacy and much of their emotional meaning. Sometimes the arrangements took so long that it was months before the victor, waiting patiently outside the gates of the city, was allowed to make his entrance. On one occasion the conquering general was kept waiting for three years, a far cry from the instantaneous and joyous celebration on the modern football field, where even three seconds would seem like a long delay. There is, however, a present-day equivalent to the delayed triumphal parade, and that is the 'home-coming' celebration of a sportsman, or team of sportsmen, who have been unusually successful in some field. The open bus-ride of the football cup-winners through the streets of their home town is a case in point. Here the ghost of Rome lingers on, as it does in the famous laurel-wreath hung around the neck of a modern motor-racing champion.

A new Triumph Display has developed recently in the motor-racing world. It consists of the victor receiving his award on a raised platform and being given a bottle of champagne which he proceeds to shake violently and then spray over the crowd below. This is done by holding a thumb over the neck of the bottle and then releasing it only slightly, so that there is still great pressure inside. The result is a long, foamy white jet of liquid which squirts down on to the heads of the watching crowd below and is strikingly symbolic of a phallic ejaculation. As such, it relates well to the dominating virility of the high status male at that moment in time.

On the opposite side of the coin are the postures of defeat. These are less obvious because most vanquished sportsmen attempt to hide their disappointment as best they can and muster a weak smile of congratulation for the winner. This only happens, however, at the end of a contest. Where there is a great moment of triumph during the course of a match, no such cheerfulness is attempted. At the moment when the footballer has scored his goal, the postures of the rival team tell their tale transparently and without any attempt at cover-up. The heads are usually lowered and may often actually stare down at the grass. The facial expressions are bleak and solemn, and the hands are often placed on the hips. This arms-akimbo posture is characteristic of exasperation and irritation generally and is seen in many such contexts.

Above: the symbolic 'ejaculation' of the triumphant racing driver. Left: the triumphant overarm downbeat of a goal-scoring footballer contrasting sharply with the dejected posture of an opponent.

CUT-OFF
Actions that block in-coming visual signals when we are under stress

Social behaviour is a matter of output and input. We send out signals with our own actions, and we take in messages from the actions of others. When all is well we achieve a balance between these two, but sometimes this equilibrium is upset. If we become starved of social contact, and feel lonely, we correct this by becoming more exploratory—by increasing our output. If, on the other hand, we suffer from too much social input, we become stressed and then try to damp down the over-stimulation in some way. This damping down process has been called Cut-off and it takes several forms.

The most primitive solution is to hide away from the social scene until we have recovered sufficiently from the glut of stimulation to return to the fray once more. One way we do this is to fall ill and take to the privacy of our beds. Another is to suffer from what we describe as a 'nervous breakdown'. A third is to take pills we call 'tranquillizers'. A fourth is to blur the incoming chaos by getting drunk or taking some other form of drug. And a fifth is to indulge in meditation, disappearing inside our own thoughts and leaving the outside world to take care of itself for a while.

Cut-off is a device that reduces stimulation from the outside world. For most of us it is no more than an occasional, momentary solution; but for some, like this mental patient (below left), it can tragically becoming a way of life. Below: the Stammering Eye. During ordinary conversation some people blink their eyes shut for much longer periods than usual— sometimes as much as several seconds per blink. This extended blinking behaviour is a special form of unconscious Cut-off.

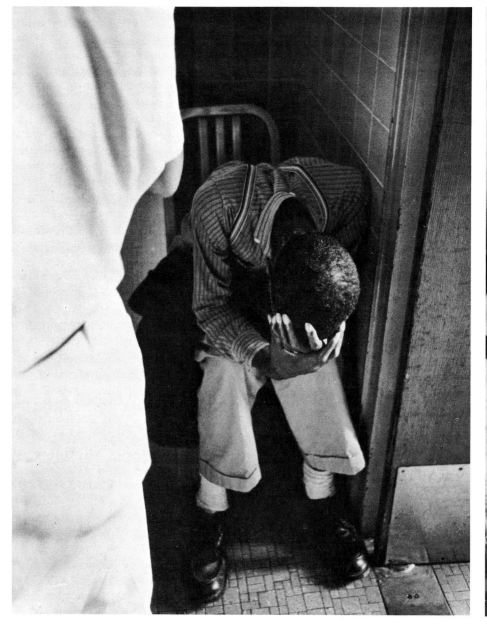

A common form of Cut-off is the closing or covering of the eyes, reducing the visual input briefly, because what is seen is either too unpleasant or over-stimulating. Too much input makes it hard to think clearly and eye-screening is often observed at moments of deep concentration.

But these procedures go far beyond the normal day-to-day Cut-off devices we all use in our social encounters. We may be driven to one or other of these major reactions occasionally, but they are drastic solutions to extreme situations. The much more frequent moments of minor stress are handled by fleeting actions of a far less dramatic kind. The most common and obvious device is briefly closing the eyes. We simply lower the shutters on the incoming visual messages. The man at a noisy party who has been asked a question and cannot remember the answer shuts his eyes tightly as he searches his memory. The mother surrounded by clamouring children clamps her hands over her ears and shouts 'I can't hear myself think!' The actor trying to learn his lines covers his eyes with his hand as an aid to concentration.

These are honest, obvious and undisguised cases of Cut-off and are readily accepted as such. But there is another special category that is more interesting because it includes four unconscious actions—small Cut-offs of which the performer is hardly aware. The first is the Evasive Eye, in which the person looks away from us for unusually long periods while in conversation with us. He can hardly bear to meet our eyes and spends ages staring at some imaginary object to one side of us or on the ground. The second is the Shifty Eye, in which he keeps glancing away and then back again rapidly, repeating the process over and over while he continues to talk with us. The third is the Stuttering Eye, in which, although he keeps facing us, as if to look us in the eye, his eyelids have spasms of flickering up and down, as if he is struggling to open and shut his eyes at the same time and succeeding in neither endeavour. And the fourth is the Stammering Eye, which, like the last, faces us squarely, but every so often drops shut for what should be a momentary blink and then seems unable to open itself again for several seconds.

All four of these forms of Cut-off are rather disconcerting and we find ourselves growing irritated by them without understanding why this should be. The explanation is that intuitively we know the person with us wants to withdraw from our company for some reason. Either he fears us, dislikes us, or is bored by us and would rather be elsewhere, but he goes on behaving in every other way as though he is friendly and fully involved in our social encounter. He sends his signals of Cut-off unconsciously and we receive them in the same way, the nonverbal communication taking place just beneath the surface of the encounter and acting as an unspoken irritant.

It is the contradiction in such cases that annoys us. If our companion would honestly admit to being in need of a little peace and quiet, we would be sympathetic. If, alternatively, he managed to shrug off his stresses and tensions and plunged whole-heartedly into the social encounter before withdrawing to rest himself, we would also be happy. But when he pretends to give us his attention and then unconsciously signals, by his fleeting Cut-off actions, that he would rather be elsewhere, we cannot avoid an undercurrent of annoyance in our reactions to him.

To some extent, this antagonism may be unfair, because his Cut-off actions may well be in response to social contact in general, rather than to us in particular. Some individuals, when reaching a peak of disenchantment with human sociability brought on by a surfeit of professional or domestic stress, find themselves incapable of reacting to any new conversational situation, no matter how exciting or amusing, with the appropriate level of personal involvement. For them, the Evasive Eye, the Shifty Eye, the Stuttering Eye, or the Stammering Eye become almost unavoidable 'tics'. These may be annoying for the rest of us, but for the person in question they may be providing tiny, momentary reminders that there is, after all, such a thing as glorious, solitary, privacy. Each split-second of Cut-off is, in a sense, a miniscule, symbolic escape from the tyranny of social responsibilities. It damps down, if only for a brief moment of time, the sensory input, and helps to correct the input-output balance so vital to us all.

AUTONOMIC SIGNALS

Actions and other changes resulting from body-stress

Every time we are roused into action a number of basic changes take place in our bodies. As we stir ourselves, the machinery of the body starts to gear itself up, ready for the increased demands that are likely to be put upon it. When eventually we relax again, the human engine is allowed to tick over quietly once more. To control these changes is the job of the autonomic nervous system.

This system is made up of two opposing sub-departments, the high-activity *sympathetic* nervous system and the low-activity *parasympathetic* nervous system: the churner-up and the calmer-down. With an ordinary, moderate level of bodily activity, these two systems keep in balance with each other. The sympathetic says: 'Keep it moving, keep going!', while the parasympathetic says: 'Take it easy, conserve your strength.' Neither message is so strong that it can overpower the other, and the human animal jogs happily along in an intermediate condition. This is the state we are in most of the time, but whenever we are called upon to perform some intense, violent activity, the sympathetic system takes over and pours adrenalin into the blood, temporarily dominating the keep-calm, parasympathetic system.

When this happens, a whole range of modifications occurs. The circulatory system is profoundly affected. The heart starts pumping faster and harder and the blood vessels change so that blood is shunted from the skin region and the viscera to the muscles and the brain. The digestive processes are slowed down. Saliva production is reduced. The rectum and bladder do not empty so easily. Carbohydrate stored in the liver is rushed out into the blood stream, stepping up the blood sugar level. Breathing becomes both quicker and deeper. Sweat production is increased.

All these changes help to prepare the body for a massive increase in activity. Tiredness slips away. Suddenly we are wide awake and straining for action—the blood-suffused brain ready for quick thinking, the muscles ready for violent movement. The heaving lungs are stepping up the oxygen intake and the sweating skin is flooded for extra cooling.

Obviously it is not the primary function of these changes to send out visual signals, but they cannot help doing so. We can see when someone is adrenalizing, and there is nothing they can do about it. If their body arousal has actually led to intense activity, their Autonomic Signals are of little importance. The activity tells us all we want to know. But sometimes this activity is blocked. Adrenalin pours out, the body prepares itself for action, but no action follows. At this point the Autonomic Signals can be very revealing.

This situation occurs when someone is in a state of conflict. Perhaps something has frightened them, but they cannot flee, or something has made them angry, but they are too inhibited to go into the attack. There they sit, their body systems churning away, but with no action able to develop. Because of the conflict they are in they would probably rather not give away their true mood of agitation and they try to appear calm, but this is not easy to do.

As an example, take the case of the guest on a television programme who is about to be interviewed. As he waits to walk on, he cannot avoid a sensation of being threatened by the millions of people who are about to study him critically. Fear is aroused, and his body automatically prepares itself for rapid fleeing. As he sits down in the guest's chair and starts to answer questions his body is still physiologically poised for flight, but he does his best to appear relaxed and comfortable. Despite his efforts the autonomic clues are still there. The most difficult to control is the breathing rate. Even if he is a professional actor and has learned to discipline his body actions extremely well, there will still be a tell-tale rise and fall of his chest that is faster and

When we adrenalize, in a state of tension, many body changes occur giving tell-tale signs that we are under pressure. One such change is a reduction in salivation—and this gives us a dry-mouth condition. This in turn causes us to lick our lips—an Autonomic Signal often observed in public speakers.

more exaggerated than normal. If he deliberately forces himself to lounge casually in his chair, this chest-heaving seems strangely out of key with his body posture. Only voluminous clothing can conceal it. In addition, the changes in his blood system will have taken blood away from his skin and left him with a slight pallor. Only studio make-up can conceal this. The decrease in salivation will have given him a dry mouth and, as he talks, he is liable to make small movements of his tongue and lips, trying to replace the lost moisture. The increase in blood to the muscles will have readied them for powerful movements, and these show themselves in an inhibited form. His body will tense itself, his limbs making small shifting movements, or clamping themselves against one another. Either he locks his hands together, each hand expressing its powered condition by grasping the other tightly, or crosses his legs firmly, each pressing into the other. Or he may do both at once. Also, his body-cooling system will be going into operation and he will be sweating more than usual, which may make him shiver slightly, with the well-known 'cold sweat' of fear. Luckily for him, the hot television lights will probably counteract this, and even provide an excuse for the sweating.

If only the man in such a predicament could express the intense activity for which his body is being prepared, then all the physiological preparations would be utilized. But they are not, and they become a surplus. The autonomic system reacts to this unbalanced condition by sending the counteracting system—the parasympathetic—into battle. Both systems are now fully activated and the autonomic pendulum swings wildly back and forth. If only the revved-up energy had been discharged, then the parasympathetic system could slowly bring the body back to a state of equilibrium, but this has not happened and so, instead, there are frantic pulls this way and that, resulting in a state of physiological turbulence. Flashes of parasympathetic activity become interspersed with moments of sympathetic dominance. In extreme cases, the results can be dramatic. A man driving a car, for instance, has seen a child rush out into the road and has slammed on his brakes and skidded into a wall. As he gets out of the car he is as white as a sheet. The panic of the moment has flooded his bloodstream

The excitement of a great occasion causes the adrenalin to flow. This results in the shunting of more blood to the brain; but if the tension persists for too long there is a backlash reaction and the blood-shunting is reversed—sometimes so strongly that it leads to fainting, especially in conditions of overheating.

If we are on the verge of coming to blows, both active fear and active hostility are accompanied by a white-faced appearance, as blood is shunted away from the skin to the brain and muscles, ready for imminent action—either fleeing or fighting. The angry, red-faced man is less dangerous than he looks, having already passed his get-ready-for-action peak.

with adrenalin but for him, as a driver, there has been no body action. Now, as he stands there, the parasympathetic system rebounds and the tightening of his bowels suddenly gives way to defecation, or his bladder action, held in check by his high-adrenalin condition, suddenly relaxes to produce a flood of urine. The blood system shunts the blood back to the skin and viscera again, resulting in a flushed face, burning skin, and perhaps vomiting. The rush of blood away from the brain at the same time may also lead to fainting. His respiration switches from one rhythm to another, giving rise to gasping, sighing and spluttering.

Sometimes it is possible to see contrasting symptoms occurring at one and the same time, with one part of the body showing sympathetic activation and another parasympathetic. Normally this would be unthinkable, but under conditions of intense shock and conflict, the two competing systems get out of phase, and the body condition becomes an extremely uncomfortable one as a result.

In less intense situations, milder but similar contradictions may occur. To return to our television guest: if he is kept waiting for an unduly long time, in a state of nervous agitation, before making his entrance, he too may start to experience a rebellion on the part of his parasympathetic system. It says to him, in effect, 'I have waited long enough for the action to start but, as nothing has happened, I am going to get your body back to a state of balance again.' But the action system is still operating, so once again there is a clash. Now, instead of being rather pale and shivery, the guest feels himself flushing with heat. Instead of a dry mouth, he finds he has excessive salivation. And there is a sudden urge to go to the lavatory. He may even feel slightly faint. These symptoms will not manifest themselves as intensely as in the case of the car-crash driver, but they may begin to show themselves slightly, if the tension and the waiting become too unnerving.

In a fighting situation much the same kinds of changes appear. If fear and aggression are mutually blocking each other, and the aroused individuals can neither attack nor flee, their threat displays are typically accompanied by many of the Autonomic Signals already listed. Here, in particular, it is valuable to note the colour of the threatening man's face. If he is pale, he is more dangerous than if he has reddened. This is because the pallor is part of the action system, and it means that he is ready either to fight or to flee. So if he is pale *and* approaching menacingly, he really is likely to attack. But if he has turned bright red, it means that he has already experienced the parasympathetic backlash and is no longer in the pure state of 'readiness-to-attack'. It is interesting that we speak of the red-faced man being in a 'rage', implying that it is he who is the really dangerous one. Admittedly, he is not to be trifled with, because the autonomic pendulum can still swing back to action again, but in his reddening we are seeing the results of an impotent internal struggle which explodes in curses and roars and which may seem alarming but is in reality a case of his 'bark being worse than his bite'. The dog analogy here is apt, as anyone who has been bitten by a dog will testify, for it is no more the furiously barking dog which sinks its teeth into you than it is the bellowing, scarlet-faced stick-waving man who actually hits you.

There is another Autonomic Signal that deserves mention. It is a puny signal for the human animal, but a signal none the less. When adrenalin floods the system of a mammal, it has the effect of making the hair stand on end. This is part of the cooling system and exposes the surface of the skin more to the outside air. For many species this has led to impressive hair erection displays, with dramatic manes, crests and tufts expanding as the animal responds. For the wretched human pelt this is of little use as a display, but our short hairs stand on end all the same when we experience a strong enough shock. We feel the reaction as a creeping sensation on the skin, especially on the back of the neck and, although this may signal nothing to anyone else, it acts as a sure sign to us ourselves that we are experiencing a powerful body change.

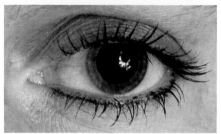

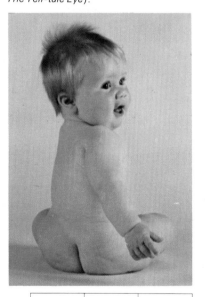

When you look at a picture of a baby, your pupils will change size very slightly. Whether they dilate or constrict will depend on your sex and your parental status. It has been found (below) that baby pictures shown to single women, married but childless women, and mothers, produced pupil dilation in all three cases. By contrast, single men and married but childless men showed pupil constriction, and only fathers responded with pupil dilation. (After Hess: *The Tell-tale Eye*).

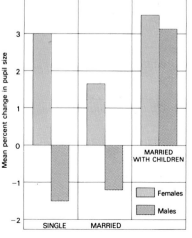

PUPIL SIGNALS
Pupil dilations and constrictions indicating changes of mood

When we look closely at a human face we are aware of many expressive details—the lines of the forehead, the wideness of the eyes, the curve of the lips, the jut of the chin. These elements combine to present us with a total facial expression which we use to interpret the mood of our companion. But we all know that people can 'put on a happy face' or deliberately adopt a sad face without feeling either happy or sad. Faces can lie, and sometimes can lie so well that it becomes hard to read the true emotions of their owners. But there is at least one facial signal that cannot easily be 'put on'. It is a small signal, and rather a subtle one, but because it tells the truth it is of special interest. It comes from the pupils and has to do with their size in relation to the amount of light that is falling upon them.

The human pupils appear as two black spots at the centres of the coloured irises and it is common knowledge that these spots are openings that vary in width as the light changes. In bright sunlight they narrow to pinhead size—about two millimetres across—and as dusk falls they widen to perhaps four times their sunlit diameter. But it is not only light that affects the pupils. They are also affected by emotional changes. And it is because emotional changes can noticeably alter pupil size when the light remains constant that pupil size-change operates as a mood signal. If we see something that excites us, whether with pleasurable anticipation or with fear, our pupils expand more than usual for the existing light conditions. If we see something mildly distasteful, they contract more than they should in the existing light conditions. These changes normally occur without our knowledge and, since they are also largely beyond our control, they form a valuable guide to our true feelings.

But Pupil Signals are not only unconsciously emitted, they are also unconsciously received. Two companions will feel an added emotional excitement if their pupils are dilating, or an added emotional dampening if their pupils are contracting, but they are most unlikely to link these feelings with the Pupil Signals they are transmitting. It is a 'secret' exchange of signs operating below the level of contrived manners and posed expressions.

A great deal of research has been carried out during the past fifteen years to try and find out how these unsuspected Pupil Signals work. The basic laboratory test has been to show people emotionally exciting pictures and at the same time to record any changes in their pupils, using sensitive apparatus. Great care is taken to ensure that there is no change in the strength of the light falling on the subjects' eyes, so that the experimenters can be virtually certain that any pupil dilations or constrictions are due solely to the emotional impact of the various pictures shown.

An early experiment involved showing photographs of human babies to single men and women, married men and women who were not yet parents, and men and women who were parents. The women showed strong pupil dilation when viewing these pictures, regardless of whether they were single, married and childless, or parents. The men, in contrast, showed pupil constriction if they were single or married and childless, but showed strong dilation if they were parents. In other words, the childless human male who coos over someone else's new baby is probably merely being polite, but the female means it. Not until the human male actually has a baby of his own does he start responding with truly sympathetic emotion to other people's infants. The human female, on the other hand, even before she has bred, seems to be primed for maternal reactions.

Sexual reactions have been tested in the same way. Pin-up pictures of naked males and naked females have been shown to both men and women, and the findings are that homosexuals on the whole show a positive pupil response—that is, their pupils enlarge—when they see the naked body of a

member of their own sex, while heterosexuals show a strong response to the opposite sex.

One interesting aspect of the sexual tests was that women as well as men found naked bodies very much more exciting than clothed ones. Men, of course, make no secret of this and it is considered quite acceptable for young men to pin up pictures of underclad females on the walls of their rooms. But photographs of underclad men rarely figure in the decorations of the rooms of young women. As a result, a myth has grown up that women, unlike men, are not much aroused by the sight of a naked body of the opposite sex. Unconscious pupil reactions tell a different story.

Another form of 'deception' was uncovered when liberally-minded people were shown photographs of black males kissing white females. Although all the subjects spoke approvingly of racial equality when questioned on the topic, their pupils split them neatly into two groups—the liberals 'at heart' whose pupils matched their stated beliefs, and the 'merely persuaded' liberals, or perhaps pseudo-liberals, who, despite their praise for racial integration, revealed pinprick pupils when confronted with the black-kissing-white display.

In another experiment, subjects were asked to state food preferences and were then shown photographs of the foods in question while their pupil reactions were monitored. Most people in this test revealed a perfect match between statement and pupil response. The more they *said* they preferred a

Both males and females react strongly to photographs of nudes of the opposite sex, when their unconscious pupil reactions are measured. The idea that females are less interested in the naked male than males are in the naked female is refuted by these findings.

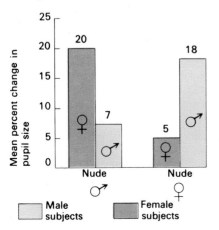

Which of these two girls do you find more appealing? Without knowing why, most people choose the girl shown above. The only difference between the two pictures is the size of the pupils. In the picture above they have been retouched to look much larger and it is this that adds the extra appeal.

food, the more their pupils expanded when they looked at a picture of the food. But a few individuals showed a poor match, which was surprising considering the innocuous nature of the experiment. Who would want to lie about food preferences? The answer came when further questioning was carried out—almost all the food 'fibbers' were dieters on strict regimes but secretly (in some cases secretly even to themselves) still longing for now-forbidden foods. Their reasoned preferences were no longer in tune with their unconsidered preferences.

A similar inconsistency was exposed when a series of pictures of different women were shown to experimental subjects. Among them were photographs of attractive pin-ups and the painting of Whistler's Mother. Needless to say, the old lady was highly rated when subjects were asked for verbal opinions, but she sank dramatically in the preference ratings when the pupil dilations and constrictions were analysed.

Intriguing as these experiments are, they tell us only what can be discovered in the laboratory, using sensitive apparatus to measure the pupil size-changes. Before we can justifiably call these pupil reactions Pupil Signals, we need to prove that they are in fact detected by onlookers in ordinary day-to-day social contacts using nothing but their own eyes, and that these emotional pupil changes are actually being used as a social communication device. A simple way to demonstrate this is to show a large audience two posters of an attractive girl, identical in all respects except that

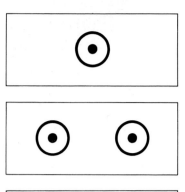

A simple eye-spot pattern can produce pupil dilation when stared at by a human subject. The double eye-spot gives rise to greater dilation than the single or treble (above). Again, if these patterns are themselves 'dilated', it is the change in the double eye-spots (below) that produces the biggest response.

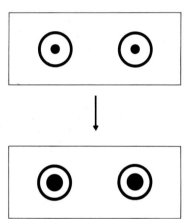

in one poster the girl has normal pupils and in the other she has her pupils artificially enlarged by over-painting them with bigger black spots. With only this one change, and with the audience unaware of what has been done, all the men present are asked to choose which girl they like the best. When a show of hands for girl 'A' is called for, only a few are raised, but when votes for girl 'B' (the one with the retouched pupils) are requested, a forest of hands goes up. Usually the audience laughs when this happens, because they still do not know why nearly all the men are choosing the same girl. They know they have been tricked, but they do not know how. The men's response was towards the girl who was 'evidently' stimulated by their presence, because she was dilating her pupils at them. She was 'excited by what she saw', expanded her pupils, and thereby made herself more attractive.

This is one of the reasons why young lovers spend so much time gazing closely into each other's eyes. They are unconsciously checking each other's pupil dilations. The more her pupils expand with emotional excitement, the more it makes his expand, and vice versa.

One experiment tested the pupil reactions of avowed 'Don Juans'—girl-chasers, men who liked to conquer a girl sexually and then move on to another, never forming a lasting, loving attachment with any one girl. These males, when tested, did not show the normal pupil dilation when viewing pictures of attractive girls. They showed a greater pupil response to girls with constricted pupils than to girls with dilated pupils. In other words, they preferred non-loving girls to loving girls. They were wary of girls who might become too clinging and therefore complicate their Don Juan life-style.

Since, in all the examples mentioned, the subjects of the experiments were unconscious of what was happening, either to their own pupils or to those of their companions, it is likely that we are dealing with a basic, inborn response of the human species. This idea is reinforced by tests carried out using schematic eye-spots instead of real eyes. A circle with a spot inside it can be drawn on a sheet of paper and shown to a person whose pupil reactions are being recorded. A single circle-with-spot or a treble—that is, three circles, each with a spot inside—prove to be less effective signs than a *pair* of eye-spots. Also, with the pair of eye-spots, the subject is more responsive when the spots inside the circles are enlarged, but there is no such increase in reaction when similar 'dilations' occur with the single eye-spot or the treble eye-spots. Apparently, a pair of circles with spots inside them has some special significance for the human animal and makes him react in a way that he cannot control, cannot learn or unlearn, and is quite unconscious of as it is happening. It is hardly surprising therefore that human babies have generally larger pupils than adults, for babies clearly have a need to muster as much appeal as they can, to ensure that they stimulate the strongest possible caring and loving responses in their parents. Any inborn signal they can emit that makes them unavoidably more lovable will obviously have increased their survival chances—and pupil enlargement appears to be just such a signal.

Finally, it is worth recording that, despite the fact that serious research into the subject of Pupil Signals has only been carried out during the past two decades, the signal was consciously manipulated in earlier times. Hundreds of years ago, the courtesans of Italy used a drug made from the Deadly Nightshade plant to drop into their eyes in order to make their pupils dilate. This was said to make them more beautiful and so the drug was called 'Belladonna', meaning, literally, 'beautiful woman'. A later example comes from the jade dealers of pre-Revolutionary China, who took to wearing dark glasses expressly in order to conceal their excited pupil dilations when they were handed a particularly valuable specimen of jade. Before this was done, the dilations were consciously watched for by the jade salesmen, as signals of interest and therefore of potentially high prices. But these are isolated examples, and most of the world has gone about its business, dilating and responding to dilations, without any such deliberate techniques.

INTENTION MOVEMENTS

Get-ready actions that signal future intentions

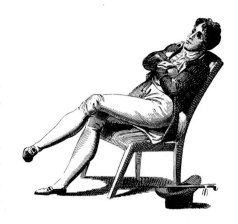

When we are about to take action, we often make small, preparatory movements. These can act as clues, revealing what we intend to do, and they are called Intention Movements. If we were prepared to plunge straight into the new activity, whatever it might happen to be, we would not hesitate, and the 'starting' movements would grow smoothly into the full pattern of behaviour. But if, for some reason, we are hesitant, then the first small piece of the action is all that we do. We start, then stop; start, then stop again. So there is a double clue: something is making us want to act, but something else is stopping us.

In social situations, the classic Intention Movement is the 'chair-grasp'. Host and guest have been talking for some time, but now the host has an appointment to keep and must get away. His urge to go is held in check by his desire not to be rude to his guest. If he did not care about his guest's feelings, he would simply get up out of his chair and announce his departure. This is what his body wants to do, but his politeness glues his body to the chair and refuses to let him rise. It is at this point that he performs the chair-grasp Intention Movement. He continues to talk to the guest and listen to him, but he leans forward and grasps the arms of the chair as if about to push himself upward. This is the first act he would perform if he were rising. If he were not hesitating, it would only last a fraction of a second. He would lean, push, rise and be up. But now, instead, it lasts much longer. He holds his 'readiness-to-rise' posture and keeps on holding it. It is as if his body has frozen at the get-ready moment.

Starting from repose.

When we wish to rise, we adopt the Intention Movement of getting up from the chair, and this posture often acts as a clue that we want to terminate an encounter. (After Siddons, 1822).

The host, in performing this extended Intention Movement, may be making a deliberate gesture, hoping that the guest will take the hint, or he may be unaware that he is doing it. The guest, if he is engrossed in the conversation, may fail to notice the change in his host's body posture, or he may see it but ignore it. A sensitive guest will, however, usually respond fairly quickly. He, too, may do this unconsciously, or he may read the sign clearly and become fully aware that he has outstayed his welcome.

The fact is that we use and respond to Intention Movements in many situations, every day of our lives, without being aware of the process. Every time we walk down a crowded street we are reacting to the Intention Movements of the other walkers around us. In this way we avoid collisions and last-minute braking actions, which can be tiring and time-wasting. Just occasionally this system goes wrong, when we mis-read the intentions of the other person who is approaching us. Everyone knows the situation where two people are about to pass each other in a narrow space. One moves to his left and the other moves to his right, so that they are forced to halt, face to face. Sensing the mistake simultaneously, they both quickly adjust and step the other way, only to come face to face a second time. At this point they usually apologize and one pauses deliberately to let the other pass. Sometimes they both pause deliberately and each waits for the other to pass. Now they have reached a stage where the simple passing action has become a verbal encounter, with each saying 'you first', 'no, you first'. This happens to everyone sooner or later in a corridor, a doorway or a street, but that it happens so rarely is a reflection of how well we read the Intention Movements of other people most of the time.

Intention Movements signal impending action. Some are performed unconsciously while others, like these outstretched hands, are deliberate. By holding out the hand as an Intention Movement of hand-shaking we transmit a signal indicating our wish to engage in a greeting ritual.

Some Intention Movements are subtle, others crude. The patient listener cornered by a bore may do no more than button a jacket, or uncross his legs. Or, in a standing encounter, he may start to edge away by backing slightly, or turning the body, while still keeping his face towards the speaker. The first clues may be missed, but the last are inescapable. Even the most self-engrossed bore cannot misread the intentions of a companion who, although still smiling and nodding, is beginning to retreat. Because bores are often tragically aware that they *are* bores, they often resort to anti-Intention Movement devices. They take the victim by the arm while talking to him, or place a hand on his arm or shoulder, so that it is more difficult for him to edge away. When we speak of 'buttonholing' someone, we visualize cornering them so that they cannot escape our attentions, but the word was originally 'buttonholding', and referred to a practice, common in previous centuries, of actually taking hold of a person's button while engaging them in conversation. Although this could not prevent the more subtle Intention Movements of escape it successfully blocked the cruder ones of deliberately edging away. Only desperate measures could overcome this device, and there is an amusing observation, dating from 1808, that 'Charles Lamb, being button-held one day by Coleridge . . . cut off the button.'

At the opposite end of the scale from Intention Movements of fleeing are those threatening actions we see when someone becomes angry. The more subtle Intention Movements of attacking are the clenching of the fists, or the whitening of the knuckles as the hand grips tightly to some inanimate object. Cruder versions include the open-mouthed snarl and the raised arm. The snarl is intriguing, because it appears to be the Intention Movement of biting, which was presumably one of our ancient methods of dealing with an opponent. Children, when very young, still resort to biting as an aggressive action, and nursery schools usually keep an eye open for the occasional, serious biter, but adults are more likely to use hands than teeth when indulging in free-for-all grappling. With them, only the primeval Intention Movement of the snarl remains, with the jaw open wide, the lips pulled back and the teeth exposed. There is perhaps a slight sex difference here. Women have much weaker wrists and hands than men and, with them, the snarl may still sometimes extend beyond the Intention Movement stage and develop into a full-blooded bite. In a recent court case, a woman was accused of biting off her neighbour's ear, when an argument got (literally) out of hand.

Rumanian Olympic gymnast Nadia Comaneci grasps her chair in an Intention Movement of rising, as she learns that she has been awarded maximum points for her performance.

The raised arm, with clenched fist, is the Intention Movement of the typical human overarm blow. In its less extreme form it consists simply of a slight upward movement of the forearm, but from this it can develop, either into the characteristic fist-shake or the fully-raised arm. The latter has become formalized as the Communist salute, where it symbolizes the aggression involved in the act of rebellion that initiated the Communist movement. Here the Intention Movement has become a fixed emblem and the gesture is an end in itself. It is no longer likely to develop into an actual blow at the moment of its performance, but indicates instead a generalized intention that expressed itself fully in the historical past and could do so again in the future.

In another form of sport, boxing, the most important form of Intention Movement is not the true starting movement, but the false one—the feint. The boxer, fully aware that his opponent is alerted to every tiny jerk of his fists or tilt of his trunk and is reading these for the subtlest signs of any Intention Movement of attack, employs false Intention Movements as a repeated decoy system. It is possible to score any boxing match on a movement-by-movement basis and to arrive at a general ratio of hits to Intention Movements of hitting. As a rule the heavier the weight of the boxers, the more this ratio favours the Intention Movements. In heavy-weight championships, where the actual blows are so exhausting, both for the attacker and the attacked, there are often whole bouts where the Intention Movements far outnumber the actual hits, and the contest becomes mainly one of feint and counter-feint.

On the athletics track, there is no feinting, but at the start of every race one sees a frozen Intention Movement as the runners 'get set'. The shorter the race, the more important this intention posture becomes. In the 100 metres race, the quality of the initial Intention Movement, the springing off at the gun, can make all the difference between winning and losing. The tension is so great that false starts often occur, with one of the runners failing to freeze his Intention Movement until the gun has fired.

There is one special category of Intention Movements, where not one but two actions are started off. There is an urge to do two things at once. The body first obeys one impulse, then the other, in an alternating sequence. If a man wants to move to the left and to the right at the same time, he cannot do both, so he chooses one—he starts to move to the left. But, as he does so, he is carried farther away from the right and this increases his urge to move right. So he checks his movement and reverses his direction. Now he is thwarting his desire to move left, so back he goes, and so on, teetering back and forth. These alternating Intention Movements, or Ambivalent Actions, often develop a special rhythm and there is nowhere better to observe them than at a speech or lecture. The speaker wishes to stay and give his talk, but he would also like to flee from his audience because all audiences, no matter how friendly, seem threatening to the lone figure standing in front of them. Instead of remaining still as he speaks, he will often start to sway from side to side. This may be only a slight tilting of the body, or it may be something stronger, an actual twisting from side to side. If he is speaking from a swivel chair, he may begin to turn it rhythmically from side to side, unaware of what he is doing, but irritating the audience in the process. For this reason, some TV studios have the swivels of their interview chairs deliberately jammed, to prevent interview subjects from setting up a back-and-forth rotation.

Anyone attending a tedious conference can pass the time by making a classification of the various speakers according to their AIMS (= Alternating Intention Movements). There is the Rocker, the Tilter, the Swayer, the Turner, the Pacer, the Teeterer and that most extreme form, the Stroller. The Stroller may go so far as to walk right off the platform in one direction, return, and then walk right off in the opposite direction. One professor used to go so far as to walk to the wall of the lecture theatre, undo a window cord, do it up again, then walk back across to the opposite wall, undo a cord there,

Intention Movements of attack are common during boxing or wrestling matches, as in this Sudanese example (left). Feints are false Intention Movements designed to confuse the opponent and are employed in many sports (above), as well as in fighting contests.

do it up, and repeat the whole process. Throughout this prolonged alternation the lecturing never ceased, but an ambulatory rhythm was established that vividly recalled an animal courtship dance. Many animals dance first to the left and then to the right, time after time, when courting a mate, as the sexual urge competes with the urge to flee. In a similar way, the professor in question expressed his conflicting desires to lecture and to escape from his audience (presumably, in his case, through the window).

This was an extreme case, but the lecturer who displays absolutely no Intention Movements during a talk is the exception rather than the rule. Nearly always, there is a characteristic speed to the rhythm of the movements, each speaker having his own personal rate of strike which can be timed with a stopwatch. One speaker who was being timed in this way happened to be talking on the subject of rhythmic displays in animals. At the very point in his speech where he claimed that primates—monkeys, apes and man—are less likely to exhibit these rhythmic movements than other kinds of animals, his own, fixed, teetering rhythm was broken and became temporarily suppressed, as if in an attempt to prove the point he was making. This observation underlines the fact that when we say we are 'unaware' of certain actions we are performing, we are really over-simplifying the situation. We may be consciously unaware, but it seems that unconsciously we must know precisely what we are doing. Perhaps it is this unconscious awareness that rewards us when we make our little, rhythmic escape movements. It is as if our body is whispering to us: 'Don't worry, you could escape if you really wanted to', and with each rhythmic reminder of this potential we feel a small wave of comfort.

There is one area of human action that takes this form of action to an extreme—we call it dancing. Nearly all human dancing is basically a long series of varying Intention Movements. To put it another way, dancing is locomotion that gets us nowhere. We take to the dance floor and we move, and we move, and we are still there when the music ends. We turn and we sway and we tilt, back and forth and round and round. Viewed objectively, the dancer is rather like a parrot in a small cage, bobbing and weaving on its perch but unable to fly away. With us, the condition is voluntary. We find it comforting to perform and even comforting to watch. The rhythm of the alternating Intention Movements has become an end in itself.

The analysis of folk-dance styles around the world (the science of choreometrics) has revealed that there are a number of basic types of body motion which relate in a general way to the cultures in which they are found. The dances consist of repetitive, abstracted versions of familiar everyday activities. Elements are taken from hunting, food-gathering and a whole variety of domestic and agricultural chores. Courting, mating and various social pursuits are also used as sources for dance sequences, and the main reward of performing these in a stylized way as part of a musical ritual is the simultaneous, joint activation of the whole group. It is as if the dancing actions, performed by everyone together at the same time and at the same pace, emphasize the consensus of feeling in the group about their patterns of living. If everyone jumps and twists together, they all feel 'as one', and the reward is in this sense of belonging, expressed physically, with full body movement. In order to achieve this quality the dance movements must not be too elaborate, and must avoid long and complex sequences of mime. (Professional dancing where the activity becomes elevated into an art form is, of course, another matter.) What has to be done in folk and amateur dancing is to provide an easily repeated series of rhythmic actions distilled from the everyday pursuits of the people, which they can express simultaneously as part of a shared, muscular experience. The way this occurs is by using those elements of movement that are most easily repeated in a rhythmic way, and these are usually the Intention Movements. Some later stages in the behaviour sequences of hunting, fighting, mating, and the rest,

will appear occasionally, but by and large it is the starting actions, the get-ready-to-go actions, that are employed. In the war-dance the warriors jerk and jump, as if about to rush into battle; in the courting dance the young partners approach each other, then turn away and approach again. In the ballroom dance the man leads the woman around the floor, as if taking her somewhere. Their embrace holds great promise of reaching a more advanced stage of intimacy, but this stage is never reached. Instead, he leads her around the floor again. And again. On the discotheque floor the younger couples do not circulate, partners preferring to face each other and make sexual Intention Movements and exaggerated locomotion-on-the-spot actions, often containing elements of turning away from the partner and then turning back to them.

If any of these dance movements went too far and burst beyond the bounds of the stylized Intention Movements, the dance arena would soon be crowded with actors rather than dancers—with people acting out work routines, courtships, matings, or fights, to music. The displays would then become dominated by the specific actions of the various sequences and would lose their collective, rhythmic quality. It is the comparative non-specificity and simplicity of the Intention Movements that enables them to feed the dance with a supply of rhythmic movements, without submerging the action under a welter of mimed complexities. When actions are starting off, the get-ready movements are typically turnings, crouchings, stretchings-out, jumps, twists, jerks, or the taking of a few steps in one direction or another. These are the actions that lend themselves to easy repetition and it is these actions that form the basis of most dance sequences for the ordinary non-professional dancers the world over, both in tribal villages and in great cities.

Dancing is largely composed of Intention Movements. The dancers twist this way and that, as in this Kenyan dance, or circle round and then circle back again, as in the case of English Morris Dancers (above).

DISPLACEMENT ACTIVITIES

Agitated fill-in actions performed during periods of acute tension

Displacement Activities are small, seemingly irrelevant movements made during moments of inner conflict or frustration.

The nervous girl waiting for an important interview repeatedly opens and closes the clasp of her bracelet. There is nothing wrong with the clasp. The bracelet was perfectly secure before she began fiddling with it. Her repeated clicking may even weaken the catch and damage it. So the function of her actions cannot be labelled as true 'costume adjustment'. It is quite different from the clicking of a bracelet that is coming loose, or is being put on when dressing. The girl is performing a Displacement Activity and, characteristically, she is probably not even conscious that she is doing it. All she knows is that she wants very much to attend the interview, but at the same time is very scared and would also like to flee the office and never return. This inner conflict makes it very difficult for her simply to sit still and wait calmly to be called. She is strongly aroused but for the moment can do nothing about it. She cannot convert her arousal into major actions—she cannot march into the interview room before she is called, neither can she dash to the exit and escape. Trapped between these two primary solutions to her conflict, she reacts by filling up the behaviour void with irrelevant trivia. She is so keyed up for action that *any* action, no matter how meaningless in its own terms, is more acceptable than gross inaction.

The secretary watching this nervous girl can easily read the signs. It is clear to her that the rhythmic clicking of the bracelet spells nervousness. She knows intuitively that fidgeting of this kind means inner conflict. In other words, Displacement Activities become important social signals, revealing to companions the thwarted urges of the fidgeters. But some displacement signals are less obvious than others. Air hostesses, for instance, are specially trained to watch out for tell-tale signs of tension in their passengers. Some are clear enough but others are disguised, because passengers often do not wish to admit that they are frightened of boarding a plane. Their fidgeting is tailored to the special occasion in an unconscious attempt to make it look less irrelevant. They repeatedly check their tickets, take out their passports and then put them away again, rearrange their hand-baggage, make sure their wallet is in place, drop things and pick them up again, and generally give the impression that they are making vital last-minute checks. The truth is that the real checks were made back in the terminal building, and an experienced hostess knows that the 'displacing' passengers are extremely tense and would like to flee the plane, if only they could.

Observations carried out at railway stations and a airports revealed that there are ten times as many Displacement Activities in the flying situation. Only 8 per cent of the passengers about to board a train showed these signs, but the figure rose to 80 per cent at the check-in desk of a Jumbo-jet flight across the Atlantic. Apart from the ticket-checking routine, there was also a great deal of face-pulling, head-scratching, earlobe-tugging and general fumbling.

Individuals who are fully aware of the revealing nature of such trivial actions find it hard to suppress them totally. Over in the corner of the airport departure lounge, there sits the 'seasoned traveller', apparently calm and relaxed. But closer inspection shows that he is smoking a cigarette in a strange way. He is employing the multi-tap-on-the-ashtray device. It is so inconspicuous that it hardly causes a dent in his image of sophisticated relaxation. But there is no ash on the cigarette he is tapping so persistently on the edge of the ashtray. In its own terms, the activity is meaningless—only as a Displacement Activity does this trivial occupation have any significance.

The ashtray on the table may bear silent witness to other forms of displacement smoking. The hardly-touched cigarette, stamped out as if it

Smoking is much more than nicotine addiction: it is a widely used Displacement Activity providing the smoker with a valuable preoccupation during times of stress.

When a puzzled man scratches his head he is performing a Displacement Activity—a small action that reflects an inner conflict. He may do this when faced with a difficult problem— or during a moment of social tension.

were being killed; the pile of back-broken matches, all neatly snapped in half; the patterns drawn in the powdered ash. The very act of smoking a cigarette is, for many, a major source of Displacement Activities. Their smoking increases and decreases, not with any narcotic nicotine-need, but with the varying tensions of the day. They are stress-smokers, not drug-smokers, and in that capacity at least, smoking can play a valuable role in a society full of minute-by-minute tensions and pressures. It is so much more than a question of inhaling smoke. There is the finding of the packet and the matches or lighter; the extraction of the cigarette from the pack; lighting-up; putting out the flame and getting rid of the lighter, match-box and cigarette packet; shifting the ashtray into a more convenient position; flicking a little imaginary ash from the front of the clothes; and blowing the smoke thoughtfully up into the air. Cigars and pipes offer even greater scope for preoccupations with trivial acts of adjustment, preparation, and organization of the smoking pattern. The smoker has an enormous advantage over the non-smoker during moments of stress, and can actually create the impression that all his fiddling and fidgeting is really part of a nicotine pleasure and therefore a sign of enjoyment, rather than an inner-conflict reaction.

This aspect of Displacement Activities in humans—the way in which the actions are unconsciously selected so as to mask the underlying emotional turmoil has led to a number of distinct social practices. Whenever we participate in 'social engagements' we are liable to find ourselves in a mild state of conflict. Whether as hosts or as guests, we are slightly uncertain of ourselves and concerned about our social performance during the encounter. Social occasions are therefore, not surprisingly, riddled with displacement interjections. The host, as he crosses the room, is rubbing his hands together (displacement hand-washing); one of his guests is carefully smoothing her dress (displacement grooming); the hostess is shifting some magazines (displacement tidying); another guest is stroking his beard (displacement

Social gatherings often create tensions—which can be relieved by the presence of displacement facilities such as (above) drinks for the un-thirsty and food for the un-hungry. A great deal of social sipping and nibbling comes into this category.

Many people develop personal displacement habits, such as jingling coins in a pocket or, as in this case (opposite), smoothing unruffled hair. It is rare to find any individual who lacks some such movement on social occasions.

Displacement sleeping during moments of inner conflict is rare, but incipient sleeping, in the form of yawning, is a common Displacement Activity.

grooming, again); the host is preparing drinks and the guests are sipping them (displacement drinking); the hostess is offering around small tidbits and the guests are nibbling them (displacement eating).

Typically, none of these actions was fulfilling its primary function. The displacement hand-washer had dry, clean hands; the displacement dress-smoother had no creases in her dress; the displacement-tidied magazines were already neatly arranged; the displacement beard-stroker displayed an unruffled beard; and the displacement drinkers and eaters were neither thirsty nor hungry. But the performance of all these actions helped to ease the tension by keeping the group occupied during the initial stages of the social encounter.

Many people develop what might be called personal displacement-habits. They each favour one particular form of Displacement Activity which they employ whenever internal conflicts arise. There is the sportsman who vigorously chews gum just before the start of an important match; the executive who predictably sucks on his spectacles or polishes them with a handkerchief before answering a difficult question at a committee meeting; the actress who twiddles a wisp of hair; the schoolboy who bites his nails; the television interviewer who carefully examines the backs of his fingers; the lecturer who repeatedly re-aligns his lecture-notes on the lectern; the chairman who doodles on his writing-pad; the teacher who picks imaginary pieces of fluff from his jacket; and the doctor who is forever winding up his watch.

The man who exhibits no such trivial actions, who is calm and serene and attends only to the primary actions in any social situation, is either socially dominant or socially detached. He is either above conflict or outside it. He might be a tyrant or a tycoon, a saint or a mystic, an eccentric or a psychotic, but he will certainly not be typical of the vast majority of human beings. The rest of us, as we go about our business, will sooner or later succumb to the need to fidget—to perform small, trivial acts that are being displaced from their usual functional contexts and injected into quite alien behaviour sequences, where they will help us to avoid the behavioural stalemate of contradictory urges.

The human species is not unusual in this respect. Many other animals also show characteristic Displacement Activities when in states of conflict. The main difference between human and non-human cases is that other animals do not utilize learned patterns of behaviour in the way we do, or show a great deal of individual variation. If one member of a species shows a particular displacement action, then it is fairly safe to predict that all other members of that species will employ the same movement when they find themselves in a similar conflict situation.

There is no such predictability with humans, although one or two examples do appear to be remarkably widespread. Displacement yawning when bored or frustrated seems to be almost universal for mankind. It is a low-intensity form of displacement sleeping, and there are intriguing reports that soldiers fighting in recent wars experienced an almost overwhelming desire to sleep at the moment they were ordered in to the attack. This was not malingering or true exhaustion. As soon as they were actually attacking they were fully awake. But just at the moment of launching the attack, there was a sudden, powerful feeling of sleepiness. This is a pattern we share with certain species of birds, which tuck their heads under their wings momentarily in the middle of hostile bouts of threatening and disputing.

Human displacement-sleeping, in a mild form, may help to explain certain cases of labour inefficiency. If a man is frustrated, or put into a state of conflict, he may become subject to uncontrollable sensations of fatigue which seriously hamper his major activities. This may be the reason why we say we are 'tired' of something, when we mean we are bored by it. A greater understanding of this mechanism might prove to be of some value in relation to the economics of work output.

REDIRECTED ACTIVITIES

Actions diverted on to a bystander

A Redirected Activity is a pattern of behaviour which is not aimed at the person for whom it is intended.

The most obvious example is redirected aggression. If someone provokes you so badly that you want to attack them, but because of your dominant position you are afraid to do so, you are liable to vent your anger on someone else who is less intimidating. This does nothing to solve your original problem, but it does at least provide some relief for your pent-up frustrations. The price of this relief, however, when viewed across a whole human community, adds up to a great deal of social damage and disruption.

Unhappily, redirected aggression is a widespread phenomenon. Indeed, it probably accounts for the majority of aggressive incidents. The reason for this is clear enough: only an individual who is fairly safe from retaliation is going to permit himself the frequent, open expression of his hostility. The boss insults his assistant, knowing that the assistant dare not reply. The assistant withdraws, smouldering, and turns on his secretary. The secretary holds her tongue for the moment, but later lets fly at the office boy. The office boy, having the lowest status in his group, has no one to turn on, hence the popular phrase used to typify redirected aggression, namely: '. . . and the office boy kicked the cat'.

The other classic picture of this type of redirection is the hostile, unsuccessful husband and his tragically cowed and battered wife. After suffering indignities at work, the husband arrives home fuming and snarling and vents his anger on his defenceless mate or his even more defenceless children. Virtually all wife-battering and child-battering is simple, redirected aggression, as is most cruelty to animals. Aggression, like blood, flows downhill, and ends up in a pool at the bottom of the dominance slope of society.

A less harmful form of redirected aggression is that in which anger is vented on inanimate objects. The angry executive pounds his desk with his fist; the furious wife smashes a vase against a wall; the small boy stamps on a delicate toy. The overpowering hostility finds an outlet, but the living do not suffer in the process. It has been reported that some factories have gone to the

Aggression directed onto the attacker's own person can lead, ultimately, to suicide, but milder forms involve no more than an angry man biting his lip. (After Lavater.)

Aggression is frequently redirected. Instead of attacking the cause of the anger the aggressive individual switches his assault to some less intimidating victim. He may attack an innocent bystander, an inanimate object, or even himself. Rape (right) is often a redirected attack disguised as a sexual action.

The least damaging form of redirected attack is the kind that vents its feelings on an object of some kind, as when an angry wife smashes a vase, or, as here, a forceful politician pounds his desk.

length of installing 'rage rooms' in which suitable inanimate effigies are providing specifically for destruction, as a safety valve for frustrated employees.

In the public sector, it is probably true to say that much of the violence witnessed in riots, rapes and muggings in our streets and parks is caused by this same mechanism of redirection. Superficial causes are usually referred to when such incidents are being reported: riots are related to political protest, rapes to sex, and muggings to theft; but beneath the surface there often lurks the deeper cause—the need to redirect unbearable frustrations that have been weighing on the attackers in their daily lives.

Sometimes the redirection process is greatly delayed in its expression. Here we are in the realm of psychoanalysis, where ancient childhood sufferings and indignities can be traced as the prime causes of later, adult violence. As a species, we seem to be all too adept at harbouring a grudge, sometimes for a lifetime. Because of this the true, redirected nature of certain hostile acts is often deeply obscured.

Aggression is not the only form of behaviour that passes through a redirected channel. Both parental and sexual love may be re-routed in this way. If a loved one dies or is removed for some reason, a substitute may be sought and loved, not for its own sake but for the extent to which it resembles the lost love-object. Since it can never match the original, the result will often be unsatisfactory, if not disastrous. The mother's-boy who seeks his mother's qualities in his young wife is an obvious example. The pseudo-parent who hopes to find in a protege the filial devotion of a true child, is another.

Redirection is a powerful process in human conduct. It can bring relief to blocked urges and provide gratifying outlets, but because it is an inherently flawed mechanism it is fraught with dangers and disappointments, and society bears both the physical and emotional scars to prove it.

RE-MOTIVATING ACTIONS

Actions which stimulate a new mood as a way of eliminating an old one

A Re-motivating Action is a device which suppresses an unwanted mood by arousing a competing one. In other words, if I wish you to stop doing something, I achieve my end by making you want to do something else. The new response I arouse in you squeezes out the old mood that I disliked. It re-motivates you.

As every mother discovers sooner or later, one of the best ways to resolve an unpleasant situation with small children is to excite their interest in something different—something as far removed as possible from the current activity. This strategy is usually much more successful in damping down fights, fears, tempers and conflicts than any more direct method could be. Attempts simply to switch off an unwanted mood by means of demands, threats, requests or pleadings, often fail where a Re-motivating Action quickly succeeds.

Re-motivating Actions succeed by replacing a companion's unwanted mood with a new, more attractive mood. The arousal of the new mood suppresses the old one. Parents often use this device to deflect the interest of their children, but the process is also employed between adults. The woman who behaves like a 'little girl' can stimulate protective, pseudo-parental feelings in a lover (below left) or in a boss.

Re-motivation operates on the concentration principle, which states that there is a mutual suppression of drives at high intensities. If we are concentrating hard on one particular activity we become increasingly unaware of other activities around us. We may be surrounded by a wide variety of stimuli, each demanding our attention, but our concentration develops a single-mindedness which makes us seemingly deaf and blind to all but our primary pursuit. Our brains operate selectively and enable us to ignore all diversions. As one highly productive artist, living in a totally chaotic studio, put it: 'If I did everything I ought to do each day, I would never get anything done.'

It is this concentration-level that the re-motivator has to exploit to change the mood of his companion. He has to increase the stimulus-level of some new element in the environment to such an extent that it begins to invade the existing cone of concentration and switch the mood to the replacement pattern. The harassed parent does this with an exciting new toy or a novel suggestion for a new play activity, the appeal of which is so strong that it sweeps aside the old preoccupation and with it the anger, fright, pain, or squabbling that has arisen in connection with it. So great is the average child's response to novelty in a play situation that this is not too difficult to do. With adults, moods are often less easily influenced, but there are several forms of re-motivation which also operate with a fair degree of success for them, and which have become characteristic patterns of social behaviour.

The most popular adult strategy is the pseudo-infantile re-motivator. Used most commonly by females towards their mates, this device involves the performance of helpless-little-girl actions as part of a wheedling process. The adult male may find such approaches irresistibly arousing his more tender, protective feelings and suppressing his more mature restraints. The adult female, by switching on juvenile signals, stimulates his paternal responses and re-motivates him from a critical companion into a care-giving pseudo-parent. Colloquial language is strewn with re-motivating phrases such as 'my little baby' and 'sugar-daddy' which, despite their literal meanings, have nothing to do with parent-offspring relations, but with the adult transactions of a mated pair. Accompanying such phrases there are characteristic gestures. The pseudo-infantile woman displays pouted lips, wide-open eyes, and child-like body postures, all borrowed from a juvenile context and put to service as adult patterns. A frequent action is the cocking of the head to one side, which is a stylized version of a child's action of laying its head against the body of its parent when being comforted. The modified, adult head-cock unconsciously transmits an appealing request for protection and, without knowing quite why, the male who witnesses the display from his mate feels a sudden upsurge of fatherly compassion.

Although less common, similar childlike patterns are also displayed by certain adult males, and females can be heard describing the appeal of a particular man as being that of 'a little lost boy'. Certain males play on their boyish appeal as a means of arousing the protective maternal urges of females they desire sexually.

Similar events occur reciprocally between young lovers, with their baby-talk, their cuddling, and their tender stroking and fondling. Like pairing birds, they often indulge in courtship feeding, exchanging morsels of food and those specialized human courtship gifts—boxes of chocolates. These mutually displayed juvenile-care patterns help to smooth the path of pair-bonding by reducing any competing fears and anxieties that may lurk beneath the surface.

Apart from these pseudo-infantile and pseudo-parental examples, there are also many cases of pseudo-sexual displays being used as re-motivators. An obvious instance is the classic advice to a young secretary: 'The more typing errors you have made, the more you should stick out your chest'. Although this is a caricature, it neatly sums up the widespread use of sexual signals as a method of reducing male aggression.

INSULT SIGNALS

Sneers and snubs—the ways we show disrespect and contempt

The ways in which one human being can insult another are many and varied. When it comes to being nasty, no other animal can match us. The range and diversity of our derogatory signals is enormous—and that is even before we have begun to open our mouths.

Almost any action can operate as an Insult Signal if it is performed out of its appropriate context—at the wrong time or in the wrong place. But the specialized Insult Signals we are concerned with here are slightly different. They are actions which are *always* insulting, no matter what the context. They set out, right from the start, to be rude, and to mock, defy; threaten, tease, snub or humiliate. They vary in intensity from mild rebuffs to attempts at savage intimidation.

They also vary from locality to locality. There are some that we can easily understand almost anywhere in the world, such as a sneering, contorted face thrust close to our own, but there are many others that we cannot even begin to interpret without special local knowledge. How, for instance, would you interpret a gesture in which the tips of the fingers and thumb of the left hand are brought together, and the straightened forefinger of the right hand is moved across to touch the ring of bunched tips? If the accompanying actions were sufficiently unpleasant, you might guess that the gesture was meant to be offensive in some way, but the precise meaning would escape you unless you happened to hail from Saudi Arabia. If you did come from there, you would be deeply insulted because you would know that the exact message is: 'You are the son of a whore'. The clue to the symbolism is given by the literal phrase 'you have five fathers', the five digits of the left hand being the five males in question.

To an outsider, local signs of this kind are so meaningless that it is possible for local inhabitants to insult foreigners without their knowledge. It can also happen that visitors to a strange country can unwittingly offend the locals by unintentionally making a rude gesture. A knowledge of the different Insult Signals is therefore doubly useful. To understand how they operate it is helpful to arrange them into a number of basic categories:

1. Disinterest Signals. It has been said that if society wishes to show its contempt, it first ignores you, then, if this does not succeed, it laughs at you, and finally, if all else fails, it attacks you. Although this is an over-simplification, it is true that the mildest, most negative form of insult is a show of disinterest. This is done by slightly reducing the intensity of the expected friendly reactions; by nodding and smiling less during conversation; by averting the eyes more than usual; or by deliberately and obviously turning away the head.

When social snobbery reached a peak in the last century, the disinterest insult achieved the status of a formal gesture: the Cut. This was reserved for encounters with people considered to be social inferiors and consisted of allowing them to see that you had noticed them and then blatantly turning your head away and ignoring them. 'Cutting someone dead' or ignoring a proffered hand-shake are still used today as exaggerated forms of disinterest in extreme cases, but they have long since ceased to play a role as a regular part of the social scene. Their impact, on the rare occasions when they are used, is therefore all the more severe. In our present anti-snobbish culture we are expected, at every friendly social gathering, to show great interest in everyone all the time, and if we fail to do so we are liable, at the drop of a smile, to transmit an immediate Insult Signal to one of our sensitive companions.

2. Boredom Signals. If disinterest fails to make its usual impact, a stronger response is to display open boredom. A favourite signal employed here is the mock-yawn. Alternatives include deep sighing, a glazed far-away expression, or repeated examination of the wristwatch. This last action can

High-status individuals tend to tilt their heads back more than lower-status companions. This has given rise to the expression 'to look down one's nose at' someone. Employed in an exaggerated way, this action can easily become insulting.

cause trouble in cases where insults are not intended. If someone has a tight schedule and is desperate to know how late it has become, he is loathe to examine his watch in case the movement will inadvertently act as a boredom insult. This leads to a variety of subtle arm-shifting techniques and secretive watch-glancings.

3. Impatience Signals. Small movements that indicate an urge to get away from the present situation are also widely used. These take the form of 'miniaturized-locomotion' actions, such as strumming with the fingers, tapping with the foot, or repeated slapping of the hand against the body. It is as if part of the body is beating out the rhythm of the get-away. The strummed fingers are like tiny pattering feet, running on the spot. The tapped foot keeps on setting forth on the first step of the escape, but gets no further and has to go on repeating its intention movement. The observer of these signals is in no doubt that the strummer or tapper would really prefer to be somewhere else. Although they have not been measured, it is safe to predict that the speed of these impatience rhythms is roughly the same as the speed of rapidly walking or running feet.

4. Superiority Signals. Many insulters perform small actions which make them appear pompous or 'superior'. The most obvious example is the tilting

back of the head, combined with half-closed eyes, which has given rise to the popular expressions 'look down upon', 'turn one's nose up at' and 'look down one's nose'. This is an exaggerated version of one of the basic high-status signals. In ordinary status displays the more dominant individuals carry their heads high, the more submissive hang their heads low. The high/low difference is usually rather slight— so slight that we are rarely aware of it consciously. Unconsciously, however, we are highly responsive even to minute differences in 'uprightness'. When a round-shouldered man enters a room he will have to work harder to gain our respect than will a vertically erect man. He will not be conscious of this and neither will we, but the undercurrent of feelings will be there none the less. At the moment when an insult is delivered the insulter, regardless of his usual status, may adopt the 'head-high' posture and may push it well beyond the usual limits.

It may seem contradictory for a low-status individual to employ an over-stressed high-status action like this, but at the moment when he flings his insult he is, as it were, stepping outside his normal status role. In a fit of pique, or 'high' dudgeon, he abandons his usual inhibitions and, as he lets fly his verbal attack, throws his head back in an unaccustomed and exaggerated high-status display. It is a fleeting elevation, but it reflects clearly his momentary loss of control.

The small child, the teenager, the pupil, the business subordinate, the servant, and others who must normally inhibit their dominance feelings in many contexts, can be observed to employ these sudden superiority displays when they are occasionally driven to breaking-point and explode with unleashed verbal insults. Storming off with heads held high, they may appear almost laughably pompous to their companions because of the sudden contrast between their usually modest posturing and the now super-dominant nose-in-air display. But for them, the incident really was a moment of super-dominance, while it was happening, and the superiority display felt entirely right.

This illustrates an important social principle: in our milder, more controlled moments, we take a long-term view of our relationships, but in our passionate, more emotional moments, we abandon this for a short-term view. The person who remains cool, while his companion loses his temper and starts throwing insults, sees the contrast between the insulter's past behaviour and his present uncontrolled behaviour, and he reacts to both the insults and the contrast. The exploding insulter himself feels only the anger of the moment. Later, when he has calmed down and has regained the long-term view once more, he will also appreciate the contrast and can often be heard apologizing for 'losing his head'.

Some individuals take superiority displays much further than this, extending their use from momentary outbursts almost to a way of life. They become characteristically aloof, sarcastic, cynical or contemptuous, wearing a nearly permanent sneer or 'bad smell' expression. Most businesses or professional groups have one or two such characters lurking in an office somewhere, ready to fling out their routine insults in response to any enquiry, whether civil or uncivil. Often laughed at behind their backs, feared and disliked, these chronic-insulters have made a long-term relationship choice to give up the relaxed, friendly interactions enjoyed by others in favour of sustained haughtiness or cynicism. For them, their superiority signals become such a regular feature of social intercourse that they lose a great deal of their impact. 'Don't mind him, it's just his way', is the sort of comment used about such people, but it is difficult not to mind, because, even though they lack the force of mood-contrast, the insults are still unpleasant to experience. Because of their very nature they are intrinsically repulsive and no amount of social conditioning can eliminate totally their antagonistic messages.

5. Deformed-compliment Signals. Sarcastic insults often take the form of distorting a compliment. A friendly response is deliberately modified to make

The Cheek Crease (1) and the Thumbnail Applause gesture (2)—both of which are Deformed-compliment Signals.

Symbolic Insults (3–9) vary greatly from culture to culture and are often meaningless outside their home range. They include: the South American Goiter sign, meaning stupidity (3), the Spanish Baby-head sign, meaning immaturity (4), the Arab Little-fingers Pull-apart movement, symbolizing the end of a friendship (5), the European Long-beard gesture, meaning you are boring (6), or the Austrian version of this (7), in which the imaginary beard is stroked with the fingers. There is also the widespread and well-known 'yakity-yak' gesture (8), where the hand mimes the speaking movements of the mouth, and the 'fed-up-to-here' gesture (9).

it unpleasant. Two common examples are the Tight Smile and the Cheek Crease. Both are deformed smiling actions in which some elements of the smile-complex occur and others are omitted. In the Tight Smile the central parts of the lips are strongly pursed, while the mouth-corners pull back as in an ordinary smile. In the Cheek Crease all normal smiling elements are omitted except for the pulling-back of one mouth-corner.

Deformed compliments of this kind are particularly unpleasant insults because they are rather like offering a reward and then snatching it away at the last moment. They show us the smile we could have had but are not getting.

There are a number of localized insults of this type. A good example is the 'thumb-nail applause' offered in certain Arab and Spanish-speaking countries as an act of derision. Instead of clapping loudly with the palms of the hands, the 'applauder' taps the back of one thumb-nail against the other. An alternative used in England and elsewhere is the super-slow hand-clap. However, as so often happens with local gestures, the same actions have different meanings elsewhere. In Panama, for instance, the thumb-nail clapping is merely a form of silent applause, lacking irony or derision; and in Russia a rhythmic slow hand-clap can be highly complimentary.

6. Mock-discomfort Signals. The insulter here uses exaggerated signs of distress to indicate the extent of his displeasure. Melodramatically beating his head with his fist, gasping or covering his face with his hands, or contorting his features into a momentary expression of agony, he deliberately over-acts as a way of stressing his outrage. In its more subtle form, this type of signal becomes the pained expression of the martyr, and is a favourite insult technique employed by 'long-suffering' parents or teachers toward their children or pupils. By exaggerating the pain they feel, they magnify, by implication, the stupidities which cause the pain.

7. Rejection Signals. Somewhere between disinterest and abuse there is an area of moderate insult in which the insulter merely makes a gesture of mild rejection. No warning of violence is involved, as with true threats. Instead, there is simply a 'go away' sign—a 'get lost' message. The Thumb Jerk is one of the most popular, but the flat hand is also widely used, pushing, flicking, flapping, or swiping away the insulted person, but without touching him. The most insulting one is the Insect Flick—with the hand brushing the companion away as if he were no more than an irritating pest.

Sticking out the tongue is a special form of Rejection Signal, originating—as already mentioned—from the infant's rejection of the breast or bottle when refusing food. This early oral movement survives as a repulsion device in older children and adults, even though they are unaware of its derivation and think of it merely as 'rude'.

8. Mockery Signals. Laughing at someone is one of the major forms of insult in our species. To understand why, it is necessary to look at the way an infant first starts to laugh. It does so originally because its mother startles it in a mild way, by tickling it or playfully swinging it through the air. The infant gets a double signal from its mother—one part saying 'there is something strange happening' and the other part saying 'but it is quite safe because it is coming from mother'. Instead of crying, as the infant might do if the tickler or swinger were a stranger, it laughs. So laughter is really a kind of relief-cry. We enjoy a laugh together as adults because we can share the mutual experience of: alarm + relief. But when we laugh directly *at* someone, we throw them a double insult. We are saying with our directed laugh: 'You are alarmingly strange, but—what a relief—we do not need to take you seriously'. This ridiculing form of insult is in one sense worse than an out-and-out threat. Threatening actions display hostility and the dangerous possibility of a physical attack, but they at least give the victim the credit of being worth a fight. Ridicule, on the other hand, displays hostility and belittles the victim at the same time. This is why open derision can so easily provoke the victim into an aggressive response. By attacking the laughing

Animal signals are often used as insults. If an animal has become a symbol of stupidity, like the donkey, then making 'donkey-ears' (top left and top right) becomes insulting. As with so many symbolic gestures it is doubtful whether the boys employing this insult are even aware of its origins. The origin of the 'cocking-a-snook' gesture (left and above) — one of the most common and widespread insults in the world — is uncertain. The earliest record of it is found in the writings of Rabelais (1532) and since then it has acquired 22 different names, suggesting a whole variety of derivations. Most explanations are unconvincing. The least outlandish include: the mimicking of a fighting cock's comb; the making of a long nose, forming a grotesque face; the performance of a deformed salute; or the mimicking of the firing of a catapult.

insulters he can hope, if not to silence them, then at least to convert their derisive laughter into threats and, in so doing, raise his own status to that of 'one worth taking seriously'.

Several forms of contrived mockery are common. Ill-concealed mirth, with the hand covering the mouth but deliberately not obliterating the suppressed laugh, is one. Another is the collusive wink given to a fellow-tormentor, but given in such a way that its usual concealment from the victim purposely fails.

9. Symbolic Insults. There are endless possibilities for symbolic gestures carrying an insulting message. As might be expected, these vary greatly from culture to culture, and many of them are meaningless outside their 'home range'. Examples that someone from an English-speaking country might find puzzling, when travelling abroad, include the following:

In certain South American countries, a hand cupped just below the chin signals stupidity. It does so because it is meant to indicate an imaginary goiter, which is itself a symbol of stupidity. In parts of Spain, the head is tilted, to rest on a supported hand, as a signal of implied immaturity. The suggestion is that the insulted person is still a baby leaning on its mother. Among Arab children, a major insult is to hook the little fingers together and then pull them apart sharply, signifying the end of a relationship. Gypsies throw an insult by squeezing an imaginary, soft object in the hand, suggesting that the insulted person is behaving in a 'soft' way.

In several European countries, a popular symbolic gesture for a male insulter is to hold a hand, palm-up in front of the chest. This is meant to show how long one's beard could grow while listening to the boring speech of the victim of the insult. A Jewish insult is to point down at the upturned palm of one hand with the forefinger of the other hand, the implication being that 'grass will grow on my hand' before the speaker's comments come true. In Austria, stroking an imaginary beard is a sign that a comment is 'old and worn'. In France, the actions of playing an imaginary flute indicate that someone's talking is going on and on and is becoming tiresome. A more widespread version of this is the 'yakity-yak' gesture in which the hand opens and shuts like a gabbling mouth.

A common symbolic gesture is the 'I-am-fed-up-to-here-with-you' sign, in which the hand taps against the throat or the top of the head. This is based on a food-refusal signal meaning: I cannot eat any more, I am full up to here. From food-refusal it has spread symbolically to mean refusal of an idea, with 'full-up' becoming 'fed-up'.

There are also many 'crazy' gestures, indicating that the insulted person is so foolish as to be mad. These usually take the form of 'bad brain' or 'dizzy brain' symbols, such as tapping the temple or screwing a forefinger against it. There may be local confusion over these actions, since in some countries, such as Holland, tapping the temple means intelligent instead of stupid, the Dutch gesture for stupidity being the tapping of the centre of the forehead.

The local varieties of symbolic insults would fill a book, but there is one further major category that deserves mention: the animal insults. Almost any animal will do, so long as it has a bad reputation and is generally considered to be stupid, clumsy, hostile, lazy, dirty, or in some way laughable or unpleasant. The much maligned donkey is a favourite model and its large ears are the basis for the 'jackass' insults. In Italy there are three versions, but only one of these is widely used, and that is the hands-to-ears flapping action. This is popular among children in many countries even though they do not always know that they are performing a donkey-mimic. Today it has spread throughout Europe and America and also into the Arab countries.

Perhaps the most popular and widespread animal sign is the 'cock's-comb' gesture called 'cocking a snook', 'thumbing a nose', or 'making a long nose', in which the thumb of the vertically fanned hand is placed against the insulter's nose. It is easy to see why this is thought to represent the hostile, erect comb of a fighting cock, but there is an alternative explanation which

Right: another Symbolic Insult—the
Spanish Louse Gesture, in which the
insulter mimes the action of squashing a
louse between his thumbnails. Far right: the
Dirt Signal of spitting, which is considered
insulting in many countries. Where spitting
is a common method of clearing the mouth,
it is not always possible to tell whether a
deflected spit is meant to be insulting, or
whether it is merely a private act. But when
it is aimed directly at the insulted person its
message becomes global.

relates it to the ancient practice of imitating grotesque, long-nosed effigies.

Less widely known are such animal signs as the Spanish 'louse' gesture, in which an imaginary louse is squashed between the insulter's thumb-nails, or the Punjab 'snake-tongue' sign, in which the insulter flickers an extended forefinger back and forth like the tongue of a snake.

10. Dirt Signals. In a survey of nearly 200 tribal cultures around the world, an attempt was made to find out whether there are any globally accepted elements of human beauty. It was discovered that the only aspect of human body appeal which applied universally was cleanliness and freedom from disease. Because filthiness means ugliness, gestures connected with dirt are obvious candidates as Insult Signals and, as expected, they can be found all over the world. Mostly they relate to human waste-products—spittle, snot, urine, and faeces, but occasionally they involve the dung of other animals.

In Syria, picking one's nostrils with the right forefinger and thumb means 'go to hell'. A similar gesture is seen in Libya, but there it is followed by a quick thrust of the stiffly extended middle finger.

Among Gypsies a final insult, ending a relationship, consists of shaking imaginary dirt from the clothes, followed by spitting on the floor. Spitting by itself is also seen as an insult in most countries, and exaggerated spitting which becomes pseudo-vomiting, is also common over a wide range.

In the USA there is a joking insult which consists of lifting the trouser-leg as if treading carefully in deep manure, and another in which imaginary dung is shovelled over the shoulder.

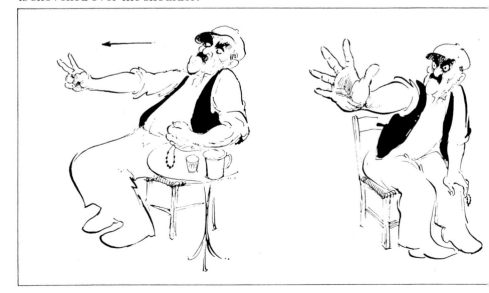

The Greek *moutza* gesture, which can be
performed at five different intensities. From
left to right: the semi-*moutza*: 'go halfway
to hell'; the single *moutza*: 'go to hell'; the
double *moutza*: 'go twice to hell'; the treble
moutza: 'go three times to hell'; the
quadruple *moutza*: 'go four times to hell'.
The most commonly used version is the
single, one-handed form. (After Papas.)

In England there is the popular faecal insult which involves pulling an imaginary lavatory chain while holding the nose with the other hand. A simpler version of this—holding the nose as if protecting oneself from a bad smell, is widely recognized as a strong insult.

In Italy, the 'tirare-saliva'—throwing-the-saliva—gesture is a threatening insult in which the hand 'pulls' saliva from the mouth and throws it at the insulted person.

Because of their basic nature, most of these dirt signals can be understood by people who do not use them and who may never have encountered them before. But there is one, in particular, that puzzles foreigners when they see it for the first time. This is the Greek *moutza* gesture, already discussed as a Relic Signal. Superficially it looks rather harmless—like someone saying 'go back' with a movement of their hand—but when performed by Greek to Greek it carries a savagely insulting meaning, harking back to the ancient practice of thrusting filth into the face of a helpless prisoner. Today, in its token form, it has several degrees of intensity: the mildest consists of a half-handed thrust, using only the first two fingers (=go half-way to hell); the standard form is the one-handed version (=go all the way to hell); and the extra-strong version is the double-handed thrust (=go twice to hell). In a sitting position, and in a slightly jokey mood, it is possible to employ one, or even both feet as additional thrusters (=go three, or four times to hell). Because of the importance of the moutza insult gesture in Greece, other hand actions which resemble it have to be avoided, a fact not always appreciated by foreign visitors who may use a simple Hand Repel action as a friendly refusal, only to find that its impact is startling and the reactions to it inexplicable.

These, then, are some of the ways in which one human being insults another. Two special forms of insult have been omitted: Threat Signals and Obscene Signals. Threat Signals deserve a separate category because their primary function is different. They are visual warnings of possible physical attack by the person who is gesturing. A true insult gesture, by contrast, is a visual substitute for a physical attack. In reality, most threats are not followed through, so they too become substitutes for actual attack, and it is this that relates them so closely to ordinary insults.

Obscene signals differ in another way. An obscenity, in modern times, is a sexual vulgarity. But there are two different categories: the obscene comment and the obscene insult. In the first, a lewd gesture may be made as a compliment or a sexual invitation, without the primary intention of being insulting. In the second, the sexual gesture is made directly at someone as a specific insult. Because obscenities therefore include both direct insults and non-insults, they too are discussed separately in the pages that follow.

THREAT SIGNALS

Attempts to intimidate without coming to blows

Threat signals are warnings of aroused aggression. They are actions which, if carried through, would lead to actual assault, but because they are stultified, remain visual displays. The movements are checked in three main ways:

First, there are the Intention Movements of attack—actions which begin but are not completed. The most familiar of these is the raised-arm threat. The angry man lifts his arm menacingly as if to strike down on to his enemy, but halts his action in mid-air. Alternatively, he may swing his flat hand out sideways, as if about to slap his victim across the face, but then drops it harmlessly to his side instead of completing the blow.

A more melodramatic Intention Movement of attack is the clawed-hands posture, where both hands are raised in front of the body, the fingers stiffly spread and half-curled, like claws about to strike. A foot may also be brought into play, one leg being swung backwards as if ready to deliver a kick. All these movements clearly signal the hostile intent of the performer and would be easily understood almost anywhere in the world.

Equally obvious are the aggressive Vacuum Gestures—actions which are completed, but without making physical contact with the enemy. These include the well-known and widely used fist-shaking movement, in which the Intention Movement of striking a blow is extended as a series of punches in mid-air. This may be done at a considerable distance from the 'victim' and has become so stylized that the vacuum-blows of the fist are mere back-and-forth jerks of the arm, quite unlike the true punch of a real fight. Even so, they are never misinterpreted.

Other Vacuum Gestures include the Italian hand-chop, where the stiffly flattened hand is jerked repeatedly towards the opponent, as if chopping off his head with an axe. There is also the expressive neck-wringing gesture, so stylized that it now looks more like wringing out a wet towel than actually tackling the enemy by the throat. Another movement, also carried out in mid-air instead of on the victim's body, is the vacuum-choking display in which straining hands encircle an imaginary throat and slowly throttle the

The stiff forefinger appears frequently in human threat displays, where it takes the symbolic role of a miniature club or a stabbing knife (above and below).

The raised-fist threat is common throughout the world. Its intimidating quality has led to its use as a special form of salute by communists and by Black Power campaigners, but it continues to be employed by anyone wishing to express a visual protest, regardless of their political role. The examples shown here come from Italy (top left) and Portugal (far left). A simple clenched fist (left), even if not raised high, always acts as a mildly threatening gesture because of the power-grip hand-posture involved. This example comes from Northern Ireland.

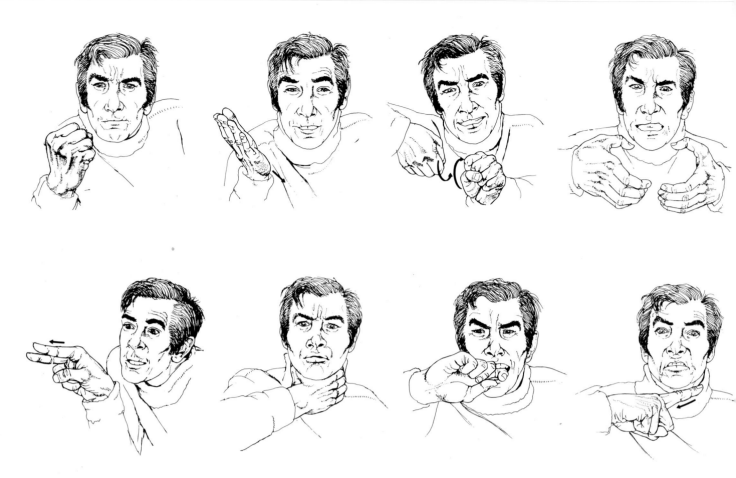

imaginary offender. In some countries the most popular vacuum attack-gesture is the stabbing of a forked hand towards the opponent's eyes. This is done with the first and second fingers aimed stiffly forward and spread apart from each other, so that in theory one would plunge into each of the rival's eyes.

A special case of vacuum-attacking is the wagging of a raised forefinger. In this display, the finger has become a miniaturized club and is beating the opponent over the head in its own symbolic way.

The third category of checked attack-movements is made up of a colourful variety of Redirection Gestures, in which the assault is carried through and makes contact, but not with the victim's body. Instead it is redirected on to some other surface, often the threatener's own body. The 'I-will-strangle-you' threat becomes a grasping of the insulter's own throat. Or he punches his own hand, bites his own knuckles, or slices a forefinger across his own throat as if to cut it.

Again, there are local variants. In Spain, a favourite is the redirected squashing movement, in which one fist grinds down the 'victim' in the palm of the other hand. In Italy, a vacuum biting-action takes the form of hooking the thumb-nail under the upper teeth and then flicking it forcibly outward towards the enemy. In Eastern Europe and some Arab countries, the gesturer squashes his own nose flat with his forefinger. In Saudi Arabia, there is an expressively savage gesture in which the threatener bites his own lip while shaking his head violently from side to side, as if trying to tear a piece off his 'victim'. And there is one redirection gesture that has a mocking tone: the threatener slaps the back of one of his hands with his other palm—a 'naughty, naughty' signal that implies the opponent is no better than a little child.

Accompanying many of these threat gestures there are several characteristic facial expressions, a tense body and exaggerated breathing. The expressions vary according to the shifting balance between the urge to attack and the urge to retreat. For both fear of injury and the urge to inflict it are

Two popular forms of Threat Signals are Vacuum Gestures, in which an attack is performed in mid-air, and Redirection Gestures, in which the attack is diverted on to the threatener's own body. Examples of Vacuum Gestures include (from top left): the Fist Shake; the Hand Chop; the Neck Wring; the Neck Choke; and the Eyes Stab. Examples of Redirection Gestures (the final three drawings) are; the Self-choke; the Self-bite; and the Throat Slit.

The facial expressions of human threat-displays (above and below) vary with the slightly shifting balance of fear and hostility. The more hostile the display the deeper the frown and the more the head is thrust forward. The mouth-corners are also brought forward, producing either a tight-lipped slit, if the mouth is closed, or a 'square-mouthed' gape, if vocal threats are added.

present in every threatener. If one mood starts to get the upper hand, then the expressions begin to change slightly. The very hostile man, whose urge to attack is stronger than his urge to retreat, will be more likely to display a tightly compressed mouth, a thrust-forward head, deep frowning, and some degree of skin pallor. If he begins to feel more frightened of his opponent, his face will change, the mouth showing a snarl that exposes more teeth than before, and he will have a more withdrawn neck, eyes that are wide-open and staring, and skin that is perhaps beginning to redden.

One common mammalian threat-display, where the human species is rather at a loss, is hair-erection. Other mammals make great play with this during hostile encounters, bristling all over, or fanning out furry crests or manes. This gives them the appearance of suddenly becoming much larger and more intimidating. A man can puff up his chest and draw himself up to his full height, but with his unhairy body there is little more that he can do to make himself look bigger and more impressive. He may be able to feel his hair 'standing on end', but as a visible threat it is useless. There seems to be only one human threat gesture that could conceivably be called 'hair-erection', and even that is erection of a rather special kind. It is a French gesture, known as *La Barbe*—literally 'The Beard'—and it consists of flicking the back of the fingers of one hand up under the chin and outwards in a curve towards the enemy. It is an insult which, when performed by a clean-shaven man, gives no clue as to its origin, but when done by a bearded male can easily be understood as a stylized form of beard-jutting. The beard is, in effect, erected at the opponent and thrust out towards him. In the human species the beard is a striking masculine gender signal, and erecting it towards a rival is saying, as it were, 'I throw my masculinity at you'. In other countries we can, perhaps, see a remnant of this display in the form of the irritated head-toss, when a man jerks his chin upwards in annoyance, accompanying it with a small 'tschick' noise, made by the tongue.

Compared with many other animals, it is clear that the human species is not particularly well endowed with basic bodily threat displays. Large numbers of birds, reptiles, fishes and mammals perform immensely impressive hostile display-patterns, shivering, jerking, quivering, inflating themselves, erecting fins, flaps and crests and dramatically changing colour. But what man lacks in bodily displays he makes up for with a great variety of cultural inventions. He threatens his rivals with verbal onslaughts, he puts on war-paint, he dresses up in gaudy uniforms, bangs drums, chants, stamps and dances, and brandishes his weapons. At a national level his threat displays reach the complex proportions of military parades. At a more informal level they express themselves in the form of protest marches, with banners, slogans, badges and ritual salutes, or in the rhythmic and colourful outbursts of football fans as they clap, chant and wave their team colours.

This last type of display has often been referred to as unruly, violent behaviour; but recent investigations into the precise details of the aggressive behaviour of football fans and other such groups has revealed that the actual amount of fighting is minimal when compared with the number of people involved and the amount of time they spend 'displaying'. Like other animals, man shows far more threat and bluff than actual cut and thrust. History books and newspapers tend to distort this picture, dwelling as they do on the tragic exceptions to the general rule. Despite the prevailing feeling today that violence is rife, we are, in truth, a remarkably peaceful species, when viewed worldwide on a day-to-day basis. To test this, you need only ask yourself how many times in your own life you have drawn blood in anger, how many physical blows you have struck, how many gougings, scratchings, bitings, or limb-breakings you have inflicted on other human beings. Compare this with the number of times you have been angered and have become involved in arguments, disputes and quarrels, and you will find that, like other animals, when it comes to aggression, you are much more of a threatener than an attacker.

OBSCENE SIGNALS

The symbolism of sexual insults

Obscene signals are sexual actions which cause offence to those who witness them. Every culture has its sexual taboos and although these vary from place to place and time to time, it is generally true that the more 'advanced' a sexual action is considered to be, the more likely it is to be forbidden in public. If one thinks of a developing sexual encounter, starting with the lovers holding hands and ending with them in the throes of orgasm, then the nearer an action is to the copulatory climax, the more readily it tends to provide a basis for an obscene gesture.

Obscenities can be observed in two distinct situations. The first is the 'vulgarly friendly' and the second is the 'deliberately malicious'. In the friendly situation, a man makes an advanced sexual gesture to a woman, or vice versa, and here the obscenity lies in the fact that their relationship has not reached the stage of intimacy where such a sign would be acceptable, even in private. Since it is often done in public, it is even less acceptable and although no malice is intended, its message is nevertheless offensive. The classic example is the customer who makes an explicit sexual gesture towards the girl serving drinks in a bar. Because of her special social role, he feels free to make an open and direct comment, with his hands, concerning the shape of her breasts. His action is not directly insulting; in fact it is meant to be complimentary, but if she takes offence she converts the gesture instantly into an obscenity.

A more common use of complimentary obscenities occurs in the 'third-party' situation. Two men are looking at an approaching girl and one man signals to the other, by jerking his hand, that he would like to copulate with the girl. His gesture is a compliment to the girl's sexuality, but if it is observed by her and annoys her because it rides rough-shod over the need for sexual preliminaries, then it too becomes an obscene gesture.

These obscenities are quite different from the deliberate sexual insults aimed straight at a victim in a mood of insolent scorn or downright anger. Here the object is to use the 'dirtiest', most taboo sign available as a symbolic form of attack. Instead of hitting the victim, the gesturer directs a sexual gesture at him. It is clear from observing such incidents that an advanced sexual obscenity carries an enormous impact and it is worth asking why this should be.

It is obvious why Dirt Signals, such as spitting or throwing faeces, should be insulting, but why should sexual activities also be the source of 'dirty words' and 'dirty gestures'? There is nothing dirty about sex, so why is there such a widespread misuse of it in this way? If we translate the usual four-letter words into their official equivalents, the strangeness of their misuse becomes even clearer. We shout insults which are the equivalents of: 'You stupid penis!', 'You stupid vagina!', or 'Copulate off!' In their four-letter versions these are familiar curses, but translated in this way they sound decidedly odd.

The explanation is that sexual actions are employed as threatening devices in a large number of species, including our nearest relatives, the monkeys and apes. A male monkey will often mount a subordinate as a method of demonstrating his dominance. Once mounted, he makes a few pelvic thrusts and then dismounts again. There is no mating contact—he merely goes through the motions. When a human male makes an obscene gesture, he is carrying out a special version of the same act. The male monkey mounts the subordinate as a way of saying: 'Since only a dominant male can mount a female, it follows that if I mount you (regardless of your sex) then I must be dominant to you'. In this manner the act of male erection or copulation becomes symbolic of male dominance and can be used as a dominance gesture in totally non-sexual situations. Indeed, it no longer has to represent *male*

The Middle-finger Jerk (above), a phallic-display gesture, is over 2,000 years old. It is still widely used today and is demonstrated (below) by an American policeman towards protesting Freedom Marchers. The man in front of him appears to be employing another obscene gesture—the Crotch Scratch, most commonly found in Mexico.

The Phallic Forearm Jerk. In this painting by Eric Scott (1976) the action is performed by females, which is unusual, but highlights the fact that either sex can use a phallic display as a gesture of dominance. In England this particular gesture is normally employed by males making a crude comment of sexual arousal.

dominance, but can come to symbolize a dominant moment for either sex, so that a human female can make a phallic gesture towards a male and still mean by it, 'You can't frighten me, I am on top of you.'

So, sexual insults are part of our animal inheritance. That does not mean, however, that the different gestures themselves are inborn. It is only the underlying mechanism that is the same in us and our primate relatives. The obscene gestures themselves are highly variable and strongly influenced by the traditions of the different human cultures in which they occur. They fall into five main categories: Male Phallic Signs; Female Genital-aperture Signs; Copulatory Signs; Masturbatory Signs; and Groping Signs.

Phallic signs are the simplest and most popular, requiring no more than some form of symbolic erection. In different countries this is done in a variety of ways, employing several parts of the body. The symbolic 'phallus' may be the tongue, the middle finger, the first and second finger combined, the thumb, the fist, or the forearm.

The most ancient phallic gesture appears to be the Middle-finger Jerk. This was known to the Romans, who referred to the middle digit as the impudent or obscene finger. As an expressive erection obscenity it has remained in active use for over 2,000 years and can be seen today in two distinct forms. In the most common version the hand is held palm-up, with all the fingers curled except the middle one. In this posture the hand is then jerked upwards into the air, or prodded in the direction of the insulted person. Arabs often reverse the procedure, holding the hand palm-down, straightening out all the fingers *except* the middle one, and then jerking this downwards, as if thrusting it into a figure beneath.

A more impressive phallus is made by jerking upwards with the whole forearm, the head of the symbolic penis being formed by the clenched fist. This, the Forearm Jerk, is extremely common today in France, Italy, Spain and Greece, where it is employed almost exclusively as a threatening insult by one male towards another. In England it is also well-known, but is used more as a sexual comment —a crude form of sexual admiration—rather than as a direct insult. The Frenchman does it towards someone who has annoyed

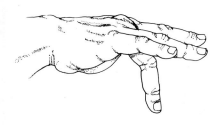

The Arab version of the Middle-finger Jerk. In this, the finger positions are reversed with the mid-finger bent and the others straight. The palm faces downward and the hand is jerked repeatedly towards the ground.

The obscene Thumb Jerk, still in common use in Sardinia, is easily confused with the friendly thumbs-up sign or the hitch-hiker's thumb-a-lift sign. The Sardinian message is 'sit on this', which has sometimes caused trouble for foreign hitch-hikers in that country. The phallic Thumb Jerk will probably disappear in time as the friendly thumbs-up gesture spreads more and more across Europe.

him, and the message is 'Go to hell!' The Englishman does it for the benefit of his male friends, when they notice an attractive girl. It is performed in the girl's general direction, but not for her benefit. Indeed, she is probably not looking at the moment when it is done. The message is: 'This (the erection) is what I would like to give to her'. This is an example of the same gesture having two distinctly different meanings in two countries, even though the action involved is based on the same type of symbolism (forearm = phallus).

A comparative rarity is the Upward Thumb Jerk. This is common enough in certain limited regions, such as southern Sardinia or northern Greece, but in many other areas it is totally unknown. Perhaps part of the reason for its failure as an obscene sign is the rise to popularity of an almost identical gesture meaning 'all's well'—the famous Thumbs-up. The Thumbs-up, which seems to have its origins in England, has now spread over a very wide area, and there is obvious confusion in those places where both the obscene Upward Thumb Jerk and the cheerful Thumbs-up are present. Foreign hitch-hikers in Sardinia can quickly find themselves in trouble if they use the usual 'thumbing-a-lift' gesture at the roadside. What they are actually signalling to the passing drivers is 'sit on this', which is the local expression that explains the obscene Thumb Jerk. Unless they switch to the local hand-waving form of hitching a lift, they are liable to be faced with a long walk.

Another complication has arisen over the use of the two-fingered V-sign. Most countries recognize this as the Victory Sign, made famous during World War II by Winston Churchill, or more recently as the Peace Sign. It has been adopted by students, rebels, politicians, sportsmen and presidents, and internationally one might expect little confusion over it. However, in England it exists in two distinct forms, one with the palm facing outwards

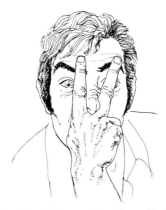

The Churchillian wartime Victory V-sign (above top) has survived as a general signal of triumph and peace, but in England it has an obscene counterpart—the Insult V-sign (above middle). In this version the palm of the hand faces the signaller, whereas in the Victory-V it faces the companion. This difference is little known in many countries and misunderstandings have arisen as a result. The obscene V-sign became more famous in England recently when a top sportsman (left) gave it to the judges of the contest in which he was competing. The origin of the obscene V-sign is uncertain, but it may be a modified version of the Arab Nose Jerk (above) in which the V of the fingers is brought up to jerk against the nose, transforming the tip of the nose into an active phallus.

and one with the palm facing the gesturer himself. Every Englishman knows the difference, and is aware that only the palm-outwards V-sign means victory or peace. The palm-inward version, he also knows full well, is the worst obscenity his hand can make. He is not sure why this is, but he knows it to be so. Englishmen wishing to hurl a gestural insult when abroad have often been nonplussed at the total failure of this sign when directed, say, towards an Italian driver. The chances are that the victim of this gross abuse will smile happily and wave, before speeding off. The explanation, of course, is that to the Italian there are no subtle distinctions to be made between the two palm postures. All he sees is the V-shape made by the first and second fingers thrust aloft, and for him this can only spell victory.

It is intriguing that the Englishman's worst obscene gesture should have such an obscure origin. He is aware that it is vaguely phallic, but beyond that he can provide no explanation for the separation of the two fingers into a V-shape. Since, unlike the kangaroo, the Englishman does not have a forked penis, the true derivation of the gesture poses something of a problem. Four possibilities have been suggested.

First is the explanation which sees it as an amplification of the Middle-finger Jerk. Before World War II there existed in England a Two-finger Jerk insult which was clearly an enlarged version of the middle-finger insult. This employed the first and second fingers, but they were not separated into a V-shape. This obscene signal is still employed today but has been largely superseded by the insult-V. The latter can be interpreted as a further 'enlargement' of the symbolic phallus.

Second, there is the possibility that the insult-V is a hybrid gesture, combining the original Middle-finger Jerk with the eye-stabbing gesture in which forked fingers are aimed at the victim's eyes.

Third is the suggestion that perhaps the Insult V-sign was a deliberate corruption of the Churchillian Victory V-sign, the rotation of the hand producing an inverted victory, that is to say, a defeat, aimed at the insulted person, rather in the way that KO is the opposite of OK. This development may well have occurred during the Second World War, but it can only have served to heighten the popularity of the gesture, since early photographs of the insult-V record that it was in use as long ago as 1913.

The fourth suggestion is perhaps the most likely, namely that the insult-V is a simplification of an obscene gesture used in certain Arab countries and elsewhere, in which the forked fingers are brought up to the gesturer's nose and jerked upwards against it. The symbolism here is copulation, with the nose representing the penis and the two spread fingers the female genitals. By abbreviating this gesture slightly, so that it fails to make contact with the nose, one is left with a perfect insult-V action. The chances are that this abbreviated obscenity was brought to England from overseas by British troops, copied endlessly, and its original form and meaning forgotten. It could be another case of a symbolic gesture becoming remote from its beginnings but managing to retain its potency none the less.

Apart from the hand and the forearm, another organ that displays a phallic potential is the tongue. Tongue-protrusion is a common rudeness, but in some cultures the movement of the tongue renders the gesture explicitly phallic. In certain Latin countries there is an expressive in-and-out action of the tongue, from the open mouth, which is specifically erotic in its meaning, and in the Lebanon there is another movement, where the tongue is wagged from side to side as an insulting proposition by a man to a woman.

Female obscene signs are less common than phallic gestures, but a number of them do exist. Around the Mediterranean, many people employ the 'squashed-circle' gesture, which looks like a partially flattened OK sign. The circle is made by the thumb and forefinger, but instead of the more rounded 'OK' ring, the vagina-sign is displayed by squashing the circle out of shape, thereby making it more reminiscent of the outline of the female genitals. In Colombia, a similar shape is made, and carries a similar female-genital

Left: the Phallic Tongue. It is difficult to be certain in every case of tongue protrusion whether the act is one of simple rudeness or one of deliberate phallic symbolism, although the context and the nature of the tongue movements will usually suggest which.

meaning, but there the squashed-circle is formed by bringing both hands together in front of the body.

Copulation gestures are of two kinds, those that emphasize insertion and those that represent pelvic thrusting. Phallic insertion is the key to the age-old Fig Sign, in which the 'male' thumb is squeezed between the 'female' fingers. This is done with a closed hand, the thumb protruding from between the first and second fingers, like a penis inserted through labia. This gesture, popular in ancient Rome, and surviving on early amulets, is now almost worldwide in distribution in the form of a 'lucky charm'. Small carved hands showing the fig-posture are sold in curio shops from London to Rio, and as in so many other cases, the wearers are probably ignorant of its true meaning. Its protective role may seem odd. Why should an obscene, copulatory gesture have come to stand for good luck? The answer appears to be that it is a 'distraction display'. For many Mediterranean peoples there is a strong belief in the power of the 'evil eye' which, if it looked you in the face, would bring you misfortune. It was not always certain who was possessed by the evil eye, and so it was wise to wear some protective device. A gesture as shocking as the Fig Sign was sure to attract the evil eye's attention and thereby save the amulet's wearer from a direct stare. This belief remains strong today in parts of Sicily, but in other regions the action of making the

There are several obscene signals based on displaying a symbolic orifice. The two demonstrated are (left) the Neapolitan one-handed version and (below left) the two-handed alternative, the latter having become more popular in Italy during recent years.

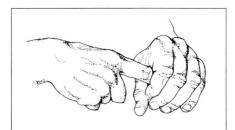

Copulatory gestures made with one or both hands are common and widespread obscene signals. They range from the obvious Forefinger Insertion gesture (above right) to the Italian Palm-banging gesture (right) and the Tunisian Hand-wiggle gesture (far right).

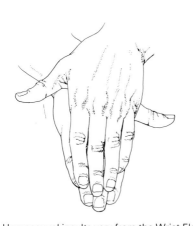

Homosexual insults vary from the Wrist Flap gesture (left) to the Colombian Bird Flap gesture (above). In the latter, the thumbs wiggle up and down like the wings of a bird. It is not clear why a bird should be equated with a homosexual, unless it is because they both take short steps when moving and are often adorned in bright colours.

Fig Sign with the hand still carries its direct sexual message. In Greece and Turkey it is a sexual insult, but in Tunisia and Holland it is mainly a sexual comment or invitation.

Copulation signals other than the Fig Sign nearly always include the element of pelvic thrusting. There are many variants of this, some one-handed and others two-handed. The fist or curled hand is jerked back and forth rapidly, or the finger of one hand is moved in and out of a tube made of the opposite hand, or one hand is banged repeatedly against the other palm. A more direct version is the forward jerking of the pelvis itself.

Homosexual insults, usually implying effeminacy, and therefore supposed weakness in men, include a widely recognized, flapping, limp-wrist display, mincing steps, and wiggling hips. More formalized gestures include the rubbing, by a male, of a licked little-finger-tip along his eyebrow—an insult popular in Lebanon, but also understood elsewhere; flicking the tip of the nose with the tip of the right forefinger, seen in Syria; or putting the hands together and waggling the thumbs like the wings of a bird, as recorded in Colombia. An extreme form of obscenity in parts of Italy is to make the hand into a tubular ring-shape and then jerk this back and forth horizontally, a sign which indicates the act of sodomy. The same gesture performed vertically is a widespread insult suggesting masturbation and implying that the insulted person can find no better form of sexual outlet.

Finally, there are the Groping Signals, usually in the form of hand-cupping gestures in which imaginary breasts or testicles are held, squeezed, fondled or twisted. Like other forms of obscene signals these actions vary greatly in significance according to the context in which they are used. If combined with other hostile behaviour they enhance and amplify the intensity of the insults; if done jokingly between friends they are little more than expressions of vulgar intimacy, or comments on shared reactions to members of the opposite sex, and as such they may be employed to increase or maintain the informality of a relationship.

Some people may find even discussion of obscene gestures offensive. Since offensiveness is the main aim of the gestures themselves this is hardly surprising, but there is one important fact to be remembered. No gesture, no matter how savage its obscenity or how lewd its meaning, ever drew blood. Although they may sometimes provoke retaliation, obscene gestures are essentially substitutes for aggression—miniature rituals that take the place of physical assault—and their social value in this respect has perhaps been underestimated in the past.

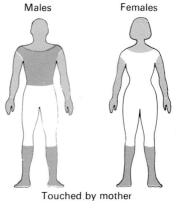

Males   Females

Touched by mother

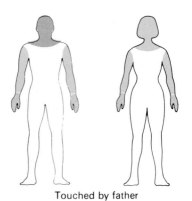

Touched by father

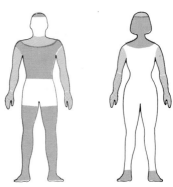

Touched by same sex friend

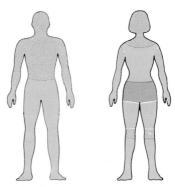

Touched by opposite sex friend

0–25%	26–50%
51–75%	76–100%

TABOO ZONES

Regions of the human body that are out of bounds

A Taboo Zone is an area of the body which a companion may not touch. Each of us has a sense of body-privacy, but the strength of this varies from person to person, culture to culture, and relationship to relationship. Above all, it varies according to the part of our body which is experiencing physical contact. If a companion touches a 'public zone', such as the hand, then no problem arises; but if the same companion reaches out to make contact with a 'private zone', such as the genitals, then the result can be anything from embarrassment to anger. Only lovers and parents with babies have completely free access to all parts of the body. For everyone else there is a graded scale of body-contact taboos.

A careful study was made recently of the Taboo Zones of college graduates in the United States. Their body-surfaces were divided up into twelve contact-zones and then they were asked how likely they were to be touched in these different areas by: (1) their mothers; (2) their fathers; (3) friends of the same sex; and (4) friends of the opposite sex. Four degrees of touch-taboo were allowed for: touched frequently, touched moderately, touched rarely, and touched hardly ever or never.

In general, as might be expected, the body zones nearest to sexual features showed the strongest taboos and those farthest away showed the weakest, but in spite of the general similarity, there were a number of clear-cut differences, according to the nature of the relationship involved. These included the following: (1) Mothers touch their sons less than their daughters *on the hair and arms.* (2) Mothers touch their daughters less than their sons *on the chest.* (3) Fathers touch their sons less than their daughters *on the hair, face, neck and shoulders.* (4) Female + Female friends touch each other less than Male + Male friends *on the shoulders, chest and legs.* (5) Male + Male friends touch each other less than Female + Female friends *on the hair, face, neck and forearms.* (6) Females touch male friends less than males touch them *on the knees.* (7) Males touch female friends less than females touch them *on the chest and pelvis.*

What emerges from these differences is that each relationship has its own unique combination of 'go' and 'no-go' areas. Some of the differences between the sexes are hardly surprising—the greater taboo on the female chest, for instance, relating to the obvious breast taboo; but others are less expected. The male graduate, whether with his father, his mother or another male friend, is clearly far less happy about having his hair touched than is his female counterpart. And this difference extends sometimes to his face, neck, shoulders and arms.

This stronger rejection by the male of caresses to the upper part of his body, by anyone other than his girl-friend, has its roots in earlier childhood, long before the sexual stage is reached. Schoolboys can often be heard muttering 'stop fussing, mother', or some similar phrase, when parental attempts are being made to smooth dishevelled hair, or tidy unruly collars. Young girls are far less hostile to such attentions. The reason behind this probably has something to do with the Western attitude to the decorative qualities of the hair and costume of young girls. To be neatly groomed, even in the pre-sexual condition of childhood, already carries effeminate values, and in this way becomes a masculine taboo.

One rather odd result of these studies is the discovery that the male pelvis is less of a taboo area to a girl-friend than hers is to a boy-friend. Both are associated with primary genital zones and no taboo differences would have been predicted. Field observations of young lovers soon provide an explanation, however. When boy and girl walk or stand with their arms around each other, the usual height differences mean that the boy puts his arm around the girl's shoulder, while she embraces his waist. In doing this,

Opposite: the Taboo Zones of American college graduates. These body zones differ in touchability both by sex and by relationship to the toucher, the percentages indicating how many graduates reported being touched in a particular body zone by different kinds of 'touchers'. (After Jourard.)

Even among almost naked tribal peoples such as these Brazilian Indians (right) there are many taboos about who may touch whom and on what part of the body. Throughout the world, it is only between lovers, in private, and between mothers and their babies (below) that all parts of the body are available for touching, without any Taboo Zone restrictions.

her hand comes to rest on his hip quite naturally, without any direct or deliberate 'groping' at his pelvis. This pelvic contact therefore develops a rather low-intensity quality, sexually speaking, and makes the male's pelvic region, as a whole, more touchable than the female's.

Of course, the precise details of this American college study will not necessarily apply to other countries or other relationships, but the general principles that emerge have wide significance. They tell us that, without thinking about it, we all have special body-taboo relationships with our different relatives and friends, and that we are reading-off these contact-signals every time we meet. If someone breaks one of the established taboos, we immediately become aware that something is amiss and start to tune in more carefully to the changing nature of the relationship. This is particularly important in the inevitably changing relationship between a parent and child. As the child grows, the total body intimacy possible at birth slowly shrinks. Sometimes it is the parent who initiates a restriction. The growing

The strictness of Taboo-zone rules varies from culture to culture. This advertisement from an English magazine showing exposed breasts broke a local taboo when the publication was imported into another country—the island of Malta in the Mediterranean. Before being released to the island's bookstalls, the offending breasts were obliterated with ink by the official Maltese censor.

child becomes exploratory and, sooner or later, will innocently investigate parental breasts or genitals, to be told: 'Don't touch me there.' Sometimes it is the child who initiates a taboo, as when he or she struggles free of a parental cuddle, with the 'let-me-go' reaction of growing independence. Gradually, step by step, the touching taboos strengthen until finally, at puberty, they harden into the adult pattern.

In some cultures this process of contact-reduction is less marked than others. Southern Europe, for instance, is on the whole less anti-contact than northern Europe. And some families within a culture are more strict with their body-taboos than others. Sometimes, one particular culture has a quite specific taboo for one particular region of the body—a region that may be thought of as innocuous elsewhere. In Japan, for example, the back of a girl's neck is as strong a Taboo Zone as her breasts, and in Thailand, the top of a girl's head is considered untouchable. The reasons in the two cases are completely different, however. In the Japanese case, the back of the neck is tabooed because of its erotic significance, while the Thailand restriction is related to religious beliefs.

In general, tribal societies are far freer with their body-contacts than urban civilizations and a great deal of the clamping down is due to the crowded, stranger-infested environments of big cities and towns. With further population increases, all forms of privacy, including body-privacy, are likely to become more and more carefully guarded, and it is unlikely that the phenomenon of Taboo Zones will show any decline in intensity in the years to come. Occasionally, there are brief rebellions against this situation, and in the 1960s the United States saw the growth of a number of group-therapy cults which introduced into their procedures various rituals of mass body-touching. These 'group-gropes', as they were called, revealed the underlying need for body contact and, at the same time, reflected the powerful restrictions being imposed on them in the community at large. But despite the great deal of interest they aroused, the movement now appears to have lost its momentum, and Western society as a whole has retained its general mood of body-privacy and contact-taboo.

Doctors also encounter varying body taboos when examining patients from different cultural backgrounds.

OVEREXPOSED SIGNALS

Going too far—breaking through the etiquette barrier

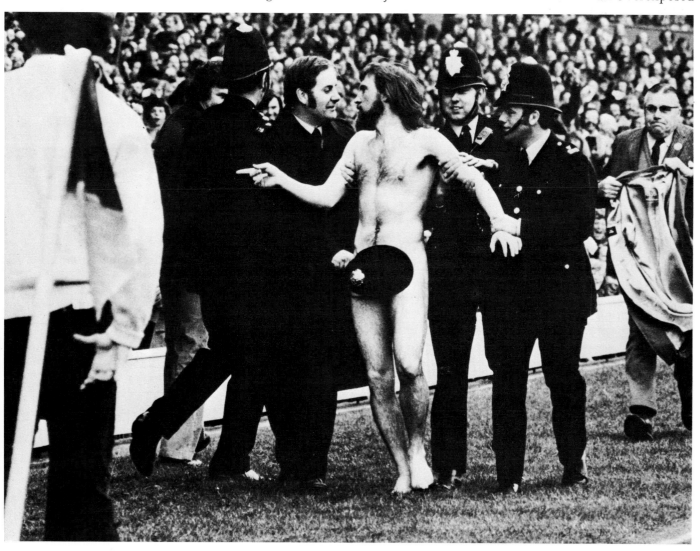

Every action has an 'exposure-rating' on a scale from totally public to totally private. When an act makes a sudden and unusual shift from private to public along this scale it presents an Overexposed Signal to those who witness it. Streaking (below) is a recent example of this and is a case of deliberate overexposure, motivated either by the desire to shock or to symbolize some philosophical stance, as in the case of the naked group (above) seen walking in the centre of London.

Every action we perform has an Exposure Rating, according to how private or public it is. We often contrast 'private' and 'public', as if these are two simple alternatives, but in reality there is a whole range of degrees of 'social exposure' between the two. At one end of the scale there are totally private, solitary acts, such as defecation, and, at the other end, totally public acts such as walking. But in between there are many intermediate actions which enjoy only a restricted exposure.

The expression of these partially public acts is usually delicately balanced against the intimacy of the social context in which we find ourselves. In general, the better we know the people we are with, the more actions we allow ourselves to perform in their presence. With less familiar companions, we become more cautious and start to omit certain acts. Alone, among total strangers, we increase still further these self-restrictions, stifling more and more of our actions until, ultimately, we become stiff and formal.

In Victorian times there was a move towards greater and greater restriction of action exposure. Endless rules were formulated demanding that this or that behaviour should be avoided 'in company'. By contrast, the twentieth century has become increasingly relaxed and informal and many actions have started creeping slowly along the private/public scale, extending their range further and further towards wide exposure. I am calling an act which has just made a move in this direction an Overexposed

Signal. It is a signal, therefore, which, although not unusual in itself, gains attention because it is being performed in a slightly more public context than expected.

There are three basic types of overexposure: the ignorant, the deliberate, and the accidental. All of us overexpose in these three ways from time to time, experiencing social 'gaffes' of one kind or another when we 'go too far' from the private to the public for some reason. And recalling the worst of such moments can still bring a pang of embarrassment even years after the event.

Looking first at the 'ignorant' type, it is clear that this is going to occur most often when we find ourselves in unfamiliar social situations, where we are ignorant of the precise conventions of conduct. A man who belches after a good meal because he comes from either a public-belching culture or a public-belching class will shock a gathering of private-belchers, but he will only become aware that he has overexposed if they react visibly or verbally to what he has done.

In a static social world such unwitting overexposures are rare. This is the major advantage of a strict code of manners. But in a rapidly changing social world, such as we live in today, conventions of any particular situation are increasingly unclear. This does not mean that we are becoming unconventional (only the insane are truly unconventional), but rather that we cannot keep up with the continual shifts in the conventional norm. In his treatment of an unfamiliar woman, a man cannot always be sure whether she is a liberated feminist, or a feminine traditionalist. If he holds a door open for the first and pushes ahead of the second, he is wrong on both counts. In a similar way, he may not be able to tell whether he is encountering a sexual athlete or an old-fashioned prude. If he acts in a courtly way to the first and is bluntly erotic to the second, again he will have been wrong on both counts.

If we are invited out for a 'social evening' we are liable to find confusion over introductions, with no one clear about who is introduced to whom, who shakes hands and who does not, when to cheek-kiss and when not to cheek-kiss, or, if we do kiss, whether we kiss on one cheek or both; there will be confusion about who sits next to whom at table; during conversation it will be unclear which are taboo subjects and which are not, and how much, if any, decorum is expected in terms of verbal censorship; and finally, it will not be clear what time we are expected to leave, or how far we should resist our hosts' polite insistence that we should stay a little longer. In short, we are faced with an evening of social tight-rope walking between the dangers of stuffy underexposure and uncouth overexposure. It is as if society has burned its bra while still wearing a Victorian corset. We like to think we have thrown off the stiff artificialities of the past — and in some important ways we have — but in many details of our social conduct we are haunted still by the ghost of etiquette past, and probably always will be.

In order to make this point, the case has perhaps been overstated, for we are all adept at rapid, almost instantaneous adjustments to a social mood. We can get through even the most confusing social events with only an occasional 'faux-pas', and we manage to keep our ignorant overexposure to a brilliant minimum, because of the hundreds of tiny social clues we respond to during our face-to-face interactions. And if we find ourselves in a totally strange and unfamiliar social setting in a far-off land, we are recognized as 'not belonging' and our unintentional overexposures are forgiven as 'quaintly foreign'.

Moving on to consider the second category of overexposure — the deliberate — we find again that it is a comparatively rare event. If a man's house burns down in the night and he must rush naked into the street to save his life, he has made an inevitable deliberate decision to overexpose, in both senses of the word. He performs a private act — going naked — in public, but is forgiven because of the extreme circumstances. If another man decides to take a nude swim in the sea when no one is about, only to return to find his

Great care is taken by most people to avoid overexposure in public contexts (top). This restriction makes it possible for a few individuals to earn a living doing little more than deliberately overexposing themselves as a form of entertainment (bottom).

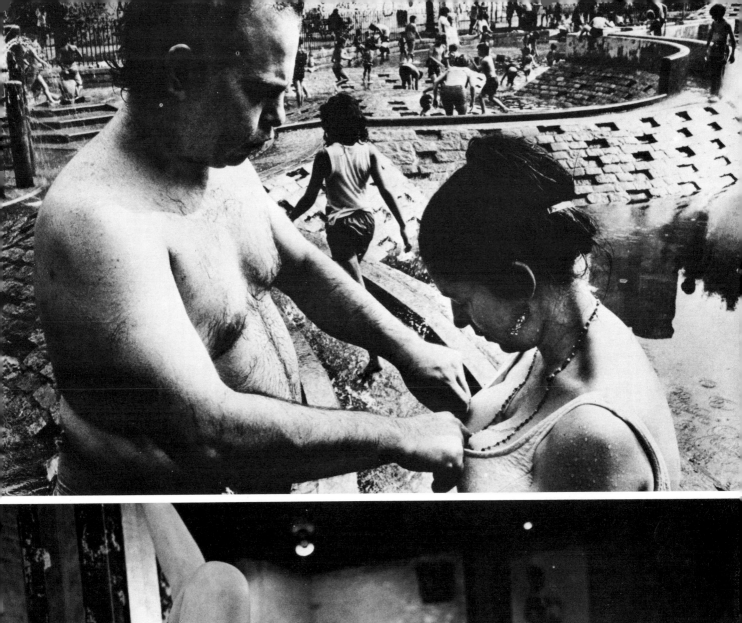

clothes stolen, then he too may be forgiven for converting private nudity into public nakedness, once his explanation has been given. But this second situation is far more embarrassing because his initial act was voluntary, rather than forced, as in the case of the fire.

If, instead, a man suddenly decides to take off all his clothes and run through a crowded street, he may be arrested for indecent behaviour. The phenomenon of 'streaking', which became popular recently, is a strange example of an act that *only* has value as a deliberate Overexposed Signal. It is a curiously symbolic activity, crystallizing in one simple act the whole trend of society towards making private actions more public. Perhaps the most striking aspect of the phenomenon has been not the bemused and rather reluctant arrests by the police, but the almost total acceptance of it by the general public, whose reaction has been one of entertainment rather than outrage. In this respect, at least, action-liberation appears to have made some small headway.

Public 'streaking' reflects similar changes that have been occurring in cinema and theatre productions, where more and more nakedness and explicit sexual activity have been displayed to the public, year by year. The overexposure steps are nearly always small ones, however, and time and again we are faced with yet another symbolic version of society burning its bra while retaining its corsets. The best example of this was a recent film in which a famous actor performed undisguised pelvic thrusts as he made love to his leading lady, but did so without removing his trousers.

Finally, there is the third form of over-exposure—the accidental. A simple example will clarify the distinction between this and the other two types. A man who belches because he is unaware of a belching taboo is overexposing ignorantly; a man who belches to be rude is overexposing deliberately; but a man who belches involuntarily is overexposing accidentally.

This last type of overexposure often involves someone who thinks he is alone, but is not. A curious example of this is the nose-picking motorist. Nose-picking, like ear-cleaning and certain other self-grooming actions, is usually a rather non-exposed action, limited to solitary individuals in private rooms. The motorist is perfectly well aware of this, but for some reason the motor-car has become a symbolic 'private room'. It is so much his personal territory that he is prepared to treat it as a sort of boudoir-on-wheels. If he has no passengers to disturb his 'solitude', he often behaves as if he is sitting in complete seclusion, although in reality he is visible to pedestrians and

Young lovers usually restrict their courtship activities in public places, and the degree of restriction varies from country to country. In some regions any advanced form of body contact is forbidden by law; in others far more is permitted. Even so, it is rare to observe postures resembling the mating act itself (below left). Some actions are more permissible for infants in public than for adults. Wayside urinating (below) is one of these, because the infant penis is solely concerned with urination, while the adult penis is also a sexual organ.

We all experience accidental overexposure from time to time, but our accidents are seldom newsworthy unless we happen to be a well-known public figure. The greater the deliberate underexposure—or decorum—of a particular figure, the greater the public reaction and interest becomes when an occasional accident does occur.

other motorists through the unscreened windows of his vehicle. In addition to picking his nose, he can also be observed performing other 'private' actions. Sometimes he appears quite demented, sitting at his wheel in a traffic jam, swinging his head from side to side, mouthing silently and beating the car with his hands. But the display is deceptive—he is merely listening to music on his car radio. Again he feels he is alone, cocooned from the outside world by the walls of his portable territory, and he disinhibits himself accordingly.

Accidental body-collision in public places is another example of this third type of overexposure. We go to great lengths to avoid this, manoeuvring around one another in crowded places with consummate skill. But despite our expertise we occasionally bump into one another. When we do, we apologize, not merely because we have inconvenienced each other, but also because we have accidentally overexposed. We have been more intimate than we intended and we have to make this clear.

If the collision is with a member of the opposite sex, the apology is usually slightly more intense, because we wish to remove any suggestion of a private, sexual body-contact having been made. Sexually desperate males sometimes make use of this situation in reverse—they press up against women in crowded places, disguising the deliberate sexual contact as accidental overexposure.

Before leaving the subject of Overexposed Signals there are some anomalies that deserve comment. The simple private/public scale is often distorted by special circumstances. Some predominantly private actions are exposable in certain contexts but not in others, and there are different rules for different performers. Roadside urinating, for instance, is less of an overexposure in the case of an infant than an adult, and there are many other similar acts that a small child can indulge in in public without causing comment. Boisterous playfulness and noisy temper-tantrums, for example, occur in public as well as private with very small children, whereas adults tend to limit such behaviour to the privacy of their own homes. Strangers observing infants behaving this way in public are often tolerant of such activities because they recognize that the performers in question have not yet learnt the exposure ratings of their actions.

As the child grows older, it switches from uncontrolled overexposing in public to the opposite extreme—to the underexposing we call shyness. Only as the years pass and further experience is gained will the 'correct' balance be achieved.

There is one special category of adults who are treated as if they are children, with regard to overexposure, and that is the sick and injured. Hospital patients and invalids are permitted to display action-exposure of an extreme kind. Their most intimate bodily actions are performed in the presence of comparative strangers. Some are too ill to care; others regress happily to the total dependency of pseudo-infancy; but others find the cultural rule-breaking of the action-overexposure an unwelcome additional strain in an already distressful situation. As a method of literally adding insult to injury, the design of the typical hospital ward deserves a special prize.

Apart from infants and invalids, there is another important category of permitted overexposers—the eccentrics. If a particular individual holds an unusually prominent place in society, either by inheritance or by talent, he is to some degree allowed to extend his private whims into public life without castigation. If he indulges in uninhibited private acts in public, his behaviour is labelled as eccentric rather than offensive, and once it has been put into this special category it ceases to be a social threat. By its isolation as a special case, it becomes 'safe'. He is then not only *permitted* to overexpose far beyond the cultural norm but, once his excesses have become familiar, is actually *expected* to overexpose on public occasions. If he fails to do so, those present feel cheated of a display. Most of us cannot get away with this because we

Overexposure is not merely a matter of revealing the more private regions of the body. Any action that is more restricted in public than in private is a potential source of Overexposed Signals. We eat more daintily in public than in private (top), so that public food-wolfing (above) can easily become a case of behavioural overexposure.

only feel the urge to 'kick over the traces' on rare occasions. Being an eccentric is a full-time social role.

In other words, you can only be excused rudeness if you are always rude and you can only be forgiven sexual blatancy if you are always sexually blatant. It is as if, for these special individuals, we make a basic correction on the usual exposure-rating scale, and then react with an appropriately adjusted tolerance. The drunken poet, the Hollywood hell-raiser, the mad genius, the notorious vamp, the insult comic, the elderly lecher, the hysterical actress, the absent-minded professor, the dotty aristocrat and the brawling crooner are some of the immediately recognizable characters who fall into this special category and whose overexposures grace our gossip columns and succeed in titillating us where others might cause anger.

We sometimes say of these wayward celebrities that they are behaving like naughty children, a comment that illustrates the way we manage to 'tame' their overexposed actions and make them acceptable. By behaving in public the way lesser mortals behave in private, they provide a spectacle for us which is at once understandable and yet outrageous, familiar and yet extreme. There are times when all of us would like to disinhibit our public selves but fear to do so, and the eccentrics act, as it were, on our behalf. We enjoy their overexposed actions by proxy. We also envy them their action-freedom, of course, and they therefore live precarious lives—at any moment, if they begin to bore us, we will turn on them. Their public playfulness and rowdiness suddenly cease to amuse, and become instead the cause for serious concern and scandal. Overnight, their licensed overexposures become revoked. Savage envy, in its official disguise as puritanism, strikes them down.

These, then, are the Overexposed Signals. For the field observer of human behaviour they provide valuable clues, revealing degrees of failure on the part of the overexposers to lock in to the private/public action-scale of their particular social scene. It has been necessary to select rather extreme examples in order to emphasize the basic principle, but in reality overexposure is a much more subtle process than the crude, all-or-none alternatives (such as public belch or non-belch, public urinate or non-urinate) which I have been giving. Public self-inhibiting is often only a matter of degree and once the field observer has sensitized himself to the different exposure-ratings of everyday activities, he can detect at a glance when someone is even slightly out of phase. This may involve no more than a small difference in the speed or intensity of a particular action. For instance, most people, when eating in public, slow down their feeding actions a little. They transfer the food from the plate to the mouth more cautiously, open their mouths less widely to receive the food, bend the head down towards the plate less, take smaller mouthfuls, and chew less rapidly. Watching diners in a restaurant, it is possible to grade them according to the degree of their 'food-gulping suppression'. The vast majority of them lock in to the cultural norm, employing a mild damping of their solitary feeding vigour, but a few do not. These exceptions fall into two groups—the public food-wolfers and the public slow-motion nibblers. The wolfers nearly always turn out to be from the extreme upper classes or the extreme lower classes, but not from the middle classes. Examples of public food-wolfing can be found in a mixed bag of certain millionaires and members of the European Aristocracy, and certain vagrants and unskilled labourers. Genteel food-nibblers, on the other hand, appear to be individuals who are underexposing because they are on unfamiliar ground. Either they are in a restaurant that caters for a clientele from a social class which is not their own, or they are unused to eating out.

We are all aware of overexposing, but once the concept has been isolated and analysed, it becomes more vivid as a cultural process and more immediately understandable. Phrases like 'Wait till I get you home', to a naughty child, or 'Now we can let our hair down', when the formal guests have left a party, fall into place and become part of a major social pattern.

CLOTHING SIGNALS

Clothing as display, comfort and modesty

It is impossible to wear clothes without transmitting social signals. Every costume tells a story, often a very subtle one, about its wearer. Even those people who insist that they despise attention to clothing, and dress as casually as possible, are making quite specific comments on their social roles and their attitudes towards the culture in which they live.

For the majority of people, Clothing Signals are the result of a single daily event—the act of dressing, performed each morning. At the top and bottom of the social scale this activity may lose its once-a-day frequency, with rich socialites changing several times daily as a matter of course, and poor vagrants sleeping rough in the same clothes they wear by day. Between these two extremes, the once-a-day routine is usually only broken for the donning of specialized clothing. The man who gets dirty wears working clothes, the sportsman wears high-activity clothes. People attending special ceremonies—weddings, funerals, garden parties, dances, festivals, club meetings, formal dinners—change into the appropriate costumes. But although these pursuits mean the doubling of the once-a-day act of dressing, the change is nearly always from 'everyday' clothes into 'special' clothing. The old pattern, in which social rules demanded the changing from 'morning dress' to 'afternoon dress' to 'evening dress', as a matter of regular routine, has now virtually vanished.

The modern trend in dressing behaviour is usually referred to as one of increased informality, but this is misleading. In reality, there is no loss of formality, merely the exchange of old formalities for new. The wearing of a pair of jeans by a young male today is as much of a formality as was the wearing of a top hat by his equivalent in a previous epoch. He may feel that he is free to wear anything he pleases, and is rid at last of the suffocating rules of costume etiquette that once dominated social life, but what he is pleased to wear is as much a uniform today as the costumes of his predecessors were in earlier times. The written rules of yesterday may have been scrapped, but they have rapidly been replaced by the unwritten rules of today.

To understand these rules we have to look back at the origins of clothing as a pattern of human behaviour. Basically, clothes have three functions: comfort, modesty and display. Comfort is, of course, the utilitarian function of garments, non-social and personal. Early man evolved in a warm climate, where his temperature control system operated efficiently. His constant internal body temperature of 37°C, combined with his naked skin surface, worked well enough without artificial aids. He was helped by several important physiological mechanisms that had the same effect as taking off or putting on a layer of clothing. He could, for example, change the flow of blood at the body surface by dilating or constricting the blood vessels in the skin, the maximum blood-flow through the skin being twenty times the minimum level. It has been calculated that pushing the hot blood to the surface in this way is roughly equivalent to the shedding of a woollen garment such as a pullover. Heat loss from the hot skin is further improved by the human ability to sweat copiously from almost the whole body surface. Early human hunters, engaged in violent physical activity, must have experienced a dramatic increase in the amount of heat produced by the internal metabolic processes of the body—something like five times the resting level—and their naked skin surface must have been a valuable aid to temperature control under these conditions, providing a large area for sweat loss and therefore for heat loss by evaporation. The human body is capable of a continuous output over an hour of up to one litre of sweat, increasing to as much as four times this rate for short periods.

With its variable heat production and its variable heat loss, the unclothed human body was—and is—capable of maintaining the constant body-

Clothing has three main functions: modesty (top), comfort (middle) and display (above). Most costumes serve all three of these functions though the emphasis shifts from case to case. But in every instance each article of clothing transmits a signal to an onlooker, telling him something about the wearer's background, mood or personality.

temperature so vital for our species, despite variations in physical activity and despite minor fluctuations in climate. But when man started to explore and strike out across the globe, to the burning hot deserts and the icy polar regions, the natural body-system could not cope with the demands put upon it. Protective clothing became essential, either to reduce heat loss from the skin surface or to shield the skin from the direct blast of the sun's rays. With the passage of time, as human activities became more and more complex, additional forms of protection were required—against sharp surfaces that could damage the skin, against intense light, against attack from sharp weapons, against loss of oxygen, and against excessive radiation. Each new demand gave rise to new forms of protective clothing, from thick shoes and heavy gloves to helmets and suits of armour, from deep-sea diving suits to space suits, from goggles and sun-glasses to snorkels and welding-masks, from overalls to bullet-proof vests.

From the very beginning, protective clothing of these different kinds created problems. Not only did they decrease the efficiency of the muscular actions of the body, but they also introduced special health hazards. They reduced skin ventilation and they interfered with the removal of sweat from the skin surface. Also they provided a haven of rest and a hiding place for a wide variety of tiny parasites. When naked, in primeval times, the human skin suffered none of these problems. The millions of microbes living on it were kept in a state of equilibrium. But unventilated, clogged with decaying sweat and besieged by parasites, the body surface quickly fell prey to all kinds of diseases. At best, there was unpleasant 'body odour'; at worst, epidemics. Unable to abandon his protective clothing, man was forced to develop the counter-balancing devices of perfumery and hygiene. Scents were widely used to mask smells, and washing, of both bodies and clothes, was used to remove them. Today, at last, with medical hygiene adding its weight to normal ablutions, modern man has managed to return to a

In many Arab countries, females must cover their entire bodies when appearing in public. Even their body shape is concealed by the loose folds of their costumes.

The changing shape of the bathing costume. In the 4th century AD, Sicilian maidens (below left) bathed much as women do today, wearing simple two-piece costumes. But during the 19th century (below) the demands of modesty forced bathers into cumbersome bathing garments totally unsuited to active swimming.

comparatively healthy skin condition, similar to that of his primeval ancestors, without resorting to the naked state.

If clothing were simply a matter of comfort and protection, then there are many occasions when we could all abandon our costumes, thanks to modern technology. We have air-conditioning, central heating and soft furnishings in our homes and could easily wine, dine, entertain and relax in the nude without any protective problems arising. The fact that we do not do so leads on to the second basic function of clothing, that of modesty. In this role, clothing acts as a concealment device. Garments are worn to switch off certain body signals. Ever since early man went upright and walked on his hind legs he has been unable to approach another member of his species without giving a sexual display. For other primates this problem does not arise. They approach on all fours and are forced to adopt a special 'presentation' posture if they wish to display their genitals. The 'full frontal' human body can only reduce the sexuality of its approach by hiding the sexual regions in some way. It is not surprising, therefore, to find that the loin-cloth is culturally the most widespread of all garments. In any social situation demanding costume-shedding, it is the last clothing barrier to fall.

An additional factor supporting modesty in dress has been the dramatic increase in population size. After millions of years living in small tribal units, mankind now moves about in huge urban crowds, surrounded by comparative or total strangers. Under these conditions direct sexual displays have to be damped down. Body signals have to be switched off. Even in hot climates this means body coverage that extends well beyond the genital region, and the reason is not hard to find. The human body is a mass of gender signals, and every curve of flesh, each bulge and contour, transmits its basic signals to the eyes of interested onlookers. The female breasts, the buttocks, the hips, the thighs, the waist, the slender neck, the rounded limbs, and the male chest, the body hair, the broad shoulders, the muscles of the

In any situation where clothing is reduced to a minimum, it is the 'fig-leaf' that covers the genital region—a loincloth (above); a one-piece bikini (below)—that is least likely to disappear.

arms and legs, all these visual elements are potentially arousing to the opposite sex. If their messages are to be reduced, then they too must be hidden by enveloping garments.

At different times and in different epochs the social rules of modesty have varied, but the basic principle has remained the same. The more anti-sexual the demands of society, the more all-covering has been the clothing. Extreme examples were the heavily veiled females of certain Arab countries, where not only was the entire body covered with clothing, including the whole of the head and face, but its shape was also concealed by the voluminous nature of the garments. Peering through the tiny slit in her heavy veil, such a female could be either a raging beauty or a hideous hag, and only her husband knew the truth, for she would never appear in public, at any time in her life, in a more revealing costume.

Today it is hard to credit some of the lengths to which civilized cultures went, only a century ago, in their quest for modesty in dress. At one point, even to speak the word 'leg' in English was considered an obscenity, and the legs of grand pianos had to be clothed for public recitals. Bathing machines, in which early bathers changed into their bulky swimming costumes, were required to have curtained steps, so that their occupants could descend into the water before becoming visible to others on the beach.

Descending from these extremes of modesty it is possible to locate a whole range of degrees of exposure, with certain parts of the body gradually dropping out of the 'concealment category'. In the world of entertainment as late as the 1930s it was necessary to conceal naked navels in Hollywood movies, and naked female nipples did not appear in newspapers until the 1960s. since then, pubic hair has sprouted on the silver screen, but if it does so in a public place its owner is still liable to prosecution. The mono-bikini swimsuit, after initial skirmishes with the police in the south of France, has now started to appear with some regularity, however, and we are back once again to the fig-leaf or loin-cloth stage in at least some of our public social contexts. In other situations the rules are still almost Victorian in their rigidity, and even the rich and powerful may find themselves expelled from certain top restaurants for exposing their naked necks, tieless, to the gaze of the other diners.

With this neck-tie rule, we move on to the third basic function of clothing, namely display. For the expulsion of tieless diners from restaurants has more to do with their refusal to wear a social label than their attempt to expose their Adam's apples. The tie, like so many other details of costume, is unimportant either as a comfort device or a modesty covering. Instead it operates as a cultural badge, slotting the wearer neatly into a particular social category. This is the most ancient use of clothing, preceding even its protective and modesty roles, and it remains today of supreme importance. The bleak, functional tunics of spacemen from the future, beloved of writers of second-rate Science Fiction, are about as unlikely as the return of total nudity. As fast as one set of decorative accessories is stripped away, it is replaced by another, and this state of affairs is likely to continue for as long as man remains a social being. Clothing is simply too good a vehicle for visual displays for it ever to become merely a bleak, protective covering.

In the past the display function of clothing has often operated with extreme ruthlessness. In 14th-century England, for example, it was not a matter of style or taste but of law, with the parliament of the day spending much of its time laying down firm rules concerning the fashions of dress permissible for each social class. If someone of a lower social station wore clothing permitted only for higher ranks, he or she might be fined or have the offending garments confiscated. The application of the laws seems to have met with some difficulty, however, such was the desire of people to display high status via their costumes, and monarch after monarch was driven to introduce more and more restrictions and heavier fines. The details are hard to believe when viewed from the present century. These extracts from a

In earlier centuries, costume rules were a matter not merely of following fashion but of obeying the law of the land. These 15th-century costumes illustrate the relationship between status and clothing. No knight under the rank of lord was permitted to wear a tunic that failed to cover his buttocks or to wear shoes with points longer than two inches. The central figure here shows both these costume features and, if he were not a lord, would be subject to a fine on both counts.

Opposite top: the Hollywood Code once banned naked navels from the cinema screen—a ruling that led to the manufacture of a wide variety of navel jewels. In more recent years, Egyptian officialdom has insisted on a similar cover-up for the bellies of belly-dancers, who must now veil their navels behind a modesty covering (opposite).

clothing-reform act in the reign of Edward IV are typical: 'No knight under the rank of a lord . . . shall wear any gown, jacket, or cloak, that is not long enough, when he stands upright, to cover his privities and his buttocks, under the penalty of twenty shillings. . . . No knight under the rank of a lord . . . shall wear any shoes or boots having pikes or points exceeding the length of two inches, under the forfeiture of forty pence. . . .' England was not alone in these restrictions. In Renaissance Germany a woman who dressed above her station was liable to have a heavy wooden collar locked around her neck as punishment; and in America, in early New England, a woman was forbidden to wear a silk scarf unless her husband was worth a thousand dollars.

These are isolated examples chosen from thousands of such regulations which together made up a vast network of limitations imposed on costume displays in earlier periods of history. They reveal not only the fact that clothing and social status were intimately linked, but also that many people were trying to improve their status by the wearing of costumes typical of their superiors and had to be penalized for transmitting Clothing Signals that were 'beyond their station'. Today there are no such laws for everyday clothes, the only surviving regulation being the prohibition of 'indecent exposure' in public places. It is still an offence, however, for a major in any army to wear the uniform of a colonel, and specialized 'costumes of office' remain as rigidly controlled as ever.

For those without official posts it might seem that the decay of the clothing laws would lead to decorative chaos, but nothing could be further from the truth. Instead of experiencing a costume free-for-all, society applied its own restrictions. At first the legal rules were replaced by rules of etiquette, carefully written down as before but now demanding obedience to good taste rather than to the laws of the land. Then, as etiquette books faded into history with the breakdown of rigid class structures, the rules went underground. They survived but they became unwritten, almost unspoken. Today, with social 'class' almost a dirty word, these rules are subtle and complex, and are often complete inversions of the earlier systems. A British earl, for instance, when asked recently if there were any benefits in holding his social rank today, replied: 'Only one—that I do not have to dress so damned smartly as my manservant.' This comment, which would have seemed sheer lunacy to his medieval ancestors, sums up in a single sentence the major trend that has overtaken male Clothing Signals in recent generations. It is a trend that has swept the world and now applies as much to Japanese bankers and Russian politicians as it does to Norwegian architects or Portuguese school-teachers.

The explanation of the new male trend is to be found in the need for a new source of high-status clothing. If any man can buy gaudy silks and satins and adorn himself like a displaying peacock, then clearly such excesses will soon become meaningless and even vulgar, and high-status seekers must turn elsewhere for their inspiration. Where they did in fact turn, back in the eighteenth century, was the sports field. High-status males were indulging in high-status sports. English country gentlemen were taking to the hunting field and adopting a sensible mode of dress for the occasion. For ease of riding, they wore a coat that was cut away in the front, giving it the appearance of having tails at the back. Big, floppy hats were replaced by stiff top-hats, like prototype crash helmets. Once this hunting outfit became established as the high-status sports-costume of the day, it became synonymous with leisure and the lack of need to work. This made it appealing as a daring form of everyday wear for the 'young bloods' of the day, and it spread from the hunting field into general social use. Gradually it became accepted, lost its daring flavour, and by the middle of the nineteenth century the slightly modified costume of 'top hat and tails' was normal, everyday wear.

As soon as this costume was commonplace it lost its high-status quality and a new sporting area had to be plundered for further 'avant-garde' costumes. This time it was the turn of shooting, fishing and golf, all costly, leisured pursuits of the well-to-do and therefore excellent sources for new costume ideas. The tough shooting-tweeds became check lounge-suits, with only minor modifications, and Billycock hats became bowlers. The softer sporting hats became trilby hats. At first the lounge-suit was still considered daring and extremely informal. Only the tailcoat was permissible for formal

The rough look of the American working cowboy (above) has been borrowed as a new source of chic fashion (above right), but the details differ. Although the fashionable male adopts a 'working' denim costume, he ensures by various subtle devices that he will not be mistaken for a working man.

The rise and fall of the Top Hat and Tails. New fashions are often borrowed from the world of sport. The Top-Hat-and-Tails costume began as an 18th-century gentleman's hunting outfit, worn solely for the chase (above). Then, during the 19th century, it became increasingly accepted for use at fashionable social gatherings, such as this Victorian garden party at Windsor (left). By the early 20th century it was employed as ordinary day wear suitable for an office interview (right) and today it has sunk to the fossilized condition of 'Formal Attire' for wedding guests (far right).

occasions, even though it was clearly beginning to lose ground. In no time at all the lounge-suit, by abandoning its loud checks and becoming more sombre in colour and pattern, was pushing the tailcoat out of all daytime social events until, as 'morning dress', it retreated into the formalized contexts of weddings and other such ceremonial events, and as 'evening dress', it retreated into a fossilized black-and-white condition for special nights on the town. Relentlessly the lounge-suit pursued it, driving it even from these strongholds, until it sank to its present relic condition as the costume of head-waiters in expensive restaurants. In its place came the ubiquitous dinner-jacket, the newly fossilized black-and-white version of the lounge suit.

No sooner had the lounge-suit reached this hallowed status than it became necessary to replace it with some new and more daring sports wear. The answer was the hacking-jacket, worn by high-status horse-riders on cross-country canters. It quickly became the everyday casual wear known as the 'sports jacket', and soon climbed the long social path to the boardroom and the executive suite. Today it is still locked in battle with the entrenched lounge-suit, but whichever choice they make, modern businessmen are, without exception, all wearing what can accurately be described as ex-sports clothing.

In recent years a new trend has appeared. With a growing distaste, in an increasingly egalitarian society, for 'privileged' individuals, it became necessary for high-status males to perform their clothing displays in an even more subtle fashion. The man who wore a smart yachting blazer with shiny brass buttons when going out for a drink at his local bar, in imitation of a rich sporting yachtsman, was now in serious trouble. Raiding high-status sports was no longer possible. Instead it became necessary to borrow costumes from distinctly low-status occupations, in order to demonstrate

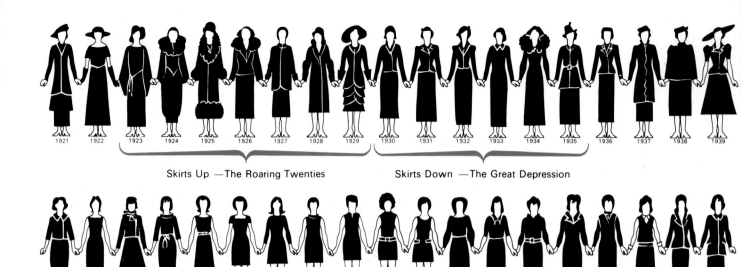

Skirts Up —The Roaring Twenties

Skirts Down —The Great Depression

Skirts Up —The Swinging Sixties

Skirts Down —The New Recession

that, even though you were rich and famous, you were nevertheless one of the 'poor boys' at heart. The earliest symptom of the 'poor boy' syndrome sprang from the fashion for taking Mediterranean holidays, where the rough shirts and sweaters of the local fishermen quickly became absorbed into the everyday wear of wealthy young males, and have since spread to almost all countries as casual clothing —hence the tieless disputes at many a restaurant door. Even more important was the adoption of the denim jackets and jeans of poor cowhands in the American West, a trend that is still spreading today in a hundred subtly varying forms.

There is, of course, a catch in this latest trend, for the costumes of these new, high-status males must somehow be distinguishable from the real working clothes of the low-status males who still wear them in their original contexts. The clothing signals must transmit the perverse message that: 'I approve of "poor boys", but I am not one myself'. This is done in several ways. The first is to wear the sweaters or denims in just those social situations where the true 'poor boy' would be climbing into his 'best clothes'. The second is to have the 'poor' clothes beautifully tailored and elaborately styled, without robbing them of their superficial 'poorness'. The third device is one that belongs exclusively to the modern world of mass media, and could not have existed before it. This is the famous-face contrast. Anyone who is rich and well-known, and whose face appears regularly in newspapers and magazines and on TV and cinema screens, can afford to wear the scruffiest of 'poor boy' clothes to even the most glittering occasions. He is then, by the contrast between his famous face and his faded denims, making a violent silent attack on his affluence-oriented culture. If he is carefully photographed alighting from his gleaming Rolls-Royce, while wearing his crumpled, 'poor boy' clothes, he must be forgiven for the inconsistency.

This is only one of the many interwoven trends that can be observed in the complex world of Clothing Signals. Some are long-term, lasting for whole decades, while others are short-term, surviving only for a season or two. Not all are easy to explain. One of the most mysterious is the relationship between female skirt-length and economic conditions. During the present century, ever since the First World War, there has been a rather precise correlation between the length of female skirts and the periods of boom and depression. On the surface, one would expect long skirts, employing greater quantities of material, to be related to the boom periods, and the skimpier, shorter skirts

Skirts Up —Active Wartime Economy   Skirts Down —Post-War Austerity

The skirt length of the modern Western woman acts as an economic barometer. As hemlines rise and fall, so does the economic condition of the country. Short skirts appear at times of high national production and long skirts during periods of austerity and recession.

to be made when money also was short. But an analysis of the facts reveals that the exact opposite is the case. As the stock market rises so too do the skirts, and when it falls they descend with it. Attempts to change this relationship have met with disaster. Back in the boom period of the 1960s the fashion houses tried desperately to increase the amount of cloth used in skirt-making by the introduction of the 'midi', a skirt almost twice as long as the 'mini' then in favour. The midi-skirt project was an expensive failure and skirts went soaring on upwards to the 'micro' level and even the 'hot-pants' peak. Only with the recession of the 1970s did the longer skirt edge its way back into fashion. The same was true of the inter-war period: in the booming 1920s, there were the short, flapper-skirts, followed by much longer garments in the deeply depressed 1930s. Skirts rose again during the 1940s and the Second World War, when national production for defence purposes was at its peak, but then sank again with the 'New Look' styles of the late 1940s, in the austerity aftermath of the wartime period. Gradually they rose to new heights in the affluent 1960s, and at the height of that boom phase were as high as they have ever been in the whole history of skirts. At the close of the 1960s designers were already talking of the possibilities of decorated crotches, but the collapse of the economy in the early 1970s robbed the male population of this particular extreme of female fashion. Now, in the late 1970s, there is already talk of the re-introduction of the mini-skirt, but whether this is achieved or not rests more with the success or failure of international politics than with the dictates of the fashion houses.

Exactly why females should want to expose more of their legs when the economy is healthier, it is hard to understand, unless a sense of financial security makes them feel more brazenly invitatory towards the males. Perhaps the general atmosphere of financial activity makes them feel more physically active—a condition favoured by shorter, less hampering skirt-lengths. Hopefully, future fluctuations will give us a clearer explanation.

More short-term variations are at work in a hundred different ways, as fashion-trends diffuse themselves rapidly around the globe. Many of these are no more than 'novelty changes', based on the need to signal up-to-dateness by the wearers. Displaying the latest mode indicates not only the social awareness of the individual but also the ability to pay for new clothes at regular intervals, and therefore has its own special status value. Each new minor trend of this type modifies or reverses the fashion of the previous season, and can often be measured with precision. The width of male lapels, for example, has been growing during the last few years, as has trouser-bottom width, tie-width, shirt-collar height, and shoe-heel height. By measuring these changes, and hundreds of others like them, it should be possible to plot graphs of shifting Clothing Signals and demonstrate the ways in which first one element and then another is modified to produce a constantly varying costume display system. Unconsciously, we all plot such graphs, all the time, and, without knowing quite how we do it, we read-off the many signals that our companions' clothes transmit to us in every social encounter. In this way clothing is as much a part of human body-language as gestures, facial expressions and postures.

BODY ADORNMENT

Social mutilations and cosmetic decorations

The wearing of clothing is only one of many ways in which the human animal decorates itself. In addition, skin may be scarred, flesh pierced, hair lopped, necks scented, nails painted, faces powdered, and teeth filed. Some of these Body Adornments persist for a lifetime while others last for only a few hours; but they all act as important human displays, indicating the social status, the sexual condition, the aggressiveness, the group allegiance, the playfulness, or some other quality of the decorated body.

The many temporary adornments, such as make-up, jewellery, nail-varnish, wigs and hairstyles, and perfume, are little more than extensions of clothing. Like garments, they can be put on and taken off at will, and do not commit the wearer to any lasting social bond. They can be used again and again, but can be varied for special moods and contexts. Or they can be discarded as fashions change.

The permanent adornments—those involving some form of body mutilation—are more typical of rigid societies, where allegiance to the group is of massive importance. These are badges that can never be taken off, and that set their owners apart from all other groups until the day they die. Frequently the application of the decoration is performed at a special ceremony, a tribal initiation, with the initiate suffering great pain in the process. This pain is an important part of the bonding—a physical horror that binds him even tighter to those who share it with him. Acquiring the status of belonging to the group is made such an ordeal, so difficult to endure, that forever afterwards it will be felt as something vitally important in his life. The very intensity of the experience helps to widen the gulf between him and those who have not shared it.

Frequently the mutilations are genital and applied at the age of puberty. For the first time the child cannot turn to its parents for protection from pain and, in this way, is turned away from them and towards the social group of the tribal 'club'.

Other mutilations are performed by parents themselves on their infants, long before the children know what is happening to them. In these cases the child, as it grows, accepts its special body qualities almost as if they are biological features making him into a different species from the members of other tribes who lack them.

The best way to study these adornments, both temporary and permanent, is to look at each part of the body in turn, and see what kind of attention it receives. Starting with the hair, there are obviously enormous possibilities for decorative modification, but always of a temporary kind, since whatever is done is soon undone by the death of old hairs and the growth of new ones.

The curious thing about human head-hair is that it is so long. If left to itself it would grow to great and cumbersome lengths in both males and females, and it seems likely that some sort of attention must have been paid to it even by our earliest ancestors. The male beard also attains great lengths if uncut, and there is a case on record of a man whose beard was longer than himself—so long, in fact, that one day he tripped over it and fell to his death. What prehistoric hunters were doing with hirsute appendages of these dimensions remains a mystery, unless they were useful specifically as an encouragement to increase social grooming. Monkeys and apes spend a great deal of time grooming one another's fur, and this action helps to cement friendly relations between them. If early man was in constant need of barbering, this could conceivably have increased his friendly grooming ritual and helped him improve his social relationships.

Whatever its original value, the head-hair of mankind has for centuries been a vital decorative organ, often being employed as an additional gender signal by dressing it differently on males and females. It has also been worn in

The use of wigs is a practice at least 5,000 years old. Many ancient Egyptians shaved their heads and then donned elaborate hairpieces for ceremonial occasions (right). At certain periods in history, wig-wearing has been secretive; at others, flamboyant. The last period for obviously artificial hairpieces was the 1960s, when fun wigs (far right) in many colours sold by the million. Wigs have fallen out of favour again in the 1970s, but certain ethnic hairstyles, almost as startling (top right), have appeared on the scene.

Like wigs, cosmetics have a long and complex history. The eye make-up of ancient Egyptians contained hydrosilicate of copper—a protection against damage from the sun's glare—but their facial adornments were also decorative and were applied with great care. Since then there have been countless styles of make-up, from the tribal extravagances of New Guinea (right) to the white face of the traditional Japanese theatre (centre). Vivid colours have also been used in the West in modern times, but a more recent trend has been to produce an artificially 'natural' look (far right).

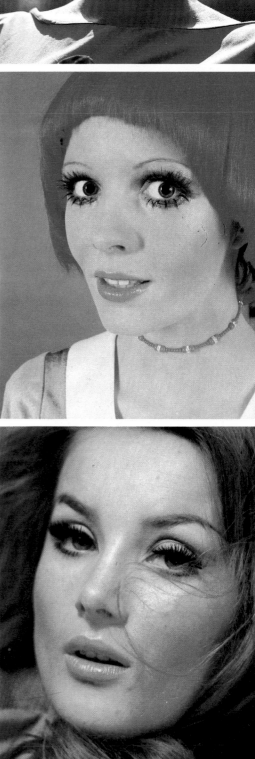

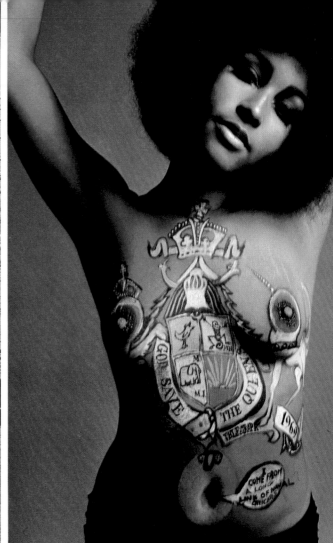

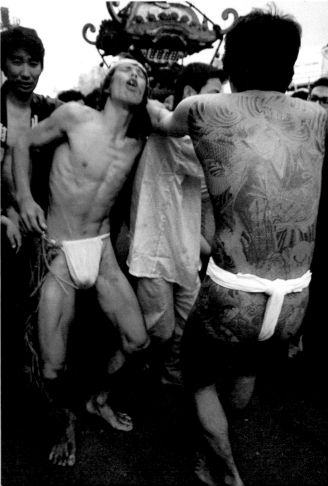

Body skin has been adorned by painting,
both in tribal societies, as with the Xingu
Indians from Brazil (far left), and in modern
Britain (left). The paint is washable and the
adornment does not lead to a permanent
display, as in the case of the Sudanese skin-
scarring (bottom far left) which the owner
must carry for life. Tattooing falls into this
last category and is a widespread form of
Body Adornment, both in the East (bottom
left) and the West (below).

a hundred different styles as a badge of age or status, and elaborated by the employment of waxes, ointments and wigs. The use of artificial hair is at least 5,000 years old. Ancient Egyptians commonly shaved their heads and then donned special wigs for ceremonial occasions. They used either human hair or vegetable fibre, holding it in place with beeswax. Wigs were also popular with Roman women, who had them made from the hair of conquered peoples. Roman prostitutes could be identified by the colour of their wigs, which were dyed yellow. Roman men, like those of modern times, wore wigs only to hide hair defects and tried to keep the matter secret.

The early Christian church hated the artificiality and vanity of wigs, and bishops refused to give a blessing by the laying on of hands if it meant touching a hairpiece that might have come from a pagan head. Even the natural flowing locks of female Christians became looked upon as tempting and devilish and in medieval times women were urged to hide their hair under tight hoods. Not until the Elizabethan age did wigs and elaborate hairstyles make a full comeback. When the great queen decided to cover her own poor hair with a full wig, she was quickly copied by other women anxious to emulate her, and the wig again became a high-status display. At the same time, in France, Henry III lost his hair as a result of dyeing it with dangerous chemicals and was forced to wear a velvet cap with tufts of hair stitched inside it. Again the courtiers followed suit and by the seventeenth century large, decorative wigs were seen everywhere in Europe. Louis XIV, becoming bald at the age of 32, kept the tradition alive with a magnificent black wig that was handed to him each morning through closed bed-curtains and was then handed out again in the same way at night, so that no one ever caught a glimpse of his royal bald pate. The Christian church was now deeply divided on the subject of these decorative aids to personal appearance, and ugly scenes occurred in vestries as wigless priests tried to knock off the wigs of their more stylish colleagues.

During the eighteenth century European wigs became more and more elaborate and over 110 different wig-styles for men are recorded from this period, the tallest being the extraordinary Macaroni wig, which was stuffed with horsehair and reached a height of 18 inches. Wigs were expensive and only a rich man could afford the really large ones, which required several real heads of hair to make them up, hence the words 'bigwig' for an important person.

Eighteenth-century wigs were so obviously false that they were frequently removed in public, to scratch the head, to wash it, or simply for comfort when relaxing among friends. As in ancient Egypt, the male head was shaved or cropped beneath the wig.

There were several advantages in wearing wigs at that date. Hygiene was poor and the removal of the wig for washing was an aid to cleanliness. Also, wigs could be changed to suit the mood or the occasion and could be sent to the hairdressers without the owner leaving his home. The wig-wearer could also go out incognito, so vast was his head-covering. But above all the wig was a display of fashion and of social status.

In the later part of the century female wigs outdid those of the males in sheer extravagance, reaching heights of 30 inches in extreme cases and requiring the lowering of carriage seats and the raising of doorways. France was the centre of inspiration, where a fashionable woman would spend half a day erecting her wig and then sleep in it for as long as a week, propping it up on special bed supports. The real hair was swept up into these creations, causing severe problems with hair-parasites and much pin-scratching of heads.

When the guillotine fell at the end of the French Revolution, the fashion for wigs fell with it and was never to be seen again in such extreme forms. At the same time, in North America, where, despite the ragings of puritan ministers and the introduction of wig-taxes, wigs had flourished for many years, the newly won independence of the United States led to similar

changes. The elaborate, old hair-styles of Europe were fading fast everywhere and a new simplicity was on the horizon. Throughout Victorian times the wig was reduced to a secretive role, employed only to remedy defects and referred to discreetly as 'an imperceptible hair-covering'. Hairstyles remained restrained in both sexes, and apart for the usual minor shifts of fashion, there was little extreme activity until recent years.

In the 1950s, synthetic hair was invented in the United States and cheap, dramatic wigs became possible. By the 1960s there was a new wig boom, with an estimated one-third of all fashion-conscious females in Europe and the United States owning a 'wig of convenience'. The fun-wigs of the affluent, buoyant 60s came in all sizes, shapes and colours, and were once again being worn openly as wigs, rather than secretly as pseudo-hair. Modern males have not, as yet, returned to this condition. Instead they have gone further and further towards creating a naturalistic hairpiece. The culmination of the trend has been the invention of hair transplant techniques, in which hair and skin is cut from one part of the head and sunk into the bald patch on the top of the skull. In 1970 an American entertainer was reputed to have paid 12,000 dollars for a hair-by-hair treatment of this type, undoubtedly the most expensive piece of Body Adornment since the construction of Marie Antoinette's finest three-foot-high court wig.

As the 1960s faded, obvious wigs once again lost favour, and women returned to a more naturalistic approach to hairstyling. But it is doubtful if we have seen the last of blatant, decorative hairpieces. As an extension of the natural hair-signals they will undoubtedly reappear before very long. They have one great advantage over many other types of Body Adornment—their conspicuousness. Today, with most of the body draped in clothing, the key sites for adornment devices are the head and hands, and artificial hair can easily take the lion's share of available space.

The next region to consider is the face. Like the hair, this has been subjected to endless forms and styles of adornment over the centuries. Ancient cosmetic boxes reveal the minute attention that was paid by early Egyptians to their facial make-up, and ancient wall-paintings show us with remarkable clarity some of the results of their labours.

Make-up does several things to the human face. It may disguise it, or protect it from the sun; it may make it look younger and healthier, or it may label it as belonging to a particular social category; it may signal aggressiveness or sexuality. As with hair adornments, there have been periods when any form of make-up has been spurned as 'unnatural', and others when to be without it would be tantamount to indecent exposure.

In tribal societies make-up plays an important role in establishing the status of the individual within the community, and gives him a cultural 'badge'. It may also be thought of as protective, defending the wearer against imagined evils, but in reality this amounts to the same thing, since the true protection it affords is that of group membership.

In ancient societies an underlying motive in using make-up was protection, not against evil but against the sun. Like modern sunbathers with their sun-lotions, the early Egyptians protected their faces against the damaging glare of the sun's rays. One of the ingredients of their famous eye make-up was hydrosilicate of copper, which acted as an immediate remedy for suppuration caused by the intense glare. But their interest in cosmetics grew beyond the purely protective and became highly decorative in its detailed application. Cleopatra, for instance, used black galena on her eyebrows and painted her upper eyelids deep blue and her lower eyelids bright green. An upper-class Egyptian lady would spend much time at her toilet, employing special elbow cushions to steady her pivoting arm as she applied the delicate eye-lines. Her toilet box included a tube of eye-pencils, a container of shadow-powder, bottles of coloured ointments, cosmetic pots and a bronze mixing dish. Some of her make-up was antiseptic as well as decorative and some was heavily scented. Some, such as face masks of egg white, were used to conceal wrinkles. A reddish ochre was used to add a healthy colour to the cheeks and carmine was added to the lips. Lipstick, often thought of as a modern invention, is in reality 5,000 years old at the very least.

There is therefore little that is new in the world of facial adornment. All that has happened over the centuries is that different cultures have approved or disapproved—exaggerated or restricted—to varying degrees, the cosmetic activities of ancient and tribal peoples. Sometimes, as in ancient Greece, the more elaborate application of cosmetics was confined to one particular class—the courtesans (both male and female)—while at others it spread from royalty downwards. Tragically, in later centuries, the chemistry of make-up became increasingly dangerous and frequently damaged the faces it was meant to improve. This led in turn to even more frantic attempts to cover up the ravaged surfaces. Disease was also playing havoc with smooth skins and marks and blemishes were repeatedly smothered in layers of powder and paint. In the seventeenth century a craze developed for 'beauty spots', small patches that were used to cover small scars and spots. Before long these had developed their own language and became specific facial signals. In London they were even used as political devices, the right-wing Whigs wearing them on the right cheek, and the (then) left-wing Tories wearing them on the left. The simple black spots soon grew into fancy shapes, such as cresents and stars, and at the court of Louis XV the precise position of these facial adornments became loaded with meaning: the corner of the eye indicated passion, the centre of the cheek gaiety, the nose sauciness, the forehead majesty, and so on, around the face.

In modern times there have been two great changes. In the first place, advanced medical care reduced the damage done to skin by disease, and in the second place advanced chemistry made modern cosmetics safe and even beneficial. The result was that the make-up of the twentieth century could, at the same time, become less of a mask and less of a danger. Caked faces became shaded faces, and skin-painting became skin-care. As before, the features, such as the eyebrows, eyes and lips, were specially modified or exaggerated, but there was now a completely different approach to the general surface of the smooth skin. Previously this had nearly always been powdered or painted white, with or without the addition of rouge. This was a high-status signal based on the fact that only low-status females would have to work out-of-doors and ruin their cheeks with a horrible tan. Since high-status females were protected from the sun, a super-white face heightened this status value. The rouge, when added, was to indicate good health. For the modern female, the situation has become completely reversed. Now, in a predominantly industrial world, it has become important to demonstrate that long holidays in the sun can be taken. The longer the sunning, the higher the status, so sun-

Tribal mutilations take many forms, but several are particularly popular and occur in widely differing areas. They include (opposite) Lip-plugs, Nose Ornaments and earrings. Earrings are popular across a wide spectrum of human societies and represent one of the few body mutilations still used among Western urbanites.

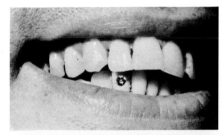

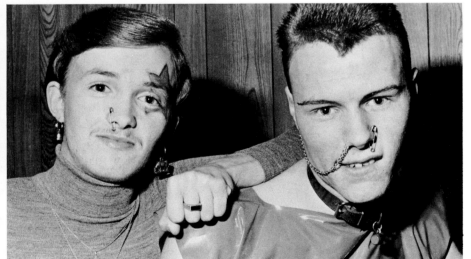

In modern Western society, deliberate body mutilations other than female ear-piercing and male circumcision are rare but do occur from time to time. Examples include diamond-studded teeth (above top) and the safety-pin nose attachments of the 1970s Punk Rockers (left). Although the safety-pin ornaments were intended to shock—and succeeded in doing so—they were not original, as the tribal scene (above) clearly shows. With body adornment it is hard to find a device that has not been exploited before.

tan, real or artificial, has become the new facial badge to wear, and cosmetics have changed from white to brown.

Another facial device belonging to recent years is the more drastic phenomenon of cosmetic surgery, involving the cutting away of sections of skin and then stretching what is left to pull out the wrinkles of old age. Face-lifts and nose-bobs are still viewed as extreme measures by most people today, but cosmetic dentistry, another modern development, is now widely accepted, as is the use of contact lenses for the eyes. The 'Bionic Man' may be an escapist fantasy, but the bionic face is almost with us already.

Apart from making modern faces look younger and healthier, and therefore more appealing, the application of careful make-up means three things: time, materials and services. Time means money, and materials mean money, and where specialized services are needed the cost is even higher; so, on these three counts: make-up = affluence = status. On this basis make-up has always been, and always will be, a facial signal saying 'I have money to burn'. Also on this basis, the more elaborate the make-up, the better. In other words, if a woman presents an elaborately made-up face of unashamed artificiality, she is performing a threat display. In the boisterous 1960s, this led to wild facial adornments in Western countries, rivalling those of tribal warriors; but in the more restrained and increasingly egalitarian social climate of the 1970s, these overt displays have receded. In their place is something much more subtle. Make-up has not vanished, it has instead become devious, reflecting a more devious attitude to affluence itself. Affluence and high status are still sought after, but they must not be *seen* to be sought after. It is an age of pseudo-puritanism, and the effect this has on facial displays is precisely what we might expect from looking back at history. It was the purity of the Ancient Greeks, the puritanism of the Christian Church, and the prudery of the Victorians that led, in the past, to the suppression of flashier styles of make-up. Only courtesans, whores and tarts were painted ladies in those periods. We are returning to those conditions now and, once again, the female face must appear fresh and innocent. The difference is that now she has a whole range of advanced cosmetics to help her look even fresher than fresh, and even more natural than nature herself can manage. To the experienced eye the adornment signals are still there, but they are no longer blatant. Like the expensively tailored, faded denims, the face cleverly contradicts itself and transmits two messages at once: 'I take care to look careless'.

Descending from the face and looking at the body skin in general, there is an obvious draw-back in fully clothed cultures, where the skin is only exposed on special occasions. In semi-naked tribal societies body painting and tattooing were widespread and, in many cases, a work of art—perhaps the *original* form of art for our species. A third form of skin ornamentation was the more drastic process of cicatrization, in which patterns of raised scars were made by rubbing charcoal and other materials into freshly cut slits on the body-surface. The bas-relief effect, like the coloured patterns of the tattooist, provided a lasting 'badge' of adornment.

Despite modern clothing, all three of these devices have continued to survive in some form. Body painting made a brief comeback in the 1960s. Tattooing has never completely vanished, but has merely withdrawn to the vicinity of naval dockyards and other sailors' haunts. Cicatrization has been less successful and its last appearance was in Germany, where it took the form of deliberately inflicted duelling-scars.

Tattooing and scarring, being more or less permanent mutilations of the skin, are essentially badges of allegiance, and it is significant that many of the designs favoured by sailors are symbols of pair-bonds (hearts and arrows) or culture-bonds (patriotic flags and national emblems). From time to time it has been suggested that tattooing should be employed on a widespread basis, specifically for its permanence; and there was a serious proposal in the last century that the tattooing of a coloured ring on the wedding finger should be

Male circumcision rituals at puberty still survive in some tribal cultures, as among the Australian Aborigines (above), but in the West this type of body-violation is now performed only on babies, whose cries of protest are more easily ignored by the adult mutilators.

Penis sheaths, such as the one worn by a New Guinea highland chief (above) are less widespread than many other forms of Body Adornment, although they once found an echo in the West when the fashion for ornate codpieces was at its height.

made a compulsory part of the marriage service. This was to defeat unscrupulous bigamists and other males who removed their wedding rings to prey on unsuspecting women. If widowed, a tattooed star was to be added; if divorced, a bar; and if re-married, a second ring. In this way no one could escape having their marital status identified. In the early part of the present century, American husbands were similarly urged to follow the custom of New Zealand natives and tattoo their wives to reveal to other men that they were married and were not to be molested.

Despite these attempts, the only widespread forms of permanent body mutilation that still survive, apart from sailors' tattoos, are the piercing of ears for earrings and the cutting-off of the foreskin in the ritual of circumcision. Tribal mutilations, such as lip-plugging, tooth-filing, ear-stretching, and the removal of parts of the female genitals, have failed to find favour in the modern world. Circumcision is, in fact, the only really severe form of primitive mutilation to have resisted the modern trend towards abhorrence of body-violation. If, as used to be the case, it was performed at puberty instead of at infancy, that too would no doubt have vanished long ago, swept away by the outrage of the initiates. But the protests of babies are more easily ignored, and with the false accolade of medical hygiene to help it on its way, the genital deforming of young males continues unabated.

One early form of infant violation that has failed to survive is the curious and previously widespread activity of head squashing. At birth the human skull is soft and easily moulded. Various cultures, in Africa, North and South America, and Europe, indulged in skull-moulding, employing a variety of tight bindings or squeezing-boards to achieve the desired shape. The most popular head-style was one with a flattened forehead, producing a tapering, pointed crown. The preference for this shape is linked to high status, like so many body adornments. The reason for the linkage in this case is that individuals with pointed heads cannot carry burdens on their heads, and display throughout their lives their inability to perform menial tasks.

European head-squashers seem to have had different motives. Like some of the Ancient Egyptians, they preferred elongated heads that ballooned out at the back of the skull, an effect easily produced by mothers binding their babies' heads tightly soon after birth. This practice was still active in certain provincial regions of France up until the last century, kept alive by the teaching of phrenologists that head shape could influence intelligence.

In modern times heads have been left unsquashed, and this particular form of body deformation has been relegated to the feet, twentieth-century shoemakers having taken over the role of human bone-crushers. This is more true of female shoes than male; but fortunately for modern women, the extremes of foot-squeezing seen in Old China are no longer perpetrated. There, the crushed feet of high-status females made walking difficult and working impossible—again a deformation to display the owner's inability to perform menial tasks. The 'elegant' pointed shoe of modern Western women is also less than perfect for hard physical work, but the foot deformities it causes are less devastating.

There are, of course, a thousand other ways in which the human animal seeks to adorn its body and enhance its display qualities. Some are exotic rarities, such as nipple-rouge and nipple-rings, male chest-wigs, and female pubic tufts trimmed to heart-shapes; others are commonplace and widespread, such as necklaces, bracelets, finger-rings and nail-varnish. Taken together they amount to a set of wide-ranging 'frozen' gestures, items of display that are long-lasting and highly efficient in relation to the actions that produce them. The visual impact of a shaken fist lasts only as long as the arm is moving, but the visual impact of the act of putting on any form of Body Adornment lasts long afterwards. It is this efficiency of the ratio of action-effort to display-impact that ensures that Body Adornments will be with us for as long as our species walks the planet.

GENDER SIGNALS

Masculine and feminine signals that label or emphasize the sex of the signaller

Gender Signals are clues that enable us to identify an individual as either male or female. In addition they may help to emphasize masculinity or femininity in cases where the sex of the individual is already known.

At birth the only obvious Gender Signal of the human baby is the shape of its genitals. Penis means boy and vagina means girl, and that is all the layman has to go on. There are other sexual differences, of course, but since these are not available to ordinary observation they cannot be classed as Gender Signals. To become a Gender Signal, a sexual difference has to be observable.

Once the newborn baby is clothed it is effectively genderless, and is often referred to as 'it'. Artificial Gender Signals (blue for a boy, pink for a girl) can be added, and a gender-linked name is given, but as far as the mother is concerned the baby is a baby and receives the same treatment regardless of its sex.

As the child grows this situation rapidly changes. Many of its Gender Signals will have to await the onset of puberty, but there are plenty of others available. Most of these are imposed on the child by the society in which it lives. Boys will be given different clothes, hairstyles, toys, ornaments, pastimes and sports, from girls. Although children are functionally pre-sexual, they are given strongly defined sexual roles. Society prepares them for the future and gives them a gender identity long before they need it for reproductive activities.

This trend has the effect of widening the 'gender gap' between the sexes so that when they become adult, boys will be not only reproductively mascline but also socially masculine, and girls will be both reproductively and socially feminine. This exaggeration of the differences between men and women has come under severe attack in recent years and some people today feel that a strong reversal of the trend should be encouraged. They argue that the gender gap belongs to man's ancient past and is no longer relevant in the modern world.

To some extent they are correct and, to appreciate why, we must consider for a moment the long period when our ancestors evolved as primitive hunters. Over a time-span of more than a million years, early man changed from the typical primate mode of feeding to a system that demanded a major division of labour between the sexes. Nearly all primates wander around in mixed bands of males, females and young, moving from one feeding site to another, picking edible fruits, nuts and berries wherever they find them. When our ancient ancestors abandoned this way of life to become hunter-gatherers, their whole social organization had to be changed. Hunting involved intensely athletic episodes and the females of the group—nearly always pregnant or nursing—had to be left behind. This meant that the group had to stop wandering and establish a fixed home base where the males could return after the hunt. The females could carry out the less strenuous food-gathering near this home base, bringing vegetable foods back from the surrounding district; but because of their heavier breeding burden, they could not become specialized hunters like the males.

As a result of this divided labour system, the male body became more and more specialized as a running, jumping and throwing machine, while the females became improved breeding machines. Consequently, some Gender Signals stem from the male hunting trend and others arise from the female breeding specializations. Male hunting features include the following:

1. Male bodies are taller and heavier than female bodies, with bigger bones and more muscle. *They are stronger and can carry heavier loads.*

2. Males have proportionally longer legs and larger feet. *They are faster, more sure-footed runners.*

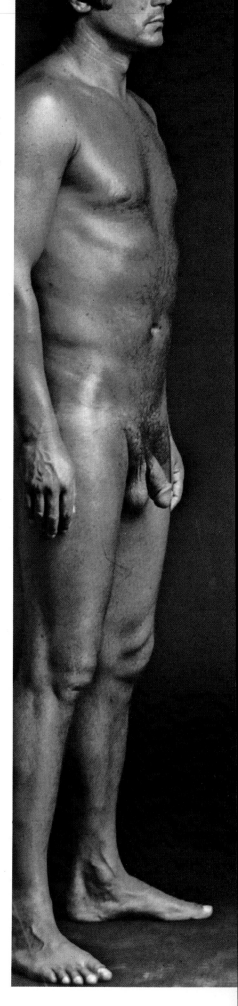

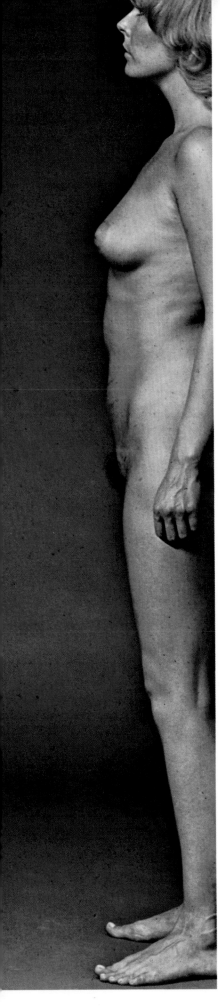

3. Males have broader shoulders and longer arms, and their forearms are longer in relation to their upper arms. *They are better aimers and weapon-throwers.*

4. Males have bigger hands with thicker fingers and stronger thumbs. *They are better weapon-graspers.*

5. Males have bigger chests housing larger lungs and hearts. Together these features mean that males can call upon a greater respiratory response, bringing with it greater stamina and quicker recovery from physical exertion. *They are better breathers and long-distance chasers.*

6. Males have stronger skulls with heavier bony ridges, and their jaws are thicker and sturdier. *They are better protected against physical damage.*

Taken together, these features explain why male and female events at modern athletic meetings have to be kept separate. The best female athletes selected from the whole world population are unable to match the running speeds or the jumping distances of the best males. In the general population, however, there is a certain amount of overlap. If the hundred strongest individuals were selected from a random group made up of one hundred males and one hundred females, the probabilities are that the selected group would consist of ninety-three males and seven females. In other words, the seven weakest out of every hundred males are likely to be weaker than the strongest seven out of every hundred females. So, even in the realm of the purely physical there is no clear-cut distinction between the entire masculine population and the entire feminine population. The physical differences are only a matter of degree, where strength is concerned. This comparatively small difference is due to the fact that from a very early stage man became a weapon-user, and whether he was hunting prey, defending himself against predators, or attacking rival males, he was relying more on his brains and his weapons than on enormously developed muscle-power. He had to become a good athlete; but there was no need to become a heavyweight.

However, even though the masculine physique is not dramatically different from the female, there are sufficient *detectable* distinguishing features to provide the sources for an impressive array of Gender Signals. Some of these are purely anatomical—the wide shoulders or the heavier hands—while others are behavioural, resulting from the various anatomical differences—the throwing actions or the long stride of the legs, for instance.

Turning to the female, there are several important Gender Signals arising from her specialized role as a child-bearer and feeder. Her pelvis is wider and rotated back slightly more than in the male. Her waist is a little more slender and her thighs a little thicker. Her navel is deeper and her belly longer. Her breasts are swollen. These specializations, which aid in the carrying of the foetus, its delivery and its subsequent suckling, alter the outline of the human female in several characteristic ways. Her protruding breasts mean that her chest, although narrower than the male's when seen from the front, is deeper when seen from the side, even at a distance. The female torso also has a distinctive hour-glass shape created by the narrow waist and the wide hips that cover the broad pelvis. Because the thighs start wider apart from each other, there is a larger crotch-gap in the female, and an inward slope to the thighs that often leads to an almost knock-kneed appearance.

Because the pelvis is rotated backwards, the female buttocks protrude more than those of the male. They are also fleshier and wider, making them much more conspicuous. When the female walks, and especially when she runs, her child-bearing anatomy gives her a special gait. The inward sloping thighs force her to make semicircular rotations of the legs. Her buttocks sway more and her body tends to wiggle in a way that contrasts strikingly with the male gait. In addition, her shorter legs mean that she takes shorter strides and her running actions generally are much clumsier than those of the male.

This last point may seem like an exaggeration, but the reason for this is that our experience of running females is gained mostly from watching female athletes or young girls. Successful female athletes *are* successful because they happen to have rather masculine figures, and young girls have not yet developed the full female proportions. If, instead, we were to watch an unselected group of racing mothers, the gender difference in gait would become immediately apparent. A middle-aged woman running to catch a bus is in much greater difficulty than a middle-aged man, and her locomotion is strikingly different from that of a female track athlete. It is not only her wide-hipped leg movements that cause her trouble, for her heavier, more pendulous breasts will also slow her down with their rapid bouncing action. The female athlete, in contrast, tends to be longer limbed, narrower hipped and flatter chested.

One small Gender Signal that is often overlooked concerns arm-bending. Because females have narrow shoulders, their upper arms are usually held closer to the sides of their chests than in the male. The broad-chested male displays arms which hang down *away* from the sides of his trunk. This is particularly noticeable in weight-lifters and body-builders, whose arms seem to dangle in space on either side of their top-heavy torsos. The typical female tends to have her elbows tucked in close to her body, and this feature is often mimicked exaggeratedly by male actors when impersonating females or male homosexuals. The effect of this upper-arm closeness, combined with the spreading hips beneath, is to make the carrying of objects more difficult. The female anatomy has compensated with an increase in the angle between the upper arm and the forearm to the extent of six degrees beyond that possible in the male. This increase can be tested by bending a woman's forearm sideways away from her body, while holding her upper arm still. If a man deliberately tucks his upper arms into the sides of his chest and then spreads his forearms out sideways as best he can, he will find himself transmitting an effeminate Gender Signal.

This arm-posture difference is only a small one and yet it is being responded to unconsciously by men and women as they look at their social companions. Many Gender Signals operate in this way, below the level of our conscious awareness, but they are important none the less in determining our behaviour towards each person we encounter. There are others, however, which are blatantly obvious and which have evolved primarily as signals of maleness or femaleness. They are not connected with the male hunting or female breeding specializations that have been discussed so far, but instead are pure display features. They include the following:

In the male: the possession of a deeper voice, a prominent Adam's apple, a beard and moustache, bushier eyebrows, hairier nostrils and ears, and a generally hairier body surface. The exception to this hairiness is the top of the head, which frequently becomes bald in later life.

In the female: spherical protruding breasts, fleshier lips, smoother, more sensitive skin, rounder knees and shoulders, bigger and wider dimples above the buttocks, and a generally much heavier fat deposit all over the body.

There are also ancient odour differences between males and females, to which we still respond but which now play only a comparatively minor role, unlike their role in other primate species. These odours are produced by special scent glands in the skin, especially in the armpit region and the crotch. The hairs in these regions act as scent traps to retain the odours and intensify them. Ladies baring their arms in evening dress or on the beach frequently shave their armpits. The reason is to reduce the natural female odour, although the motive is usually expressed differently, the hair being referred to as 'unsightly', rather than as potently odoriferous.

Not all the attempts to reduce olfactory Gender Signals are so cryptic. Body deodorants are used deliberately by many people today. There are dangers in this procedure. The skin does not always take kindly to having its natural processes interfered with chemically. But there is a good reason why this trend has developed. The answer in a word is: clothes. The wearing of clothing tends to trap the stale sweat and other skin secretions, and the odour produced rapidly deteriorates and loses its gender attractiveness. Exposed to

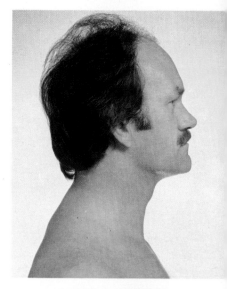

The heavier male jaw with its jutting chin, the facial hair, the larger Adam's apple, the thicker neck and the receding hairline all act as masculine Gender Signals—as does the male crotch-bulge. The female's legs are set farther apart, and this produces a distinctively female crotch-gap.

Smoothness of skin is a powerful female Gender Signal—emphasized (right) by the artist Bronzino in rendering his female subject as totally lacking in body hair.

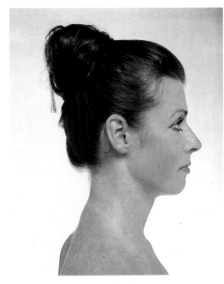

the air and the sun, the skin's odour-cycle is quite different, but that is a thing of the past, and modern man—and woman—can only try to regain something approaching the natural condition by repeated washing. Skin experts feel that this alone should be enough and that chemical deodorants are an unnecessary and potentially damaging addition. Damaging or not, they certainly defeat one of our most ancient forms of Gender Signalling.

While the females are busily de-gendering their odours, the males are hard at work each morning scraping off their facial Gender Signals—their beards and moustaches. There are, admittedly, large numbers of bearded and moustachioed males to be seen today, but the habit of male face-shaving has a long and ancient history, has appeared at many different historical periods, and is widespread across the face of the globe. It is more than a local, fashionable whim, even if it is not inevitably present in every culture. Why this particular form of de-gendering should be so popular has rarely been discussed. When it does receive comment it is usually described either as an improvement in cleanliness when eating or drinking, or as a status symbol indicating that the shaven males have time to spare for their toilets, or as a distinguishing feature separating shaven males from their hairy neighbours in the tribe next door, or merely as a whim of fashion.

There are elements of truth in all these explanations but they remain superficial, none the less. Underlying them are two more basic reasons, one visual and one tactile. The visual advantage of clean-shaven male faces is that they can transmit with greater subtlety the nuances of facial expression. Mouth movements and postures are extremely complex in the human species and visual signalling from the mouth region is enhanced by the removal of surrounding or overhanging hair. The tactile advantage concerns the erotic value of skin-to-skin contact during sexual encounters. A male pressing his face to the skin of his sexual partner will receive much more sensitive tactile signals if he is clean-shaven. But against both these advantages must be set the loss of an ancient male gender signal, so the hairy/hairless pendulum continues to swing back and forth from culture to culture and from epoch to epoch.

Still on the subject of hair, it has been remarked that it is curious that the male's whole body surface should be generally hairier than the female's. If, as seems likely, the male lost his heavy coat of fur as part of an improved cooling system, counteracting the overheating of strenuous hunting behaviour, then he is the one who should be the less hairy of the sexes. The answer to this is that once the human fur had been reduced to *functional* nakedness, with the skin effectively fully exposed, it made little difference as far as cooling was concerned whether there were a few small, straggling hairs left on the surface. So the slightly hairy male body is no worse off, as regards overheating, than the female. What remains to be explained is why the female went even further, if her extra de-hairing was not connected with temperature control.

The answer appears to be the same tactile one as in the case of the shaven male face, namely an improvement in skin sensitivity during erotic body-contact. One authority, talking of erogenous zones on the human female body, has declared that the delicate, naked skin of woman does not *have* erogenous zones—it *is* an erogenous zone, the whole body surface being so sensitive as to make gentle contact in any region a potentially sexual experience. This has been given as the reason why women, in particular, enjoy the touch of velvets, furs, silks and other soft fabrics.

Whether or not this explains the origin of the greater reduction in feminine body-hair, the fact remains that smooth, seemingly hairless skin is a powerful female Gender Signal in our species, and women with slight moustaches, or hairy arms or legs, are automatically looked upon as rather masculine. A great deal of private depilation occurs as a result of this, and there are thriving clinics dealing exclusively with the removal of 'unsightly' body-hair.

The reverse process operates on the tops of male heads, where elaborate procedures have been adopted to replace hair lost with encroaching baldness. Baldness transmits a double signal: maleness and advancing age. The toupees, wigs and hair-transplants are not concerned with the male signals, but rather with the age signals, and the fact that a masculine Gender Signal is being lost with the replacement of head-hair is considered of no importance alongside the aging display of the bald pate.

Another male Gender Signal that falls into this age-linked category is the development of the pot-belly. This is something which a primitive tribesman might wear as a proud badge of success in the hunt but to the modern male it spells 'lost youth' just as clearly as a bald head. Young males nearly all have flat, lean bellies, and because the pot-bellied profile grows later in life, it is once again a Gender Signal of an older male, and therefore to be avoided. Hence the existence of male diets, male exercises and even occasionally male corsets, which attempt to defeat the aging outline of the middle-aged spread.

The observation that the pot-bellied look is predominantly a male Gender Signal reflects the fact that women have a rather different distribution of body fat. They not only have *more* fat on their bodies, but they have it in different places. Regions where this increased adipose layer creates visible Gender Signals are: the shoulders and the knees, the breasts and the buttocks, and the thighs. The enlarged, rounded buttocks appear to be an ancient sexual signal, the human equivalent of the sexual swellings of other primate species. In monkeys and apes these swellings increase and decrease in size with the monthly cycle of the females, rising to their maximum dimensions at the time of ovulation. In the human female there is no such change, the buttocks remaining 'swollen' throughout the adult breeding life-span and the females remaining sexually responsive at all times.

The rounded hemispheres of the female buttocks are echoed by the rounded hemispheres of the breasts and, to a less obvious extent, by the roundedness of the shoulders and knees. It is almost as if 'smooth

Buttocks protrude more on females than on males, and this Gender Signal can be seen in extreme forms in prehistoric 'mother goddess' figurines, in Hottentot women and in Victorian bustle-wearers.

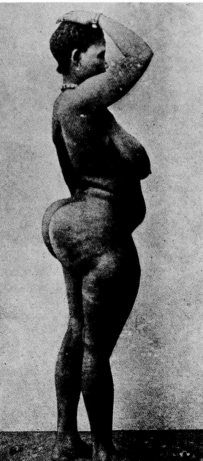

The larger, fleshier lips of the female have been further magnified in size, colour and texture by the application of lipstick—a practice known to be at least 4,000 years old.

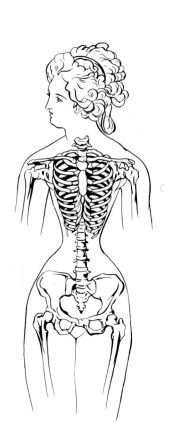

The narrower female waist has often been exaggerated by tight corsetting. This has sometimes led to drastic rib compression and other internal deformities.

hemispheres of flesh' are the key female Gender Signal for the human species, and there is every reason to believe that the male response to this basic shape has become an inborn reaction. There is no way of proving this, of course, but it would be rather careless of our species to have given up a genetically controlled Life Insurance Policy of this kind.

In some ethnic groups the buttock signal is taken to much greater extremes than we are used to in the West. Among the Bushmen and the Hottentots of Africa there is a condition known as steatopygia, in which the buttocks become enormous, fatty protrusions, several times the size of ordinary buttocks. Interestingly, the small figurines carved by prehistoric artists also frequently show this condition, so that it must have existed in ancient times in Europe and Asia as well as Africa. It seems probable that for early human females steatopygia was the normal rather than the rare condition, and that the present-day Hottentot and Bushmen females are merely the last remnants of the original shape of womankind as she was seen some thousands of years ago. Perhaps the modern male response to female 'hemispheres' owes its strength to this ancient condition, when the female must have been transmitting such powerful Gender Signals from her buttock region.

These, then, are the natural biological Gender Signals of our species—the hunting features, the breeding features and the pure display features. Add to them the visible, primary genital differences—the male penis and testicles and the female vulva (detectable in clothed adults as either the presence or the absence of a crotch-bulge)—and there is clearly a wide range of clues available to the human being concerning the gender of his or her companions. But even these are insufficient, judging by the ways they have been artificially amplified and added to by cultural invention.

Almost every natural Gender Signal mentioned so far can be discovered in an artificially exaggerated form in one culture or another. The greater height of the male has often been amplified by the wearing of tall headdresses; the broader shoulders of the male have frequently been increased further in width by the wearing of padded jackets or tunics with epaulettes; the narrower waist of the female has often been exaggerated by the wearing of tight corsets; the protruding breasts of the female have been made to protrude still further by the wearing of brassiere cups and padding. Women have also added padded hips and bustles to their larger hip measurements and their already bigger buttocks. Their large, fleshier lips have been exaggerated by the wearing of lipstick. Their small feet have been made to look even smaller by the wearing of tight shoes, or, in the Orient, by ruthless and painful foot-binding. Their smoother skin is made even smoother by powder and cosmetics. The list is a long one.

It becomes even longer when one adds the pure cultural inventions which have little or nothing to do with the basic anatomical differences between the sexes. Invented Gender Signals are so numerous, so diverse, and often so short-lived, that they can change from generation to generation and even from season to season; they can alter as one moves from country to country or even from district to district. Their most interesting feature is that they *are* so common. It is as if every human being feels the constant need to remind companions of his or her gender, despite the fact that there are perfectly adequate natural Gender Signals available to do the job.

A few obvious examples of invented signals are: short hair versus long hair; skirts versus trousers; handbags versus pockets; make-up or no make-up; and pipes versus cigarettes. These are entirely arbitrary and although, at the time and place they are used, they seem to be basically masculine or feminine, there is nothing that links them inevitably to one sex or the other, beyond local fashion. Head hair is long in both sexes; it is a species signal, distinguishing us from other primates, but that is all. Here there is no difference between the sexes at a biological level, and the only reason short hair has become associated with males is because of long-standing military anti-parasite regulations. Skirts have often been the male attire and trousers the female garment, if one casts one's net widely enough across different cultures and epochs. In the same way, all the other invented signals can be shown to vary and even reverse roles at different times and places.

I have chosen obvious examples, but if one moves to a strange culture then there are many local invented signals that are meaningless to the casual visitor. And it is easy to make mistakes. In certain hot countries where people fan themselves to keep cool, the shape of the fan used is a Gender Signal: rectangular fans are male and curved ones are female. To pick up the wrong gender of fan would be thought as funny as a man putting on a skirt, or a woman smoking a pipe. Anthropologists encounter similar small differences between male and female custom in every tribe they visit.

Sometimes an apparently arbitrary difference has an underlying biological explanation. An intriguing one is the answer to the age-old question: Why do males button their jackets left over right, while females button them right over left? This behaviour has been going on for centuries and is usually referred to simply as traditional. The true explanation, however, appears to be that males prefer left-over-right because it means they can tuck their right hands into the fold of the garment. This began in a pocketless epoch and was supposedly a way of keeping the dominant weapon-hand warm and ready for action, and has persisted ever since. Females, by contrast, preferred the wrapping over of the longer right side of their garment because they tended to carry their babies more often on the left breast than the right, and it meant that they could wrap the long fold over the infant as it slept or sucked. Again the pattern is thought to have persisted long after the original reason for it became obsolete.

If behaviour can influence clothing, clothing can also influence behaviour.

When a man and a woman have to squeeze past each other, the man twists towards the woman, while she twists away from him. This does not happen every time (see chart—after Collett and Marsh), but the contrast is great enough to provide another gender difference.

MEN

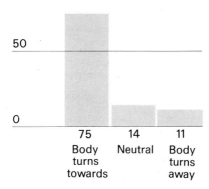

100%		
50		
0		
75	14	11
Body turns towards	Neutral	Body turns away

WOMEN

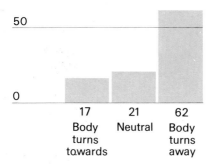

100%		
50		
0		
17	21	62
Body turns towards	Neutral	Body turns away

Top left: the leg-cross posture of the man on the left is used by both sexes, but the ankle-on-knee cross of his companion is typically male. The legs-spread sitting posture (above left) is a masculine Gender Signal and is rare even for trousered females. Left: the female leg-twine posture in which one leg is crossed over the other, with the free foot resting against the supporting leg. Men hardly ever sit like this.

If an arbitrary garment difference exists for some reason of fashion, then it may lead to subtle changes in the postures or movements of the wearers, even without their realizing it. The wrist-flapping of the modern female is a case in point. Limp wrist movements are so typically feminine that they are often used by males when pretending to be effeminate. But the origin of these movements is not understood by anyone who has not worn historical costumes. Actresses who have been forced for reasons of authenticity to work in the heavy, tight-sleeved dresses of earlier periods report that their arm movements when gesturing are so impeded that they find themselves gesticulating from the wrists. Without even meaning to do so they start to accentuate the wrist actions, and it is easy to see how this can have developed into a gesturing style which, like left/right jacket buttoning, survived after the passing of the clothes with which it originated.

The wearing of skirts also clearly influences sitting postures. The legs-spread position is typically male, for obvious reasons, as is the ankle-knee cross. Even when wearing trousers modern females tend to adopt these postures less than males, although the danger of underclothing exposure is no longer present. It is as if their trousered legs are still wearing a ghost-skirt,

The skirt is intrinsically neither masculine nor feminine. It is an arbitrary Gender Signal and in the past has often been typical male attire, as revealed in the Tudor portrait (above) and in the traditional Greek military uniform (below).

and if skirts disappeared completely from our culture, the entrenched skirt-postures might well outlive them.

Another leg-crossing posture also transmits a Gender Signal, and that is the feminine leg-twine. Women often sit with one leg wrapped around the other, a position which men never adopt. The key factor in this posture is the touching of the crossed leg with the cross-over foot. This is probably not a clothing-influenced difference, but rather a consequence of the differing leg structure in the two sexes.

The leg-twine is an example of a Gender Signal which, although immediately feminine in flavour once attention has been drawn to it, is nevertheless operating unconsciously when men and women look at one another. Until scientific observers began to analyse the ordinary everyday postures and movements that people make as they go about their daily business, such signals went unremarked. Now, more and more are coming to light, and it is clear that in a hundred small behavioural ways, the male signals his maleness and the female her femaleness.

For example, a recent research study of the way people move through the streets in crowded shopping centres revealed that men and women behave differently when they have to pass close to one another. Hidden cameras showed that the woman usually turns away from the male as she pushes past him, whereas the male is more likely to turn towards the female when he has to squeeze past. The reason is clear enough: the women are protecting their breasts, or, at least, avoiding passing them too close to the male's body in case they brush against him accidentally. It is easy to see *why* there is a difference, but the point is that, until the research observations had been made, no-one was even aware that the difference existed. The fact that it did was undoubtedly being registered by the eyes of the male and female shoppers, and they were all unconsciously clocking up their scores of Gender Signals as they passed through the crowd, but they never stopped to analyse how they were doing it.

In the same way most people are unaware of the fact that women spend much more time touching their hair with their hands than men do, or that they adopt certain hand-clasp postures more frequently, or that men are more likely than women to fold their arms across their chests, or to perform shoulder embraces when walking or standing side-by-side. These and a hundred other small differences are beginning to emerge from modern observational studies, and the true complexity of human gender differences—and therefore Gender Signals—is slowly being revealed.

This tends to make nonsense of the 'unisex' philosophy that wishes to eliminate all but the basically reproductive differences between men and women. It is hard to stop doing something when you are not aware you are doing it. Of course, many of the deliberate, brutishly masculine or simperingly feminine adornments and actions can be reduced or even swept away. The modern male has stopped prey-hunting and the modern female has drastically reduced her breeding burden. The world is overcrowded and urbanized, and the pressures that originally made men and women split into hunting-humans and breeding-humans are gone. Social adjustments will have to be made to accommodate the new situation. But the inherited qualities of more than a million years of human evolution cannot be cleared away overnight. The modern male may no longer chase and kill antelopes, but he still hunts down symbolic prey in his urban businesses, and the modern female is still subject to deep-seated maternal urges. Artificial, invented Gender Signals may come and go, but those stemming from the human genetic inheritance may prove stubbornly resistant to social progress. Change they no doubt will, but the hard fact is that the process may take another million years of evolution to become a genetic reality. In the meantime the Gender Gap, though narrowing, will retain much of the fascinating complexity that pervades and influences so profoundly our ordinary everyday lives.

BODY SELF-MIMICRY

Ways in which we imitate ourselves anatomically

Body Self-mimicry occurs when one part of the human body acts as a copy of some other part of the anatomy.

When a female monkey or ape gives a sexual display to a male, she does so by presenting her rump-region to him as conspicuously as possible. In one species, the gelada baboon, the female has on her chest a remarkable copy of her rump signals. On her rump there is a brightly coloured genital region of pinkish-red skin, bordered by white papillae and with a bright red vulva at the centre. This is the primary female sexual signal of the species, and the intensity of its colouring increases when the female is 'on heat' and ovulating. On her chest there is a similar patch of naked, pinkish-red skin, also bordered by white papillae. At its centre lies a mimic of the vulva, created by the bright red nipples, which have moved from their more usual positions until they are close together in the midline of the chest, looking like a pair of red, genital lips. The whole chest display increases and decreases in intensity, its colour becoming brighter and duller, in synchrony with the changes in the true genital patch on the female's rump. These animals spend a great deal of time sitting on the ground, and their curious self-mimicry means that a male approaching from the front can tell whether a particular female is in sexual condition or not simply by looking at her chest region.

A similar evolutionary process appears to have taken place in the case of the human female. If she were to present her rump region to a male as conspicuously as possible, what he would see would be a pair of pink labia surrounded by two swollen, fleshy, hemispherical buttocks. The act of protruding the female buttocks is still seen occasionally as a sexual invitation signal, but this is usually confined to moments of rather theatrical playfulness, and it is much more usual for a sexually active adult female to be facing the male. In fact, during most social encounters, it is the *underside* of the human body that is visible. Because of our uniquely vertical locomotion posture, our undersides have become our fronts and our fronts have become our most readily available display areas. It is not surprising therefore to find genital mimics on the front of the human female body. The pink labia are imitated by the everted, pink lips and the rounded buttocks by the rounded breasts.

It has been argued that the fleshy lips of our species are necessary for infantile sucking, but other primates suck efficiently without possessing *everted* lips. It is this eversion, the turning inside-out of our human lips, that makes them unusual and renders them permanently visible. It has also been suggested that our lips evolved as kissing organs, but again apes can kiss well enough without permanently everted lips. The special design in the human case does appear to be a visual signal, rather than a tactile one, and it is worth recording that, like labia, the lips become redder and more swollen during sexual arousal and, like them, they surround a centrally placed orifice. The fact that males also possess visible lips need not be an objection. Males also possess nipples, but this does not mean that nipples are not primarily female.

Even if, despite these arguments, it is hard to accept the pink lips of the adult human female as evolved labial mimics, it cannot be denied that culturally they have often been viewed in this way. They have been artificially reddened with lipstick for thousands of years, and the deliberate use of suggestively gaping lip postures in films and advertisements frequently underlines their role as a 'genital echo'. Moistening of the lips, or the wearing of glistening lipstick, adds an extra hint of genital lubrication. Also, the positioning of phallic-shaped objects so that they appear to be ready to pass between the lips is a device often employed by commercial advertising.

Turning from lips to breasts, it has been argued that the hemispherical

The Body Self-mimicry of the female Gelada baboon. In this species the sexual rump-display is mimicked on the female's chest, where the nipples have come to lie close together, copying the labia, and are surrounded by naked skin similar to the coloured rump-skin. The female can therefore display sexually from the front, while sitting down.

The ancient rump-display of the sexually active female is rarely used in the human species. Exceptions are found in theatrical contexts—as in the famous can-can dance—and in certain advertisements, such as this one, seen in Italy. It is far more common for human females to display sexually from the front, with the breasts acting as buttock substitutes.

shape of the human breast is important in connection with its role as a feeding device and milk-container. Although this has been the generally accepted view, it is difficult to defend. Other primates do not have *rounded* breasts, yet they feed their young with great efficiency. Furthermore, their chest regions are only swollen with milk when they are nursing. Adult females of our species have large protuberant breasts from the time they become sexually mature, regardless of whether they are nursing infants or not. So the shape of the breasts coincides with sexual maturity, not with maternal nursing, and the *shape* must therefore be primarily a sexual signal, rather than a parental one. If anything, the rounded shape creates problems for the human baby, which finds it much easier to suck from a long-teated bottle than from a short-nippled hemisphere.

A criticism of the idea that female breast-shape has evolved as a mimic of female buttock-signals is that breasts sag too much and do not echo efficiently enough the roundedness of the female rump. This view is based on observations of breasts that have passed the peak of sexual signalling. The human female matures sexually at about 13, but because of the need for extended education in our complex, modern societies, her sexuality is played down as much as possible until she is considerably older. It is during the early teenage years of sexual maturity that her breast shape is at its most firm and rounded, and this is biologically her most vital phase for sexual display. In modern societies, it is no accident that older females, in their twenties, thirties and beyond, employ artificial means to create the impression of firm rounded breasts, doing so by wearing uplifting garments of various kinds, and even, in special cases, by having silicone injections. The modern brassiere not only lifts but 'holds', recreating both the shape and the firmness of the younger breast.

Even without these improvements the adult breast is still sufficiently like the rounded buttock for its sexuality to be transmitted as a frontal signal. Mimics do not have to be precise in order to operate successfully. The essential feature of the buttocks is their smooth roundedness, and any other part of the body that possesses this particular visual quality will be available as a sexual display organ. The breasts, even when sagging, have this quality, except in very old females, and so, too, do the smoothly rounded shoulders and knees of the adult female. The shoulders are sometimes given an extra mimic-boost by the wearing of an off-the-shoulder garment which isolates them more as hemispheres, or by the adoption of an erotic shoulder-raising posture, often with the cheek pressed gently against the rounded flesh. Rounded knees are also exposed or positioned in a similarly provocative way, and advertising photographers have become expert at exploiting these and various other body-echoes.

Below far left: breasts as buttock-mimics. The human species is the only primate in which the female possesses hemispherical breasts and buttocks. The similarity between the two regions is further enhanced by certain kinds of clothing which push the breasts up or exaggerate the cleavage between the paired hemispheres. The navel (below left) has occasionally been viewed as a genital echo. By adopting a belly-stretching posture photographic models have been able to convert a 'round navel' into a vertical slit, improving its genital-orifice mimicry in the process. This special form of posing has increased in recent years to six times its earlier frequency.

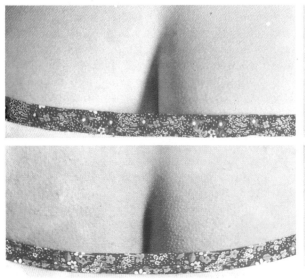

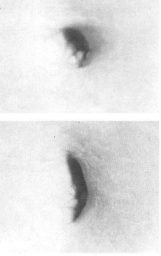

Core!

soft-hearted lipstick with the brushed-on look
clearer, sheerer than any you've ever worn.

Once upon a time colour th
stand up in a stick. No
sheeny, pearly core in a ri
blending into a thin, brigh
just barely there, can't eve

The role of the female lips as labial-mimics has often been emphasized by advertisements (left) employing phallic-shaped objects approaching the open mouth, or by the use of gently parted lips, moistened and reddened, in erotic or sexually teasing photographs (above).

Pin-up photographs recently have emphasized a new kind of genital echo. By using certain belly-stretching postures, the girls acting as models have been able to change the shape of their navels from a rounded hole into a vertical slit. In doing this, they have consciously or unconsciously rendered their navels more 'genital' in terms of body mimicry. This does not mean that navels have evolved their special shape as genital echoes, but merely that in trying to make pin-up photographs more sexually appealing the photographers and their models have somehow arrived at the idea of making the navel shape more of a vertical, labial slit than it used to be. Taking 200 female nudes at random from the whole of art history, it emerged that there were 92 per cent rounded navels and only 8 per cent vertical ones. A similar analysis of modern pin-up and actress photographs shows a shift to 54 per cent rounded and 46 per cent vertical, an increase of nearly six times for the vertical, 'genital-echo' navels.

Other artificial genital echoes occur in erotic clothing, with genital elements built in to the details of the costume design.

Switching from female to male genital echoes, the arguments become less convincing, but many suggestions have been put forward at various times by both poets and scientists. Here the major element of Self-mimicry is thought to be the nose. In another species, the mandrill, this is obvious enough and is clearly an evolved genital echo. The male mandrill's face has a long red nose with swollen blue cheeks and yellowish beard, imitating in a

The basic sexual signal of the human female body is a smooth, rounded hemisphere of flesh. This ancient buttock-sign is echoed not only by the female breasts but also to some extent by the female knees and the female shoulders—especially when these are held in a posture that accentuates their visual qualities, as when the knees are hugged or one shoulder is raised to touch the cheek.

remarkable way his genital colouring with its red penis, blue scrotal pouch and yellowish genital hair. The face of the human male also copies his own genital region to some extent, but whether this is the result of evolution, or whether it is simply a matter of symbolic thinking, is not clear. Artists have certainly made the equation on a number of occasions, seeing the protruding, fleshy nose as mimicking the male penis.

A number of male facial elements have been interpreted in this way. The swollen nose-tip has been seen as the glans of the penis, with nose-dimples, when they occur, as mimics of the urethral slit. The nose-alae, the bulbous lobes on either side of the nose-tip, have been likened to scrotal-mimics, and the flaring of the nostrils has been interpreted as a 'phallic threat'. The fact that the nose is small in females and infants and larger and more bulbous in adult males has been cited as added support for this view. It has also been pointed out that male facial hair, from eyebrows to beard, is bushier, coarser and more coiled and wiry than head hair, and is in fact much closer to pubic hair in texture, as if the male face were trying to provide a hairy, pubic setting for its genital mimicry. The cleft chin has also been mentioned as an additional scrotal mimic.

It could be that during the course of evolution the male face has become modified to some extent in this direction as a site for Self-mimicry, making it possible for a male to give a phallic threat display from his head region during face-to-face interactions. Phallic threats are common among primates and this idea is not too outlandish when viewed against the behaviour of our near relatives. But, as with female genital echoes, there can be no argument that the mimicry has been employed culturally, even if the evolutionary argument is rejected.

Other cultural devices employing male genital echoes include the use of the protruded tongue as a penis-mimic and the use of fingers or fists in place of the erect penis in phallic threat gestures and insults. Male costume has also played its part, with codpieces and sporrans providing mimics of the erect penis and the pubic hair-patch respectively.

The third major category of Self-mimicry is that of Infantile echoes. The face of the adult female is more babyish than the face of the adult male, and it has been suggested that this is an evolutionary device which enables the adult female to stimulate protective parental feelings in adult males. In a similar way male shaving, apart from its other functions, can be seen as a cultural attempt to switch off assertive, masculine signals. The clean-shaven male is, in a sense, pseudo-infantile. The young boy approaching puberty looks forward eagerly to sprouting his first masculine chin-hairs, but no sooner does he have them than he is chopping them off and returning to a bare-faced condition once more.

There is also the hotly debated question of male baldness. Two totally opposing views have been put forward to explain this genetically controlled male display. One sees it as yet another case of infantile mimicry. The human baby has a large forehead and may also be bald. The adult male has a hairy head. The elderly male has a bald head again, returning to a babyish condition. The large-domed head of the older male is therefore seen as a signal that arouses feelings of parental care and protection for the old and infirm. If many bald males today feel reluctant to be classed as 'elderly' and in need of pseudo-parental sympathy, this may be because the human life-span has been so enormously stretched in modern times, compared with primeval conditions.

Against this view, however, must be set the fact that old males do not lose their beards. The beard is the most intensely masculine hair-signal, and should be the first to go, as baldness approaches. But it survives stubbornly to the end, making nonsense out of elderly, babyishly bulbous, domed foreheads. It is true that a clean-shaven, Churchillian head looks remarkably baby-like, and this may well arouse warm parental feelings, but it is hard to see this as an evolutionary explanation of the development of baldness.

The colours of the face of the male Mandrill mimic the pattern of his genital region, where there is a bright red penis, pale blue scrotal pouches and yellowish hair. Similar genital echoes have been suggested for the human male, whose fleshy, protuberant nose has often been likened, by writers and painters, to the human penis, as in this painting by Barbara Millett (below).

Below right: nipples as eyes. The brown areolar patches surrounding the human nipples—in both sexes—are unique to our species and have never been explained. The surrealist painter Magritte here employs them suggestively as eye-spots.

The opposing view is not much more convincing. This sees the bald head as permitting a greater display of mature male anger and dominance, via the red, skin-flushing display. The more naked skin the angry male has exposed on his head, the greater impact will his furious flushing make on his opponents. This interpretation is also hard to swallow, because the adult male needs his threat displays most when he is at his peak of activity, in early adulthood when his head is fully haired. So the question of whether male baldness has any survival value beyond that of a simple Gender Signal must, for the moment, remain unsettled.

Another suggested example of human Self-mimicry concerns the brown or pink pigmented patches of skin surrounding the nipples of both male and females. These patches, the areolae, have never been satisfactorily explained. They look remarkably like eye-spots, as if the human trunk were attempting, at a distance, to appear like the face of some huge animal. This is a device employed by many moths and other animals, and it works well. A hungry predator sees a small, juicy meal and then, just as it is about to attack, the moth flicks open its wings and flashes a huge pair of eye-spots, which frighten the killer away. These big 'eyes' make an impact because they suggest a much larger animal, one that would be a hundred times bigger than the tiny moth. At a distance the human body, standing vertically, also bears a certain resemblance to a huge head. Viewed with alien eyes, the nipple patch 'eye-spots' would tend to convert the trunk into a vast face, with a navel-nose and a genital-mouth. This curious echo has been exploited by at least one major surrealist artist with startling effect, but it is difficult to envisage it as explaining why the unique nipple-patches of our species should have evolved. It seems more likely that they are simply nipple exaggerators, the areolae acting as 'false-nipples' of greatly increased size. But again it remains to be established why adult males and females should need to super-nippleate themselves in this way.

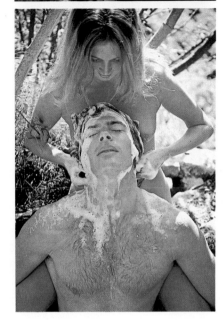

SEXUAL SIGNALS

The courtship and pre-copulatory sequence of the human animal

Sexual Signals function in four important ways: finding a mate, choosing a mate, arousing a mate, and bonding with a mate.

First, finding a mate. With the arrival of sexual maturity there is a sudden increase in certain special kinds of social activity. In addition to fixed events, such as dances and parties, teenage males and females develop a powerful urge to go out 'on the prowl' in the absence of parental supervision. The invention of the chaperon, in an earlier epoch, was necessary to limit this urge and control it, wherever mate-selection had been taken out of the hands of the mates themselves for economic or status reasons.

In most modern societies there are informal arrangements for the coming together of young unmated males and females, which take on the quality of an Arena Display. There is the 'promenade', the parade and the stroll. Young females walk along, often arm in arm, not going anywhere in particular and pretending not to notice the boys who are sitting watching them go by or following them at a distance. The girls display signals of shyness, with much giggling and face-covering, whispering and joking. The boys often adopt truculent postures, feigning a lack of interest, lounging, spreading their legs wide in a primate crotch display, or alternatively calling out aggressively and sometimes insultingly. There is a marked male-with-male and female-with-female clustering. It takes a considerable effort for an individual to make the break with his or her own-sex group and cross the gender-divide. The selection will be made in the course of general social activities, but usually the actual contact will be effected later, in a less inhibiting atmosphere, when third parties are absent.

The fixed occasion, such as the dance, speeds up this process by giving a

Finding a mate. Young males and females develop a powerful urge to explore and patrol their social scene. They spend a great deal of time strolling, standing and watching in male-groups or female-groups (right). From these vague beginnings, individual male-female contacts are eventually made and the long 'sexual sequence' of our species is initiated. The young couples, as they form, start to isolate themselves from the groups, and there follows a pattern of increasing body intimacy (above), with often prolonged bouts of touching, kissing and embracing.

social reason for making contact with a member of the opposite sex. Even so, most teenage dance floors are ringed with clusters of one-sex groups, still eyeing potential partners from a distance.

For many young adults, these mate-finding problems are solved by virtue of modern co-educational arrangements, or work situations involving a similar mixing of the sexes. Males and females are thrown together in these instances and cannot help but get to know one another socially. Despite this, dances, parties and other forms of social gathering remain as popular as ever. They persist as a way of providing a greater mixing of individuals and a greater range of mate-choice.

Choosing a mate depends on many factors. Physical appeal is obviously important, with the various gender signals playing a role, but behaviour is also vitally significant. There are many small signs by which one person indicates attraction to another. Some are obvious, others are not, but they all make their mark. 'Warm' gestures include: looking a little longer than usual into the other's eyes; making any small, touching movements, such as letting a hand rest against the other's body; moving towards the other person slightly more than usual; smiling more than usual, with the mouth open, looking in turn at different parts of the other's body; nodding the head vigorously in agreement; sitting directly facing the other, with an 'open' body (that is, with no body-protection signals or barrier signals); using rather more frequent hand movements to illustrate speech than at other times; taking fast glances at the other person, checking their reactions more than usual, with the eyes rather wide open and the eyebrows high up on the forehead; and using more tongue-play than at other times, the lips being moistened more often.

Consciously or unconsciously, the partner recognizes from these signs that the other person likes him or her. In addition, the verbal exchanges have a special flavour. Characteristically, the exchange of information will be a search for common attitudes and shared likes and dislikes. Often, if physical appeal is strong, there will be a deliberate suppression of personal likes and attitudes in order to avoid a verbal clash. A verbal question will bring an immediate agreement which, although false, helps to promote further intimacy. If, however, there are too many of these suppressed disagreements, they may, in the end, swamp out the positive physical attraction between the pair.

This process of mate selection may be aided by specifically erotic displays, such as the body movements of dancing, where sinuous actions accentuate the gender signals and the individual qualities of the potential mate. Sexual intention movements and mimicked copulatory actions also appear on the dance floor, helping to suggest the patterns of behaviour yet to come. Dancing action vary from 'comings and goings' of partners, as in much folk dancing, to stylized embracing, as in most ballroom dances, and to actual imitations of pelvic thrusting, as in modern go-go dancing. The female is at a special disadvantage in this last role, because during copulation it is normally the male who makes the most vigorous body movements. Go-go dancing girls solve the problem by performing male copulatory movements with the pelvis, thrusting it repeatedly forwards in a masculine fashion. The origins of female belly-dancing are rather different. Originating from the actions of harem girls servicing almost immobile masters, the belly dance has developed as a distillation of female pelvis gyrations calculated to bring a moribund male to orgasm with the minimum of male pelvic movement. This gives the belly dance a marked advantage as an erotic display over all other female dance forms.

Once a bond has started to form between a male and female, there follows an escalating sequence of bodily intimacies. The partners do not normally move straight from introduction to copulation except in the special case of prostitution. By moving through a gradually ascending scale of intimacies, the partners have the opportunity of abandoning the courtship at any stage.

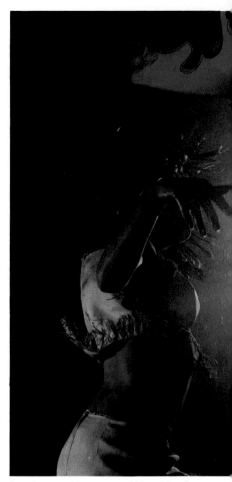

Dancing provides opportunities either for body contact or for visual display. Female go-go dancers, like the one seen here, perform male pelvic thrusts as part of their routine, this masculine movement being the most characteristic element of the human mating act.

Overleaf: during the advanced stages of the sexual sequence, skin contact between male and female is increased to the maximum, aided by complete nudity and conditions of privacy. The entire body surface then becomes a sensitive erogenous zone.

Many mating postures are employed by the human species, but the face to face position is especially common and widespread. It has sometimes been called the 'missionary position', implying that it is strictly European in origin; but this is mistaken, as ancient erotic art objects such as this Pre-Columbian American pottery couple reveal.

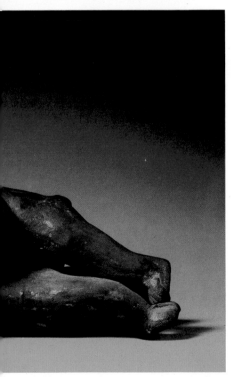

If their mutual bonding is not proceeding smoothly, they can break off long before they have reached the stage of a possible fertilization. Since the development of modern contraceptive techniques, however, this has become less of a problem, with the result that many courtship sequences now run through in minutes what would once have taken weeks or months. But even in the era of the pill, most people are still reluctant to rush headlong to the culmination of the sexual sequence. The preliminaries provide time for careful judgements to be made, judgements that may be hard to form once the massive, shared emotional impact of double orgasm has been experienced. This powerful moment can act as such a tight 'bonder' that it may well tie together two people quite unsuited to each other, if they have not spent sufficient time exploring each other's personalities during the sexual preliminaries.

The ascending scale of intimacies—the Sexual Sequence—varies from case to case but a typical sequence is: (1) Eye to body: the looking stage. (2) Eye to eye: the mutual gaze condition—catching the other's eye. (3) Voice to voice: the talking stage—an exchange of personal information and attitudes. (4) Hand to hand: the first touching stage—often started with a disguised act of 'supporting aid', 'body protection' or 'directional guidance'; the partner helps to take off or put on a coat, lingering a little too long in the process, or takes a hand to guide the other across a street or through a door. (5) Arm to shoulder: the bodies come into slightly closer contact, again often starting with a body 'guidance' subterfuge. (6) Arm to waist: a slightly more intimate action, bringing the male hand nearer to the female sexual regions. (7) Mouth to mouth: the kiss—the first seriously arousing intimacy. If prolonged, it may lead to female genital secretions and male penis erection. (8) Hand to head: caresses are added to the kissing, with the hands exploring the partner's face and hair. (9) Hand to body: the hands start to explore the partner's body surface, fondling and stroking. If this stage is passed, the courtship sequence has reached the pre-copulatory stage, and the chances are that arousal will be so great that copulation will occur. (10) Mouth to breast: now, in a strictly private context, with clothing removal, the partners begin to explore with their mouths the naked skin surfaces of each other's bodies. Elaborate embracing occurs at this stage and, in particular, the exploration of the female breast by the male lips. (11) Hand to genitals: finally, the hands move to the genital region, where they explore and stimulate. By this time both the male and female genitals are fully aroused and ready for intromission. (12) Genitals to genitals: genital contact is made, accompanied by rhythmic pelvic thrusting from the male until orgasm is reached.

Naturally, this sequence of sexual behaviour varies considerably. Preliminary stages may be shortened or omitted, especially in cases where the partners are well known to each other and have mated many times before. It is not even necessary to wait for female arousal to take place, if some form of artificial lubricant is used.

There are also changes in the sequence, resulting from set social conventions. The goodnight-kiss ritual can bring this form of intimacy forward in the sequence considerably, just as accepting an invitation to dance can bring forward a waist embrace to an early stage in courtship. Between puritanically minded partners the final genital-to-genital contact may be made before the more arousing preliminaries have been performed. In some extreme cases, these may never occur, with sexual interaction reduced to the absolute minimum required for procreation.

On the other hand the Sexual Sequence may be made highly elaborate if the mating couple are sexually uninhibited. Oral-genital stimulation may then be added to the list of arousing actions, along with a wide variety of other sexual explorations such as variations in mating postures and mating contexts.

It is sometimes argued that such elaborations are 'unnatural' and that any sexual behaviour that goes beyond basic procreative needs is wrong.

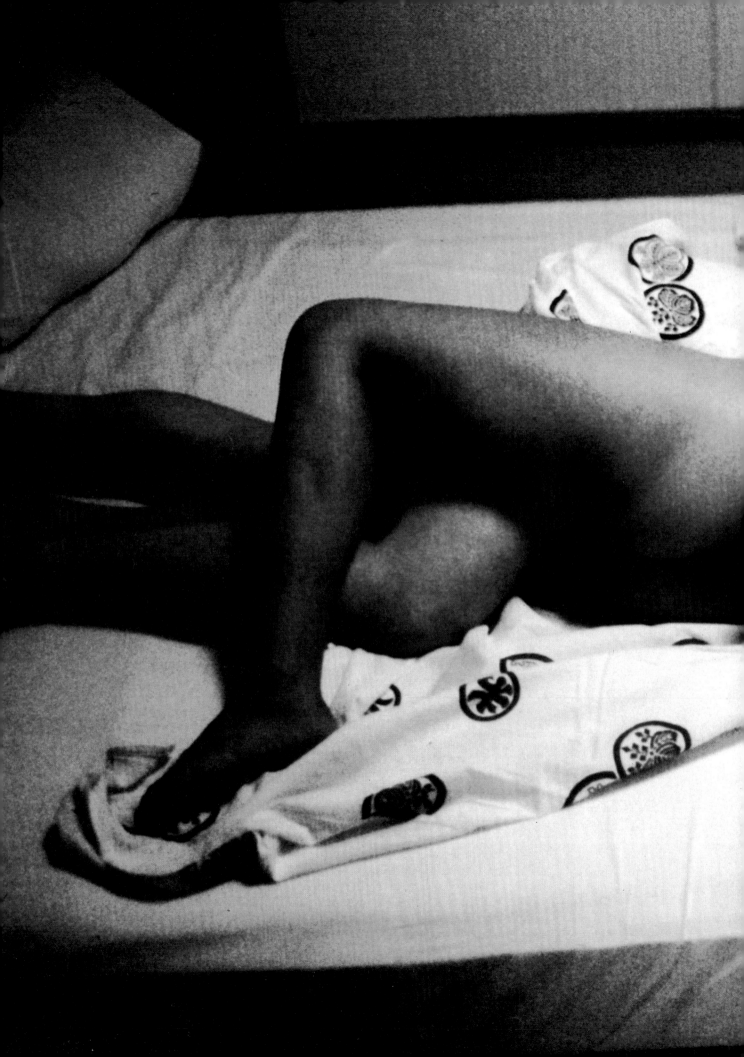

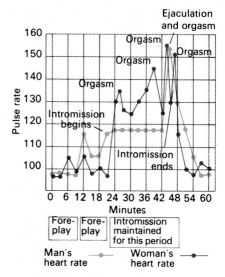

There are dramatic changes in pulse-rate during the course of human copulatory activities. During foreplay the male pulse-rate slowly increases; then, with intromission, it reaches a high plateau level and finally peaks at around 150 with ejaculation. The female pulse-rate follows a similar course but shows a more dramatic jump at the moment of intromission and then fluctuates more rapidly with mounting orgasmic experiences. (After Ford and Beach.)

Following from this, it is argued that artificial forms of contraception are wrong, too, because they permit sexual activity without the possibility of fertilization. This view is not only mistaken for our particular species, it is also dangerous, because it overlooks the fourth main function of sexual signalling, namely *bonding*. Each sexual preliminary not only helps to find, choose and arouse a mate, and to synchronize the arousal of the male and female so that they share an orgasmic climax, but it also helps to cement the loving bond between them, the bond that will keep them together successfully as parents of a family unit.

The human parental burden is enormous, and the offspring immensely demanding. Like other species with a similar problem, the human animal indulges in a mutual-aid system, with male and female partners acting as a parental combine. Together, the father and mother can raise the offspring their sexual activities have produced. If left to the mother alone, the problems would be overpowering. Sexual rewards from extended erotic sequences help to maintain this vital bond of love.

The puritan answer to this is that there should be sufficient 'loving' from the procreative acts alone, without any further erotic 'boosts'. The biological evidence, however, clearly suggests otherwise. In other species of primates there is a brief period of sexual excitement at the time of ovulation. Each month, when the female comes into heat and sheds an egg, her whole physical appearance changes. Her genital region becomes swollen and redder and she is both attracted to, and attractive to, the males in her troop. At other times, when she is not ovulating and cannot therefore conceive, she ceases to be either interested or interesting sexually. In other words, for monkeys and apes there is sexual activity when it can lead to procreation, but not at other times. This is an oversimplification, but essentially it represents the situation that exists for our non-human relatives.

Moving to the human sphere, the whole sexual scene changes. Now the female remains sexually attractive all through her monthly cycle, regardless of whether she can be fertilized or not. Indeed, without a great deal of trouble, it is impossible for a male to tell whether the female with whom he is copulating is ready to conceive or not. Only if he has kept careful records of the dates of her menstruations or employed repeated thermometer checks to find out if she is showing characteristic changes in body temperature can he have any assurance that his ejaculation will be procreatively functional. To put it another way, our species has lost the ancient primate link between sexual activity and egg-production. The human female's sexual responsiveness is always potentially arousable and she is always physically stimulating. Her body signals—the swollen buttocks and breasts—do not rise and fall dramatically with her monthly cycle. They are there throughout her long years of sexual maturity, and she is even responsive during pregnancy and nursing phases. There are only brief periods of non-sexuality, around the time of giving birth. Even after the menopause she remains sexually active.

Clearly, then, one of the main functions of sexual activity in our species is pair-bonding, and any code of morals which serves to reduce spontaneous sexual expression between a mated pair is indeed therefore a danger to successful family life. Particularly notorious is the muddleheadedness that has dogged the question of female orgasm. Because the female orgasm is quite unnecessary for successful procreation, it has often been looked upon as no more than a 'pleasure-seeking indulgence'. In reality it is a unique human evolutionary development of the utmost importance, and one that ensures— in an uninhibited relationship—the mutual reward of human sexual partners that gives such intense support to the loving process of bond-forming and bond-maintenance. Monkey females do not experience massive copulatory arousal leading to orgasm and, unlike females of our species, typically do not form lasting pair-bonds. In addition, they do not indulge in elaborate pre-copulatory sequences of prolonged body-intimacies. So, to describe the human species as the 'sexiest of all the primates' is not a comment on modern

The orgasmic response of the human female is unusual for a primate species. The females of other primates do not experience similarly intense peak moments. The human female is therefore more powerfully rewarded by the culminating moments of her sexual encounter and in this way becomes more strongly bonded to her male partner.

styles of love-making, it is a comment on the basic biological nature of the human animal.

If we are so much more sexually intimate than other primates, where do our sexual actions themselves originate? The answer is that most of our adult, sexual body-contacts are borrowed from the intimate contacts we experienced in our infancies, with our parents. Then, too, we were establishing a loving bond, and we did it via extended cuddlings, fondlings, kissings and strokings. As we grew older we reduced these patterns. As school-children we reached the point where we wanted to break free from parental intimacies and increasingly came to resist them. Then, having withdrawn from our infantile body-ties and having stood apart from our parents, in every sense, we were ready to approach our own sexual maturation. Once achieved, this drew us back again into the loving world of body-intimacy, this time with a prospective mate. Now the reductions of infantile intimacy were put rapidly into reverse and all the old touchings and embracings reappeared, growing more and more abandoned until, naked again in the arms of a lover, we were at a stage of body intimacy unknown since we were naked babies in our mother's arms.

This process has been turned upside-down by the Freudian concept of infantile sexuality. This sees the extravagant body-contacts of infancy as being an early manifestation of adult sexuality, when in reality it is the adult body-contacts that are patterned on the infantile. The primary bonding between mother and baby grows out of their close physical involvement, and the same system goes to work again between young lovers, who treat each other to those contacts which have come to mean loving and caring. The inverted account has done untold harm, giving many parents a sense of guilt when they find themselves enjoying the embraces of their offspring and causing them to be restrained in their physical expressions of love. If this restraint is the lesson they have taught their young, it may take those children much longer to discover the importance of elaborate body-intimacy as part of their own adult sexual relationships. A loving childhood makes for a loving adulthood, and a loving adulthood makes for a stable family unit, with expressive sexuality at its core.

PARENTAL SIGNALS

Maternal and paternal messages of loving care and safety

Unless a human baby is extremely unlucky, all Parental Signals spell care and protection.

There is no greater assurance of protection than the mother's womb, and during the later stages of pregnancy the baby is sensitive to both touch and sound. There is still nothing to see, taste or smell, but it can feel the snug embrace of the uterine walls, the heat of the mother's body, and can hear the pounding rhythm of her heartbeat, thumping away at 72 beats per minute. These are the primary impressions of human life on earth, and they make a lasting impact. Even if, after birth, the mother is unloving towards her baby, she will have given it at least these three signals of parental care. For every child, warmth, embraces, and the heartbeat sound-signal will always suggest comfort and security.

When the baby is born it experiences a sudden loss of these vital signals. In a typical delivery it is jettisoned into a bright light, assailed with the metallic clanking of medical instruments, feels sudden cold and loss of surface contact, and may even be held upside down and smacked to make it take its first breath. Small wonder that the first signal it gives in response to this treatment is a panic-stricken outburst of crying. For some inexplicable reason, these signs of distress bring a proud smile to the faces of the listening adults. Masquerading as 'normal delivery procedure', the behaviour involved could in some ways be compared to a primitive initiation ritual.

Only when the baby is snugly wrapped in warm, soft material and placed in the mother's arms, next to her heart, does it regain some of its uterine comfort-signals. Once again it feels warmth and an embracing contact on its skin, and can hear the familiar heartbeat rhythm. But there is really no need for it to have to wait for this condition, while passing through moments of pain and anguish. Recently developed delivery techniques in France have shown how much more 'parental' a birth can be. As the baby emerges from the birth canal, the room is kept dimly lit, all sounds are reduced to a minimum, and the baby's body is not taken out of contact with the mother's. The doctor's hands gently move it up and round on to the mother's belly, keeping its body surface in close contact with warm skin. Provided there are no complications, it is allowed to lie there passively until, of its own accord, it has started to breathe. Then, very gently, it is moved up towards the mother's waiting arms, where she can embrace it to her heart while it is still

The tortured face of a newborn baby when held aloft by the doctor, contrasted with the peaceful repose of the infant who is allowed to remain in contact with its mother's body.

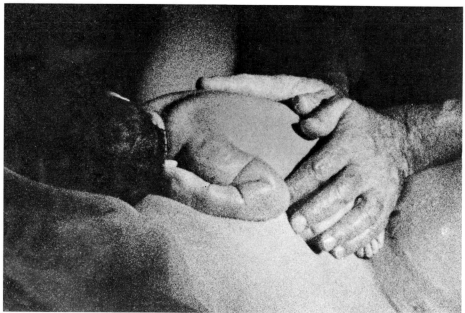

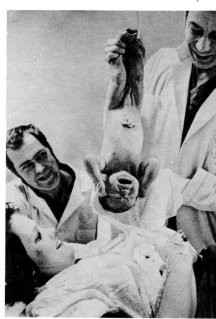

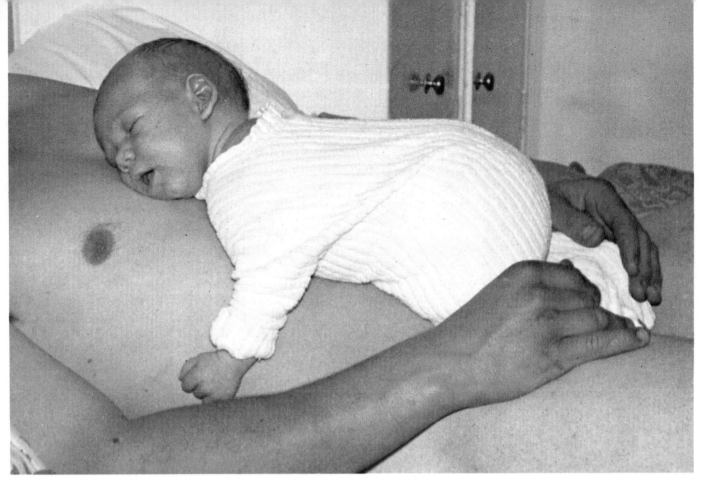

To a young infant the sound of a steadily beating heart acts as a soothing, reassuring signal. Here, utterly relaxed and fast asleep, an infant son rests on his father's body.

wet. Warmly wrapped, it can wait there for a while until it has recovered from the shock of the powerful muscular expulsion from the womb. Only then are other matters attended to.

This method is extraordinary to watch because the baby does not scream and writhe. It is not forced to breathe before it is ready to do so. It is not washed and cleaned while still in a state of birth shock. And its cord is not cut prematurely, before it has ceased to function. Throughout the calm moments following delivery it continues to gain comforting contact from its mother's body: its parental signals are not lost at this crucial time.

Whether or not a baby is fortunate enough to enter the world in this way, it is soon sleeping peacefully and when it awakes it can look forward to many weeks of maternal embraces. Some mothers are better embracers than others. The good ones are calm, lacking in jerky, nervy movements, and intuitively give the baby as much body surface contact as possible. The bad embracer only holds the baby and fails to envelop it.

Added to the maternal embrace there is often a rhythmic rocking movement and a soft cooing and humming. These gentle sounds help to soothe the baby and the rocking reinstates another characteristic womb-signal—the heartbeat rhythm. At first sight one might be forgiven for thinking that the swaying motion of the rocking action was recreating the swaying of the mother's body when she walked, but the speed is wrong. Rocking is performed at a slower rate than the average walking pace. In a typical mother, it is done at something very close to heartbeat speed, although she is quite unaware of this herself. Experimental cradles set to rock at different rates were ineffective as soothing devices when moved too slowly or too quickly, but when they were activated at between sixty and seventy rocks per minute the movements had a much greater calming effect on the baby, with a great reduction in crying. It seems as if the 72 beats per minute of the human heart can make its impact not only by sound, but also through movement.

The sound of the heart also remains important, however, and observations of mothers holding their babies reveal that 80 per cent of them intuitively

It was recently discovered that in the great majority of madonna-and-child paintings the infant is cradled against its mother's left breast, as in this picture by the Flemish artist Robert Campin.

cradle their infants in their left arms, next to their hearts. This is not a matter of being right-handed. Left-handed mothers behave in the same way. If left-handed mothers alone are observed, the figure is still very high—78 per cent. The 80-per-cent figure was even found to hold good in a survey of Madonna-and-child paintings drawn from all periods of art history. In 373 of the 466 paintings examined, the child was shown supported on its mother's left arm.

Babies in a hospital nursery were tested to see if the playing of a recording of a maternal heartbeat would act as a calming lullaby. The results were dramatic. Crying fell to almost half the usual level. Older infants aged between 16 and 37 months were also observed, to see if the heartbeat impact was still operating. They were watched to see how long they took to fall asleep at bedtime under different sound conditions. The average times were as follows: with no sound: 46 minutes; with a metronome beating at 72 beats per minute: 49 minutes; with recorded lullabies: 49 minutes; but with recorded heartbeat sounds: 23 minutes.

The heartbeat sound clearly has a special quality as a soothing signal. It is a little surprising that the metronome fared so badly, but perhaps it is the 'thumping' property of the beating heart that is important, in addition to its speed. This may account for the pleasure obtained in later years from the rhythmic thumping of the base drum in so much popular music. The more comforting popular tunes are those played slowly, at about heartbeat speed, and it may be no accident that we speak of 'rocking to the beat' of the music, and that the word 'heart' appears so frequently in the lyrics of the more romantic songs. When the music is faster than heartbeat speed it no longer calms but excites, and ceases to be music for cheek-to-cheek lovers.

There is another parental signal that reappears in a new form later in life, but in this case it can cause trouble. In its original form, it is sucking at the breast. At feeding time, the mother becomes a warm shape pushed into the baby's mouth, and a sweet taste. The nipple (or teat) and the milk become massive signals of parental care to the baby. As it grows up, whenever a little comfort is needed, this can be obtained by acts which unconsciously recreate these signals. This means either putting something warm into the mouth (a cigarette, a pipe stem, a cigar), or tasting something sweet (candy, chocolates, sweet drinks, and other sugar-rich foods). Ironically, those of us who over-employ these particular comforting devices ultimately suffer the discomforts of black lungs or fat bodies.

In addition to rocking us, feeding us, embracing us and keeping us warm, our mothers also perform other parental intimacies during our infancy. They

The rewarding contact with the mother during breast feeding—or bottle feeding—is never totally forgotten and will be recaptured during the child's adult life by means of a variety of substitutes—for example, sweet-sucking, lip-touching with the hand or the smoking of cigarettes.

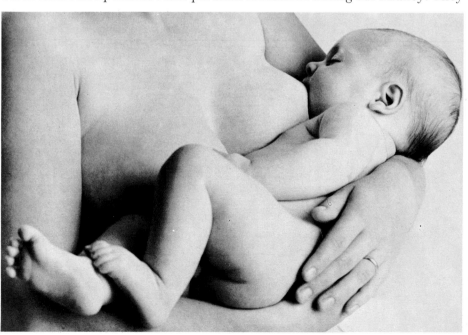

The smiling face of the mother is usually identified as belonging to one particular person during the fifth or sixth month of an infant's life. Constant exposure to loving parental intimacies is essential to the infant's well-being.

fondle us, caress us, wash us, clean us, stroke and pat us. While they are doing these things they often smile softly at us. For the first five months of our lives we care little who does these things for us, but soon afterwards we start to be selective. After the first year of life, all healthy babies can recognize their own mothers and see them, not simply as a friendly smile, but as *the* friendly smile. From now on a tight bond of attachment will develop and strengthen with every loving intimacy. Later in childhood, the mother will be the safe place to which the infant runs when in trouble; the safe place from which it sallies forth to explore the world briefly before returning to base; the safe place where there is protection, comfort and aid.

As the years pass and the child discovers that it is male or female, it also discovers that it has two parents, one of its own sex and one of the opposite sex, and it begins to match its unconscious imitations more and more with the parent of its own sex. It will learn readily from both parents and will imitate both in many ways, but will show an increasing bias in favour of its matching parent. Parental signals that are copied at this stage are not merely the skills and manual dexterities, the tones of voice, and the mannerisms of walking, sitting and moving, but also much deeper similarities—in emotional balances and rhythms, levels of enthusiasm and pessimism, motivation and energy direction.

Unless they have been cursed with particularly unloving parents, most children, by the time they reach adolescence, are already remarkably like their parents. The absorption-like process of intuitive copying that has been going on for years, has endowed them, at a deep level, with many of their parents' special qualities. Superficially there may be many differences, and at adolescence these differences are often exaggerated in a 'teenage rebellion'. This is the mechanism of 'leaving the nest', so vital to young adults, and it gives them a sense of being totally different from the previous generation, especially their parents. The truth is rather different for, beneath the surface, all those Parental Signals have made their mark and are firmly lodged in the developing brain. Sooner or later they resurface in a hundred different forms. Above all, they show themselves when the children eventually become parents, in their attitudes to their own offspring.

INFANTILE SIGNALS

The babyface syndrome, and the signals of crying, smiling and laughing

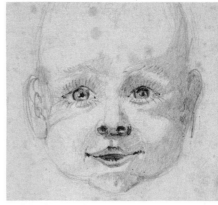

The Babyface signal is a powerful stimulus releasing a flood of protective feelings. It includes a flatter face, bigger eyes, a more-domed forehead, a smaller nose, rounder cheeks and a more receding chin — as compared with the adult facial pattern. The original name given to this anatomical signal was Kinderschema (=child pattern).

Just as parents send signals of care and protection to their offspring, so children send signals to them which help to stimulate their loving attention.

The very shape of a baby acts as a powerful stimulus, releasing a flood of parental emotion. In particular, the configuration of the face is important. Compared with an adult, an infant's flatter face has proportionally: greater width from ear to ear; larger eyes set below the midline; more-dilated pupils; a larger, more domed forehead; a smaller, less protrusive nose; a smoother, more-elastic skin; rounder, fleshier cheeks; and a smaller, more-receding chin. The whole head is much larger in relation to the infant body, which is generally more rounded. The limbs are shorter relative to the trunk, and all body movements are clumsier.

Together with the child's small size, these Infantile Signals trigger off a massive maternal (or paternal) reaction, creating an overpowering urge to smile at, touch, caress, embrace and care for the object possessing them. Indeed, the parental response is so strong that it is even unleashed by the sight of non-human objects bearing the same features. Pet animals, dolls, toys, puppets, and fictional cartoon characters possessing big eyes, flat faces, rounded shapes, and the other infantile characteristics, are immediately appealing. Cartoonists and toy-makers exploit this response by exaggerating these characteristics even more, to produce super-infantile images. Also, human adults whose faces happen to be wider and flatter and bigger-eyed than average often benefit from this unconscious reaction. This is why we like 'sex kittens' more than females who are 'catty'. It also partly explains why women sometimes add to their adult appeal by smoothing their skin with cosmetics, adopting a look of 'wide-eyed innocence', and pouting with their lips and cheeks.

But although the shape of the human body is an important visual sign, anatomy is not enough. Other Infantile Signals must be added to step up the appeal and ensure greater parental devotion. The 'Big Three' are crying, smiling and laughing, which appear in that order. Crying starts at birth, smiling at about five weeks, and laughing during the fourth or fifth month. Crying we share with many other animals when in pain or insecure, but

The three most important infantile action signals are crying, smiling and laughing. All three tend to bring the mother and the child closer together. Crying, which starts at birth, is an alarm cry common to many species of animals. It is followed, about five weeks after birth, by smiling, and then, about four to five months later, by laughing.

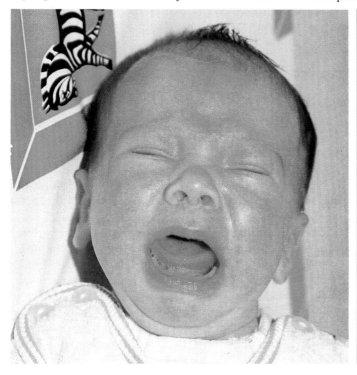

smiling and laughing are uniquely human signals. Another difference between them is that crying is switched *off* by parental attention, whereas smiling and laughing are switched *on* by it. Crying *gets* the parent, and smiling and laughing *keep* the parent.

During crying there is considerable muscular tensing, a reddening of the skin, watering of the eyes, opening of the mouth, pulling back of the lips, and exaggerated breathing with intense expirations. With babies there is thrashing of the limbs and with older children there is running to the parent and clinging. These visual elements that accompany the typical, high-pitched, rasping vocalizations are remarkably similar to those seen during intense laughing, and someone who has suffered from an uncontrollable bout of laughter often says 'I laughed until I cried'. The similarity is no accident. Despite the different subjective feelings that accompany the two actions, it seems that they are, in reality, very close to each other. It looks as if the laughing reaction evolved out of the crying one, as a secondary signal. Laughter arrives on the infantile scene at just about the time the offspring has become capable of recognizing its own mother. As someone once said: it is a wise child that knows its own father, but it is a laughing child that knows its own mother. This is the key to the origin of the action. At an earlier stage babies may burble and gurgle, or they may cry, but they do not laugh. They gurgle when contented and cry when discontented. But once they have identified their mother as a personal protector, they are in a position where they can experience a special kind of conflict. If she does something that startles them, like tickling them or swinging them playfully up into the air, they get a double message. They say to themselves, as it were: 'I am startled, but the source of my fear is my protector, so there is nothing to worry about.' This contradictory feeling that there is danger, but no danger, creates a response that is part alarmed crying and part contented gurgle. The result is what we have called laughter. The facial expression is similar to crying, but less intense, and the sound is still rhythmic, but loses its high pitch.

Once this stage has been reached, the baby is able to signal with its laughter 'I am happy that what seems to be a danger is not real'. The mother can play with it in a new fashion. She can deliberately frighten it in the mildest of ways, by pretending to drop it, by playing peekaboo, and by making funny faces at it. The infant soon starts to encourage this type of behaviour by play-fleeing, so that it can laugh at the 'safe shock' of being

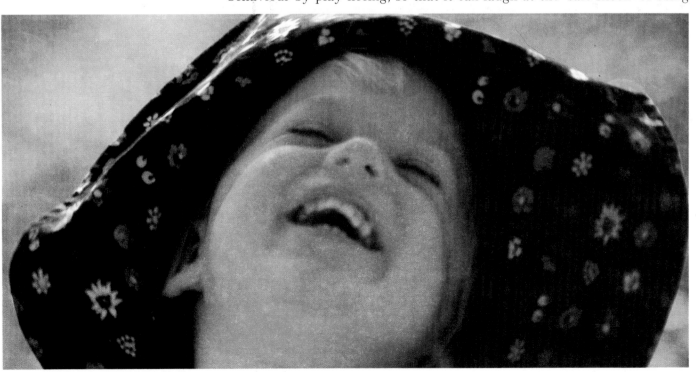

The facial signals of the growing child tell its parents exactly how it is managing to balance its conflicting moods. If parental play becomes too vigorous or frightening, the child responds with alarm and starts to cry. If the actions are slightly less worrying, the child produces a signal which is halfway between the cry of panic and the contented gurgle—the laugh. In this picture, the swinging action of the parents, carrying the child high in the air, has made it momentarily serious, but no doubt there was laughter again, an instant later.

caught by the mother, or by play-hiding, so that it can suddenly be discovered. If, as occasionally happens, the parent goes too far and frightens the child too strongly, then the balance between security and fear tips over in favour of crying, and the infant dissolves into sudden wailing. This narrow borderline between laughter and tears broadens as we grow older, and we become far less likely to switch rapidly from one condition to the other, but the underlying relationship is still there. It is the basis of most forms of humour. When we laugh at a visual or verbal joke, the essential element of the joke is that something strange or shocking has occurred, something abnormal and therefore slightly frightening. But it is not to be taken seriously and so we laugh, just as the child laughed when it was running away from its mother. In other words, laughter makes us feel good because it is an expression of a danger encountered but escaped.

Although it is tempting to think of smiling as a low intensity expression of laughing, this is a mistake that must be avoided. Smiling develops earlier than laughing and is a separate infantile signal of great importance. A young monkey or ape has a great advantage over a young human—it can cling to its mother's fur. It has this physical way of ensuring close contact with its parent. The human baby is too weak to cling to its mother for hours on end and in any case she lacks body fur to cling to. It must rely instead on signals that will make her want to stay close. A good bout of crying can attract her attention, but something extra is needed to keep her near, once she has arrived. The answer is the friendly smile.

In origin the smile is an appeasement gesture. Hostile expressions pull the lips forward, while frightened ones pull the lips back. In smiling, the mouth is stretched back, and originally this was a simple sign of fear. But being fearful means being non-aggressive and being non-aggressive means being friendly. This was the way the 'nervous smile' evolved into the 'friendly smile'. It changed slightly in the process, with the mouth-corners pulling not only backwards but also upwards. This upward curve of the lips created the unique friendly sign of our species, the smiling face that at first keeps the mother happily close to the baby, and then, in later life, acts in a hundred different ways to signal our amicable feelings towards our companions. We smile in sympathy, in greeting, in apology, and in appreciation. It is without doubt the most important social bonding signal in the human gestural repertoire.

Because both smiling and laughter have originated from a mixture of slight fear and positive attraction, they frequently occur together, in the same social context. But there are occasions when they occur separately, and the distinction between them is then clear. This is obvious during a greeting, where no matter how intense the signal becomes it does not grow into a full laugh. The greeting smile, as it increases in intensity, develops instead into a broad grin or a beaming smile. In a joke-swapping situation, by contrast, the friendly smile grows rapidly into full-blown laughter as the intensity increases.

As the infant grows it begins to add hostile signals to its repertoire. These begin simply as rejection movements—a turning away of the head, writhing of the limbs, pushing away or throwing away of objects, and a special form of angry crying with more broken, irregular screaming. Before long the temper tantrum puts in an appearance, with the addition of hitting, biting, scratching and spewing. Eventually directed threat signals arrive on the scene. The tight-lipped glare comes into use, with the lips pursed into a hard line, the mouth-corners held forward rather than pulled back, the eyebrows lowered in a frown, and the eyes fixating the 'enemy'. With its fists firmly clenched, the small child has reached the stage of vigorous self-assertion. This creates a new relationship between the infant and its parent, with the latter no longer able to offer total care and protection. Now an element of discipline creeps in, with the assertive Infantile Signals meeting resistance and attempts at parental control and restraint.

Before long the situation changes again, with the development of that unique human ability—speech. By the age of two, the typical child can already utter nearly 300 different words. By three it has tripled this figure, and by four it can manage nearly 1,600. By the age of five, the child has a vocabulary of more than 2,000 words, all learnt at an astonishing rate and providing it with a form of infantile signalling that permits ever-increasing complexity in its relationships with its parents and its other human companions. But despite the possession of this unparalleled communication system, the old visual signals persist and continue to play a vital role. The talking child remains a crying, smiling, laughing child, even though it can speak freely about its emotional conditions. The possession of words adds a whole new dimension to human interactions, but it does not replace the old one.

ANIMAL CONTACTS

From predators to pets—human involvement with other species

Man has viewed other species of animals in many lights. He has looked upon them as predators, prey, pests, partners and pets. He has exploited them economically, studied them scientifically, appreciated them aesthetically and exaggerated them symbolically. Above all, he has competed with them for living space, dominated them, and all too often exterminated them.

From his earliest days he has feared certain species as killers. Some, such as lions, tigers, leopards, wolves, crocodiles, giant snakes and sharks, he has pictured as savage man-eaters, hungry for human flesh. Others he has labelled as aggressive poisoners—the venomous snakes, deadly spiders and scorpions, and stinging insects. In every case his fears have greatly magnified the true dangers. None of the supposed man-eaters has ever had mankind as the main dish on its menu. Only on very rare occasions and under special circumstances have they turned to human flesh, as a tasty, ready-plucked supplement to their natural diet. Big cats that have taken up man-eating have nearly always done so because of injury or illness. A wounded leopard, unable to catch its usual, fleet-footed prey, may be driven to prowling around a native village where, once in a while, it may be successful in bringing down a human victim. When this happens, word spreads quickly and in no time at all leopards everywhere are under attack as potential man-killers. Wolves have been even more unjustly condemned as a bloodthirsty enemy of man. Endless, bloodcurdling stories have been told about them, but hardly ever have these been authenticated. In a district of North America where such tales were rife, a reward of $100 was once offered for any proven case of an unprovoked attack on man, but after 14 years the reward remained unclaimed. Everywhere, myth has dominated fact, and the wolf is now nearly extinct.

Man the Hunter (below left) and Man the Farmer (below). The hunting scene depicts a successful foray in Assyrian times (8th Century BC). Farming had already arrived as a more efficient feeding device, but the hunting urge still found expression—and continues to do so in many places, even today. For some the kill remains a real part of the modern 'hunting sequence', but for the vast majority it has been possible to satisfy the hunting urge with a symbolic kill—'shooting' animals with cameras (below right) instead of guns, and carrying home the spoils as photographs rather than as carcasses.

In a similar way, poisonous animals have been pictured as a major threat, attacking man whenever possible. Again, fiction has overwhelmed fact. No poisonous snake attacks, it merely defends itself. It needs its venom to subdue its prey, which it then swallows whole. Since no venomous snake is large enough to swallow even a small human baby whole, it follows that to strike at a human target is a waste of precious venom. It is a course that is taken only as a last resort, in a desperate attempt at self-protection. This has not stopped snakes becoming the most feared and hated of all animals. They are destroyed ruthlessly wherever they are encountered.

Prey species have also suffered, but in a rather different way. Instead of being hunted to extinction, they have been transformed into domestic breeds. With the great switch from hunting to farming that took place about ten thousand years ago, the most important prey species were brought under human control and herded, penned and slaughtered at will. Selective breeding gradually changed them. As food animals they became improved stock, not only more conveniently available but also more efficiently meaty. The result of this was a dramatic reduction in the number of animal species on the human menu. Whereas the early hunters killed anything they could catch, and ate a wide variety of animal forms, the farmers and their descendants, right down to the present day, have restricted their 'prey' to relatively few types, mostly goats, sheep, pigs, cattle, rabbits, chickens, geese and ducks. With a few minor additions, such as pheasant, guineafowl, quail, turkey and carp, this is the modern man's short prey-list of domesticated species. Countless millions of these animals now live out their brief lives under strict human control, while their wild ancestors have in most instances dwindled dramatically in numbers or completely vanished.

Animal pests have been more persistent, but even with these there has been a steady decline. Vermin and parasites keep fighting back, but advances in pest control, hygiene and medical care are slowly winning the day. Pests remain the only group of animals that can expect no aid from the modern movement of Conservation of Wildlife.

Animal partners (or symbionts) naturally fare better. They fall into several categories, the most ancient of which is the hunting partner. Dogs, cheetahs, falcons and cormorants have all been employed as hunting companions since early times. Of these, only the dog has become fully domesticated, and it has been selectively bred in several specialized directions. Some have been improved for rounding up stock (the sheepdogs), others for scent-tracking (the hounds), others for chasing prey (the greyhounds), others for spotting prey (the setters and pointers), others for finding and carrying prey (the retrievers), others for vermin killing (the terriers), and still others as guard dogs (the mastiffs). No other symbiotic species has ever been exploited in such a wide variety of ways. Some dogs have even been bred as body-warmers, the Mexican hairless breed, with a very high skin temperature, having been developed by New World Indians as a primative version of a hot-water bottle, for use on cold nights. Then there are mine-detecting and drug-detecting dogs, snow-rescue dogs, police tracking dogs, and guide dogs for the blind. Despite all our technological advances, the dog still remains man's best animal friend.

A second symbiotic category is that of pest-destroyers. From the beginnings of agriculture, man has had problems with rodents invading his stored foodstuffs. Cats, ferrets and mongooses were encouraged as rodent-killers and both cats and ferrets became fully domesticated species. Although they can still serve a useful function on farms, they have never been as fully exploited as dogs, and today are rapidly being replaced by modern rodent poisons.

A third category is that of beast of burden. Horses, onagers, donkeys, water buffalo, yak, reindeer, camels, llamas and elephants have all been forced over the centuries to bear the weight of human toil. The onager, an Asiatic wild ass, and one of the first to be exploited in this way, was in use 4,000 years

ago in ancient Mesopotamia, but it was soon eclipsed by the more easily controlled horse, which went on to become the most important of all burden species.

Fourthly, there are the animal-producers: species which give part of themselves without having to give their lives. We take milk from cattle and goats, wool from sheep and alpaca, eggs from chickens and ducks, honey from bees, and silk from silk-moths.

Finally, there is the special case of the message-carrier—the domestic pigeon. This bird's extraordinary homing ability has been exploited for thousands of years and has been so valuable in times of war that counter-symbionts had to be developed in the shape of interceptor falcons.

In all these cases man gives food, care and protection in exchange for the different services the animals have to offer. They cease to be our rivals and do not suffer the gradual extermination inflicted on so many other species; but although this means that their numbers increase dramatically, they do so at a high cost. The price they pay is their evolutionary 'freedom', for in most cases they have lost their genetic independence and are now subject to our breeding whims and fancies. They may be our partners, but we remain very much the senior members of the firm.

These then are the economic forms of Animal Contact indulged in by our species. For the vast majority of city-dwellers they may seem rather remote, but they continue to operate none the less. The urbanites continue to swallow and wear countless animals every day, but the actual contact—the keeping and killing—has become the work of specialists, the farmers and slaughterhouse men. The man in the street is now mainly concerned with other, less ancient approaches to Animal Contact—namely, the scientific and the aesthetic. Both these involvements are the result of man's intense exploratory urge—the urge to investigate and study the world around him. Via books, films and television he is transported into the world of zoology. He watches programmes on animals in the wild state and learns their ways. He looks at animal paintings and illustrations and marvels at their beauty. He goes snorkeling, bird-watching, and safari 'hunting' with a camera. He visits zoos and game parks. In these ways he continues to express his interest in the animal world, a world that once, when he was a hunter or a primitive agriculturalist, was a daily involvement and a matter of life and death.

In addition, man uses animals as symbols. Here we enter the fascinating and complex world of animal idols, gods, images, emblems, and the increasingly widespread world of pet-keeping. Here animals are not allowed to be themselves, but instead are representatives of some human concept, or substitutes for a human relationship. This is the anthropomorphic approach to animals. It is strongly criticized by scientists because of its tendency to obscure or distort the true facts about the animals concerned. And for the scientist this is fair comment, because he aims to be as objective as possible in his studies of animal life; but man remains a symbolizing species and nothing is going to stop him from employing animal images in a symbolic role or as a caricature of himself. If a species looks fierce it becomes a war-symbol, and if it looks cuddly it becomes a child-symbol. It makes no difference whether the species concerned are truly fierce or genuinely cuddly. In reality they may be just the opposite, but the symbolic equation loftily ignores this. The hyena and the Bald eagle are good examples. The hyena has become the epitome of an ugly, scavenging coward, cackling with villainous, hideous laughter, as it goes about its despicable business. The eagle, in contrast, is lauded as a brave, dignified warrior, swooping down from the skies, bold and fearless, to destroy its enemies. To call someone a hyena has become a gross insult, while the Bald eagle reigns supreme as the proud emblem of the United States of America. In reality, scientific studies have shown us that the hyena is predominantly a bold hunter, while the Bald eagle is largely a robber and a scavenger. Discovery of these facts has done nothing to weaken their symbolic roles, although there was a brief attempt, back in the 18th century, to switch the

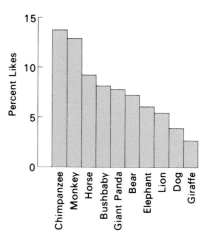

The Top Ten Animal Loves—based on results obtained from 4,200 British children aged 4–14 years. All animals on this top-ten chart are mammals and are well endowed with humanoid features.

As children grow older, their animal favourites change. Small animals such as the bushbaby and the dog become increasingly popular, while bigger animals such as the elephant and the giraffe decline in popularity. This reflects the symbolic roles of animals in the life of the growing child, which shift from that of parent-figures for infants to that of offspring-figures for older school-children. (All charts after Morris and Morris.)

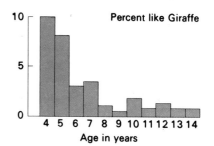

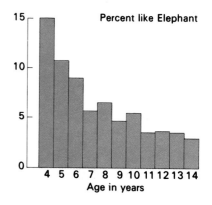

American National Emblem from the eagle to the rattlesnake. It was pointed out (reputedly by Benjamin Franklin) that because the rattlesnake always gave generous warning to an enemy and never started a fight, but, if provoked, defended itself fearlessly, it was the perfect symbol for the American nation. Scientifically this was correct, but symbolically it was doomed to failure. Anthropomorphically, eagles are lordly creatures and snakes are lowly, 'slimy' things, and in the world of symbolism false beliefs are more important than scientific facts.

In order to analyse the way in which we develop our subjective animal 'loves' and animal 'hates', a detailed enquiry was recently carried out involving 80,000 British children between the ages of four and fourteen. They were asked to name the animal they liked most and the one they disliked most. The results are revealing, as can be seen from the charts on this page. The top ten animal loves all have humanoid features. They are clearly not being chosen for their economic or aesthetic values, but for the ways in which they remind the children of people. They all have hair rather than feathers or scales. They also tend to have rounded outlines, flat faces, facial expressions, and a body posture that in some way or other is vertical, either because they are tall, or because they can sit up or stand on their hind legs. In addition they are often good at manipulating things—the primates with their hands, the panda with its front paws, and the elephant with its trunk.

Although no birds reached the top-ten level, the two top birds turned out to be the penguin and the parrot, both vertical in body posture, and with the parrot capable of picking up small objects in its claws and raising them to its mouth, not to mention its ability to talk in a human voice, and its appearance of having a flattened 'face'.

Only two killers managed to squeeze into the top ten animal loves—the lion and the dog. The reasons for this are obvious enough: the lion, alone among big cats, has a face that appears flat because of the huge ruff of fur that surrounds it. If the male lion lacked this mane, it is doubtful if the species would be so respected, because its face would then seem much more pointed and less humanoid. The dog, of course, was not being seen as a savage wild dog, but as a friendly pet. To most children the dog is not a killer but a protector, and benefits accordingly. It also benefits because of the extraordinary distortions that man has heaped upon it by selective breeding over the centuries. Its face has been artificially flattened, its fur artificially lengthened. Its legs have been shortened, so that it becomes more clumsy and child-like. It has been neotenized (selected for a tendency to carry infantile behaviour patterns into adulthood) so that it remains more puppy-like and playful. Its size has been altered so that it has become more cuddly, either as a vast shaggy sheepdog, or a a tiny, silky pekinese. In reality, the dog is a wolf in pet's clothing—a hated enemy converted into a trusted friend. There it sits, flat-faced, soft to the touch, smooth and rounded to the eye, expressive of face and playful of mood. Even its lack of verticality can be cured by teaching it to sit up and beg. Its popularity is secure, its vulpine ancestry a blur.

If we look at the way the animal loves change with the age of the child, a curious feature emerges. The smallest animals are more favoured by older children, the largest animals by younger children. The tiny bushbaby rises in popularity from 4.5 per cent with four-year-olds to 11 per cent with fourteen-year-olds and the dog rises in a similar way from 0.5 per cent to 6.5 per cent. The elephant and the giraffe by contrast, decline with increasing age, the elephant from 15 per cent to 3 per cent and the giraffe from 10 per cent to 1 per cent.

In other words, very small children are looking for *big* symbolic animals—presumably parent-substitutes—and the older children are seeking *small* symbolic animals—presumably child substitutes. The name 'bush*baby*' seems particularly apt here.

It is not enough, therefore, for an animal to be merely humanoid—it must

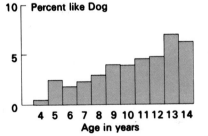

Percent like Dog

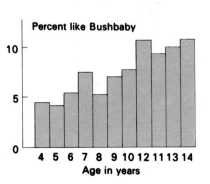

Percent like Bushbaby

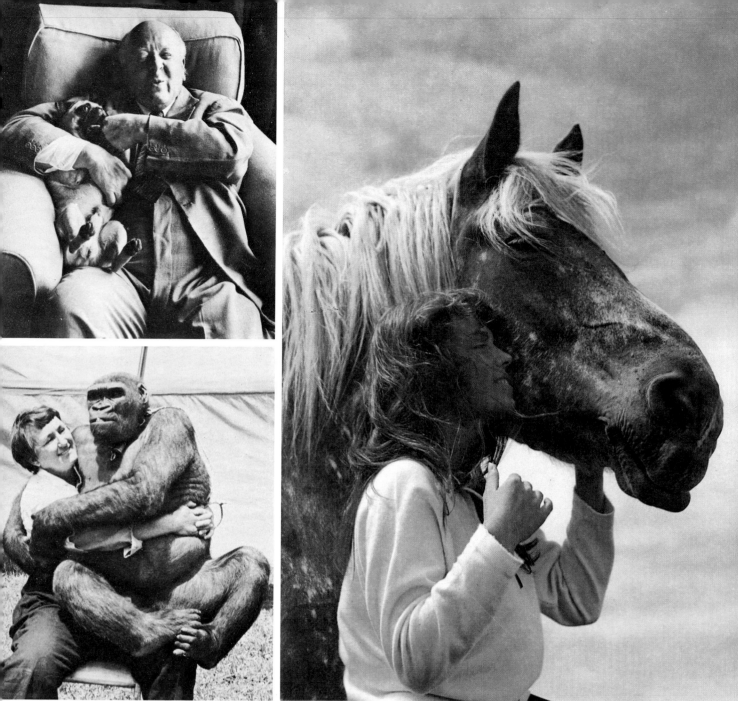

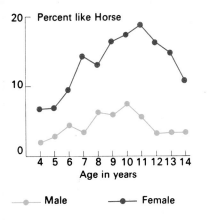

20 ┐ **Percent like Horse**

10

0

4 5 6 7 8 9 10 11 12 13 14
Age in years

⚬— Male   ●— Female

Above: horse-love among British children. The adoration of the horse shows an unusual pre-puberty peak and a striking sex difference, with girls roughly three times as responsive as boys.

also represent a particular kind of human. Virtually all pet-keeping can be seen in this way as a form of pseudo-parentalism, with the animals standing in for missing human infants, either because the 'parents' are too young to have real children, or because for some reason they have failed to become parents as adults, or because they have had children but are now without them. These are the conditions in which pet-keeping is at its most intense.

The horse provides an interesting exception to the general rule about older children liking smaller animals. This shows a peak of appeal just before the age of puberty. If the figures for girls and boys are separated, then the curves for 'horse love' reveal something else, namely that this animal is three times as popular with girls as with boys. It is interesting to speculate on this gender element in the response to horses. No doubt the open-legged posture of the rider and the rhythmic movements of the horse's body has a sexual undertone and this, combined with its size, strength and power, gives it a massive but unconscious appeal for girls approaching puberty.

Leaving the animal loves and turning to the animal hates, we find a very different picture. Here, there is one hate that outstrips all the rest—the snake. It accounts for 27 per cent of the total sample. In other words, more than a quarter of British children dislike snakes more than any other animal, despite the fact that in Britain they are more likely to be struck down by lightning than bitten by a snake in the countryside.

The top ten hates all have one special feature—they are dangerous, or believed to be so. Most of them lack anthropomorphic features, with the exception of the lion and the gorilla. The lion is the only species to reach both the top ten loves and the top ten hates, and he does it because he is both dignified and apparently flat-faced on the one hand, and a savage killer on the other. The gorilla, although very humanoid, looks permanently angry and fearsome, simply because of the structural arrangement of his facial features. In real life he is a gentle giant, but despite excellent field studies establishing this point, he continues to frighten children. If this seems perverse, it should be remembered that even a beloved parent can frighten a child when playing a 'monster' in a party game. The knowledge that the gorilla is really a shy, retiring creature in the wild does nothing to reduce the impact of his accidentally hostile appearance, and symbolically he must continue to play his role of 'hairy monster'.

Snakes and spiders, the two main hates of children, were frequently described as 'slimy and dirty' and 'hairy and creepy', respectively. Myth again dominates science, the snake being smooth, dry and clean to the touch, and the spiders 'hairs' being his long legs. True, spiders have small hairs on their bodies, but the 'hairs' the children hate are the long, spindly, moving legs as the spider walks along. No distinction is made between harmless and venomous snakes, or harmless and poisonous spiders. All are hated equally, without any rational element entering into the response. Snake hatred reaches its peak at six years of age and there is little difference between the sexes—and *no* dramatic change at puberty, as might be expected on the basis of the snake's ancient role as a phallic symbol. It almost looks as if the snake reaction in human children is inborn, an idea that is given support by observations of apes with snakes. Chimpanzees and orangutans both have been seen to respond with panic to real or toy snakes under certain circumstances, sometimes without any prior experience of them during their infancy.

As regards spiders, there is an astonishing sex difference, with girls at puberty showing a huge leap in their levels of spider-hatred compared with boys, so that by the age of fourteen spiders are twice as hated by girls as by boys. Before puberty this difference is absent, implying something sexual about the reaction. It is difficult to understand this, but it may have something to do with the hated 'hairiness' of spiders. At puberty both sexes begin to sprout body hair. Adult males appear more bristly to small girls than do adult females, so perhaps at puberty body-hairiness becomes, in a secret

Left: the Pet Lovers. Human beings employ a variety of species as sources of 'loving contact'. Pets are nursed like babies, hugged like children, caressed like lovers and even kissed on the mouth.

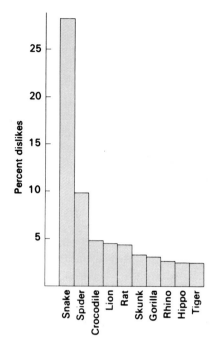

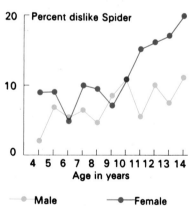

The Top Ten Animal Hates (above) — also based on results obtained from 4,200 British children aged 4–14 years. The snake reaction is massive, despite the rarity of venomous snakes in Britain. The spider response is also powerful although, again, poisonous spiders offer no threat to the British child. (After Morris and Morris.) The great distaste shown for spiders involves a curious sex difference. Although younger boys and girls dislike spiders equally, there is a dramatic rise in the response at puberty for girls. Boys do not show this change — a sex difference not accounted for by any previous theories of animal phobias.

Percent dislike Spider

Age in years

Male   Female

way, something frightening to a girl, and the spider is the animal embodiment of this feeling.

All these different forms of Animal Contact can be summed up in a simple table depicting what might be called the Seven Ages of Animal Reactivity:

1. *The Infantile Phase.* We are completely dependent on our parents and react most to very big animals, seeing them as parent-substitutes.

2. *The Infantile-Parental Phase.* We are beginning to compete with our parents and become 'little parents' ourselves. We prefer smaller animals and enjoy pet-keeping.

3. *The Objective Pre-Adult Phase.* Exploratory interests supplant the symbolic and we turn to bug-hunting, microscopes and aquaria.

4. *The Young-Adult Phase.* We are now at our least animal-oriented, concentrating most·strongly on our purely human relations. Animals are relegated largely to economic roles.

5. *The Adult-Parental Phase.* As parents, we see the return of pets into our lives, this time for our children.

6. *The Post-Parental Phase.* We lose our children and may replace them with animal substitutes — the third phase of pet-keeping.

7. *The Senile Phase.* We are facing our personal extinction, so we become more intensely interested in species struggling for survival. This is the age of preservationism and conservationism.

These are of course merely shifts of emphasis rather than major changes of direction, and there are many individual exceptions. But the Seven Ages listed here do go some way towards explaining the various moods of man in his many and complex involvements with other species. The extent of the involvement is truly extraordinary, especially where pet-keeping is concerned. In the United States more than 5,000 million dollars is spent every year on pets of different kinds. In Britain the figure is 100 million pounds, and in West Germany 600-million deutsche marks. In France some years ago the figure was an annual 125 million new francs, and that must have multiplied several times by now. Cats and dogs account for most of this cost — in the United States there are about 100 million of them and they continue to be born at the amazing rate of 10,000 per hour. Other figures for dogs include: France, 16 million; West Germany, 8 million; and Britain, 5 million. The figures for cats would exceed even these.

Pets are obviously fulfilling some very basic need for modern human populations, and that need seems to be primarily for loving contact. Whether it is a child-substitute or a friend-substitute, the important thing for a pet-owner to do is to *touch* his pet. Pets are not for looking at, for studying, or for admiring at a distance. They are for petting — for fondling and cuddling, thereby replacing intimacies that are in some way missing from the ordinary lives of the pet-owners. An analysis of a large sample of photographs showing owners in contact with their pets (of all kinds) revealed that over 50 per cent were holding the animal in their arms as if it were a baby. In 11 per cent of cases they were patting the pet, in 7 per cent they had one arm around it in a semi-embrace, and in 5 per cent they were engaged in a mouth-to-mouth kiss with it. The act of kissing ranged from a lady with a budgerigar to a girl with a whale, showing that if you cannot hold the pet, there is always some other way of contriving to make body contact.

It has been argued that this passion for Animal Contact is an unfortunate trend, because the human love involved is being misdirected. Dubbed 'petishism' by one author, it is seen as a perversion of human loving and a possible cause of neglect for other members of our own species. There is little to support this view. For many people in an increasingly bleak world of concrete and steel, full of impersonality and urban stress, the loving relationship provided by Animal Contact may be of inestimable value. Many people without children or without friends may well find a supportive bond in such relationships — symbolic and anthropomorphic and unscientific and romantic and irrational as they may be.

PLAY PATTERNS

Play signals, play rules and playfulness

Play is activity which is unproductive. It is a way of testing the possibilities of the environment and the capabilities of the player.

It is important to distinguish play from specific training. A child in the water can be trained to swim, or can teach itself to swim, but this is not play. Water-play, splashing about in the waves, is not organized towards a specific goal. It is an end in itself. But the more a child does it, the more at home he is in the water. He gains incidental insights into the properties of the liquid and into the range of abilities of his own body. His play enables him to acquire a generalized experience of the water, rather than accomplish the direct improvement of one particular skill.

This is important for an opportunist animal such as man. Like all opportunists, he survives, not by having one big trick, but by having many small tricks. He is not limited to one habitat, or to one rigidly followed way of life. He goes anywhere, does anything, and solves whatever problems the environment can throw at him. This is the secret of his success, and to make it work he has to have the back-up of as wide a range of prior experiences as possible. For a human child, a sheltered, narrow, inactive life is a disaster. To be really successful as an adult, he must be super-active in childhood, and it is his natural playfulness that encourages this and, under normal conditions, ensures that it will happen.

Play Patterns have a number of characteristic qualities. They are usually

Play bouts (above) often include a special play signal, such as the smile on the face of a fighting boy, or the uneconomically exaggerated movements employed during interactions. Small girls frequently exaggerate their play actions by 'over-acting' when mimicking adult behaviour (right).

accompanied by a special 'play-signal', which says: 'This is not serious, I am only playing.' Popular play-signals include smiling, laughing and fun-screaming. These have been called 'Metasignals', and are discussed more fully in the next chapter.

Play also commonly includes an element of over-acting. Playing groups overstress their interactions, each movement being made more conspicuously than is strictly necessary. Even in solitary play there are similar exaggerations. The small girl tucking her dolls up in bed dramatizes her movements, making each one more expressive than is required. If there were a serious, functional end-point to these sequences of behaviour, then the individual actions used would become subordinated to this goal. They would become more efficient and less showy. But since the essence of play is that it is activity for activity's sake, each action can become its own master, and the movements can be capriciously magnified.

Another consequence of the lack of 'end-point' directedness is that Play Patterns, like dreams, get their events out of order. There are repetitions and sequence changes—'let's start again', and 'just once more'. In aggressive play there is a special case of this, namely, Role Reversal. The attacker suddenly switches to become the attacked; the chaser suddenly flees. These mercurial changes occur with such speed that they give play-fighting and play-chasing an entirely different quality from their serious equivalents. They reveal that the underlying mood of a play-fighter is neither aggressive nor fearful, but simply playful. If real hostility or real submissiveness was present, it would be impossible for the 'fighters' to exchange roles so freely. They would be locked into their primary mood, and only a dramatic and prolonged struggle would see a shift from one role to another.

One of the striking features of play is that it puts dominance relationships temporarily out of action. The dominant father playing with his small son may totally abandon his usual role of authority and become, for a few moments, the down-trodden subordinate jumped upon, sat upon and squashed flat by his small 'play-rival'. In a similar way, stronger individuals playing with weaker ones— older brothers with younger brothers, for instance—will introduce self-handicapping as a means of destroying the natural imbalance between 'rivals', and in this way will permit a much more prolonged and elaborate play interlude.

Another way in which Play Patterns are intensified is by selecting a special kind of 'play object'. Whether a toy, a piece of sports equipment, or simply a carefully chosen setting, the play object operates on the principle of Magnified Reward. To put this in the simplest possible terms: when you tap a toy balloon, it travels farther than most objects of its size. In other words the amount of work you do is small compared with the result. This is the appeal of roller-skates, ice-skates, trampolines, swings, bouncing balls, beach balls, frisbees and a whole variety of other toys, each of which creates a bigger movement than might be expected from the amount of effort expended. The reward in every case is magnified by the special properties of the play-object. This is why children enjoy toys that roll along on smooth-running wheels. A small shove produces a large displacement. The toy car goes on a long journey. It also explains the appeal of splashing in water. A single sweep of the arm and the water is cascading through the air. A similar sweep of the arm against solid material is far less spectacular. Jumping up and down on the ground is fun, but bouncing on a trampoline or a springy mattress is that much better. This is another side of the whole exaggeration process of Play Patterns.

With games and mechanical toys, the principle of Magnified Reward often operates symbolically. An obvious example is the scoring system on pin-ball machines. The player's ball hits a target and the machine clocks up, not one point, but 100, or 1000 points, giving the feeling of a vast achievement. The very latest pin-ball machines have taken this process even further and it is now possible to score hundreds of thousands of points in a single game.

Right: play bouts involve sequence-changes and action-repeats not seen in 'serious' contexts. Roles can shift from second to second and complete 'role reversal' may occur, with normally dominant individuals assuming subordinate postures. Below right: the play principle of Magnified Reward. Any play object that gives a large reward relative to the effort expended on it by the player has a special attraction. This is why modern pinball machines give scores registering hundreds of thousands of points. Bottom: exploratory behaviour and play behaviour are related but are not the same. The exploratory urge may account for the initial stages of a new play bout, when novel objects are first investigated, but then order is imposed and a 'game' stage is reached, where rhythmic or patterned repetitions begin to dominate.

Similarly, in table games, winning and losing often involves huge sums of toy money, millions of pounds being won and lost in a few minutes.

It is important to make a clear distinction between exploratory behaviour and play behaviour. They are related, but they are not the same. Imagine a group of children released into an unfamiliar room full of toys. Everything is new to them and they go through a series of play-phases:

1. *They investigate the unfamiliar until it has become familiar.* This is the true exploratory stage of the play, with curiosity dominating the scene. The actions are rather chaotic and fragmented, with each examination interrupted by the sight of some other exciting object. There is a great deal of manipulation and testing, but little rhythm or organization. The powerful *neophilic* urge of the human animal—the urge to investigate the new and the novel—drives the players on.

2. *They impose rhythmic repetition on the familiar.* This is the game stage of play. Having explored the novel objects, the players begin to impose a structure on their activities. Rules are invented—either formally or informally—and out of the exploratory chaos grows a systematic pattern of action.

3. *They vary the repetitive pattern.* Before long, repetition begets boredom, and the basic theme is subjected to variation. In make-believe play, the empty box that, following the initial explorations, became a boat in which to sail an imaginary sea, now becomes a car for a journey across a fantasy land. Later, it will become a house, or a cave, or a cot, as its basic 'container' theme is run through a series of imaginative variations.

4. *They select the most satisfying of these variations and develop these at the expense of others.* One way of playing a particular game proves to be more rewarding, and this is the one which will be amplified and reinforced. Players may return to it repeatedly on later occasions, while other variations, once tried, are abandoned for good. In this way, some children's games have lasted for centuries, others for no more than minutes.

5. *They combine and re-combine these variations with one another.* Ideas from one type of play can be brought in to improve another.

6. *They make a sudden, major switch in play activity.* Without warning, a game becomes stale. A few moments ago it was all-absorbing. Now it and all its variations are of no interest whatever. Parents who buy expensive toys for their offspring are all too aware of this rule. Frequently they bewail the ingratitude of their children but in so doing they are misunderstanding a basic play-rule. If play is an experience-gaining process, then it follows that there must be repeated shifts of interest. These shifts are not 'fickle' or 'scatter-brained', but part of the vital exploratory process. There is a constant need for novel stimulation, and the major switch mechanism ensures this.

These six play-rules apply to all types of play, regardless of whether it is social or solitary, physical or make-believe.

Turning to the types of play themselves, there is a bewildering variety of activities in the human animal. A kitten may be playfulness itself, but its types of play are strictly limited. The human child knows no such limitations, but there are, nevertheless, certain favourite styles of playing that can be identified as major preoccupations. The most common is Locomotory Play, in which gross body movements are the main ingredient. Included here are running and racing play, prancing and jumping, leaping and climbing. Tree-climbing is so popular with children all over the world that it has given rise to a special theory of play which sees it as the recapitulation of earlier ancestral patterns of behaviour. The powerful urge to climb trees is then seen as a brief re-living of our primeval, arboreal past. Appealing as this idea is, it is hard to accept when one looks at the enormous variety of locomotory play-patterns employed by children. There are plenty of activities which bear no relation to our ancestral past.

A special form of locomotory play is Vertigo Play. This is a kind of thrill-playing, with the child exposing himself more and more to extremes of body motion. The thrill comes with a momentary loss of balance and feeling of giddiness—the body going out of control, but in a situation known to be basically safe. Included here are spinning games, rolling over and over, cartwheeling, hand-standing and acrobatics. Playgrounds and fairgrounds provide specialized apparatus that amplifies the sensation of vertigo in a variety of ways. There are slides, swings and roundabouts, big dippers and giant wheels, rotating drums and aerial rides. In each case the body is flung into violent motion and the excitement comes from experiencing the limits to which this kind of vertiginous experience can go without causing actual bodily harm.

More energetic still is Muscle Play. This involves pitting the body against other bodies rather than the environment. Each species of animal that play-fights does so in a particular way, and we are no exception. Of all the possible variants there are certain favourites. They include: Pinning (throwing to the ground, getting on top, and holding down); Struggling (bear hug, neck lock, arm twist, leg pull, trip, tackle, kick, push and pull); Piling-on (in which play-fighters end up in a heaped mass of bodies); Chasing (threat display, running, peekaboo, pouncing, hiding, falling down, mock stealing, catching); Throwing (aiming, ducking, catching); and Water-play (splashing, squirt-ing, dunking, diving, wading, and jumping).

Observations of play-fighters reveal that wrestling is far more popular and widespread than punching and hitting. The grappling patterns listed above seem to be of worldwide occurrence, whereas playful fist-fighting is restricted in range. When it does occur, there is remarkably little face-hitting, and punches are nearly always pulled, so that blows are delivered into the air or, if they strike the body, do so very lightly. Arm-grappling, by contrast, is often quite violent, but seldom leads to injury.

Love Play in the broadest sense (rather than the narrowly sexual sense), is common between mothers and infants, where a great deal of kissing, nibbling, nuzzling, hugging, rocking and tickling takes place. It is also common between younger children, but vanishes as they grow older and does not reappear until the teenage courtship phase. Symbolic love play, between children and dolls (or other soft toys) is common at all pre-puberty ages, especially in girls. Play with pets takes a similar course.

Mechanical Play starts early, with the first attempts to take things to pieces, and gradually shifts in the opposite direction—putting things together. It culminates in model-building and 'making things'.

Fantasy Play is a late starter in childhood, but becomes increasingly important as time passes. It ranges from charades to cowboys-and-indians, and from dressing-up to day-dreaming. Here it is the acting out of adult roles that is important, rather than the actions themselves.

Clever Play begins early and shows a steady increase. This is the world of tricks and puzzles, of board-games and contests of mental agility, of jig-saws and crossword puzzles, of chess and card-games.

Creative Play is also an early starter, beginning with scribbling and banging, and ending with painting and music, and the other art forms.

This list is by no means complete. Human play is so varied and so vigorous that virtually all forms of behaviour are represented in a play version. But the types identified here cover the major areas and are the ones which preoccupy children through much of their childhood. It is worth repeating that, in all cases, they have to do, not with specific practice, but with general 'knowing'. In our species, more than any other, it is vital to be a 'knowing', experienced child, if adult success is to follow. There is an old saying that children do not play because they are young, but rather that they are young so that they may play. This sums up neatly the enormous importance of play behaviour for the human animal. We often contrast 'play' behaviour with 'serious' behaviour, but perhaps the truth is that we would be better off treating play as the most serious aspect of all our activities.

There are eight different types of human play—among them: Locomotory Play (top left); Vertigo Play (top right); Clever Play (right); and Muscle Play (far right), where wrestling usually dominates the scene.

METASIGNALS

How one signal can tell us about the nature of other signals

A Metasignal is a signal about signals. It is a signal that changes the meaning of all the other actions being performed. An example will help to clarify this. If two men are fighting we can tell at a glance whether they are serious or playful. We do this by reading two Metasignals. First we check to see if they are smiling or laughing. If they are, we can be sure that the fight is really a mock-tussle. The amused expressions on their faces act as Metasignals telling us that all the other—apparently aggressive—actions are to be re-interpreted as play rather than as hostility. The smiling faces convert the whole, long, elaborate battle-sequence into a harmless play-bout.

If they are not smiling as they continue to fight, they may or may not be serious. Sometimes, in a play-fight, the protagonists adopt mock-savage faces and suppress their smiles, as part of the game. To be certain of the true mood, we must check a second Metasignal: lack of action economy. In serious fighting no energy is wasted on wild or exaggerated movements— every muscular act in the sequence is trimmed to maximum efficiency. In play-fighting, by contrast, the movements are deliberately uneconomic and melodramatic.

Animals employ similar Metasignals when fighting. To give just three examples: chimpanzees stretch their lips over their teeth in a special play-face when indulging in mock-fights; badgers give a little head-toss before starting a bout of mock-wrestling; and giant pandas roll over or turn somersaults when inviting play-struggles. In each case there is also the typical lack-of-economy of playfulness, a feature which seems to be of ancient origin.

Less ancient are other human Metasignals, such as winking. A wink to an accomplice, before a bout of teasing, acts as a selective Metasignal, operating for the accomplice but not for the victim. Once the wink has been given, the meaning of all the insulting actions which follow it will be quite different for the other two involved. The accomplice will read them as counterfeit, the victim as real.

Other Metasignals are less deliberate. An angry man, attempting to be polite, may ruin a long series of pleasantries merely by giving-off unwittingly one single Metasignal of anger, such as a blanched face or a too-rigid trunk posture.

General body-posture, or 'bearing', is one of the most widespread and common of all human Metasignals. The way a man holds himself while going through a long sequence of interactions with a companion will provide a basic

Gaze direction is an important Metasignal. The man on the left is directing hostile comments at the woman on the right, who takes them seriously; but the woman in the middle is not intimidated. She can hear the comments, but the gaze direction qualifies their message, telling her that she herself is not under attack.

A Metasignal is a signal about signals. It qualifies what we are doing. If we smile as we attack someone, the smile acts as a friendly Metasignal transmitting a message that our attacking actions—strangling (above), punching (below) or raising our fists (bottom)—are not to be taken seriously.

'reading' for the whole set of other signals that he transmits. Just as the striding gait of a dominant monkey makes all its other actions more impressive to its companions, so a human swagger or briskness in movement can modify the message of all his other social activities. Individuals who lack what might be called 'muscular charisma' will fail in encounters where other succeed. They can often be heard complaining afterwards that they did everything that was required of them and that, since they had greater knowledge and experience than their more successful rivals, they cannot understand their failure. It is difficult to convince such a person that, in certain contexts, a buoyant stride, or a bounce in the step, is worth ten years of technical education. Such is the power of the Metasignal.

For humans, unlike other animals, there is one special way of overcoming this problem: the donning of a badge of office or a uniform. Virtually all clothing acts as a Metasignal, transforming the significance of the wearer's actions, but uniforms with a rigidly accepted authority are a special case. Put a perfectly ordinary young man, with negligible body-personality, into a policeman's uniform and his every act becomes immediately more authoritative, more power-laden.

An entirely different kind of Metasignal is gaze-direction. When we witness a violent argument between two strangers, our curiosity may be aroused, but we do not feel personally threatened. We hear the aggressive words and see the aggressive actions, but we know that they are not intended for us because of the gaze-direction of the quarreling pair. Because they face each other and fixate each other, we know where the hostile signals are supposed to be registering.

This is obvious enough, but in a crowded social world it is nevertheless a vitally important way of qualifying our actions. If we were unable to direct and limit our activities in this way, social intercourse in a crowded room would become intolerable. The Metasignal of gaze-direction says: 'All my actions from now on are for you and for you only; others can ignore these signals.' An expert lecturer can exploit this type of Metasignal in a special way, by letting his gaze scan slowly across his audience as he speaks, making each one of his listeners in turn feel that they, in particular, are the object of his attention.

In a sense, the whole world of entertainment presents a non-stop Metasignal, in the form of the proscenium arch around the stage of a theatre, or the edge of the cinema or TV screen. It is only our knowledge that the murders and thefts we witness on the stage or screen are play-crimes that enables us to enjoy them as entertainment. The actors may aim at maximal reality in their dark deeds, but no matter how convincing they are, we still carry at the back of our minds (even as we gasp when the knife plunges home) the Metasignal of the 'edge' of their stage.

On very rare occasions, this rule has been broken with startling effect. Certain theatrical presentations have permitted dramatic events to occur among the audience—'staged' but not 'on stage'. The shock reaction of finding themselves apparently physically involved in these events proved too much for some audiences. A famous example from radio was the 'invasion of America from outer space', an imaginary event presented with such documentary realism that many people in the country panicked seriously. Radio, of course, lacks the visual Metasignals of the other media and the deception was therefore much easier.

It has been said that many a true word has been spoken in jest, and this thought requires a final comment as regards the more playful Metasignals. The fact is that they are often only surface-modifiers. Although a Metasignal smile may indicate that a fight is for fun, the fun-fight itself may be concealing real but suppressed hostility, rather than the advertised 'high spirits'. The joking rough-house may be all that the aggressor can permit himself as an outward expression of inner hostility. But whether this is so or not, the Metasignal still fulfils its special function—as a signal about signals.

SUPERNORMAL STIMULI

The creation of stimuli stronger than their natural equivalents

Many toys and children's fictional characters provide an intense array of Supernormal Stimuli. Here a Disney-style character with enlarged eyes, a domed head, a small nose, and a receding chin—all infantile qualities—approaches a small boy. The use of Supernormal Stimuli in this way has been exploited now for several decades.

A Supernormal Stimulus is one that exceeds its natural counterpart. In nature, every animal is a system of compromises. To take a simple example: if an animal is camouflaged as a method of hiding from prowling killers, it may be inconspicuous when displaying to a mate. If it is brightly coloured as a method of attracting a mate, then it may be too conspicuous when hiding from a predator. A balance has to be struck. For most species, this compromise puts limits on the extent to which the different features can develop. Experiments with dummy animals, having one feature artifically exaggerated, reveal that it is possible to improve on nature and make that one feature more stimulating and more effective. If wild animals cannot afford to do this, man can. He can improve on his own physical features in many ways and can similarly 'super-normalize' the world around him by artifical means. If he wishes to improve his height, he can wear high-heeled shoes; if he wishes to improve the smoothness of his skin, he can wear cosmetics; if he wishes to appear more frightening, he can wear savage masks with magnified aggressive expressions.

There is no end to the many ways in which he has amplified his body-signals as a means of improving his sexual displays, his hostile displays and his status displays. But he has also gone beyond his own body and attempted to super-normalize other elements in his environment. He likes bright flowers, so he breeds brighter ones, more gaudy than anything seen in nature. He likes the taste of food, so he makes it spicier and richer by developing elaborate cuisines. He likes a soft bed to lie on, so he develops super-soft pillows and mattresses. He likes vividly marked animals, so he interferes genetically with the natural fur-patterns of his domestic animals and pets, creating a dramatic array of black, white and piebald forms that would never be able to survive in the wild state.

To stroll around any supermarket is to be confronted with a hundred different kinds of supernormalizing devices. There are toothpastes promising a supernormal smile, soaps promising supernormal cleanliness, sun-tan oils promising supernormal browning of the skin, shampoos promising supernormal softness of the hair. The modern pharmacy is full of similar devices: sleeping pills to produce supernormal sleep, pep pills to produce supernormal alertness and laxatives to produce supernormal defecation.

Wherever we want more of something, more is offered. Sometimes the

Technology enables man to improve on nature. He does this by inventing supernormal versions of normal stimuli. For example: he likes brightly coloured flowers, so he breeds extra-bright ones (left). He likes a soft bed to sleep on—so he develops the water-bed and a whole range of other super-soft surfaces (right) on which to rest and relax.

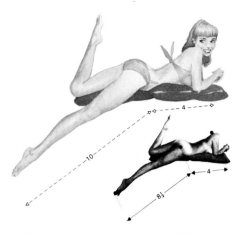

Many Western artists depict beautiful girls as having supernormally long legs. This becomes clear whenever a pin-up drawing is compared with its original model. The reason for this improved leg-length appears to be connected with the fact that as schoolgirls reach sexual maturity they undergo dramatic leg-lengthening; and the artists, by extending this process, make girls seem even more sexual and therefore appealing.

Works of art depicting the human body often show supernormal properties. Drawings by young children always depict individuals with exceptionally large heads. In most contexts, the head is the supremely important part of the body, with a range of decreasing importance as you travel down from head to toe. The drawing (right) reflects this scale of values, the body-parts also getting proportionally smaller from head to toe. Ancient artifacts, such as the Pre-Columbian pottery figure from Peru (centre), also frequently show a large head in relation to the rest of the body, as does the African tribal figurine (far right).

claims are bogus, but the urge to improve on natural functions drives people on. There are over nine hundred recorded aphrodisiacs, each of which supposedly produces heightened sexual energies. Few if any have the slightest effect on performance, but the demand is so great that they continue to be sold the world over.

In many cases, the Supernormal Stimuli are to be found in the packaging rather than its contents. The vast industry of commercial advertising is concerned almost entirely with the question of magnifying the visual appeal of the products. Since many of the actual products are virtually identical, this requires expert attention to presenting them in a more stimulating way than their rivals. The shape, texture, pattern and colour of objects becomes a matter of vital concern. If one package is eye-catching, the next one must be even more so. If one soap powder washes white, the next must wash whiter than white.

The essential quality of any Supernormal Stimulus is that it must be commanding and clear-cut. This means that certain elements —those considered most important in a particular case—must be exaggerated, while others are not. To supernormalize too many details at one and the same time can lead to confusion. The solution is the development of Stimulus Extremism. Some elements are increased while others are reduced. This double process heightens the impact of the selected features. Irrelevant features are eliminated or played down and the magnified elements therefore appear even more striking. This is the essence of the process we call dramatization. It is the basis of most forms of entertainment in books, films and plays. Everyday actions, spaced out as they happen in real life, would be weak in their impact, and so dramatists develop the technique of subtly enlarging the important moments and reducing the rest. If they go too far, the exaggerations become transparent and cease to impress us. We reject the fictions as melodramatic, but if the supernormalizing is expertly done, we experience in a short period of time emotional responses that excel anything in our daily lives. In some areas, such as opera and ballet, and cartoon films, we ignore this rule and enjoy the deliberate rush to the limits of artificial exaggeration. There is no attempt to conceal the supernormal process and we consciously accept it as a special 'convention'. The same is true with many children's toys, dolls and puppets, where stimulus extremism is the order of the day. It is significant that this applies mostly to the toys of younger children. The older child, approaching the age of reason, seeks more realistic toys, suited to the scientific attitudes of advanced education.

A similar trend can be observed in the drawing of children as they grow older. The figures depicted by very young children are full of supernormal elements, as are the art-products of most ancient and tribal cultures. Heads are important parts of the body, so heads are shown bigger than normal. Eyes are important, so huge eyes stare out of the drawn or sculptured heads.

Demi Lashes   Natural Full

Cluster Lashes   Tassel Lashes

Winged Underlash   Raggedy-Plus

Winged Raggedy   Starry-Full

Super Sweeper   Wispy Lashes

The beauty salon is full of supernormal aids, such as these artificial eye-lashes. They help to exaggerate the size of the eyes and the fluttering movements of the lids. By contrast, female eyebrows are rendered supernormal by depilation, because this exaggerates the gender differences between the thicker male and the thinner female eyebrow patches.

Only when children are approaching adulthood do they begin to reduce these exaggerations to an approximation of the natural proportions. And, in adult art, only on a few occasions in the history of painting and sculpture have the goals of artists been to reproduce as accurately as possible the outside world. In a picture, man is freed from the demands of reality to a supreme degree. If a figure is running, it can have incredibly long legs; if it is mating it can display a huge, abnormally long penis; if it is threatening, it can open a vast mouth to reveal impossibly large fangs. Artifical exaggerations applied directly to the real human body are limited, ultimately, by considerations of weight and mobility, but on the drawn or painted figure such considerations can be ignored, and elements selected for supernormal treatment can be magnified a hundredfold.

The art of caricature is entirely concerned with the process of stimulus extremism. By looking at each human face as a slight distortion of an 'ideal' face and checking which features are slightly longer, wider, bigger, or fatter, the caricaturist can increase the impact of his drawing by taking these natural enlargements several degrees further, at the same time reducing the weaker features. The quality of his work will depend, in the end, not on how ridiculously far he takes this process, but on the harmony he manages to achieve between the different exaggerations he makes in the same face. This is basically the same process as seen in the art of young children and primitive artists, but in the case of the caricaturist the concern is with individual differences rather than general human characteristics.

The definition of a Supernormal Stimulus can be extended to include objects for which there is no natural counterpart. To take two contrasting examples: since a girl's legs grow longer as she approaches sexual maturity, it follows that long legs can be seen as sexy. Pin-up artists therefore exaggerate the leg-length of the girls in their drawings and paintings. Measurements of such drawings, alongside the real models on which they are based, reveal that this increase in length can result in legs which are one-and-a-half times as long as the flesh-and-blood equivalent. This is a straightforward improvement on nature, starting from a biological feature and then magnifying it. But supposing, instead, the starting point is a man-made product, such as a motor-car. Here there is no natural starting point, yet there are, undeniably, supernormal cars on display each year in the showrooms of the motor industry. Car designers are as concerned as pin-up artists with the business of producing a supernormal reaction in the people who look at their work. But what is normal for an artificial object such as a car? There are no 'natural' cars, and there is no biological base-line against which to measure the supernormal specimens. The answer is that, with human artifacts, there is usually a 'commonplace' form, against which improvements can be measured. At any stage in the history of the motor-car, there has been a common and therefore 'normal' type of vehicle. The base-line is not fixed, as with the legs of girls. It changes season by season. With each new advance, the whole standard of normality has to be changed. The situation is therefore much more fluid than in the case of supernormalized natural objects, but the principles involved remain much the same.

Throughout the whole of our world there are artificial trends of this kind taking place. We are tireless exaggerators of almost every feature of our environment. Frequently we render particular features so intensely stimulating that we suffer from stimulus indigestion. We long to flee from the over-spiced curry of life back to simple, plain food for thought. Uncontrolled by the survival compromises that limit the activities of other species, we repeatedly find that our more outlandish excesses, wildly exciting at first, become garish, lose their appeal, and must be replaced. Having exhausted one line of supernormality, we switch to another, selecting a new element for improvement and dwelling on that until it too has become stale. In other words, we ring the changes, which gives us the very basis of what we call 'fashion'.

AESTHETIC BEHAVIOUR

Our reactions to the beautiful—in nature and in art

Aesthetic behaviour is the pursuit of beauty. This is easy to say but difficult to explain, because beauty is such an elusive quality, especially when viewed biologically. It bears no obvious relationship to any of the basic survival patterns of the human animal, such as feeding, mating, sleeping or parental care. And yet it cannot be ignored, because any objective survey of the way people spend their time must include many hours of beauty-reaction. There is no other way to describe the response of men and women who can be found standing silently in front of paintings in an art gallery, or sitting quietly listening to music, or watching dancing, or viewing sculpture, or gazing at flowers, or wandering through landscapes, or savouring wines. In each of these cases the human sense-organs are passing impressions to the brain, the receipt of which appears to be the only goal involved. The advanced wine-taster even goes so far as to spit out the wine after tasting it, as if to underline that it is his need for beauty that is being quenched and not his thirst.

It is true to say that virtually every human culture expresses itself aesthetically in some way or other, so the need to experience the beauty-reaction has a global importance. It is also true to say that there are no absolutes involved. Nothing is considered to be beautiful by all peoples everywhere. Every revered object of beauty is considered ugly by someone, somewhere. This fact makes nonsense of a great deal of aesthetic theory, and many find it hard to accept. There is so often the feeling that this, or that, particular form of beauty really does have some intrinsic value, some universal validity that simply must be appreciated by everyone. But the hard truth is that beauty is in the brain of the beholder and nowhere else.

If this is so, then how can any statement be made about the biology of beauty? If everyone has their own idea of what is attractive and what is ugly, and these ideas vary from place to place and time to time, then what can possibly be said about the beauty-reaction of the human species, other than that it is a matter of personal taste? The answer is that in every instance there do appear to be basic rules operating. These rules leave open the precise nature of the object of beauty, but explain how we came to possess a beauty-reaction in the first place and how it is governed and influenced today.

If we ignore man-made artifacts for the moment and concentrate on the response to natural objects, the first discovery to be made is that beauty-objects are not isolated phenomena—they come in groups. They can be classified. Flowers, butterflies, birds, rocks, trees, clouds, all the environmental elements we find so attractive, come in many different shapes, colours and sizes. When we look at any one specimen we are seeing, in our mind's eye, every other specimen we have met before. When we see a new flower, we see it against our background knowledge of every other flower we have encountered previously. Our brain has stored away all this information in a special file labelled 'flowers', and as soon as our eyes settle on a new one, the visual impact it makes is instantly checked against all that stored data. What we are seeing really only *becomes* a flower after this complex comparison has been made.

In other words, the human brain functions as a magnificent classifying machine, and every time we walk through a landscape it is busy feeding in the new experiences and comparing them with the old. The brain classifies everything we see. The survival value of this procedure is obvious enough. Our ancient ancestors, like other mammals, needed to know the details of the world around them. A monkey, for instance, has to know many different kinds of trees and bushes in its forest home, and needs to be able to tell which one has ripening fruit at any particular season, which one is poisonous, and which is thorny. If it is to survive, a monkey has to become a good botanist. In the same way, a lion has to become a good zoologist, able to tell at a glance

Classical ideas of aesthetics involved set rules of proportion and composition (below), but different epochs and different cultures (above) fail to agree on precisely what is beautiful and what is ugly. In reality there are no absolutes, and a great deal of aesthetic theorizing is meaningless if a broader, worldwide view is taken.

Underlying aesthetic behaviour is the powerful human urge to classify the elements of the environment. This *'taxophilic urge'* manifests itself in several distinct forms, one of which is the human passion for 'collecting' (right).

which prey species is which, how fast it can run and which escape pattern it is likely to use.

Early man also had to become a master of observation, with an acute knowledge of every plant and animal shape, colour, pattern, movement, sound and smell. The only way to do this was to develop a powerful urge to classify everything met with in daily life. I am calling this the *taxophilic* urge (literally: arrangement-love) and I am suggesting that it became so important that it developed its own independent existence. It became as basic and distinct as the need to feed, mate or sleep. Originally our ancestors may have classified berries or antelopes as part of their food-finding activities, but eventually they came to do so without reference to hunger — they classified for the sake of classifying. The survival value of this development is clear enough: if, from early childhood, there is a strong urge to arrange and organize all the elements of the environment somewhere 'at the back of your mind', then, when an emergency occurs, the relevant elements can be rushed to 'the front of your mind' and the knowledge brought into immediate service.

School-children can often be heard complaining about the vast quantities of seemingly useless information that they are forced to memorize as part of their education. Had they been the children of Stone Age hunters, they would have learned such lessons at first hand, where the impact would have been much greater. In the abstract world of the classroom, botany can seem remote, geology boring, entomology meaningless. Yet despite these complaints, the taxophilic urge is strong enough to ensure that even in the detached, rarified atmosphere of the schoolroom, young humans can and do commit to memory huge assemblages of facts on topics that they hardly ever encounter at first hand. This astonishing ability becomes even more vivid when the child is moved into a context where taxophilia has more meaning. Ask a child apparently bone-headed at school to name all the latest football fixtures, scores, team-members or club colours, and, if he is an enthusiast, he will immediately pour out an astonishing stream of facts, all carefully classified in his head. Ask another child to name all the recent record releases, song-titles, and the names of all the singers and musicians over the past few years, and if she is involved in that particular pastime, she will pour out names, dates and titles. The process starts surprisingly young. Make a game of, say, car-spotting, and a four year old will soon be able to identify over 100 makes of motor car. So the human animal is a master-classifier of information—and almost any classifiable information will do, providing it is encountered in the real environment and seen to be part of the world in which the child lives.

It is this taxophilic urge that is at the root of our response to beauty. When we hear a new bird-song for the first time, or walk into a garden we have not seen before, our response to the sounds or to the arrangement of flowers may be intensely pleasurable and we say: 'How beautiful!' The source of the pleasure seems to be the song itself, or the garden itself, but it is not. It is the new experience as checked against all previous experiences in its particular

category. The new song is instantaneously compared with all similar songs we have heard before, the garden with all previous gardens we have seen. If we find beauty, it is comparative, not intrinsic; relative not absolute.

But if beauty is a matter of classifiable relationships, then so is ugliness, and it is still necessary to define the difference between the two. The answer lies in the way we have set up our 'classes' when classifying the world around us. Each class or category is recognized because certain sets of objects have common properties which make them similar but not identical. Lumping them together on the basis of their shared properties is the way we arrange them in our minds. The more properties they share, the closer we juxtapose

The modern international bathing beauty competition attempts to find a globally acceptable winner but is doomed to failure owing to the huge variety of human body-types (above). If the Venus figures of today are compared with those of the distant past (above left), the contrast becomes even more striking. Miss World contestants of the present (left), display average dimensions of: chest 35″, waist 24″, hips 35″. In the Prehistoric Miss World parade—from left to right: Miss Willendorf, Miss Indus Valley, Miss Cyprus, Miss Amlash, and Miss Syria—only Miss Syria approaches the modern shape.

them in our taxophilic scheme of things. This is frequently an unconscious process and we may not even be aware we have done it, but it is vitally important none the less. What it amounts to is the establishment of a set of rules about what constitutes 'a song' or 'a flower-garden'. When we encounter a new song or a new garden we are then unconsciously analysing how well it plays the game according to our pre-set rules. If we have decided that bird-song is to be defined as a long sequence of pure notes of varying pitch, then we will find a new song beautiful if it excels in these particular qualities. If it is harsh, short and repetitive we are likely to call it a poor or ugly song. If we have decided that flower-gardens should be a riot of colours, with large blooms of pure and contrasting hues, then again we can easily measure any new garden against such scales of values.

Supposing, by contrast, we prefer more subdued, delicate bird-song, or more restrained, quieter colours in our flower-beds, what then? Our scale of values will differ, and our response to the new song or the new garden will not be the same. We will find them overbearing or gaudy. The arbitrariness of beauty becomes immediately apparent. It all depends on the previous experiences that have been fed into the brain and which have established the rules of the song-game or the flower-game. But if we have all lived in the same kind of world, how can such differences arise? The answer is a process called 'stimulus generalization'. To give an example: if a small boy is bitten by a dog he may come to hate all dogs. His fear of that one dog spreads to include all members of that breed of dog, and he then generalizes even further to include all other kinds of dogs as well. Suddenly all dogs are nasty, savage, smelly brutes, whereas previously they were a carefully classified set of objects of varying appeal and beauty. Before the attack he could make subtle distinctions, like most other people—not as well as the judge at a dog show, perhaps, but with a reasonably graded scale of values, nevertheless. Now, however, his personal assessments are heavily biased. For him there can no longer be such a thing as a beautiful dog of any sort. This stimulus-generalization process can apply in virtually any case and in any category. If a girl is brutally attacked in a rose garden, roses can become ugly overnight. If another girl falls in love in a rose garden, the reverse process may go into operation.

There are many other such influences at work. If someone we despise is passionate about bird-song, we are liable to find the sweet warbling turning into an irritating cacophony. If someone we respect loves pigs, we may soon find beauty in a grunting sow. If an object that was once cheap and commonplace becomes rare and expensive, its beauty may at once become apparent, and we wonder why we never noticed it before.

If, stated baldly like this, these comments seem rather obvious, it must be remembered that the cherished idea that there is such a thing as intrinsic beauty still clings on, tenaciously and against all the evidence. Nowhere is this more vividly encountered than in the world of 'feminine beauty'—the world of the human female form, of beauty contests and artists' ideal models. For centuries men have argued over the finer points of feminine perfection, but no one has ever succeeded in settling the matter once and for all. Beautiful girls still persist in changing shape as epoch succeeds epoch, or as the girl-watcher travels from society to society. In every instance there are fixed ideals which are hotly defended. To one culture it is vitally important that a girl should be extremely plump; to another it is essential that she should be slender and willowy; to yet another she must have an hour-glass shape with a tiny waist. As for the face, there is a whole variety of preferred proportions with almost every feature subject to different 'beauty rules' in different regions and phases of history. Straight, pointed noses and small, snub noses; blue eyes or dark eyes; fleshy lips or petite lips; each has its followers.

Because of these variations, an extraordinary situation develops when attempts are made to find cross-cultural beauty queens, as in the Miss World

When people marry, mate selection is often based on the partner's beauty-rating rather than on their qualities as life-long breeding companions. As a result such pair-bonds are frequently unsuccessful.

and Miss Universe contests. These competitions encourage contestants to enter from cultures where the beauty ideals are clearly different from one another and then proceed to judge them as if they all originated from one single society. In world terms, the results of such competitions are nonsensical and are insulting to all those non-Western cultures that participate. Non-Western girls have to be chosen by local selectors not on the basis of their true local beauty features, but on the degree to which their proportions approximate to the current Western ideals. If a black girl wins, it is because she is a white-shaped black; if an oriental girl wins, it is because she is abnormally Caucasian in proportion. Those girls coming from cultures where protruding buttocks, an elongated clitoris, or unusually large labia are the most prized features of local beauty need not apply. They would never reach the semi-finals.

The only measurements quoted for the current Miss World contestants are their so-called 'vital statistics'—their bust, waist and hip measurements. The average, in inches, for a typical 1970s contest works out at 35–24–35. If we turn the clock back to prehistoric times we cannot compare these figures with the real females of the past, but if we assume that the carved figurines of ancient females that have survived represent the ideal of those earlier times, then some startling differences emerge. One of the very earliest of all 'beauty queens' is the Venus of Willendorf, a small stone carving from central Europe. If we consider her as Miss Old Stone Age of 20,000 BC, then, had she lived, her vital statistics would have been 96–89–96. Moving forward to 2000 BC, Miss Indus Valley would have measured 45–34–63, and in the Late Bronze Age, Miss Cyprus of 1500 BC would have registered 43–42–44. Later still, Miss Amlash of 1000 BC would have offered the startling proportions of 38–44–78, but Miss Syria of 1000 BC, only a short distance away, would have measured an almost modern 31–26–36.

Clearly, whether we move across space or time, these are dramatic variations in the female body ideals, and all hope of finding an intrinsically perfect feminine beauty must be abandoned. This does not, of course, mean that there are no basic human female signals, nor does it mean that human males are necessarily lacking in inborn responses to such signals. Gender signals and sexual invitation signals are present in our species, just as in any other. But sexual body signals of that kind are present in *all* human females, regardless of how ugly or beautiful each individual may be considered to be by local rules. An ugly girl can own a complete set of female anatomical features, possess efficient reproductive organs, be an excellent friend, and have a charming personality, and yet despite all this a human male may find her so visually unattractive that he cannot bring himself to mate with her.

This would be hard for a monkey to understand. A male monkey does not consider the comparative beauty of a female of his species. To him, a female is a female. There are no ugly monkeys. But the human male sees his females both as members of the opposite sex *and* as beauty-rated individuals. His highly developed taxophilic urge invades almost all of his areas of interest, classifying and grading remorselessly as it spreads, and his response to human females is no exception. The result is that a tiny variation in, say, the tilt of a nose, or the curve of a cheek, can make all the difference between attraction and repulsion.

Obviously, the precise set of the face or, for that matter, the exact measurements of the female breast, make little difference to the qualities of a female, in practical terms, as a lifelong breeding partner. But these are the subtleties that have arisen as important elements in human beauty-rating and which frequently play a part in mate-selection.

This invasion of the sexual arena by our powerful aesthetic tendencies has led to a number of social curiosities. At one end of the scale there are the thriving industries of plastic surgery, beauty culture and cosmetics, which enhance local visual appeal, so that females who may in reality be bad cooks, poor mothers and selfish companions are able to promote themselves as

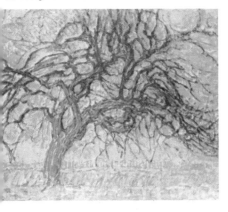

Below: the visual artist, regardless of his style, always imposes a rigid formalization on his work. Even if, like the Dutch painter Mondrian, he moves from depicting trees to fragmented trees to abstract patterns, he still inflicts strictly controlled limitations on the visual themes he employs. His success depends, in the end, on how brilliantly he manages to vary the severe thematic rules he has given himself.

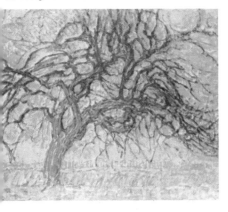

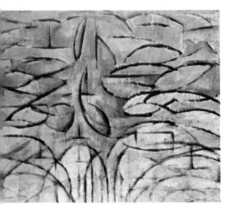

potential mates of the highest order. At the other end of the scale are the lonely-hearts clubs that cater for at least some of the many isolated and rejected females who although they might be good cooks, excellent mothers and wonderful companions nevertheless remain alone and unmated merely because of their plain features or unacceptable figures.

If this trend were to grow it would eventually lead to an increasingly wide gulf between the 'beautiful people' and the 'uglies', as beauty married beauty and ugly married ugly, producing offspring of strengthened super-beauty or super-ugliness. Several factors help to prevent this, not the least of which is the fact that a 'rich ugly' may sometimes be preferred to a 'poor beauty'. Also, many individuals refuse to allow their compulsive beauty-ratings to dominate mate-selection when the final, crucial moment of decision arrives. Instead they make their choice on more appropriate grounds, even though they have always paid lip-service to the aesthetic appeals of the human body. Even after establishing a mateship such individuals may continue to play the human beauty-game, when assessing film stars, pin-ups, or passers-by in the street, but they relegate it to their fantasy worlds and do not permit aesthetic invasions to overpower their real-life breeding systems.

Turning to the question of invented aesthetics, we move into the area usually designated as *Art*. Art can best be defined as man-made beauty, and it appears in two main forms: the Performing Arts and the Plastic Arts. The Performing Arts provide an aesthetic event; the Plastic Arts provide an aesthetic object. In both these cases, the sense of beauty comes primarily from our subtle comparisons and classifications of set themes, as it did with natural objects. The difference, of course, is that with natural beauty the theme is merely selected from the world around us. We do not invent it, we only isolate it. In the case of the arts, however, we create it ourselves.

This gives rise to a new problem: how to arrive at a theme, so that its variations can then be enjoyed. If, for example, we were going to enjoy the beauty of wild animals or wild flowers, there was no creativity involved. They existed already, and evolution had done the creative work for us. But if we now decide to compose music or paint pictures we have to impose our own evolutionary forces on the works we invent.

For the painter staring at a blank canvas or the composer sitting in front of a silent piano, there is total responsibility. He starts from nothing, or, rather, from everything. His initial choice at the beginning of a work of art is theoretically completely open. *Any* shape can be drawn. *Any* note can be played. This is the special, additional challenge for the artist, as opposed to the individual reacting to natural beauty. How does he meet it?

The answer is that he quickly imposes on himself a highly restricted form. In a word, he formalizes. Any form will do, just so long as it contains the potential for a complex set of variations. He may copy the form from nature—a tree, for instance—or he may steal a scale of notes from bird-song. Or he may take a geometric pattern from some geological structure as his starting point. Once he has begun to experiment with forms he has wrested from nature, he can then rapidly shift his themes further and further away from the natural starting point until the themes he employs are relatively abstract. With music this process took place long, long ago. The visual arts are, by contrast, only recently beginning to explore the more abstract possibilities of painting and sculpture.

Either way, whether staying close to imitated natural objects, or creating entirely novel abstracted compositions, the artist's work is judged, finally, not on any absolute values, but on the basis of how ingeniously he manages to ring the changes on the themes he has employed. The quality of the beauty will depend on how he manages to avoid the most obvious and clumsy of possible variations, and how he contrives to make daring, subtle, amusing, or surprising variants of the theme without actually destroying it. This is the true nature of invented beauty and it is a game that the human animal plays with consummate skill.

LATERALITY
Lefthanded versus righthanded

A great deal of human behaviour is asymmetrical. Laterality is de-monstrated whenever an action demands more from one side of the body than the other. Every time we wave, wink, clap, shake a fist, cock an eyebrow, put an eye to a telescope, fold our arms, or cross our legs, we are forced to favour one side more than the other. Each such action requires a clear-cut decision, usually instantaneous and unconscious, to activate the two halves of the human body in different ways. Indecision and fumbling would mean inefficiency.

The problem starts early in infancy and goes through a strangely complex series of stages. At 12 weeks babies usually use both hands with equal vigour, but by 16 weeks they mostly favour the left hand when making contact. By 24 weeks they have changed again and show a strong shift back to the bilateral use of both hands. Then at 28 weeks they become unilateral once more, shifting this time to the right hand. At 32 weeks they are again bilateral. When they reach the age of 36 weeks, there is yet another shift, this time with the majority favouring the left hand. Between 40 and 44 weeks the right hand predominates once more. At 48 weeks some infants show another shift back to the left hand and then, between 52 and 56 weeks, the right hand takes over yet again.

The pendulum has not yet ceased to swing. At 80 weeks, confusion is back and the right hand loses its dominance, with the return of bilateral actions. When the infant reaches the age of 2 years, the right hand takes over again, but, between $2\frac{1}{2}$ and $3\frac{1}{2}$ years, bilateral activity resurfaces. Stability begins, at last, at around the age of 4 years, and grows in strength until, finally, at the age of 8 years, the child is fixed in its permanent condition, with one hand strongly dominant over the other.

The most peculiar feature of this long sequence is that the end result is a population of human beings showing a strong bias towards right-handedness. Roughly 9 out of every 10 school-children are naturally right-handed and 1 out of 10 is naturally left-handed. No one has ever satisfactorily explained why this curious ratio should be typical of our species. It remains one of the minor mysteries of human life.

It is an untidy arrangement. 50:50, or 100:0 would be much easier to accept, and yet there it is, unavoidable, all over the world, with one-tenth of the population refusing to join the majority group of right-handers. Inevitably, the majority have repeatedly attempted to suppress the unfortunate minority (even though, today, there must be somewhere in the region of 200 million left-handers). Left-handedness has been ridiculed, punished and banned with varying degrees of strictness. Many cultures in the past—and some, even today—have encouraged their school-teachers and their parents to force their left-handed children into righteous ways.

What do all the famous figures above have in common? Left to right, from the top: Julius Caesar, Harry S. Truman, Judy Garland, Hans Holbein, Leonardo da Vinci and Paul McCartney. The answer is that they all are, or were, left-handed. Each of us has a bias favouring one side of the body, with roughly ten per cent of the world population being naturally 'left-handed'. This applies even when clapping (left); most people applaud with their right hand uppermost, but every audience contains a small number of left-handed clappers.

Enlightened education authorities in many countries have now abandoned this policy and permit children to follow their natural tendencies; but, even so, the left-handers are still looked upon as slightly odd and, in both senses of the word, not quite 'right'.

Many languages contain insulting words for the left-handed individual. *Sinister* comes from the Latin word for left-handed. The French word *gauche* not only means left, but also awkward or clumsy. There is the Italian *mancino*, also meaning crooked or maimed, the Portugese *canhoto*, also meaning weak or mischievous, and the Spanish *zurdo*, from *azurdos*, meaning to go the wrong way.

The Bible makes it clear that God is right-handed and the Devil is left-handed. It is the sheep that are invited to sit on the right hand, while the goats must sit on the left, where they are cursed and sent off to the everlasting fire. In the Hindu, Buddhist and Muslim religions, it is the right hand that is clean and the left hand that is unclean. And in a British court of law today you are still instructed to 'take the book in your right hand' when swearing an oath.

At a more mundane level, there are many every-day objects that are designed specifically and exclusively for right-handers, from scissors and sewing-machines to potato-peelers and fountain-pen nibs. At table the wine-glass is always on the right and the wine is served from the right. We all shake hands with the right hand and salute with the right hand when we join the army. For the millions of left-handers there is nothing to do but accept this right-handed tyranny for the sake of social conformity.

To some (presumably right-handed) writers on the subject of left-handedness, the minority group are seen, not merely as odd, but downright belligerent. Although the evidence of careful child-studies clearly shows that left-handed children develop their laterality quite naturally, without even being aware of the way their bias is going until it is pointed out to them, these authorities claim, with great vigour, that left-handers are 'stubborn and wilful ... domineering, overbearing and openly rebellious ... obstinate introverts'. This interpretation can presumably be explained by the left-hander's natural reluctance to give up his or her urge to use the left hand when put under pressure to do so.

Inherent in all general discussions of left and right handedness is one gross oversimplification. This is the equating of leftness and rightness with the act of writing. The very term 'right-handed' has become synonymous with holding a pen or pencil in the right hand, despite the fact that there are many other one-sided actions being performed throughout any ordinary day. To eliminate this shortcoming, a study was made covering no fewer than 45 different one-sided actions. Ten people were photographed doing each of the 45 movements and then their left/right score was calculated to find out if any one of them was totally left-biased, or totally right-biased.

Briefly, the answer was that not one of them performed all the 45 actions with a bias favouring the same side of the body. The most intensely right-sided person only managed 40 right-biased actions, and the most left-sided person only managed 32 left-biased actions, out of the 45. Nevertheless, all ten subjects showed a marked degree of bias one way or the other, and no one came close to the 50:50 balance mark. The nearest was a girl who scored 15 left-actions to 30 right-actions, so that even for her there was a two-to-one bias in favour of one side.

Three basic kinds of actions were tested. First, there were the various one-handed movements, such as beckoning, writing and scratching. Nine of the ten subjects showed a strong bias to the right, while one showed an equally strong bias to the left. Second, there were various 'non-handed' actions—such movements as cocking the head to one side and jutting out one hip. Again, the same nine people showed a right bias, even though quite different body organs were involved, and the same solitary left-sider continued to favour the left. Third came the two-handed actions, such as striking the

When we speak of being left-handed, we think of the act of writing, but there are many ways in which we must make a left or right choice during our ordinary daily lives. Every time we stand with more weight on one leg (left), we stick out one hip more than the other. Are you left-hipped or right hipped? Every time we put our hands behind our backs (right), one hand becomes dominant and holds the other. Which do you do? In the picture showing prisoners-of-war on camp parade, one man differs from all the rest.

Are you left-eyed or right-eyed? There is a simple test to answer this question. Stare at a small object in front of you and then quickly bring your finger up, so that it is dead in line with that object. Now close one eye; now open that eye and close the other. When you are looking at the object with your dominant eye, the tip of your extended finger will stay in line with it. When you switch to the other eye, the fingertip will appear to move to one side of it. The two pictures here show a left-eyed man (below) and a right-eyed man lining up on the camera that is taking their photograph.

palm with a closed fist, or threading a needle. In these cases, both sides of the body were used, but one hand was active and dominant while the other was passive and usually more or less static. Even with motionless postures, such as sitting with one hand clasped in the other, it is possible to distinguish between the active, clasping hand and the passive, clasped hand. With these two-handed actions, the left and right bias of the subjects was far less clear-cut, and two of the 'right-handed' subjects actually switched to become predominantly left-sided.

Detailed tests of this kind reveal that the way we each become fixated on certain patterns of movement is by no means simple. It is obviously too easy to speak of people as belonging to two totally distinct groups. Every right-hander, it seems, has his left-handed moments, and vice versa, and many of the actions are so automatic that few people are fully aware of how they are operating their own bodies.

It is worth carrying out a simple test on yourself to see just how left-sided or right-sided you are. You will, of course, know in which hand you hold a pen; but how far does this bias in your body extend? Are you left-eyed, or

right-eyed? Left-eared or right-eared? Are you a left-handed clapper or a right-handed clapper? Here is a simplified 10-point test you can apply to yourself:

(1) Imagine the centre of your back is itching. Which hand do you use to scratch it? (2) Interlock your fingers. Which thumb is uppermost? (3) Imagine you are applauding and start clapping your hands. Which hand is uppermost? (4) Wink at an imaginary friend straight in front of you. Which eye does the winking? (5) Put your hands behind your back, one holding the other. Which hand does the holding? (6) Someone in front of you is shouting but you cannot hear the words. Cup your ear to hear better. Which ear do you cup? (7) Count to three on your fingers, using the forefinger of your other hand. Which forefinger do you use? (8) Tilt your head over on to one shoulder. Which shoulder does it touch? (9) Fold your arms. Which forearm is uppermost? (10) Fixate a small, distant object with your eyes and point directly at it with your forefinger. Now close one eye. Now change eyes. Which eye was open when the fingertip remained in line with the small object? (When the other eye, the non-dominant one, is open and the dominant eye is closed, the finger will appear to move to one side of the object.)

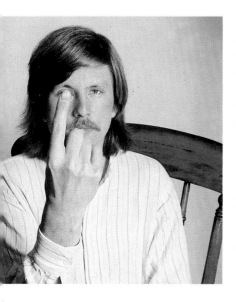

If you have always spoken of yourself as right-handed or left-handed, you will probably now have discovered that your body is less than total in its devotion to its favoured side. If you are right-handed the chances are that you were not able to answer 'right' ten times. If you are a parent or a school-teacher, then this is something worth bearing in mind whenever you feel tempted to criticize a left-handed child. (You may argue that such criticism is unlikely today but according to recent reports school-children in most Communist countries of the Eastern world are still being forced to write with the right hand, regardless of their natural tendency.)

LOCOMOTION

The twenty basic ways of moving from place to place

Man's great urge for mobility has led to an astonishing variety of artificial aids to locomotion, from large animals and land vehicles to aquatic vessels and aircraft. But although these advances have made modern man slightly less athletic than his tribal ancestors, they have added to, rather than replaced, his ancient, bodily modes of locomotion. The artificial techniques are all essentially concerned with long-distance transportation, and over short distances we can still observe the whole range of typical body-movements of our species. There are many local and individual variations, but viewing people as a whole, the man-watcher in the field can detect twenty basic ways in which people manage to move their bodies from A to B, without the use of artificial aids.

1. The Slither. This is the very first way in which we manage to move ourselves about as tiny babies. Like reptiles, we slide ourselves along the ground on our bellies, using our limbs to tug and shove our bodies along as best we can. As adults we hardly ever use this laborious method, unless we are forced to advance while keeping flat on the ground. Soldiers are trained to do this efficiently for creeping up on an enemy, children may employ it when playing hiding games, and naturalists may adopt it as a stalking-device to avoid detection by a nervous animal. A wounded man may drag himself to safety by slithering along the ground, and cave explorers and engineers may be forced into this posture when moving along narrow passages. But apart from these specialized uses, the Slither is essentially an infantile pattern that we leave behind in the nursery.

2. The Crawl. One stage up from the Slither is the body Crawl on all fours. This too is predominantly infantile, but it does not generally appear until we are ten months old. It is our version of the quadrupedal locomotion typical of most other mammals. But, because we have such long legs, it is extremely difficult for us to crawl on hands and feet and we nearly always use hands and knees instead. For the child approaching the age of one, this is an exciting new form of high-speed movement and he uses it to increase his explorations of the fascinating world around him. As he enters his second year of life and conquers vertical movement, the Crawl begins to fade in importance. In adult life it reappears only rarely—when picking up small objects scattered on the floor, when giving children rides, or when moving under low obstacles.

3. The Totter. The Totter can be defined as unsteady, slow, vertical locomotion. When the human infant approaches the age of one it can Totter, or toddle, with the support of a parental hand. In the months that follow, the legs rapidly become stronger and by the age of fifteen months the child can at last stand up and Totter along unaided for short periods. This unsteady and hazardous form of locomotion is repeated in later life only by the injured, the invalid and the intoxicated, where, for one reason or another, the adult legs become as unreliable as the infantile ones.

4. The Walk. This is the crowning glory of human bodily locomotion. It is an action we all take so much for granted and yet, when analysed as a mechanical operation, it emerges as an immensely complex process—so complicated, in fact, that muscle experts are still arguing today over the finer points of how it operates, and how we manage to stride along so successfully. The human stride is unique in the animal world. There are hundreds of different mammals trotting along on four legs in much the same way as one another, and there are plenty more, like the kangaroos and wallabies, hopping on their hind legs. And there are quite a number, like the bears and apes, which can rear themselves up into a vertical position to stagger for a short while before collapsing back into the comfort of their more usual four-footed posture. But only man strides out for long periods, with the bipedal Walk as his normal, basic gait.

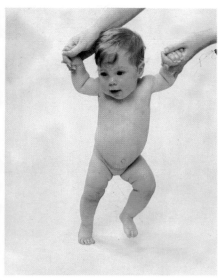

Top: the Crawl and the Totter. Above: the Slither. Left: the Walk.

Overleaf: the Hurry; the Stroll; the Jog; the Run; the March; the Goose-step; the Sprint; and Acrobatics—represented by a cartwheel'.

Walking at average speed, most people progress at a rate of two strides per second. Even an unathletic city-dweller could keep this up for several miles without too much trouble, at a rate of about three miles an hour. Athletes can, of course, maintain this for huge distances, the current record for a non-stop walk being just over 300 miles at a rate of about 2½ miles an hour. Walking with rest periods produces even more spectacular results, the Trans–Asia record being 6,800 miles covered in 238 days, giving an average speed, including rests, of just over one mile an hour. Even though these are specially prepared events, they nevertheless give a clear idea of how comparatively easy it was for mankind to spread across the whole face of the globe long before artificial travel aids were available.

Without going into technical detail, the essential elements of the human Walk are as follows: with each stride, the foot is placed on the ground heel-first. Then, as the other leg is bent up and swung to the front the supporting foot rocks forward until the pressure is taken by the ball of the foot just behind the big toe. The heel has now left the ground and the supporting foot is ready for the final moment of push-off from the toes. But this push-off does not take place until the other foot has touched the ground. So, during the process of walking, there is always either one or two feet on the ground at any one time. The walker is never airborne. This is the essential difference between walking and running.

5. The Stroll. The Walk is usually described as a single type of locomotion and then contrasted with running; but careful observation of people moving about in public places reveals that there are several distinct types of walking, and that they do not all grade smoothly into one another as a continuum, but instead each show their own special, typical intensity. Strolling is a particular form of slow walking, usually performed at a rate of about one stride per second, and where there is clearly no desire to arrive somewhere, but merely to travel. The stroller's journey is an end in itself. This is the saunter of the social occasion—the garden party, or the park on a sunny afternoon—where people are 'taking a turn' or 'promenading' or 'parading'. It is the opposite of the brisk walk, frequently involves pauses to look or talk, and is often combined with body-contacts with walking companions—arm-in-arm linking, hand-in-hand, arm-around-shoulder, or arm-around-waist. In addition to being a social walk, the Stroll is also the gait of the man pacing up and down, deep in thought, or reading a book.

6. The Shuffle. This is the hobbling gait of the aged and the infirm, in which the speed of movement is drastically reduced and the feet are slid cautiously along the ground. There is no heel-to-toe action, the feet being kept flat on the ground and hardly raised off it at all. Each forward movement is a very short stride, with the foot 'skidded' forward, making the typical scratchy, shuffling sound of this laborious type of locomotion. Progression is at a snail's pace, but the shuffler does eventually arrive, and by using this technique manages successfully to avoid total immobility.

7. The Hurry. Going to the other extreme, the Hurry is the fast walk of the man who is desperate to get somewhere quickly, but who has not yet been driven to the extreme of breaking into a run. In any crowded street, the hurrier can easily be distinguished from the ordinary walkers. He is not merely walking slightly faster than the other people, he is moving as fast as he can go without running. When one is hurrying oneself, the subjective feeling is that one is taking more strides per second to achieve the higher speed, but usually this is not the case. What happens is that the hurrier still walks at the standard rate of about two strides per second, like the normal walker, but what he does do is to increase the length of each stride. This means that the legs are moving faster, as they cover more space, but the stride rate stays much the same.

In any typical street scene one can spot strollers, walkers, shufflers and hurriers, all navigating their routes, weaving in and out among one another with great dexterity, and hardly ever colliding. It feels so simple to do, and

yet it involves limb movements and visual checking actions of great subtlety and complexity. And one of the unconscious processes at work as we move about in such a crowd is the automatic classification of each person we see into one of the locomotion categories. Without being aware of it, we tag each person as a stroller, a shuffler, a walker, or a hurrier and then make unconscious calculations concerning where their gaits will bring them, relative to our own movements. In this way we can anticipate and avoid collisions more efficiently. If people did not employ these characteristic and identifiable gaits when moving about in public, we would find manoeuvring among them much more difficult than it is.

8. The Run. Turning from walking gaits to running gaits, we come to the next major division in human locomotion. Here the individual becomes airborne and the whole sequence of striding changes. There is no longer a moment when both feet are on the ground at the same time, but instead there is a moment when both feet are off the ground together and the runner is 'sailing through the air'. This has the effect of increasing the length of each stride considerably and, even if the rate of striding does not rise above that of a brisk walk, the ground covered is greater. When the foot touches the ground it is not in front of the body, as in walking, but immediately underneath it. This helps to propel the runner forward more vigorously. The way the foot hits the ground is also different. Instead of striking it heel first and then rocking forward on to the toes, it tends to smack itself down almost flat-footed. This, at least, is the case with medium-speed running.

For the man-in-the-street, running, even at moderate speeds, is a short-lived affair, soon leaving him overheated and breathless. For the trained athlete it is a different matter, and a non-stop run has been recorded in which a distance of over 120 miles was covered at a rate of more than five miles an hour.

9. The Jog. Jogging is a deliberately slowed down version of the Run, carrying the jogger along at little more than a brisk walking pace, but providing him with a more complete form of body exercise and avoiding the sharper tensions of the very rapid walk on the one hand and the heart-pounding exhaustion of the full run on the other.

10. The Sprint. In this, the high-speed version of running, the feet strike the ground not flat, but at the toe-end, with the heels hardly making contact at all. The stride rate is dramatically increased so that for a trained athlete there are as many as four to five strides per second. At the short distance of 100 yards, the world champions can maintain a sprinting speed of over 22 miles an hour. For the non-athlete this form of locomotion seldom extends for more than a brief dash, such as when sprinting to catch a bus or a train.

11. The Tiptoe. Advancing on Tiptoe is a hybrid between very slow walking and sprinting. The speed and foot-sequence are taken from the slow walk, with one foot touching the ground before the other one leaves it, but the foot posture is taken from the sprint, with the ball of the foot and the toes being the only parts to make contact. Because of the smaller area of ground-contact, this mode of progression is less noisy than ordinary walking, and is used for a stealthy approach towards an unsuspecting victim, or when trying not to waken a sleeper.

12. The March. In this, the military version of the Walk, the pace is lengthened and the gait is balanced by stronger swinging of the arms, producing a surprisingly efficient mode of travel for long-distance journeys. Cross-country hikers sometimes unconsciously adopt a semi-marching gait, finding it valuable as an aid to maintaining a good speed for long trips.

13. The Goose-step. Some armies, more for show than for efficiency, have trained their troops to adopt a strange, stiff-legged, forward-kicking action when marching. Christened the Goose-step at the end of the 18th century, it was last seen in a prominent role in the march of the Nazis in the Second World War.

14. The Jump. The act of leaping across or over some kind of natural

obstacle was obviously of importance to our early ancestors, either when escaping from predators or when pursuing fleet-footed prey. The Jump is achieved either by springing from a standing start, or by combining this spring with a sprinting run-up. Used by many a schoolboy for crossing a stream, on a country ramble, this form of locomotion reaches its extreme expression in the high jump and long jump of the athletics field, where a height of over $7\frac{1}{2}$ feet (2.3 metres) and a length of nearly 30 feet (8.9 metres) have been achieved.

15. The Hop. Repeated hopping as a mode of progression, kangaroo-style, is almost non-existent in human behaviour, but one-legged hopping is sometimes efficiently employed by an individual with a damaged leg, and it is also seen in certain children's games, such as hop-scotch.

16. The Skip. A skipping progression is achieved by hopping alternately, first on one foot and then the other. This, too, is a rarity, as a form of locomotion, confined largely to children's games and simple dances.

17. The Climb. When faced with moving upwards or downwards, instead of along the surface of the earth, the human animal is capable of reasonably agile climbing actions, employing the hands to grasp and pull, or support, and the legs to push upwards or reach down for a foothold. But the large size and heavy weight of the human body means that, compared with the smaller primates, man is less than athletic in the tree-tops. Mountaineers valiantly combat this disadvantage and clearly show the extent to which our ancient climbing ancestry has not been totally eclipsed. And particularly striking is the way in which tree-climbing repeatedly re-surfaces in the play of school-children.

18. The Swing. Our ancient ancestors, before they left the trees and came down to live on the ground, were almost certainly efficient brachiators—that is, overarm swingers, propelling themselves along the underside of branches with their arms held above their heads, grasping alternately left hand and right, swinging from side to side as they moved along. Children climbing on apparatus in playgrounds can still be seen to use this method of locomotion in their play periods.

19. Acrobatics. Trained acrobats manage to develop specialized locomotion skills, progressing by cartwheeling, forward rolling, backward rolling, and walking on the hands, but these are forms of locomotion rarely if ever seen outside professional performances. They contribute nothing to the domestic scene, but nevertheless remind us of the enormous variety of locomotion techniques of which the human frame is capable.

20. Swimming. The human animal is capable of developing impressive locomotory skills in the water, and these are discussed at length in the chapter that follows.

Viewing these twenty forms of human locomotion, it is clear that man is a complex mover, but with walking as his dominant locomotory feature. He might justly be described as a 'Striding Ape'. Nearly all his major activities involve walking at some stage and, despite his incredible technological advances in the field of transportation, there is still no sign of a lack of demand for shoe-leather. Even if, in the centuries to come, a miniaturized anti-gravity device is developed, enabling a human being to float effortlessly in any direction he cares to choose, for as far as he likes, it still seems probable that walking will survive, if only as a limited activity. For the act of walking, apart from its role in body health, is vitally important in providing a form of progression that operates as an integral part of an environment-checking and assessing system. By walking through a setting we are exposed to it in an ideal manner for imprinting its details on our minds. We take it in at a natural pace. We feel it and we respond to it. To walk through a landscape is to explore it. To drive through it in some form of vehicle is merely to traverse it. This, perhaps more than any other reason, is why Twentieth-century man has retained his body-mobility and avoided restricting himself to totally passive modes of transportation.

Top: the Hop. Left: the Jump. Above: the Swing.

The human animal is undeniably attracted to water. He drinks it, cools off in it, plays in it, leaps into it and swims in it. But does all this water activity reflect something more than man's general interest in the world around him? The Hardy Theory of Aquatic Man considers the possibility that mankind was once much more aquatic than he is today.

AQUATIC BEHAVIOUR
Was man more aquatic in his ancient past?

There is no doubt that water is of extreme importance to the human animal. When he is thirsty, he drinks it in large quantities; when he is dirty, he washes with it; when he is hot, he cools himself in it; when he is feeling playful, he splashes about in it; when he is hungry, he searches for food in it; and when he is attacked by a savage animal, he may occasionally even flee into it. Unlike his close relatives, the Great Apes, he is an excellent swimmer and diver, able to swim many miles without a rest (the record swim in a river being 288 miles, and in the ocean 90 miles) and to reach great depths merely by holding his breath (the record is 282 feet). Skin divers can stay under the water for several minutes (the record being 6½ minutes), giving them time to search for and collect various food objects.

Man is clearly at home in the water, and it has recently been suggested that he was once even more aquatic than he is today. This idea, the Hardy Theory of Aquatic Man, proposes that back in our primeval past we went through a phase of much closer association with the water, and that this helped to shape many of our rather unusual anatomical features. The orthodox view sees man evolving from a fruit-picking forest-dweller to a hunter on the open plains, but the Hardy Theory envisages an intervening aquatic stage coming between these two phases, and providing an explanation for how we managed to achieve this difficult transition.

We know from recent field studies that forest-dwelling apes occasionally kill small animals and eat meat in the wild. If our forest-living, early ancestors also had a hankering for an occasional meaty supplement to their fruit-and-nut diet, then this could easily have been amplified by a little judicious shoreline searching. The shoreline and river bank are fertile sources of small animal life, as any exploratory schoolboy knows, and the creatures living there are comparatively simple to catch. With this as an encouragement, the Aquatic Theory sees early man becoming more and more engrossed in his dabblings and divings, living in tribal groups close to the water's edge and slowly adapting to this new pattern of living.

This phase is seen as a long one, occurring during the vast, ten-million-year hot-spell of the Pliocene period, which ended about two million years ago. It is envisaged as having lasted so long that the human body began to adapt itself to the watery life and to change considerably, before our ancestors began to drift back to the open plains and a more advanced form of hunting. The improvements in prey-catching developed in the water are seen as having given us great advantages in this final transition, and to have equipped us with bodies better suited to tackling larger, land-living species. At this point, with the co-operative bands of human hunters tracking down and killing large mammals on the plains, we are back again with the more orthodox story of human evolution.

Opponents of the Hardy Theory say that there is no direct evidence for this aquatic interlude—this conjectural baptism of the human species—and they see no need for it. The change from forest-dwelling to plains-living and hunting is not, according to them, one that requires any special intermediate condition. They picture the transition passing through a phase of scavenging, egg-stealing and killing of small prey, followed by the attacking of larger and larger prey until the stage of full-blown co-operative, big-game hunting is finally reached. Against this, the Hardy Theory points out that shorelines and river banks have changed drastically and that it would be extremely difficult today to find any direct evidence. Its absence is not therefore to be taken too seriously. Furthermore, it is pointed out that the indirect evidence is highly persuasive.

The matter is still an open one. Man is undeniably a water-loving animal, but he also spends a great deal of time flying in the air and burrowing beneath

the ground. This does not necessarily mean that he went through flying or burrowing stages in his evolution—merely that he is ingenious and exploratory to the extreme. Could his modern obsession with water simply reflect yet another of his explorations of his environment, or is there more to it than that? Since there is no certain answer at present, here are the major points made by the Aquatic Theory, from which each reader can draw his own conclusion. Where criticisms have been levelled against any particular point, they are appended, to give both sides of the story:

1. Few terrestrial mammals can rival man in swimming below the surface. Many can 'dog-paddle' along, but few who are not at least semi-aquatic can move efficiently beneath the water surface. Yet man can twist and turn elegantly, when searching for sponges or pearls.

2. Human babies can swim when only a few weeks old. Even when dropped into a swimming pool, young babies do not panic. If placed in the water in a prone position they do not struggle, but make reflex swimming movements which actually propel them forward. They show breathing control, inhibiting their respiration when submerged. Young apes tested in this way failed to show these reactions and had to be removed quickly from the water.

This remarkable human ability soon fades. By the time they are four months old, babies have lost the automatic swimming response. They rotate into a supine position, struggle, and clutch at adult hands for support. Within a few years, however, infants are once again at ease in the water and by the age of four years can, after rapid learning, swim with great efficiency and over considerable distances, including underwater swimming. Only children whose experience of swimming is limited to brief annual holidays at the seaside are frightened of the water. Any child living near the sea can become a proficient swimmer and diver by the age of five years, and should then be capable of picking up small objects from several feet below the water. Although parental teaching is usually involved at this stage, the infantile swimming capabilities of our species are far beyond what might be expected purely on a basis of human intelligence and curiosity.

3. Man, alone among primates, has functionally naked skin. Hair loss is characteristic of many aquatic mammals, such as dolphins, whales, dugongs and manatees, and semi-aquatic species such as the hippopotamus. An objection here is that other aquatic mammals, such as beavers, seals, sealions and otters, have not lost their fur; but it is pointed out that these are basically cold-country animals which need their fur to keep them warm when they come out on to land. Early man lived in a hot climate, where streamlining in the water would have been more important than keeping

Human babies can swim when only a few weeks old. They do not panic when dropped into the water, but this soon changes. By the time they are four months old, this remarkable ability has been lost.

The human infant makes contact with the water for the first time. Is this a purely exploratory interest, or is there the awakening of some primeval response from man's ancient past?

warm out of it. The retention of hair on top of the head is interpreted as a protection from the sun's rays.

4. The hair-tracts on man—the directions in which the hairs lie on the skin—differ from the arrangement found in the apes. In man they follow the directions which water would flow past the body during forward swimming. This means that before the human body-fur was lost it had already undergone a change which would have helped smooth progress through the water. This is envisaged as an intermediate stage in body streamlining.

5. The shape of the human body itself shows improved streamlining, when compared with that of other primates. Compared with a chimpanzee, the naked body of a man has the smooth curves of a well-designed boat.

6. Only man, among all the primates, has a layer of blubber beneath the skin. This subcutaneous fat is typical of aquatic mammals but not of land mammals. Its function is to keep the body warm in the water. For a water-living species it takes over the role of the usual coat of fur, having the advantage that it can reduce heat-loss without impeding locomotion.

An alternative explanation is that when man became a hunter he suffered from overheating. He needed a cooling system that would prevent this without making him suffer from cold when at rest, especially at night time. By losing his fur and gaining a fat-layer and copious sweat glands, he could keep cool on the chase and warm when still. This system could have developed without the aquatic factor. On the other hand, it could have developed *because* of the aquatic factor. In other words, the streamlining process could have given him the right kind of temperature control system for later use as a terrestrial hunter.

7. Man has an erect posture. The Aquatic Theory sees this developing naturally as a by-product of moving into steadily deeper water in search of food. The support of the water would have been a great aid in making the difficult transition from quadruped to biped. In other words, man waded before he could run.

8. Man has highly sensitive hands, ideally suited to exploring rock-pools and seabeds for food objects. His broad nails grow faster than those of apes and are ideal for rough scratching at rocks and pebbles and for prising open shellfish. The Aquatic Theory sees this feeding behaviour as leading to tool-use. One of the few tool-using mammals is the sea-otter, which employs a stone when breaking open sea-urchins, and this is imagined to be the way in which man first began his long path of tool-using and eventually tool-making.

These are the original eight points of the Hardy Theory of Aquatic Man, and they stand up to close examination remarkably well. Other authors have added to them, sometimes fancifully, and additional points can be listed as follows:

9. Man is a speaking animal, and speech is basically 'exaggerated breathing'. Diving meant breath control, and this in turn meant more effortless production of intermittently released groups of sounds. Furthermore, hunting for food in the water required more co-operation and a signalling system that relied less on gestures. The hands were too busy swimming to be pointing directions. Bobbing to the surface with exciting news about what was down below, it would be natural to want to use vocal clues. In this way, an aquatic existence would favour the development of a more elaborate system of vocal signals, leading eventually to speech.

10. Man has slightly webbed hands. They are proportionally much wider than ape hands and there is a characteristic web of skin between the thumb and forefinger—enough to add a small increase to the pushing surface of a swimmer's spread hand, but not so much that it would start to interfere with manipulation activities. Human feet also show some residual webbing. Of a thousand schoolchildren examined, 9 per cent of the boys and 6.6 per cent of the girls were found to have webbing between the second and third toes and in some cases the webbing extended between all the toes. Perhaps, with these

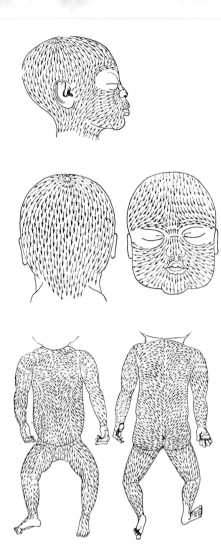

The human hair-tracts, shown here in a diagrammatic representation of a foetus, lie in a pattern which differs from that of other primates such as the apes. In man there is claimed to be evidence of streamlining. (From Hardy; originally from Wood-Jones.)

skin-folds we are seeing remnants of human features that were once more marked than they are today.

11. Man exhibits the 'diving reflex' known to exist as an aid to breath-control underwater in other aquatic species. When a seal dives, for instance, some of its body-processes slow down, reducing the oxygen demands temporarily. In particular, the heartbeat speed is reduced, a mechanism known as brachycardia, and this enables the seal to lower its oxygen consumption sufficiently to permit longer periods below the surface. The existence of this mechanism in man is hard to explain unless he, too, has been at least semi-aquatic in the past.

12. Man has a protruding nose-shield. Unlike most other primates, the human nose sticks out on the face and turns the nostrils through ninety degrees. Instead of facing forward, our nasal apertures face down. When swimming this would clearly reduce the unwanted intake of water through the nostrils; but against this idea must be set the fact that other aquatic mammals solve the problem much more efficiently by having nostrils that open and shut. If aquatic man was improving this feature as an adaptation to water-living, it can only be said that he did it rather badly.

13. Man is the only weeping primate. The production of copious salty tears is widespread among marine animals, as a mechanism for disposing of excess salt, but it is extremely rare among land animals. The Aquatic Theory sees this as yet another factor supporting the idea that mankind has experienced a more marine past. Against this must be set the fact that we do not use tears in this way. We only weep copiously when emotionally disturbed, not when we have been sea-swimming and have swallowed the occasional, accidental slurp of salty water.

14. Before they have mated, human females possess a hymen, a fold of skin that is regarded by the Aquatic Theory as a protection for the vaginal passage against the intrusion of abrasive sand. As with the human nose argument, the answer to this is that it is not a very efficient solution. Not only does the hymen become useless for a mated female, but even before that it may do more harm than good. Since it does not close the genital aperture completely, it may actually help to retain any abrasive sand that has found its way into the genital passage.

15. The human species has protruding, fleshy buttocks. These, the Aquatic Theory sees as helping to tuck the genital region away from harm, on the sandy, rocky seashore, in addition to providing a comfortable cushion. But if this is true of the seashore, then it would also be equally true of other sitting surfaces right away from the beaches, and it cannot really be used as an argument in favour of a water-dwelling life-style.

Other ideas that have been put forward to support the Aquatic Theory are too far-fetched to be considered, and only do harm to what is otherwise a brilliant speculation. No doubt more arguments against the original Hardy Theory will be brought forward, as the idea receives further attention, but it is difficult to see at present how all the points assembled to back the suggestion can be explained away. On balance, it does look as if our species went through a temporary water-loving phase, and spent a great deal of its time fishing around beneath the surface. Hopefully, future fossil-hunters will unearth some evidence to resolve this question. We know virtually nothing about human evolution during the major part of the Pliocene heatwave. Even taking into account the very latest discoveries, there is a gap of over five million years, during which we have not one single piece of fossil evidence about the human story. From 5.5 million years ago, back until 11 million years ago, no hominoid bones have so far come to light. Before and after that phase there are plenty; during it, nothing. If aquatic man did exist, that will be the period when he was splashing happily about in his warm, primeval waters. There are many suggestive features, as listed here, to make us suppose that this is precisely what he may have been doing. All we need now is some hard, tangible evidence to clinch the idea.

FEEDING BEHAVIOUR

How and where and what we drink and eat?

In origin, man is a fruit-picking primate who turned hunter. His feeding behaviour today reflects this dual personality. In many ways he is still a harmless sweet-tooth, but in others he is a prey-killing carnivore.

When the human feeding story began, our early ancestors were searching the forest trees for nuts, berries and fruits, like present-day monkeys and apes. They were highly sensitive to the many changing colours, textures, shapes and tastes of their food objects. Once found and picked, the food often required special preparation before it could be eaten, but each member of the tribe acted for himself in all respects. There was no food-sharing, no concerted effort. The group would move about together, shifting from food site to food site, but beyond that, feeding was a personal problem.

The switch from the trees to more open ground and the adoption of a hunting life-style changed all this. The adult males became the prey-killers, setting off from a fixed home base and returning with the kill. The females, the young and the elderly confined themselves to food-gathering nearer the home base, continuing to collect roots, berries and nuts in the old primate way.

This new pattern of feeding brought several major social changes in its wake. The most important was co-operation. The male hunters had to co-operate to bring down large prey. They had to co-operate to get it home. They had to share the kill. Also, the division of labour between males and females meant that they had to share as well—meat for vegetables and vegetables for meat.

The human hunter is often depicted as a savage killer, but this is strictly a prey's-eye view. Within the human community itself, the change to hunting meant a change to mutual aid and friendly co-operation—the very opposite of 'savagery'. It also meant that feeding occasions became social events, rather than personal activities.

How are these ancient origins reflected in our modern eating habits? We still follow the mixed-diet pattern of meat plus vegetables. This remains the typical human menu the world over. The fact that 10,000 years ago farming took over as the dominant method of obtaining food has not altered our dual interest in plant and animal substances.

Man is a fruit-picking primate turned hunter and prey-killer. For more than a million years primeval male hunters set out on the chase, rather as some remote tribesmen still do today (above), while the women continued to gather fruits, berries and roots from sites near the home camp.

This mixed, meat-and-veg diet is still enjoyed by the vast majority of modern eaters and ghosts of the old division-of-labour system still survive. Meat is still 'male food', to be carved by the man, and vegetables are still 'female food' to be served by the woman.

What farming did do, however, was to start a major trend towards more and more specialized food production. Instead of everyone being involved in finding food, it now became a task for farmers only. The rest of the population could concentrate more on other matters, until, with today's vast urban communities, the business of obtaining food is reduced to the un-adventurous act of shopping in food-stores.

This situation has robbed the modern feeder of some of his ancient behaviour patterns. Gone are the excitements of the hunt—the thrill of the chase, the cunning of the trap, the plotting of the strategy, the climax of the kill, the risk-taking and uncertainty, and the comradeship of the all-male hunting group. When the modern female goes food-gathering at the green-grocer's, she also stops off at the butcher's. Unlike her ancient counterpart, she brings home the bacon as well as the beans.

As a result of this, the modern male is a huntless hunter, a tracker without a quarry, a chaser with nothing to pursue. He solves the problem by indulging in symbolic hunting. For many males, 'working' takes on the qualities of a hunt, with manoeuvres and stratagems, tactics and traps. He plans business campaigns and he makes 'killings' in the city; he sits on all-male committees that replace the old hunting groups, and he speculates. In taking chances and working towards a climax, he manages to re-live, in the symbolism of the business world, the ancient excitements of the hunt.

If his working situation lacks these qualities, he can resort to other means. He can join all-male clubs, he can gamble, or he can indulge in some kind of sport. These activities replace at least some of the missing hunting pattern. The clubs provide the male comradeship, the gambling involves risk-taking and a climax, and the sporting events manage to recreate almost the complete behaviour sequence of the whole hunting pattern.

When he does finally sit down to a meal, the modern male pseudo-hunter may not have caught and killed the prey that is being served up for eating, but he has at least filled in the 'hunting hours' before the meal with a suitable substitute for the chase. At the table, his hunting role survives in a few relic patterns. He sits at the head of the table and it is he who carves the meat (the 'male' food) while his mate passes around the vegetables (the 'female' food). At a restaurant, it is the male who controls the waiter, places the orders, and tastes the wine.

The timing of meals also owes something to our ancient hunting past. As primeval fruit-pickers in the tree-tops, we must have been non-stop snack-takers, like other 'vegetarian' primates. For them, feeding is not a case of sitting down to a big meal, it is a matter of nibble-here, nibble-there, and

The butcher's shop has become the modern hunting ground, but now it is the woman who carries home the 'kill', while her male engages in symbolic hunting, called 'work'.

Primitive hunting led to food-sharing, which can still be seen today, at the tribal level (far left), or in the Western style (left). Feasting and food-sharing and the whole business of sitting down together at a special mealtime are part of our 'hunter inheritance'. The solitary diner (right) is a lonely figure, often forced to eat and run, rather than linger.

keep on nibbling. But when we switched to become hunters, these minute-by-minute snacks were replaced by the great feast. Like lions, early hunters gorged and then rested, gorged and then rested, alternating massive feeding sessions with long foodless intervals. When hunting gave way to farming, and food-stores were developed, there was once again a ready supply of morsels for non-stop nibbling to reassert itself, but the prolonged period of hunting had left its mark, and we never again abandoned our carnivorous, 'big meal' approach to feeding.

For modern man, this means an average of three meals a day—breakfast, lunch and supper. There is no need for us to follow this routine, but we seem reluctant to abandon it. We have the technology to replace it with regular, balanced snacks, every hour on the hour, which would put far less strain on our stomachs, but we do not do so. This would rob us of the 'hunter's feast' quality of the meal. In particular, it would rob us of that most essential feature of the hunting world—the act of food-sharing. Meals are social events. We go to a great deal of trouble to avoid eating alone. The solitary diner always has a curiously forlorn, self-conscious quality. And it is said that the very best way of losing weight is to avoid eating in company.

The food-sharing quality of the modern meal is the reason why so much social entertaining is done in the form of lunch-parties and dinner-parties. These are today's food-sharing rituals and represent a major survival from our hunting past. Even casual social encounters—the arrival of an unexpected guest—involve offerings of food: 'Can I get you something, a drink perhaps?' Drinks are, after all, only liquid foods, and the drink-sharing ritual is as basic as the formal food-party.

In one way we do still revert to our very ancient fruit-picking past. In between our main meals we often indulge in minor nibblings. We take coffee-breaks or tea-breaks. We munch biscuits, crunch apples, chew candy and suck sweets. We have whole shops devoted to the sale of these objects, and as food morsels they all have one thing in common: their sweetness. The essential quality of wild fruits and berries that makes them attractive is their process of ripening and becoming sweeter and sweeter. This is what appeals to the primate fruit-picker, and this is what we still look for in those modern-day replicas of our old tree-top food-objects.

Only when we sit down to a big, hunter's meal do we switch our food goals from sweet to meat. At lunch and supper, the sequence of the meal is revealing: we start with meat and end with sweet. We make the 'main dish' the hunter's triumph, the food-sharing social food, but then we like to finish off the meal with sweeter tastes that can linger on and satisfy our persistently

surviving 'sweet tooth'. Smaller meals tend to be generally sweeter, with the main meat course omitted. This is true of most breakfasts and afternoon teas. Where a bigger breakfast is taken—the British breakfast, for example—the meal starts sweet (porridge or cereals), then moves to meat (kippers or eggs and bacon), and ends sweet (toast and marmalade or jam). This follows the same pattern as lunch and supper, except for the addition of a sweet course at the beginning of the meal. It seems as if, emerging from sleep into another active day, the modern feeder cannot immediately throw himself into the role of a hunting-eater. He has to start off with a little simple 'sweet-toothing'. And for most, the breakfast will go no further. For those that do follow up the initial mouthfuls with a full-blown meal, there then follows the standard sequence of meat/sweet, to complete the repast.

The predominance of sweetness in the breakfast diet relates to the fact that this is the least social of meals—the least talkative and the least concerned with food-sharing. Breakfast parties have always been much rarer than lunch or dinner parties, and are likely to remain so. Breakfasts are also likely to retain another special quality: monotony. We nearly always eat the same thing for breakfast, but usually try to vary the midday and evening menu as much as possible. This is because we are at our most insecure in the morning, with all the unknowns of the day ahead of us. When we wake, we need the reassurance of something familiar to see us through the first moments, and this familiarity is provided by the unvarying breakfast menu.

The greatest food-sharing event of the year for early agricultural communities was the moment when the long winter phase passed its mid-point. This was the moment to break out the food-stores for a special celebration. After months of harvesting and hoarding, it was at last possible to risk a major exchange of food-gifts and a feast to herald in the new year. During these yuletide festivities early farmers gave one another presents of food, and our modern custom of giving Christmas presents is a descendant of this ancient practice, just as our modern Christmas dinner is a descendant of the ancient pagan feasting.

When food is brought to the table, it is met with a concentrated 'food-stare', especially at the moment when it is being placed on the diner's plate. It is almost as if we are watching the ancient hunter sighting his prey.

Other primitive survivals from our ancient eating past include a strong preference for foods with the colours of ripe nuts, fruits and roots—whites, reds, browns and yellows. If we are offered the same foodstuffs dyed blue, we find them instantly repulsive. Even today, we eat remarkably few blue foods despite advanced technology.

Another survival from the past is our curious reluctance to eat blue foods or drink blue drinks. Turn the pages of any illustrated cook-book, and there are hundreds of reds, yellows, greens, browns and oranges—but not a blue in sight. Even the rare exceptions are hardly true blue. Blue cheese is predominantly yellow and blueberry is almost black. This is not because we lack blue colouring. Cake-shops occasionally offer confections covered in a blue icing. But for some reason we do not exploit this colour where eating and drinking are concerned. And we seldom employ blue colours in the wrappings of foodstuffs. Other products, at the pharmacy or the ironmongers, are often swathed in blue, as are cleaning materials such as detergents and soaps, but food and drink remain stubbornly anti-blue.

The blue taboo appears to be a throwback to our primitive eating habits. Natural foods were nuts and seeds (brown and yellow), fruits and roots (orange, red and white), leaves and shoots (green); with hunting added, there was also the white of fish and poultry, and the red and brown of the various meats. But no blue. And so it remains today, with the ancient bluelessness of food surviving into an epoch that can play with food colours in almost any way it likes.

Another ancient survival is the strange business of 'backs to the wall' when feeding in public. Observe diners arriving at any restaurant and you will see them make a bee-line for the wall-seats. No one ever voluntarily selects a centre table in an open space. Open seating positions are only taken when all the wall-seats are already occupied. This dates back to a primeval feeding practice of avoiding sudden attack during the deep concentration involved in consuming food. It is a moment when it is easy to be taken off-guard, and the eater always tries to make it possible for himself to see the whole space around him. To get the best, most protected view, he must have his back against a wall, and this is why many restaurants put up small screens around their centre tables. By providing partitions to every table, they give a sense of security to their customers as they munch their food. A well partitioned restaurant provides an almost 100 per cent 'backs-to-the-wall' facility, making it the most attractive proposition for modern diners haunted by ancient fears, even though, in the process, it makes the serving of food by waiters extremely awkward and cumbersome.

The concentrated food-stare is never so acute as at the moment of the 'plate arrival'. As the diner's food approaches, his eyes are glued to the heaped dish being placed in front of him. No better moment could be chosen to assassinate an enemy, so rivetted is his attention at this second. Even if he is deep in conversation at the moment of plate arrival, his eyes still fixate the steaming dish, as if his very life depended upon seeing it now, at this first possible instant. To watch a modern diner sighting his dish is rather like seeing a cat sight a mouse, and it is tempting to see in this reaction the ghost of an ancient hunter spotting his prey.

Because there is a certain tension involved in eating in public, restaurants employ two major trends to exploit the mood of their diners. The expensive restaurant, to justify high prices, has to overcome the tensions. It does this by shielding, screening and partitioning and also by keeping lights dim, often with orange-red glows, sounds muffled, with thick carpets and soft drapes, colours soft, with neutral or pastel tones, and movements slow, by having more staff than usual so as to reduce waiter-speeds, and frequently fires visible, to give a sense of cosiness and warmth. In this way, the top restaurant makes its clients relax and feel at peace with the world. Lingering over their meals, they are prepared to pay the large sums eventually demanded. The cheap restaurant uses the opposite device of making the eating space as harsh and unappealing as possible, in order to rush its customers through their eating. In this way its low prices can be balanced by a rapid turnover. To make its eaters flee the eating-site, it uses intense strip-lighting, harsh, bright colours, clanking metallic trays and hard, uncovered table surfaces. No sooner has the food been hurriedly consumed, than the table is thankfully

The slight tension caused by eating in public, surrounded by strangers, is overcome by the screening of tables, to give a backs-to-the-wall sensation, and the use (as seen here) of dim lighting. Cheap restaurants use harsher lights to hurry customers through their meals and thereby ensure a rapid turnover.

vacated, making way for another customer and another payment for food.

Being a primate fruit-picker turned meat-eater, the human animal has had certain problems with his teeth. Since he has essentially remained an omnivore, it has been important to keep rather general-purpose dentition. Tough carcasses of freshly killed prey have therefore given him something of a headache. He has solved this difficulty in two main ways: cutlery and cookery.

Cutlery began hundreds of thousands of years ago, with simple blades used to skin carcasses and slice flesh. Eventually stone gave way to copper, copper to bronze, bronze to iron, and iron to steel (with silver and gold invading the sequence at high levels). Early metal knives were nearly always pointed and had a double function—cutting the food and then spearing it for delivery to the mouth. Unfortunately this also made them dangerous weapons and, in 1699, Louis XV of France, fearing assassination, banned the making of sharp-pointed table-knives, a prohibition that has remained with us voluntarily ever since. The blunter knives naturally increased the popularity of that other essential piece of cutlery, the fork. Forks had been slowly gaining ground at table, with two-handed tool-using gradually taking over from the more primitive one-handed style. Because the more ancient knife had already become established as a right-handed implement, the fork had to make do with the left hand. In some areas—the United States for example—there was a resistance to this. There the fork was held in the left hand to steady the food object being sliced by the knife, but once the cutting was completed, the knife was put down and the fork laboriously transferred from left hand to right for the final spearing and delivering of food to the mouth. This brave attempt of the fork to invade the knife's righteous position has proved too cumbersome for most cultures. Almost everywhere, the two-handed operation survives—fork-in-left, knife-in-right. A major exception occurs in the Orient, where chopsticks dominate. This is because, in a comparatively table-free eating context, the diner must hold the food-bowl in his hand and must deal with its contents one-handed. Although chopsticks are less efficient than the two-handed knife-and-fork combination, they remain more effective than any other form of one-handed eating, and have survived well. But as high-table eating gradually invades the East, we can expect to see their slow eclipse.

Knives and forks, along with spoons and tongs and various other food-tools, lie on the modern table like metallic super-teeth, extending our bite, our grind and our chew. Together they give us every kind of tooth in the text-book of evolution, without so much as a sliver of bone being added to our real jaws. Aiding and abetting this process is the business of cooking. The use of fire—and, even before that, the simmering of food in the waters of natural hot springs—is an ancient practice that has served to tenderize a wide variety of food objects and reduce the demands made on our unspecialized teeth. Baking, boiling, roasting, grilling, stewing and poaching, we attack our plant and animal foods. We break down the hard cell-walls of vegetables, we soften hard grain, and we weaken meat fibres. In the process, we not only tenderize, but also improve flavour and destroy parasites. And perhaps by serving hot, we rekindle the memories of the natural heat of freshly killed prey and the body-warmth of our first and most comforting foodstuff—milk from the breast.

As an extension of food-hoarding we have developed smoking, pickling, drying, preserving, bottling, canning, refrigeration and, more recently, deep-freezing and freeze-drying. With our cutlery, our cookery and our preservation techniques, we have become super-gnashers, super-chewers and super-hoarders. We each eat about a ton of food a year, so that we get through more than sixty tons in an average lifetime. To observe this process in action is to watch a fascinating combination of ancient habits and modern skills, a complete amalgam of primitive feeding patterns and technological inventions.

SPORTING BEHAVIOUR

The biology of sport—a modern hunting ritual

Sporting activities are essentially modified forms of hunting behaviour. Viewed biologically, the modern footballer is revealed as a member of a disguised hunting pack. His killing weapon has turned into a harmless football and his prey into a goal-mouth. If his aim is accurate and he scores a goal, he enjoys the hunter's triumph of killing his prey.

To understand how this transformation has taken place we must briefly look back again at our ancient ancestors. They spent over a million years evolving as co-operative hunters. Their very survival depended on success in the hunting-field. Under this pressure their whole way of life, even their bodies, became radically changed. They became chasers, runners, jumpers, aimers, throwers and prey-killers. They co-operated as skilful male-group attackers.

Then, about ten thousand years ago, after this immensely long, formative period of hunting their food, they became farmers. Their improved intelligence, so vital to their old hunting life, was put to a new use—that of penning, controlling and domesticating their prey. The hunt became suddenly obsolete. The food was there on the farms, awaiting their needs. The risks and uncertainties of the hunt were no longer essential for survival.

The hunting skills and the hunting urges remained, however, and demanded new outlets. Hunting for sport replaced hunting for necessity. This new activity involved all the original hunting sequences, but the aim of the operation was no longer to avoid starvation. Instead the sportsmen set off to test their skill against prey that were no longer essential to their well-being. To be sure, the kill may have been eaten, but there were other, much simpler ways of obtaining a meaty meal. The chase became exposed as an end in itself. The logical extension of this trend was the big-game hunter who never ate his kill, but merely hung its stuffed head on his wall, and the fox-hunter who has to breed foxes in order to release them to hunt them down. Here there is no longer even any pretence that the chasing and killing are a means to an end. They are openly accepted as their own reward.

For centuries the sporting world was dominated by blood sports of this kind and the bloodless sports, so popular today, were restricted to a very minor, inferior role. An early dictionary definition of sport is: 'a pastime afforded by the endeavour to take or kill wild animals.' But as civilizations grew and flourished, their populations became too large for more than a small

Sporting activities are modified forms of hunting. As a hunter in disguise, the footballer uses a harmless football as his 'killing weapon'.

In this painting by the 15th-century artist Uccello the hunt is clearly no longer a matter of survival but has become a pastime—and it is only since the late 19th century that such bloodsport pastimes have ceased to dominate the whole field of sporting activities.

The essence of most sports—here represented by basketball (left) and baseball (right)—is the act of aiming, very much a matter of life and death in the world of the ancient hunter (above).

minority—the rich and the powerful—to indulge in the full pattern of hunting down prey as a pastime. For ordinary men, the ancient urge to hunt was frustrated. The Roman solution was to bring the hunt into the city and stage it in a huge arena, where thousands could watch the prey-killing at close quarters. This solution has survived even to the present day, in the form of the Spanish bullfight.

An alternative solution was to transform the activities of the hunting pack into other patterns of behaviour. Superficially these new activities did not look like hunting, but beneath the surface all the basic elements were there. The key to the transformation lies in the fact that there was no longer any need to eat the prey. This being so, then why bother to kill an edible animal? Why indeed kill any animal at all? A symbolic killing is all that is needed, providing the thrill of the chase can be retained. The Greek solution was athletics—field-sports involving chasing (track-running), jumping, and throwing (discus and javelin). The athletes experienced the vigorous physical activity so typical of the hunting scene, and the patterns they performed were all elements of the ancient hunting sequence, but their triumph was now transformed from the actual kill to a symbolic one of 'winning'.

In other parts of the world, ancient ball-games were making a small beginning: a form of polo in ancient Persia, bowls and hockey in ancient Egypt, football in ancient China. Here the element of the primeval hunting sequence to be retained and amplified was the all-important hunter's action of aiming. Whatever the rules of the game, the physical act of aiming was the essence of the operation. This more than any other, has come to dominate the world of modern sport. There are more aiming sports today than all other forms of sport put together. One could almost define field-sports now as competitive aiming behaviour.

Among the bloodless sports there are two basic kinds of aiming: aiming at

an undefended object, such as a target, a skittle, or a hole, and aiming at a defended object, such as a goal or a wicket. Thinking of these actions as transformed hunting patterns, it is clear that a defended object is more like the real prey and aiming at it therefore provides a better substitute for the primeval activity. The real prey is not going to make matters easy for the hunter. As an object to be aimed at, it is going to defend itself as best it can, by making sudden movements, by fleeing, by attack, or by any other means at its disposal. So it is hardly surprising that the most popular of all the modern field-sports are those in which the aimers must attack a defended object.

Viewed in this way, a game of football becomes a reciprocal hunt. Each team of players, or 'hunting pack', tries to score a goal by aiming a ball, or 'weapon', at a defended goal-mouth, or 'prey'. Because the defended goal-mouth is more unpredictable than an open goal-mouth would be, the hunt becomes more exciting, the action more rapid and athletic, the skills more dazzling. It is this type of sport that attracts huge audiences, content merely to watch the drama. The other basic type of sport, where the target is undefended, draws smaller crowds, but can still be intensely satisfying to the aimers themselves, because of the skill and precision required.

Popular sports of the first type include not only football but also cricket, badminton, basketball, hockey, hurling, ice-hockey, netball, polo, water-polo, tennis, table-tennis, volleyball and lacrosse. Examples of the second type include bowls, golf, archery, darts, skittles, skeet, tenpin, quoits, curling, croquet and billiards. All of these sports and many other are dominated by the human urge to aim at something. Surprisingly, this aspect of sport is often overlooked when underlying motivations are being discussed. Instead, the competitive element is stressed, and is usually expressed as a total explanation. Certainly competitiveness finds an outlet in sport, there is no doubt of that. But it could equally find an outlet in cake-baking competitions or flower-arranging. This would not make these activities sports, however. Of all the hundreds of forms of competition we indulge in, only sports have the special properties of chasing, running, jumping, throwing, aiming and prey-killing. This is why, ultimately, only the transformed-hunting explanation will do.

For modern man, bloodless sports have become a major form of recreation. Amost every large human settlement throughout the world has its sports centres and stadiums. Millions follow the details of sporting activities in the press and on television. This high level of interest today exceeds anything from previous eras, and the reason is not hard to find. Following the industrial revolution, the vast majority of adult males in the swollen human populations were even more remote from their hunting heritage. Mass-production and industrialization led to increasingly boring, monotonous, predictable and repetitive labour. The essence of the ancient hunting pattern was that it involved a great deal of physical exercise combined with risk and excitement. It involved a long sequence, with a build-up, with strategy and planning, with skill and daring and ultimately with a grand climax and a moment of triumph. This description fits well the activities of a sportsman such as a footballer, but it is a far cry from the life-style of a worker at a factory-bench or a clerk in an office.

The nineteenth-century male, locked in his unvarying routine, experienced a new level of hunter-frustration. The result was, predictably, an explosion of interest in organized sports. Nearly all the most popular sports of today were either invented or at least formalized during the nineteenth century. They include the following:

Tennis (below) and cricket: two further sports demanding aiming ability of a high order—and the physical condition and eye-hand co-operation that this implies.

1820—Squash—England	1858—Australian Football—Australia
1823—Rugby Union—England	1859—Volleyball—USA
1839—Baseball—USA	1860s—Lawn Tennis—England
1846—Association Football—England	1870s—Water Polo—England

1874—American Football—USA
1879—Ice Hockey—Canada
1891—Basketball—USA

1895—Rugby League—England
1895—Tenpin Bowling—USA
1899—Table Tennis—England

Some of these games had been in existence before, but were converted into their modern forms, with fixed rules and regulations; others were invented from scratch. Throughout the century, more and more people played these games and watched them being played. They were thought to be recreational because of the physical exercise involved and the fresh air that was breathed by the participants, but it was the hunter's brain as well as his body that was crying out for help. The popularity of the pseudo-hunt was due, in large part, to the sense of excitement kindled by the nature of the actions involved in the sporting events. They were not merely exercises, they were chasing and aiming exercises—the chasing and aiming of the primeval hunter.

The twentieth century, surprisingly, has not seen the development of new types of sports, but involvement in the existing ones has risen to a new pitch and they have spread, as industrialization has spread, to almost all parts of the globe. There are now more people than ever who find their daily work boring and lacking in variety and unpredictability. For them the dramatic sporting occasion brings an immediate reward.

For the more successful males in modern society there is rather less demand for this type of outlet. This is because the work-style of the successful male is much closer to the primeval hunting pattern. His work involves a hunt for ideas—he chases after solutions, he captures contracts, he talks of the *aims* of his organization. His life-style is full of the excitement of one pseudo-hunting sequence after another. All that is missing in his version of transformed hunting is the actual physical exertion of the hunt. His pursuits and aims and killings have all become abstracted, and the result is that his body often suffers for it.

A corrupted form of sport that requires special mention is warfare. In the early days, when weapons were young, one form of blood sport was as good as another. If hunting for real food-prey was no longer a major preoccupation, then the selection of a substitute-prey was wide open. Any victim that provided the necessary hunting challenge would do, and there was no reason why a human prey should be excluded. Early wars were not total wars, they were strictly limited affairs, conducted with rigid rules just like sporting games. The male warrior-hunters used the same kind of weapons that were originally employed in a real hunt, and in the special case of cannibal-warriors there was even the similarity of eating the prey after it had been killed. And we know that in some wars rain stopped play, just as it does with cricket. Of course group competition was involved, as in other sports, but again this does not seem to have been the whole explanation. There appear to be plenty of cases of 'unprovoked' warfare, where the warriors give the superficial impression of having the uncontrollable urge to 'go looking for a fight'. This has led some authorities to the unfortunate conclusion that man has an inborn urge to kill his fellow-men. If, however, these warring groups are seen not as savage man-killers, but, like sportsmen, as transformed hunters pursuing substitute-prey, then their behaviour becomes immediately more understandable.

Tragically, warfare was a form of sport that rapidly got out of hand and escalated into bloody massacres. There were two reasons for this. On the one hand technology advanced to the point where weapons no longer required bravery and physical field-skills. The hunter-warrior became a slaughter-technician. On the other hand, the human populations grew and grew until they became seriously overcrowded. This led to immense social pressures and hitherto unimaginable competitive demands. The ancient sport of war-hunting exploded into the uncontrolled savagery of modern, total war.

For the future, the lesson to be learned from this is that to reduce the chances of war breaking out it may not be enough simply to solve the

Until the last century sport was an almost exclusively male pursuit; but as it has grown farther away from its bloody hunting origins, it has also become a popular pastime for both women and children.

The battle as a corrupted form of bloodsport, before it escalated into the technological slaughter of total war.

problem of overcrowding and the social stresses it creates. In addition it may be necessary to re-examine the working life-styles of post-industrial men, to see if they can be brought nearer to the hunter condition—the condition to which our ancestors adapted genetically over a period of at least a million years. If work is repetitive and lacks variety, excitement and climax, then the primeval hunter embedded in modern man will remain dangerously unsatisfied. Football on Saturday afternoons may help, but it may not help enough. In planning future work-styles, attempts to involve workers in a pseudo-hunting sequence of some kind would seem to be essential, if we are to avoid the damaging alternatives of riots, violence and total war.

Finally, there is one other aberrant form of sport that deserves a brief comment. This is the sport, not of man-killing, but of 'lady-killing'. Another early dictionary definition of sport is 'amorous dalliance' and the pursuit of females has often been likened to a hunt. The normal courtship sequence of the human species has many of the characteristics of a symbolic chase, culminating in the climax of copulation as a symbolic kill. In real sexual relationships this climax heralds the development of a pair-bond, a deep bond of attachment between the mated pair that will see them through the rigours of a breeding cycle that lasts, in our species, for many years and makes heavy demands on both parents. In the pseudo-sexual relationships of 'girl-hunting' the reaching of the climax of copulation virtually ends the sequence. The male who uses females as substitute prey and who talks of scoring rather than of adoring, quickly loses interest once the prey has been successfully 'speared' with the symbolic weapon. He must now move on and search for a new prey. He may, of course, find himself succumbing during the chase to the influences of normal pair-formation, and what started out as a sport may grow into a true courtship despite his intentions. But, tragically, he may simply create a one-sided pair-bond and leave his female victim stranded with a loving attachment to her pseudo-hunter. Worse, he may accidentally fertilize his prey and leave her with the beginnings of a 'parental sequence' in which he feels no emotional involvement. As a sport, girl-chasing, like war, has dangerous consequences for society.

In seeking substitutes for the primeval hunt there are many pitfalls, and cultures which make poor choices, or play the game badly, do so at their peril. The nature of the sporting behaviour of mankind clearly deserves greater attention than it has received in the past.

RESTING BEHAVIOUR

The postures of relaxation and the nature of sleeping and dreeming

Much of the day is spent locked in to the social scene. As the hours pass, our social roles change. We may be parent to child, husband to wife, customer to salesman, patient to doctor, worker to boss, performer to audience, or prisoner to guard. We may be busy interacting with colleagues, friends, workmates, rivals, relatives, or partners. In all these situations, the excitements of our social involvements bring with them stresses and strains. From time to time we need to withdraw from these endeavours, and our Resting Behaviour takes several forms.

Major 'rests' demand a total removal from the social scene that is stressing us, but minor 'rests' can be taken on the spot. The tired companion lets his mind wander, or go blank, while continuing to nod and smile automatically. Outwardly he appears to remain locked in to the social interaction, but his brain is coasting. He has put it out of gear. After a few moments, he stirs himself and returns to the mental fray, hoping that he has not missed some vital point in the argument.

Alternatively, he can adopt a *relaxed posture*. Again, he can do this without withdrawing. The problem here is that the more relaxed he allows his body to become, the more he risks insulting his companions. If they expect polite attentiveness, they are going to require an alert posture to go with it. Relaxed postures can only be risked if the relaxer is either extremely dominant and does not have to care about the thoughts of others present, or if he is in the company of extremely close friends and relatives in a highly informal situation. Indeed, among close friends, the adoption of a fully relaxed posture can be used as a positive sign of friendship—a signal that the relationship has no need of tense alertness and can survive without respecting the niceties of polite manners.

There is a whole range of relaxed postures. For standing companions, there is the Vertical Lean, in which the body is supported against a wall or some other surface. Then there is the Arms Support, in which either the hands are thrust into the pockets, or the forearms are resting on some easily available surface. Going one step further, there is the Head Support, in which the head is allowed to rest on a hard surface or propped up on a hand or forearm.

Relaxed postures of the human species: the Vertical Lean (above) giving relief to tired leg muscles; and the Head Support (right), which relaxes tired neck muscles.

The Prone and Supine Lie-down. Here the resting postures employed facilitate maximum exposure of skin surface to the cosmetic action of the sun.

The Prone and Supine Lie-down. Here the resting postures employed facilitate maximum exposure of skin surface to the cosmetic action of the sun.

We often speak of 'squatting on the ground' as a resting posture as if it were a single action, but in reality it is not. The following variants exist: the Squat-kneel and the Flat-footed Squat (below) and (right, top to bottom) the Tiptoe Squat, the Squat-sit, the Legs Fold, the Lotus Position and the Legs Side-curl.

Sitting Down is itself a major relaxation posture, and this can be amplified by the Body Slump, in which head, arms, wrists, shoulders and legs are permitted to go limp and lose their usual alert tension. Taking the slump even further, there is the full Limbs Sprawl. Here, the essence of the action is the unbending of the limbs and the resting of them against supportive surfaces. The natural extension of this posture is the Lying-down action, either prone, supine or side.

With this, we have reached a level of relaxation that is too extreme for all but a few social occasions. Friends may chat while sprawled out across the furniture, but to lie down is to move into a new phase of 'interaction withdrawl'. Only in open-air situations, such as picnics, can the full lie-down be adopted socially, while still continuing with the interactional flow; and even there it is usual to see a certain amount of elbow-propping to keep the body up out of the total recline.

The basis of all these relaxation postures is that they relieve the relaxer of

Infants sleep more than adults. During their first three days they are asleep for two-thirds of the time, but this decreases rapidly, and as adults they will spend only one-third of the day in slumber.

the task of maintaining verticality. The vertical posture of man, which is such an important part of his life-style, is much more of a burden for him than the standing postures of his four-footed animal relatives. Because we do it so often, we tend to take the difficult business of Standing Up very much for granted. In reality it requires a constant balancing trick and any action that can briefly excuse us from 'standing duty' is a valuable source of rest. Apart from the common examples already listed, there are a number of specialized postures of relaxation. There is the One-leg Stand, a stork-like position adopted by certain African tribesmen. There is the Knee-kneel of the boxer recovering from a blow that has knocked him to the canvas (not to be confused with the submissive knee-kneel of a subordinate). There is the Double Knee-kneel of the exhausted athlete, who sinks to his knees after passing the finishing line, and there is the even more abandoned All-fours Rest of almost total exhaustion.

In less dramatic situations there is the Squat-kneel, in which the buttocks sink down to become supported by the backs of the kneeling legs. Related to this is the common Squat, in which the knees are off the ground, and the feet take their place as the main supporting organs, while the thighs sink down to touch the backs of the legs. There are two versions of this, the flat-footed squat and the tiptoe squat. The flat-footed squat, common among certain tribesmen, is, like the one-leg stand, difficult for many people to maintain as a true resting posture.

Going further with this type of action, there is the Squat-sit, in which the buttocks reach the ground and become a supportive area, but the legs remain bent. This grows into the full Legs-fold posture often adopted by school-children when sitting in groups on the floor, and the Lotus Position assumed by students of yoga. A less complicated version is the simple Legs Side-curl, often seen in parks and on beaches.

Briefly, these are the main postures of relaxation of our species, leaving out such oddities as yogal head-standing, and other localized developments. They may be adopted fleetingly or may be held for several hours, according to the context. They may occur within the social scene of tension and interaction, or they may be assumed outside it, in recognized 'rest periods' or 'breaks' in the serious action. The only other type of Resting Behaviour which can occur within the social flow is the 'snooze', 'catnap', or 'forty winks'. If grandfather drops off to sleep during an afternoon family gathering, the group may continue to interact almost as if he is still actively involved with them. They talk around him and do not attempt to remove him to bed and therefore outside the social context of the 'gathering'. Dozers at lectures and theatres are treated in a similar way until they snore or give other intrusive signs of their condition that cannot be overlooked.

Beyond the act of dozing lies the full sleeping pattern, our major form of social withdrawal; but it is important to realize that there are many types of Resting Behaviour available to us other than sleep. They operate to some extent on the basis of 'a change is as good as a rest', but the condition changed *to* is important. Included here are the 'breaks' we give ourselves, from brief coffee-breaks and tea-breaks to lunch hours, to nights out, to weekends off, to holidays and annual vacations. In all these cases we are allowed to escape

The postures of sleep. We each vary our sleeping position many times during the night. In a typical night there are between 40 and 70 body shifts, helping to prevent cramping of the limbs.

Some adults require a longer sleep period than others, but most fall in the seven to eight hour range. The elderly tend to sleep for slightly shorter periods at night—about six hours—but supplement this with daytime naps.

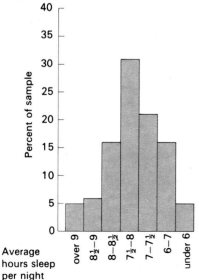

Average hours sleep per night

from our usual social roles and momentarily to adopt an entirely new persona—the drinker, the diner, or the tourist. In each case we gain a rest, even though our new activity may be comparatively energetic. But the essence of these resting roles is that *we* are in charge. We do what we want to do, not what some one else tells us to do. In all instances we are spenders, rather than sellers. The serious working hours of our social lives are concerned primarily with selling, either ourselves, or our services, or our products. To rest from this means switching to the buyer role, but not in relation to so-called 'necessities'. The buying must always have a slight air of luxury and frivolity about it—whether it be a drink in a bar, or a visit to a holiday hotel.

Valuable as these breaks are, they still do not give us total 'role release'. Many a holiday collapses under the weight of arrangements and responsibilities—the planning and the organizing causing unexpected levels of irritability, simply because it is precisely planning and organizing from which the holiday is meant to be providing an escape.

The only total escape is provided by long periods of nightly sleep. Attempts to survive without this nocturnal release have quickly led to severe mental as well as physical collapse. This is because sleep is even more important as a brain-rester than it is as a body-rester. We can relax our tired muscles by massage and the act of lying-down for lengthy periods, but this does little to re-charge our mental batteries. By the end of every day, we have built up such a confusion of new ideas and thoughts and experiences that we need hours of sleep to permit this new input to be filed away in our memory banks. And it is more than mere filing—it is also a matter of sorting through the various contradictions that have arisen, attempting to resolve the conflicts that have beset us, and generally tidy up the 'office of the mind'. This is what dreaming is all about. Persistent, worrying 'filing' causes persistent, repetitive dreams. Intense new experiences lead to vivid bouts of dream-time. What we remember afterwards as our dream story is merely the tip of the nocturnal iceberg. Modern studies of sleepers have revealed that we are actively dreaming in repeated bouts every night, regardless of whether we have dream memories when we awaken or whether we feel we have spent a dreamless night of totally blank sleep.

Babies sleep more than adults, and the middle-aged sleep more than the

elderly. There is a good reason for this. Infants are faced with a whole new world to comprehend. The input into their brains is enormous, and they need correspondingly long periods of dream-time to file away all their new information. The elderly, by contrast, are usually rather set in their ways, with not a great deal of new information arriving, and they can get by with fewer bedtime hours. During the first three days of life, the average baby sleeps for 16.6 hours out of 24, varying from 23 to as little as 10.5 in extreme cases. The average adult sleeps for 7 hours and 20 minutes. The elderly make do with only 6 hours plus a few daytime catnaps.

The newborn baby sleeps in short bursts all through the night and day, but by the time it is six months old it has reduced its daytime sleeping to short naps and increased its night-time sleeping to one prolonged bout. Its total sleep time is now about 14 hours, and this goes on shrinking. The daytime naps become reduced to two, one in the morning and one in the afternoon. Then during the second year the morning nap vanishes and the average total is 13 hours. By the age of five, the child abandons daytime naps altogether and the night-time total stands at about 12 hours. This figure is reduced gradually until, at 13, the usual night's sleep for the teenager is nine hours, dwindling eventually to the fully adult pattern of 7½ hours.

During a typical adult night there are from 40 to 70 shifts of body posture. Serial photographs taken of sleepers tend to make them look agitated and restless because of these shifts, but even the deepest sleeper undergoes these natural changes of position, which prevent cramping of limbs and other parts of the body.

Also, during a typical night, there are four or five 'dream-times'. The first occurs about 90 minutes after falling asleep, and the others follow at intervals of about 60 to 90 minutes. Altogether they add up to about 1½ hours of our total sleep time. During these special bouts of dream-sleeping some contradictory things happen. In some ways we act as if alert—we perform rapid jerky movements of our eyes behind our closed lids, as if we are watching something intently; our brain-waves are more like waking waves; our heart-rate and blood-pressure become irregular, as if trying to cope with some emotional experience; and our oxygen consumption is increased, again as if we are preparing for action. Completely opposed to all these changes is the fact that our muscular tone becomes lower than during ordinary sleep, and we are more difficult to rouse. This peculiar condition has, for this reason, been called Paradoxical Sleep. The body is deeply withdrawn from consciousness, but at the same time seems geared for action. The action it is geared for, of course, is the vital business of dreaming, and if sleepers *are* roused from this special sleep condition they will be able to remember their dreams vividly. If they are roused only a few minutes after a special dream-sleeping phase has ended, then they remember only vague elements of the dream story. If woken ten or more minutes after, they usually remember nothing and report that they have not been dreaming at all. This explains why some people deny dreaming, despite the fact that we all do it four or five times nightly. They are the ones who awaken from the ordinary, non-dreaming phases of sleep. If we are left to wake up naturally, this is what usually happens. But if we are woken, while still tired, by an early-morning call or an alarm clock, we are more likely to have our dreaming interrupted, and therefore to be able to remember the dream story.

Dreaming does not, as was once thought, occur in a flash. If experimental sleepers are awoken at the beginning of a period of dreaming-sleep, then they report having had only short dreams. If they are woken later in the dream-sleep phase, they recall longer dreams. So it is safe to assume that the total of 1½ hours of Paradoxical Sleep we have each night really does represent 1½ hours of actual dreaming. This means that by the time he reaches old age the average man will have dreamed for a total of about 35,000 hours. Only in this way can he keep the computer inside his skull in good working order, ready to cope with the complexities of the day.

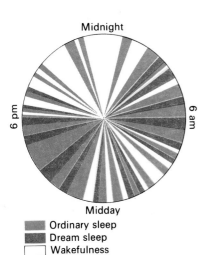

Adults normally sleep only once during a 24 hour period, but babies sleep in short bursts. This one had 18 periods of sleep totalling 17 hours out to the 24

REFERENCE

Although quoting specific references is normal practice for academic publications, it is irritating in a book for the general reader, breaks the flow of words and adds confusion to the page; but credit must be given where credit is due. The following selected lists also present suggestions for extended reading.

General Works

Argyle, M. 1969. *Social Interaction*. Methuen, London.

—— 1975. *Bodily Communication*. Methuen, London. (Michael Argyle's research studies into interpersonal behaviour, although laboratory based, have dealt with aspects of behaviour closely related to the subject of Manwatching.)

Barakat, R. A. 1975. *The Cistercian Sign Language. A study in non-verbal communication*. Cistercian Publications, Kalamazoo, Michigan. (Robert Barakat's field studies have provided valuable compilations of gesture repertoires in several widely differing social contexts.)

Birdwhistell, R. L. 1970. *Kinesics and Context. Essays on body motion communication*. University of Pennsylvania Press, Philadelphia. (Ray Birdwhistell's extensive studies of human body movements have led to comparatively little published work, but he remains a major influence in the field.)

Brun, T. 1969. *The International Dictionary of Sign Language*. Wolfe, London. (A modest, non-academic work which nevertheless contains many useful examples of regional gestures.)

Critchley, M. 1975. *Silent Language*. Butterworths, London. (A useful general survey of the subject of human gestures by a distinguished neurologist.)

Davis, F. 1971. *Inside Intuition. What we know about non-verbal communication*. McGraw-Hill, New York. (A popular report on modern American research in non-verbal communication.)

Efron, D. 1972. *Gesture, Race and Culture*. Mouton, The Hague. (David Efron's pioneer study, first published in 1941, has been a model for many later investigations.)

Eibl-Eibesfeldt, I. 1972. *Love and Hate. The Natural History of Behavior Patterns*. Holt, Rinehart and Winston, New York. (An important popular work by the leading German authority on human ethology.)

Ekman, P., Friesen, W. V. and Ellsworth, P. 1972. *Emotion in the Human Face*. Pergamon Press, New York.

Ekman, P. (Editor). 1973. *Darwin and Facial Expression*. Academic Press, New York. (Paul Ekman's research team in San Francisco have published many papers, concentrating largely on the detailed analysis of facial signals.)

Fast, J. 1970. *Body Language*. Evans, New York. (A popular account of non-verbal research studies, which brought the term 'body language' into common usage.)

Goffman, E. 1963. *Behavior in Public Places*. Free Press, New York.

—— 1967. *Interaction Ritual*. The Penguin Press, London.

—— 1969. *The Presentation of Self in Everyday Life*. The Penguin Press, London.

—— 1971. *Relations in Public*. The Penguin Press, London. (It is difficult to single out any one of Erving Goffman's books, but the four listed here are perhaps the most important. Together they present an inspired analysis of the micro-dramas of day-to-day living.)

Guthrie, R. D. 1976. *Body Hot Spots. The anatomy of human social organs and behavior*. Van Nostrand Reinhold, New York. (A lively and original study of the 'social anatomy' of the human body.)

Key, M. R. 1975. *Paralanguage and Kinesics. Nonverbal communication*. Scarecrow Press, Metuchen, N.J. (A useful report based on a lecture course, including a 65-page bibliography.)

Morris, D. 1967. *The Naked Ape*. Cape, London.

—— 1969. *The Human Zoo*. Cape, London.

—— 1971. *Intimate Behaviour*. Cape, London. (Three general works on human ethology, presenting a zoologist's view of the human animal.)

Morris, D., Collett, P., Marsh, P. and O'Shaughnessy, M. 1978. *Gesture Maps*. Cape, London. (An extensive international field-study of regional variations in human gestures.)

Ruesch, J. and Kees, W. 1969. *Nonverbal Communication*. University of California Press, Berkeley and Los Angeles. (A general survey of human visual signalling systems.)

Saitz, R. L. and Cervenka, E. C. 1972. *Handbook of Gestures: Colombia and The United States*. (A valuable catalogue of gestures, comparing the repertoires in North and South America.)

Scheflen, A. E. 1972. *Body Language and the Social Order*. Prentice-Hall, Englewood Cliffs, N.J.

—— 1973. *How Behavior Means*. Gordon and Breach, New York. (Reports summarizing the findings of Albert Scheflen's painstaking field observations in New York.)

Tiger, L. and Fox, R. 1972. *The Imperial Animal*. Seckerand Warburg, London. (An anthropological study of the biological basis of human society.)

Wildeblood, J. 1973. *The Polite World. A guide to English manners and deportment*. Davis-Poynter, London. (An historical survey of the formalities of social life, from medieval times to the twentieth century.)

Wolff, C. 1945. *A Psychology of Gesture*. Methuen, London. (One of the earliest of modern studies on the subject of gesture.)

Early Works

Listed here are some earlier studies of particular historical interest to the subject of human gesture and action.

Bulwer, J. 1644. *Chirologia; or the Naturall Language of the Hand. Whereunto is added Chironomia: or, the Art of Manual Rhetoricke. London*.

—— 1648. *Philocophus; or the Deafe and Dumbe Man's Friend. London*.

—— 1649. *Pathomyotomia, or a Dissection of the Significative Muscles of the Affections of the Minde. London*.

—— 1650. *Anthropometamorphosis; Man Transform'd; or the Artifical Changeling*. London. (Re-issued in 1654 as: *A View of the People of the Whole World*.) (John Bulwer was the first person to make a systematic study of human gestures. He is an isolated, pioneer figure whose work was strangely advanced for his time.)

Austin, G. 1806. *Chironomia; or, a treatise on rhetorical delivery*. London. (Gilbert Austin's long and detailed account of human gestures was primarily concerned with improving the impact of public speakers.)

Bell, C. 1806. *Essays on the Anatomy of Expression*. Longman, Hurst, Rees and Orme, London. (The first serious study of the relationship between the musculature of the face and facial expressions.)

Siddons, H. 1807. *Practical Illustrations of Rhetorical Gesture and Action*. London. (Henry Siddons, the actor son of Sarah Siddons, adapted the German treatise by M. Engel on Gesture and Theatrical Action.)

De Jorio, A. 1832. *La Mimica Degli Antichi Investigata Nel Gestire Napoletano*. Napoli. (The first attempt to publish a detailed gesture repertoire of one particular locality.)

Darwin, C. 1872. *The Expression of the Emotions in Man and Animals*. John Murray, London. (Darwin's study was the forerunner of modern ethology and was the first work to relate human expressions to their evolutionary background.)

Wundt, W. 1900. *Volkerpsychologie. Volume One: Die Sprache*. Stuttgart. (Chapter 2 of this first volume of Wilhelm Wundt's great 10-volume work on comparative psychology was called: 'The Language of Gesture' and presents the most important theoretical discussion of human gestures prior to the modern period. It has been reprinted in English as a separate book by Mouton, The Hague, 1973.)

Special References

Many books and papers were consulted during the preparation of *Manwatching*. Only the most important are listed below on a section-by-section basis. Where General Works or Early Works have a special relevance, they are mentioned again without full reference.

Actions. (1) Eibl-Eibesfeldt, I. 1970. *Ethology, The Biology of Behavior*. Holt, Rinehart and Winston, New York. (chapter 18); (2) Eibl-Eibesfeldt, 1972; (3) Morris 1967; (4) Morris 1969; (5) Neville, H. 1900. 'Gesture' in *Voice, Speech and Gesture*. Deacon, London; (6) Nierenberg, G. I. and Calero, H. 1971. *How to Read a Person Like a Book*. Hawthorn, New York; (7) Strobridge, T. R. and Nalty, B. C. 1963. 'Hand Salute'. *Leatherneck* XLVI (No. 7) p. 76–77; (8) Wildeblood, 1973.

Gestures. (1) Aubert, C. 1927. *The Art of Pantomime*. Paris; (2) Barakat, 1975; (3) Brun, 1969; (4) Cody, I. E. 1972. *Indian Talk*. NEL, London; (5) Ekman, P. 1967. 'Origins, usage and coding of nonverbal behavior.' Centro de Investigaciones Sociales, Buenos Aires, Argentina; (6) Ekman, P. 1969. 'The repertoire of nonverbal behavior. *Semiotica* 1 (1), p. 49–98; (7) Elworthy, F. 1895. *The Evil Eye*. John Murray, London; (8) Elworthy, F. 1900. *Horns of Honour*. John Murray, London; (9) Huber, E. 1931. *Evolution of Facial Musculature and Facial Expression*. The Johns Hopkins Press, Baltimore; (10) Jones, H. 1968. *Sign Language*. EUP, London; (11) Lavater, J. C. 1789. *Essays on Physiognomy*. John Murray, London; (12) Meri, L. 1964. *The Gesture Language of the Hindu Dance*. Blom, New York; (13) Munari, B. 1963. *Supplemento al Dizionario Italiano*. Muggiani, Milan; (14) Papas, W. 1972. *Instant Greek*. Papas, Athens; (15) Saitz and Cervenka, 1972; (16) Tomkins, W. 1969. *Indian Sign Language*. Dover, New York.

Gesture Variants. (1) Morris, D. 1970. *Patterns of Reproductive Behaviour*. Cape, London; (2) Morris et al, 1978.

Multimessage Gestures. (1) Morris et al, 1978.

Gesture Alternatives. (1) D'Angelo, L. 1969. *How to be an Italian*. Price, Sterne, Sloane, Los Angeles; (2) Brun, 1969; (3) De Jorio, 1832; (4) Morris et al, 1978; (5) Saitz and Cervenka, 1972.

Hybrid Gestures. (1) Cody, I. E. 1972. *Indian Talk*. NEL, London; (2) Morris et al, 1978.

Compound Gestures. (1) Darwin, 1872. (p. 264–272).

Relic Gestures. (1) Critchley, 1975. (p. 118); (2) Darwin, 1872. (p. 261); (3) Papas, W. 1972. *Instant Greek*. Papas, Athens; (4) Saitz and Cervenka, 1972. (p. 136); (5) Smith, W. J., Chase, J. and Lieblich, A. K. 1974. 'Tongue-showing: a facial display of humans and other primate species.' *Semiotica* 11 (3), p. 201–246.

Regional Signals. (1) Morris et al, 1978.

Baton Signals. (1) Efron, 1972. (p. 96); (2) Ekman, P. and Friesen, W. V. 1972. 'Hand movements'. *J. Communication* 22, p. 353–374; (3) Napier, J. 1962. 'The evolution of the hand.' *Sci. Amer.* 207, (6), p. 56–62.

Guide Signs. (1) Austin, 1806. (Appendix V); (2) Brewer, E. C. 1962. *Dictionary of Phrase and Fable*. Cassell, London. p. 902.

Yes/No Signs. (1) Cody, I. E. 1972. *Indian Talk*. NEL, London; (2) Jakobson, R. 1972. 'Motor signs for 'Yes' and 'No'. *Lang. Soc.* 1, p. 91–96; Tomkins, W. 1969. *Indian Sign Language*. Dover, New York; (4) Brun, 1969; (5) Darwin, 1872 (p. 273); (6) Morris et al, 1978.

Gaze Behaviour. (1) Argyle, M. and Cook, M. 1976. *Gaze and Mutual Gaze*. Cambridge University Press, Cambridge; (2) Morris, 1967. (p. 163); (3) Yarbus, A. L. 1967. *Eye Movement and Vision*. Plenum Press, New York.

Salutation Displays. (1) Eibl-Eibesfeldt, 1972; (2) Firth, R. 1973. *Symbols, Public and Private*. Allen and Unwin, London. (chapter 9); (3) Goffman, 1971. (p. 73); (4) Kendon, A. and Ferber, A. 1973. 'A description of some human greetings.' In *Comparative Ecology and Behaviour of Primates*. Academic Press, London; (5) Morris, 1971. (chapter 4).

Postural Echo. (1) Condon, W. S. and Ogston, W. D. 1966. 'Sound-film analysis of normal and pathological behavior patterns.' *J. Nerv. and Ment. Disorders*. 143, p. 338–347; (2) Davis, 1973. (p. 104 and 114); (3) Kendon, A. 1970. 'Movement coordination in social interaction.' *Acta Psych.*, 32, p. 100–125; (4) Scheflen, 1972. (p. 53).

Tie-signs and Body-contact Tie-signs. (1) Eibl-Eibesfeldt, 1971. (p. 134–141); (2) Goffman, 1971. (p.

194–237); (3) Morris, 1971; (4) Wickler, W. 1969. *The Sexual Code.* Weidenfeld and Nicolson, London. (chapter 29).

Auto-contact Behaviour. (1) Morris, 1971. (chapter 8).

Nonverbal Leakage. (1) Ekman, P. and Friesen, W. V. 1969. 'Nonverbal leakage and clues to deception.' *Psychiatry* 31 (1), p. 88–106; (2) Ekman, P. and Friesen, W. V. 1972. 'Hand movements'. *J. Communication* 22, p. 353–374; (3) Ekman, P. and Friesen, W. V. 1974. 'Detecting deception from the body or face.' *J. Personality and Soc. Psych.*, 29 (3), p. 288–298; (4) Goffman, 1971; (5) Goffman, E. 1974. *Frame Analysis.* Penguin, London.

Status Displays. (1) Caine, M. 1960. *The S Man: A Grammar of Success.* Hutchinson, London; (2) Korda, M. 1975. *Power: How to get it, how to fight it.* Random House, New York; (3) Maclay, G. and Knipe, H. 1972. *The Dominant Man.* Delacorte Press, New York; (4) Morris, 1969. (chapter 2 and p. 100); (5) Packard, V. 1960. *The Status Seekers.* Longmans, London.

Territorial Signals. (1) Ardrey, R. 1966. *The Territorial Imperative.* Collins, London; (2) Hall, E. T. 1959. *The Silent Language.* Doubleday, New York; (3) Hall, E. T. 1966. *The Hidden Dimension.* Bodley Head, London; (4) Hutt, C. and Vaisey, M. J. 1966. 'Differential effects of group size on social behaviour.' *Nature* 209, p. 1371–1372; (5) Letourneau, C. 1892. *Property: Its Origin and Development.* Scott, London; (6) Mackenzie, N. 1967. *Secret Societies.* Aldus, London; (7) Morris, 1967. (p. 182); (8) Morris, 1969. (chapter 1); (9) Scheflen, 1972. (chapter 2); (10) Sommer, R. 1969. *Personal Space.* Prentice-Hall, N.J.

Barrier Signals. (1) Davis, 1973. (p. 106); (2) Kendon, A. and Ferber, A. 1973. 'A description of some human greetings'. In *Comparative Ecology and Behaviour of Primates*; (3) Scheflen, 1972. (p. 21).

Protective Behaviour. (1) Ferm, V. 1959. *American Superstitions.* Philosophical Library, New York; (2) *Hill, D. 1968. Magic and Superstition.* Hamlyn, London; (3) Howes, M. 1975. *Amulets.* Hale, London; (4) Hunt, W. A. and Landis C. 1936. 'The overt behavior pattern in startle.' *J. Exp. Psychol,* 19, p. 312; (5) Knowlson, T. S. 1934 *The Origins of Popular Superstitions and Customs.* Werner Lauris, London; (6) Morris, 1967. (chapter 8); (7) Morris, D. and Morris, R. 1965. *Men and Snakes.* Hutchinson, London. (chapter 9); (8) Radford, E. and Radford, M. A. 1961. *Encyclopedia of Superstitions.* Hutchinson, London.

Submissive Behaviour. (1) Firth, R. 1973. *Symbols, Public and Private.* Allen and Unwin, London. (chapter 9); (2) Maclay, G. and Knipe, H. 1972. *The Dominant Man.* Delacorte Press, New York; (3) Morris, 1967. (p. 163); (4) Morris, 1971. (p. 131); (5) Wildeblood, 1973.

Religious Displays. (1) Morris, 1967. (p. 178–182).

Altruistic Behaviour. (1) Dawkins, R. 1976. *The Selfish Gene.* Oxford University Press, Oxford.

Fighting Behaviour. (1) Blurton-Jones, N. G. 1967. 'An ethological study of some aspects of social behaviour in children in nursery school.' In *Primate Ethology.* Weidenfeld and Nicolson, London; (2) Morris, 1967. (p. 173); (3) Morris, 1969; (4) Wise, A. 1971. *The History and Art of Personal Combat.* Evelyn, London.

Triumph Displays. (1) Frazer, J. G. 1932. *The Magic Art and the Evolution of Kings.* Vol. 2. Macmillan, London. (p. 174); (2) Morris, 1971. (p. 121).

Cut-off. (1) Barsley, M. 1970. *Left-handed Man in a Right-handed World.* Pitman, London. (p. 41); (2) Chance, M. R. A. 1962. 'An interpretation of some agonistic postures: the role of 'cut-off' acts and postures.' *Symp. Zool. Soc.*, 8, p. 71–89; (3) Morris, 1969. (p. 219).

Autonomic Signals. (1) Cannon, W. B. 1929. *Bodily Changes in Pain, Hunger, Fear and Rage.* Appleton-Century, New York; (2) Cobb, S. 1950. *Emotions and Clinical Medicine.* Norton, New York; (3) Kuntz, A. 1946. *The Autonomic Nervous System.* Bailliere, Tindall and Co., London; (4) Morris, 1956. 'The feather postures of birds and the problem of the origin of social signals.' *Behaviour* 9, p. 75–113; (5) Morris, 1967. (p. 148).

Pupil Signals. (1) Coss, R. 1965. *Mood-provoking Visual Stimuli.* University of California; (2) Hess, E. 1975. *The Tell-tale Eye.* New York.

Intention Movements. (1) Lomax, A. 1968. *Folk Song Style and Culture.* AAAS, Washington. (chapter 10); (2) Morris, 1967. (p. 153, 154, 160 and 161); (3) Siddons, 1807.

Displacement Activities. (1) Eibl-Eibesfeldt, I. 1970. *Ethology: the Biology of Behavior.* Holt, Rinehart and Winston, New York; (2) Morris, 1967. (p. 168–172). (3) Morris, D. 1970. *Patterns of Reproductive Behaviour.* Cape, London; (4) Rackham, A. 1975. Report on passenger reactions for Aer Lingus; (5) Tinbergen, N. 1951. *The Study of Instinct.* Oxford University Press, Oxford. (p. 113–119, 210).

Redirected Activities. (1) Bastock, M., Morris, D. and Moynihan, M. 1953. 'Some comments on conflict and thwarting in animals.' *Behaviour* 6, p. 66–84; (2) Morris, 1967.

Re-motivating Actions. (1) Carthy, J. D. and Ebling F. J. (Editors). 1964. *The Natural History of Aggression.* Institute of Biology, Symposium 13. Academic Press, London; (2) Morris, 1967. (p. 157–158 and p. 167–168).

Insult Signals. (1) Barakat, R. A. 1973. 'Arabic gestures.' *J. Popular Culture* p. 749–787; (2) Brun, 1969; (3) Critchley, 1973. (p. 118); (4) Efron, 1972; (5) Morris et al, 1978; (6) Munari, B. 1963. *Supplemento al Dizionario Italiano.* Muggiani, Milan; (7) Papas, W. 1972. *Instant Greek.* Papas, Athens; (8) Saitz and Cervenka, 1972; (9) Wildeblood, 1965. (p. 162); (10) Wundt, 1900.

Threat Signals and **Obscene Signals.** (1) Barakat, R. A. 1973. 'Arabic gestures.' *J. Popular Culture* p. 749–787; (2) Brun, 1969; (3) Marsh, P. 1977. D.Phil Thesis, Oxford University; (4) Morris, 1967. (p. 159–162); (5) Saitz and Cervenka, 1972.

Taboo Zones. (1) Argyle, 1969. (p. 92); (2) Gunther, B. 1968. *Sense Relaxation.* MacDonald, London; (3) Jourard, S. M. 1966. 'An exploratory study of body accessibility.' *Brit. J. soc. clin. Psychol.* 5, p. 221–31; (4) Morris, 1971.

97

Clothing Signals. (1) Bogatrev, P. 1971. *The Functions of Folk Costume in Moravian Slovakia.* Mouton, The Hague; (2) Broby-Johansen, R. 1968. *Body and Clothes.* Faber, London; (3) Flugel, J. C. 1930. The Psychology of Clothes. Hogarth Press, London; (4) Laver, J. 1963. *Costume.* Cassell, London; (5) Laver, J. 1969. *Modesty in Dress.* Heinemann, London; (6) Mecheels, J. 1963. 'The physiology of clothing.' *Panorama*, June 1963. p. 4; (7) Morris, 1967. (p. 85); (8) Morris, 1969. (p. 214); (9) Owens, R. M. and Land, T. 1975. *American Denim.* Abrams, New York; (10) Rosebury, T. 1969 *Life on Man.* Secker and Warburg, London; (11) Rudofsky, B. 1971. *The Unfashionable Human Body.* Doubleday, New York; (12) Strutt, T. 1842. *The Dress and Habits of the People of England.* (Reprinted, Tabard Press, London, 1970, Vol 2).

Body Adornment. (1) Angeloglou, M. 1970. *A History of Make-up.* Studio-Vista, London; (2) Broby-Johansen, R. 1968. *Body and Clothes.* Faber, London. (p. 11); (3) Bulwer, 1654; (4) Cooper, W. 1971. *Hair: Sex, Society, Symbolism.* Aldus Books, London; (5) Flugel, J. C. 1930. *The Psychology of Clothes.* Hogarth Press, London; (6) Parry, A. 1933. *Tattoo: Secrets of a Strange Art.* Simon and Shuster, New York; (7) Reynolds, R. 1950. *Beards.* Allen and Unwin, London; (8) Rudofsky, B. 1971. *The Unfashionable Human Body.* Doubleday, New York.

Gender Signals. (1) Collett, P. and Marsh, P. 1974. 'Patterns of public behaviour: collision avoidance on a pedestrian crossing. *Semiotica* 12 (4) p. 281–99; (2) Morris, 1967; (3) Morris, 1971.

Body Self-mimicry. (1) Guthrie, 1976. (chapter 13); (2) Morris, 1967. (p. 71); (3) Morris, 1971. (chapter 2); (4) Wickler, E. 1963. 'Die Biologische Bedeutung Auffallend Farbiger Nackter Hautstellen und Innerartliche Mimik der Primaten. *Die Naturwissenschaften* 50 (13) p. 481–82; (5) Wilson, G. and Nias, D. 1976. *Love's Mysteries.* Open Books, London. (p. 124).

Sexual Signals. (1) Morris, 1967. (chapter 2); (2) Morris, 1969. (chapter 3); (3) Morris, D. 1970. *Patterns of Reproductive Behaviour.* Cape, London; (4) Morri, 1971; (5) Wilson, G. and Nias, D. 1976. *Love's Mysteries.* Open Books, London.

Parental Signals. (1) Leboyer, F. 1975. *Birth without Violence.* Wildwood House, London.; (2) Morris, 1967. (chapter 3); (3) Morris, 1971. (chapter 1); (4) Salk, L. 1966. 'Thoughts on the concept of imprinting and its place in early human development.' *Canad. Psychiat. Assoc. Jour.*, 11, p. S296–305.

Infantile Signals. (1) Morris, 1967. (chapter 3); (2) Morris, 1971. (chapter 1).

Animal Contact. (1) Caras, R. 1975. *Dangerous to Man.* Holt, Rinehart and Winston, New York; (2) Matthews, L. H. 1964. 'Animal Relationships.' *Med. Sci. and Law.* p. 4–14; (3) Morris, 1967. (chapter 8); (4) Morris, 1971. (chapter 6); (5) Morris, D. and Morris, R. 1965. *Men and Snakes.* Hutchinson, London; (6) Morris, D. and Morris, R. 1966. *Men and Apes.* Hutchinson, London; (7) Morris, D. and Morris, R. 1966. *Men and Pandas.* Hutchinson, London; (8) Szasz, K. 1969 *Petishism.* Holt, Rinehart and Winston, New York; (9) Zeuner, F. E. 1963. *A History of Domesticated Animals.* Hutchinson, London.

Play Patterns. (1) Aldis, O. 1975. *Play Fighting.* Academic Press, New York; (2) Bruner, J., Jolly, A. and Sylva, K. (Editors). 1976. *Play. Its Role in Development and Evolution.* Penguin, London; (3) Groos, K. 1898. *The Play of Animals.* Chapman and Hall, London; (4) Holme, A. and Massie, P. 1970 *Children's Play.* Joseph, London; (5) McLellan, J. 1970. *The Question of Play.* Pergamon, Oxford; (6) Millar, S. 1968. The Psychology of Play. Penguin Books, London; (7) Morris, 1967. (chapter 4).

Metasignals. (1) Altmann, S. A. 1962. 'Social behaviour of anthropoid primates; an analysis of recent concepts.' In *Roots of Behavior.* Harper, New York. (p. 277–85); (2) Ruesch and Kees, 1969. (p. 7, 64, and 72); (3) Wilson, S. C. and Kleiman, D. G. 1974. 'Eliciting play: a comparative study. *Amer. Zool.* 14, p. 341–70.

Supernormal Stimuli. (1) Morris, 1969. (p. 198); (2) Tinbergen, N. 1951. *The Study of Instinct.* Oxford University Press, Oxford. (p. 44).

Laterality. (1) Barsley, M. 1966. *The Left-handed Book.* Souvenir Press, London; (2) Barsley, M. 1970. *Left-handed Man in a Right-handed World.* Pitman, London; (3) Gesell, A. and Ames, L. B. 1947. 'The development of handedness.' *J. Genetic Psychology* 70, p. 155–75; (4) Humphrey, N. and McManus, C. 1973. 'Status and the left cheek.' *New Scientist*, 23 August, p. 437–39; (5) McManus, I. C. and Humphrey, N. K. 1973. 'Turning the left cheek.' *Nature* 243, p. 271–72.

Locomotion. (1) Dyson, G. 1973. *The Mechanics of Athletics.* University of London Press, London; (2) McWirter, N. and McWhirter, R. 1975. *The Guinness Book of Records.* Guinness Superlatives, London; (3) Shirley, M. M. 1933. *The First Two Years, a Study of Twenty-five Babies.* Vol 2. Intellectual development. Inst. Child Welfare Monographs, Serial No 8. University of Minnesota Press, Minneapolis; (4) Well, K. F. 1966. *Kinesiology.* Saunders, Philadelphia.

Aquatic Behaviour. (1) Fleming, S. 1976, 'Man emerging (1) The first 33 million years.' *New Scientist* 71, p. 6–9; (2) Hardy, A. 1960. 'Was man more aquatic in the past?' *New Scientist* 7, p. 642–5; (3) McGraw, M. 1939. 'Swimming behaviour of the human infant.' *J. Pediatrics* 15, p. 485–90; (4) Morgan, E. 1972. The Descent of Woman. Souvenir Press, London. (chapter 3); (5) Morris, 1967. (p. 43).

Feeding Patterns. (1) Hutchinson, R. 1906. *Food and the Principles of Dietetics.* Edward Arnold, London; (2) Morris, 1967. (chapter 6); (3) Pyke, M. 1970. *Man and Food.* Weidenfeld and Nicolson, London; (4) Renner, H. D. 1944. *The Origin of Food Habits.* Faber, London; (5) Watson, L. 1971. *The Omnivorous Ape.* Coward, McCann and Geoghegan.

Sporting Behaviour. (1) Anon. 1975. *Encyclopedia of Sports.* Marshall Cavendish, London; (2) Suffolk et al. 1897. The Encyclopedia of Sport. Lawrence and Bullen, London; (3) Strutt, J. 1801. The Sports and Pastimes of the People of England. London. (Reprinted 1965).

Resting Behaviour. (1) Anon. 1965–66. *Concepts of Sleep.* Roche, London; (2) Evans, C. 1967. The stuff of dreams. *New Scientist* 18, p. 409–10; (3) Kleitman, N. 1963. *Sleep and Wakefulness.* University of Chicago Press, Chicago; (4) Morris, 1967. (p. 110); (5) Oswald, I. 1966. *Sleep.* Penguin, London; (6) Schwartz, B. 1973. 'Notes on the sociology of sleep.' In *People in Places.* Nelson, London.

INDEX

Absorbed Actions 18–21 23
abstract thinking 10
Acrobatics 21 293
acting 28 108–9 112 116–7 156–7 166–7 237 273 276
Actions 10–23
Aesthetic Behaviour 171 278–83
afterlife 151–2 153
aggression 12 16 125 183 197 203
Air Grasp 58
Air Hold 58
Air Kiss 42
Air Punch 59
All-fours Rest 313
Allo-contact 102
Alternating Intention Movements 175
Altruistic Behaviour 153–5
Ambivalent Actions 175
Ambivalent Signals 112
amulets 140–1 202
Animal Contacts 260–6
animals 138 151–2 199 260–7 272
animal insults 191
Animal Reactivity 266
apes 19 198 239–40 278–9 282
aphrodisiacs 276
applause 189
Aquatic Behaviour 294–8
Arena Display 245
arm-folding 17 102 135
Arm-link 94 95
Arms Support 311
artifaction 10 158
athletics 175 307
Auto-contact Behaviour 102–5
Autonomic Signals 112 166–8

badges 128 197 228 273
baldness 225 234 243–4
Barrier Signals 133–5
bathing machines 216
Baton Signals 56–63
beauty 278–83
beauty-contests 281–2
beauty spots 227
beckoning 66–7
belching 208–10
birth 252–3
blood-sports 305–7
blown kiss 81
boasting 124
Body Adornment 197–222–9
Body Baton 61
Body-contact Tie-signs 92–101
Body-cross 133–5
body fat 234
Body-guide 93
body hair 232–3
Body Jerk 61
body-lowering 142–8
body mutilation 222
body odours 232
Body Point 64
Body Self-mimicry 239–44
Body Slump 312
Body Support 101
Body Sway 62
body-turning 238
Boredom Signals 186–7
bowing 143–4 146 148
boxing 136 175
breasts 231 232 236 239–40
Breast Cup 42
Breast Curve 41
buttocks 234 240

Caress 101
cattle signs 29–30
Cheek Crease 189
Cheek Kiss 81
Cheek Pinch 42
Cheek Rub 109
Cheek Screw 41
Cheek Stroke 41
Cheek Support 102
Chest-wigs 229
child-substitutes 263
Chin Flick 53–4 70

Chin Stroke 109
Chin Support 102
chopsticks 304
cicatrization 228
circle-sign 39 140
circumcision 229
Cleopatra 226
Clever Play 270
Climb 293
Close Display 81–2
clothing 19
Clothing Signals 213–21
clubs 128 222 300
cocooning 132
Coded Gestures 34–35
codpiece 243
Compound Gestures 45–46
context override 40
contraception 247–50
Contradictory Signals 112–5 119
cooking 304
co-operative behaviour 155 159
Co-operative Lie 107
Copulatory Signs 199 202–3
cosmetics 226–7
coyness 115
Crawl 288
Creative Play 270
Crooked Smile 115
crying 256
curling-up 142
curtsey 144 146
Cut 186
cutlery 304
Cut-off 164–5

dancing 176–8 197 246
Deadly Nightshade 172
Deaf-and-dumb Sign Language 35 43
deception 106–8
defecation 168 207
Deformed-compliment Signals 188–9
deities 148–52
denims 220
dentition 304
desks 135
Dirt Signals 192–198
Disinterest Signals 186
Discovered Actions 17–18 21
Displacement Activities 179–81
Display Rules 117
Distant Display 80–2
Dominance Mimicry 123–4
dreaming 315

Earlobe Pull 109
ear-stretching 229
eccentricity 211
erotic clothing 241
Evasive Eye 165
Evil Eye 76 140–1 202
exploratory behaviour 269
Expressive Gestures 26–28
Eye Touch 41 53
eyebrow flash 13 80
Eyebrow Scratch 109
Eyes Point 65

Facial Expressions 112 115
Family Territory 129
Fantasy Play 270
fashion 216–21 277
fear 137–8 196–7
Feeding Behaviour 212 299–304
feint 175
Female Genital-aperture Signs 199 201–2
feminine beauty 281
fidgeting 166 181
Fighting Behaviour 12 16 156–9
Fig Sign 43 140 202–3
Finger-by-finger Beckon 67
finger-crossing 33 140
Fingertips Kiss 42
fist-shaking 36 195
Fixed Action-Patterns 14
flags 127
flop-out 19–21
folk-dancing 177–8
food-sharing 301
football 129 136–7 161–2 308
Foot Baton 62
Foot-flap 113
Foot Signals 106
foot-squeezing 229

Forearm Jerk 43 199
Forefinger Baton 60
Forefinger Beckon 67
Forefinger Hop 65
Forefinger Point 64
Forefinger Wag 70 196
frowning 13
frozen gestures 140 229
Frozen Smile 116
Full Embrace 95

gambling 300
Gaze Behaviour 71–76
Gender Signals 230–8
genetic influences 16 17 153–4
genital contact 247
genital echo 241–2
Gestures 24–36
Gesture Alternatives 41–42
Gesture Maps 53
Gesture Variants 36–38
Gift Display 82
Goose-step 292
Greeting Ritual 77
Grooming Display 82 134
Groping Signs 199 203
Guide Signs 64–7
gypsies 192

hair 109 222–5 233–4 236 243 296–7
Hair Clasp 102
hair erection 168 197
hair tracts 297
Hand Batons 43 58–61
Hand Beckon 66–7
Hand Bow 70
Hand Chop 58
hand-clapping 63
Hand Downbeat 67
Hand Extend 59
Hand Flap 67
Hand-in-hand 97
Hand Jab 58
Hand Nod 70
Hand Lift 62
Hand-on-heart 42
Hand Point 65
Hand Purse 38
Hand Repel 67
Hand-ring 43
Hand-ring Chop 43
Hand-shake 79 93 97
Hand Shrug 110
Hands Scissor 58
Hands-together 60
Hand-to-head 100
Hardy Theory 294–8
hats 144
Head Baton 61
Head Beckon 67
Head Cock 48 185
Head Dip 61
Head Nod 68
Head-on-hands 24
Head Point 65
Head Shake 50 68 70
Head Support 311
Head Sway 68 69
Head Tilt 80
Head to-head 100
Head Toss 69 70
Head Twist 69
heartbeat signals 252–4
homosexuality 18–19 91 169
homosexual insults 203
Hop 293
horses 263–5
horse sign 30
hunting 230 305–10
Hurry 289–92
Hybrid Gestures 43
hymen 298
hypnosis 147

Identified Hand Gestures 112 114
Impatience Signals 187
Inborn Actions 12 14–16 21
Incidental Gestures 24–26 27
Inconvenience Display 79–80
infantile echo 243
infantile sexuality 251
Infantile Signals 256–59
inheritors 121–2
Insect Flick 189

Insult Signals 186–93
Intention Movements 173–8 195–
Intention Power-grip 58
Intention Precision-grip 58
Italian hand-chop 195

Jaw Support 102
Jog 292
Jump 292–3

Kiss 42 51 98–100 145
kowtow 145–6 148
Knee-kneel 313

lady-killing 310
Laterality 284–7
laughing 45–6 190 257
Leakers 108–9
left-handedness 284 7
Leg and Foot Signals 112 113–4
leg-crossing 21 22 104
leg-hugging 104
Legs Fold 313
Legs-side Curl 313
leg-twine 238
Limbs Sprawl 312
Limp Wrist movements 237
lip-plugging 229
lips 239
Lips Press 109
Locomotion 176 269 288–93
Lotus Position 313
Love Play 270
lying 106–11
Lying-down 312

Magnified Reward 268
Manual Gesticulation 27
March 292
masturbation 105
Masturbatory Signs 199
Mechanical Play 270
Metasignals 268 272–3
micro-expressions 110
microsynchrony 85
Middle-finger Jerk 43 199–201
Mimic Gestures 28–9
mimicked copulatory actions 246
mini-skirts 221
Miss World 281–2
Mixed Actions 21–23
Mock-attack 101
Mock-discomfort Signals 189
mock-yawning 186
Mockery Signals 189
Moustache Twist 42
Mouth Cover 109
Mouth Touch 102
moutza 47 140
mugging 125 183
Multimessage Gestures 39–40
Muscle Play 270

Napoleon 142
navels 241
neoteny 151 263
nervous breakdown 164
nervous system 166–8
nipples 244
nipple-rings 229
Nonverbal Leakage 106–11 119
nose 243 298
nose-picking 200
nose-piercing 229
Nose Tap 53
Nose Touch 109–11
nudity 210

Obscene Signals 43 193 198–203
odour differences 232–3
OK-sign 39
One-leg Stand 313
On-off Smile 116
orgasm 250
overarm blow 157
Overexposed Signals 207–12
Overkill Signals 118–9

pageantry 121
pair-bonding 245–50
panic 167
Paradoxical Sleep 315
parasites 214
Parental Signals 252–5

parent-substitutes 263
Partial Mimicry 29
Pat 93
patriotism 154
peck-order 121
Performing Arts 283
perfume 214 222
Personal Space 130–1
pets 262 266
Phallic Signs 199–201
Plastic Arts 283
play behaviour 269 276
play-fighting 272
Play Patterns 185 267–70
pointing 64–6
Pope 145
Postural Echo 83–5
pot-belly 234
priests 149 152
Primary Gestures 24 26
Professional Non-leakers 108–10
prostration 145 148
Protective Behaviour 136–41
Punjab 'snake-tongue' sign 192
Pupil Signals 169 72

Raised-forefinger Rotation 67
rape 125 183
Redirected Activities 182–3
Redirection Gestures 196
Regional Signals 53–5
Rejection Signals 189
Relic Gestures 47–52 98
Religious Behaviour 144 148–52
Re-motivating Activities 184–5
Resting Behaviour 311–5
restricted display 122
right-handedness 284–7
Role Reversal 268
Run 292

Salutation Displays 77–82
Schematic Gestures 29–30
screaming 137
Self-intimacy 102–5
Semaphore Language 35
Separation Ritual 77 81
sexual gestures 198
Sexual Sequence 247
Sexual Signals 185 245–51
sexual taboos 198
Shakespeare 119
Shifty Eye 165
Shortfall Signals 116–8 119
Shoulder Embrace 94 98
Shrug 46
Shuffle 289
signal-blunting 106–7
skip 293
Slither 288
smiling 256 259
smoking 179–80
snakes 138 260–1 265
snarling 174
Social Mimicry 28
Spanish 'louse' gesture 192

speech 259
spiders 139 265
sporran 243
Sporting Behaviour 129 161–2 175 231 300 305–10
Sprint 292
squashed-circle gesture 201
Squat 313
Squat-kneel 313
Squat-sit 313
Stammering Eye 165
startle pattern 136
Status Displays 120–5 144 163 188 227
Status Sex 125
steatopygia 235
Stimulus Extremism 267–7
Stroll 289
stupidity gestures 31 191
Stuttering Eye 165
Submissive Behaviour 142–7 148 188
Substitute Signals 70
sucking 13 15 50 254
Superiority Signals 187–8
Supernormal Stimuli 274–77
Superstition 139–40
sweet-tooth 301–2
Swimming 293 294–8
Swing 293
symbolic ejaculation 163
Symbolic Gestures 30–33
Symbolic Insults 191

Taboo Zones 204–6
talents 121 124
tantrum 259
tattooing 228–9
taxophilic urge 279 281
Technical Gestures 33–4 35
Temple Support 102
Temple Tap 30
Territorial Behaviour 126–32
Theatrical Mimicry 28–9 30
thigh-clasping 104
Threat Signals 193 195–7
Thumb-and-forefinger Touch 58
Thumb Jerk 189
Thumb Point 65
Thumbnail-applause 189
thumb-sucking 50
Thumbs-up 55 65–6 200
Tic-tac Language 35
Tie-signs 86–101
Tight Fist 58–9
Tight Smile 189
Tiptoe 292
tongue protrusion 50 201 243
Totter 288
Trained Actions 21 23
transactional behaviour 155
Tree-climbing 269
Tribal Territory 127
Triumph Displays 161–3
Trunk Signals 112 114
Two-finger Beckon 67
Two-finger Jerk 67
Two-handed Telescope 41
typical form 36
typical intensity 36

Unidentified Gesticulations 112 114
uniform 273
Upward Thumb Jerk 200
urbanization 154 206 215
V-sign 114 140 161 200–1
Vacuum Blow 58
Vacuum Gestures 56–9 195–6
Vacuum Mimicry 29 30
Vacuum Power-grip 58–9
Vacuum Precision-grip 56–8
Vertical Lean 311
Vertigo Play 269–70

Waist Curve 41
Waist Embrace 97
Walk 288–9
war-dances 178
Wave 80–1
weapons 158 197
weeping 298
Whole-body lying 107–109
wigs 222 225 234
winking 21 24 191

yawning 181 186
Yes/No Signals 68–70

AUTHOR'S ACKNOWLEDGEMENTS

Many people have been helpful since I first began the Manwatching project. Some, like myself, are zoologists who have become interested in studying the human animal; others were anthropologists, psychologists, sociologists, psychiatrists and artists, already professionally involved in human studies and who kindly tolerated the invasion of their world by a zoologist specializing in comparative ethology. Still others are friends and colleagues whose comments, criticisms and advice have done much to improve these pages.

In compiling a list of names I am haunted by the fact that, since my Manwatching project has taken some years to complete, there will be some omissions. For these I offer my apologies. My gratitude is due to all who have helped me, especially the following: Tom Adams, Michael Argyle, David Attenborough, Robert Attenborough, Robert Barakat, Priscilla Barrett, Mark Boxer, John Brennan, Jerome Bruner, Michael Chance, Peter Collett, Tony Colwell, Ann Davies, Richard Dawkins, Michael Desebrock, Irenäus Eibl-Eibesfeldt, Paul Ekman, Robin Fox, Falco Friedhoff, Herman Friedhoff, Polly Friedhoff, Erving Goffman, Jan van Hooff, Peter Hutchinson, Janey Ironside, Andrew Ivett, Annick Jorand, Andrew Lawson, Peter MacPhail, Domenic Magri, Gilbert Manley, Graham Marsh, Peter Marsh, Tom Maschler, Jason Morris, Ramona Morris, Philip Oakes, Kenneth Oakley, Marie O'Shaughnessy, Victore Pasmore, Trisha Pike, Michael Rand, Vernon Reynolds, Diana Rigg, Claire Russell, W. M. S. Russell, John Sanders, Albert Scheflen, Kimiko Shimoda, Anthony Storr, H. A. Swan, Lionel Tiger, Niko Tinbergen, E. B. Wayne, Pat Williams, Maurice Wilson, and Mohammed Zeribi. In addition, I would like to thank the Harry Frank Guggenheim Foundation for its support of a major joint field study from which the present volume has benefited.

PICTURE CREDITS

Unless otherwise stated, all the illustrations on a given page are credited to the same source.

All-Sport Photographic Ltd 305, top
Alecio de Andrade (Magnum) 18 right, 46 bottom, 51 top, 132, 194 top
Eve Arnold (Magnum) 6, 12 top left
Ashmolean Museum, Oxford 305 bottom
Micha Bar-Am (Magnum) 287 top
Bruno Barbey (Magnum) 25, 45 bottom, 63 bottom, 77 bottom, 162 top, 274 bottom, 278–9 bottom, 290 top left, 295 bottom
Priscilla Barrett 11 bottom two, 16 bottom, 17, 29, 30–1 bottom, 39 top and middle, 43 bottom, 53, 56, 93, 158, 188, 189, 192 top, 196 top, 199 bottom two, 201 bottom, 202 bottom, 203 top left and bottom, 312 right two, 313 left.
M. Bateman (Cartoon from Tatler) 118 bottom
Beaverbrook Newspapers 296
Ian Berry (Magnum) 156 bottom, 191 top, 280–1 top
John Bolton 276 top
John Brennan 76 bottom
British Broadcasting Corporation 49 bottom
René Burri (Magnum) 23 bottom, 78 bottom, 121 bottom, 127
Bryn Campbell 28 top, 61 top, 137 left, 160 top
Cornell Capa (Magnum) 183, 197 top, 264 top left
Robert Capa (Magnum) 48
Henri Cartier-Bresson (Magnum) 4 bottom, 11 middle top, 62, 71 top, 73 left, 78 top right, 83 top, 96 top and bottom left, 103, 107, 108–9, 125 bottom, 152, 180 top, 186–7, 218 top
Central Press Photos Ltd 22 bottom, 144 bottom, 145 top
Eric Crichton 169 top two, 230, 231, 232, 233 top 235 top
Carolyn Curtis 253
Daily Telegraph Colour Library 2, 8, 10, 20 top, 86–7, 104, 105 top, 121 top, 123 bottom, 151 bottom left, 165 top, 179 middle, 194 bottom right, 216 bottom, 223 bottom middle, 224 top right, 257
Bruce Davidson (Magnum) 60, 209 bottom
Derek Davies 224 bottom right, 260 right, 273 middle
L. Dukas (Magnum) 23 top
Editorial Everest 90 bottom
Mark Edwards 110 bottom, 111, 117, 130–1 bottom, 166, 181, 207 top, 209 top, 320
Elsevier 198 top, 206 top, 233 middle, 276 bottom left
Ed van der Elsken 215 bottom, 245 bottom, 248–249
Elliott Erwitt (Magnum) 45 top, 50 bottom, 57, 269 middle, 279 top, 290 top right, 312 top
Robert Estall Photographs 84 bottom, 290 bottom left
Mary Evans Picture Library 234 right, 310
Paul Forrester 240, 286 bottom, 287 bottom, 302 bottom, 303
Leonard Freed (Magnum) 61 bottom, 94 top right, 112–3, 119 middle, 128, 136 bottom right, 147, 190 top, 195 bottom, 225, 275
John Freeman 234 middle
Falco Friedhoff 19 bottom, 46 top, 49 top left, 59 top, 95 bottom, 100 bottom two, 110 middle, 133 top, 154 bottom, 290 middle left
Gÿsbert Friedhoff Snr 256 top
Paul Fusco (Magnum) 15 top right, 52 top, 245 middle, 267 top left
Gala Cosmetics 240 right
Richard Geiger 33 bottom, 35 bottom left, 204, 220, 221
Gemeentemuseum, The Hague 283
Burt Glynn (Magnum) 123 top, 142, 175 bottom, 180 bottom
Mark Gofrey (Magnum) 37 top right
Roger Gorringe 65 middle and bottom
Ray Green 126 bottom, 308–9 top
Ernst Haas (Magnum) 50 top, 110 top
Sonia Halliday Photographs 150 left, 214 bottom left
Charles Harbutt (Magnum) 45 middle, 138, 164 left, 292–3 top

Robert Harding Associates 58 bottom, 78 middle, 99 top, 101 top, 143 bottom, 146 top, 173 bottom, 213 middle, 214 top, 226 middle, 291 bottom left, 294
Michael Holford Photographs 150 right, 223 top left, 260 left
Thomas Hopker (Magnum) 77 top, 164–5 bottom, 271 top left, 272–3 top
David Hurn (Magnum) 101 bottom, 223 bottom right, 242 bottom left
Philip Jones Griffiths (Magnum) 15 top left, 139 top, 223 bottom left
Richard Kalvar (Magnum) 63 top, 80, 88 top, 118–9 top, 134 bottom, 160 bottom left, 272 bottom
The Kobal Collection 18 top, 182 bottom, 216 top
Josef Koudelka (Magnum) 153
Kubota (Magnum) 156 top
Kuoni Travel Ltd 261
Andrew Lawson 16 top two, 19 top, 22 top right, 33 middle, 39 bottom, 47 top, 54 top right, 64, 69 top, 76 top, 95 top, 98 bottom right, 140 top, 201 middle, 210, 210–1 right, 213 top, 234 left, 236, 237 right, 280 top left, 284 bottom, 300 bottom
Frederick Leboyer (Birth without Violence) 252
Bill Leimbach 15 bottom right, 44, 148, 149 top, 205, 224 top left, 227 middle, 229, 300 top left
Erich Lessing (Magnum) 302 top, 304
London Express News and Features Service 79, 102 top, 133 bottom left
Sergio Lorrain (Magnum) 135 top
Danny Lyon (Magnum) 198 bottom
P. MacPhail 33 top, 78 top left, 202 middle right
Magnum 92
Constantine Manos (Magnum) 49 middle left, 273 bottom, 311 top
Roger Malloch (Magnum) 4 top, 156–7 bottom
The Mansell Collection 214 bottom right, 218 middle and bottom left, 219 bottom left
Graham Marsh 65 top, 66 top and middle, 67 middle and bottom

Marshall Cavendish Ltd 24
George Melly 244 bottom left
Menil Foundation, Texas 244 bottom right
Wayne Miller (Magnum) 245 top, 271 bottom right
Anthony Moore 106, 115, 168
Desmond Morris 37 left three, 38 bottom, 40 right, 47 bottom, 54 top left, 68, 74, 87 top, 89 bottom, 94 top left and bottom, 98 top right, 141, 200 top, 202 top right, 203 top right and left middle, 239 bottom, 264 middle right, 276 bottom middle and right, 295 top
Museum of Modern Art, New York 143 top
National Gallery, London 233 bottom, 254 left
Oxford Illustrators Ltd 66 bottom, 67 top and bottom, 169 bottom, 170 bottom, 237 left, 307 top
Jean-Paul Paireault (Magnum) 36, 88 bottom, 194 bottom left
Gilles Peress (Magnum) 149 bottom, 311 bottom
Picturepoint Ltd 151 top, 170 top, 171, 238 bottom, 246 top
Pitt Rivers Museum (V. A. Narracott) 40 left, 140 bottom, 191 bottom
Popperfoto 15 bottom right, 97 top, 113, 116, 120, 122 top

124, 133 bottom right, 144 top, 146 bottom, 211 top, 264 bottom right, 284 right top, middle and bottom, 285 top and middle
Mary Quant Cosmetics 242 top
Guy le Querrec (Magnum) 71 bottom, 90 top
Rex Features Ltd 134 top
Marc Riboud (Magnum) 11 top left, 100 top left, 300 top right
Khepri van Rijn Gallery, Amsterdam 246–7 bottom
George Rodger (Magnum) 269 bottom
Science Museum, London (Theatrum Arithmeticum Geometricum) 34
David Seymour (Magnum) 145 bottom
Marilyn Silverstone (Magnum) 267 middle
Society for the Propagation of the Gospel 154–5 top
Spectrum Colour Library 169 next to bottom
Doreen Spooner (Magnum) 201 top
David Steen 251, 254 bottom
Dennis Stock (Magnum) 26, 301
Homer Sykes 178 top, 219 bottom right, 285 bottom, 286 top
Syndication International 20 bottom left and middle, 21 top, 72 top, 75, 96 bottom right, 99 bottom, 119 bottom, 133 bottom middle, 137 right, 161, 162 bottom, 163, 175 top, 176, 177, 200 bottom, 207 bottom, 223 middle right, 227 top and bottom, 255, 280 bottom, 290 bottom right, 292 bottom
Nicholas Tikhomoroff (Magnum) 271 bottom left
John Topham Picture Library 22 middle, 46 middle, 49 top right, 83 bottom, 98 top left, 136 bottom left, 160 right, 195 middle, 196–7 bottom, 206 bottom, 297
Transart 35 top left and right and bottom right, 277
Transworld Features Syndicates Ltd 122 bottom, 125 top, 256 bottom right, 306, 307 bottom, 308 bottom, 314 top three, 315 top
Nicholas Treadwell Gallery 199 top
B. Uzzle (Magnum) 73 right, 130 top, 274 top, 288–9 middle, 293 bottom, 299 bottom
Visual Art Productions 54 and 55 bottom, 82, 139 bottom, 262, 263, 265, 266, 314 bottom, 315 bottom
Walker Art Gallery, Liverpool 238 top
Maurice Wilson 30 top two, 31 top, 38 top, 43 top, 69 bottom, 70, 239 top
Michael Williams 41, 42
Graham Wood 20 bottom right, 167, 202 top left
Zefa Picture Library UK Ltd 15 middle left and right, 27 top left and right, 58 top, 59 bottom, 72 bottom, 84 top left and right, 89 top, 97 bottom, 102 bottom, 105 bottom, 126 top, 135 bottom, 151 bottom right, 157 right, 159, 174, 178 bottom, 179 top and bottom, 184, 190 bottom, 212, 213 bottom, 215 top, 219 top, 223 top right, 224 bottom left, 226 top and bottom, 228, 241, 242 bottom right, 244 top, 256 bottom left, 258, 264 top right and bottom left, 267 bottom, 269 top, 271 top right, 278 top, 282, 288 top and bottom, 289 top, 291 top and bottom right, 299 top, 313 top right

Some of the line drawings in the book are taken from the following sources: p. 26 right Charles Aubert (1927) The Art of Pantomime; p. 9 and 55 right A de Jorio (1832) La Mimica Degli Antichi Investigata nel Gestire Napoletano; p. 12 four right I. Eibl-Eibesfeldt (1970) Ethology, The Biology of Behavior and p. 13 and p. 81 (1972) Love and Hate; p. 26 bottom left E. Huber (1931) Evolution of Facial Musculature and Facial Expression; p. 32 top, 114, 182 top; J. C. Lavater, 1789 Essays on Physiognomy; p. 21 bottom H. Neville (1900) In Voice, Speech and Gesture; p. 192–3 bottom W. Papas (1972) Instant Greek; p. 298 The New Scientist, Vol. 7; p. 32 bottom, Maurice Sand (1915) The History of the Harlequinade; p. 6–7, 173 two, H. Siddons (1807) Practical Illustrations of Rhetorical Gesture and Action; p. 52 top Wolfgang Wickler (1962) The Sexual Code; p. 217 T Strutt (1842) The Dress and Habits of the People of England.

The Publishers have attempted to observe the legal requirements with respect to the rights of the suppliers of photographic materials. Nevertheless persons who have claims are invited to apply to Elsevier, Oxford.